The Transformation of Liberalism in
Late Nineteenth-Century Mexico

The Transformation
of Liberalism in Late
Nineteenth-Century Mexico

Charles A. Hale

PRINCETON UNIVERSITY PRESS

PRINCETON, NEW JERSEY

Copyright © 1989 by Princeton University Press
Published by Princeton University Press, 41 William Street,
Princeton, New Jersey 08540
In the United Kingdom: Princeton University Press, Guildford, Surrey

Library of Congress Cataloging-in-Publication Data
Hale, Charles A. (Charles Adams), 1930–
The transformation of liberalism in late nineteenth-century Mexico / Charles A. Hale.
p.   cm.
Bibliography: p.
Includes index.
ISBN 0-691-07814-9 (alk. paper)
1. Mexico—Politics and government—1867–1910—Philosophy.
2. Liberalism—Mexico—History—19th century. I. Title.
F1233.5.H35 1989
972.08'12—dc20

This book has been composed in Linotron Caledonia

Clothbound editions of Princeton University Press books
are printed on acid-free paper, and binding materials are
chosen for strength and durability. Paperbacks, although satisfactory
for personal collections, are not usually suitable for library rebinding

Printed in the United States of America by Princeton University Press,
Princeton, New Jersey

For Elizabeth, Charles, Roger, and Caroline

Contents

Preface

THIS BOOK began as an exploration of the intellectual transformation that took place in Mexican political life following the Reforma, the great civil and ideological conflict of 1854 to 1867. My initial conception was that the transformation could be traced in the rise of positivism, which had frequently been labeled the official philosophy of the regime of Porfirio Díaz from 1877 to 1911. As I proceeded, I came to realize that positivism, while of immense importance in late nineteenth-century Mexico as a set of philosophic and social ideas, was not precisely a theory of government. Thus my focus changed to the contemporary concept of "scientific politics," which was drawn ultimately from European positivism but also from other intellectual sources and political models, mostly of liberal orientation. In fact, I increasingly discovered that to understand Mexican politics after 1867 it was necessary to begin with liberalism, a subject that had already engaged my attention for many years.

My new project became an attempt to unravel the tangled relationship between liberalism and scientific politics in an intellectual environment permeated with positivism or "positive philosophy." Although my central concern (and thus the conceptual heart of the book) was the relationship between liberalism and scientific politics, I also found that I had to study positivism itself in depth, that is, the philosophy of the era as it was manifested in the refashioning of higher education and in aspects of social policy. My initial pursuit of political ideas therefore led me into philosophical and social topics rather than into economic thought and policy, which many would regard as the more pertinent direction for the historian of Porfirian Mexico to take. In making this choice, I in no way denigrate the importance of economics, but rather I hope to bring into relief other aspects of the period that may be of roughly equal importance.

As a work that purports to aid in understanding post-Reforma politics and policy assumptions, it departs from most existing studies in two principal ways. First, it places at center stage the ideas of the intellectual and quasi-governmental elite, which I term the "liberal establishment," rather than the actions of major politicians, particularly presidents. Benito Juárez, Sebastián Lerdo de Tejada, José María Iglesias, Manuel González, and Porfirio Díaz do not loom large in this work as political actors and personalities. Second, this book approaches the period from the point of view of the liberal and conservative past rather than from the perspective of the revolutionary future. Most studies of the post-Reforma era treat it implicitly or explicitly as an old regime, a prelude to revolution.

This is true even of those studies that emphasize (quite properly) the continuities between the Porfirian and the postrevolutionary state. To examine late nineteenth-century Mexico without being cognizant of the Revolution, if indeed it were possible, would be of course to engage in pure antiquarianism. At the same time, the revolutionary lens can be distorting, and it may be that a perspective from the past can provide a useful corrective. Thus the substantive treatment of ideas in this book virtually ends in the 1890s, the moment at which scientific politics and positivist higher education reached their ascendancy, and also the moment at which the consensus within the liberal establishment began to break down. Nonetheless, the intellectual legacy of this moment for contemporary Mexico is significant and I will return to this legacy in chapter 8.

In approaching the nineteenth-century political process through ideas, I have drawn recurrent inspiration from a traditional source, the work of the French historian Élie Halévy (1870–1937). His method as a historian of ideas is a model. Halévy proceeded with exceptional analytical rigor, he penetrated to the heart of a conception or idea that gave form to doctrines and even to political or social movements, and he repeatedly identified the contradictory elements or the dialectic existing within a body of thought. Not only have I found Halévy's method inspiring, but his substantive contributions have been useful as well. His discovery of the dialectic within utilitarianism (or philosophic radicalism) between the natural and the artificial identification of interests helped me see the contradiction within classic Mexican liberalism between laissez-faire and statist anticorporate reform. In the present study, Halévy's essay on Saint-Simonian doctrine provided the point of departure for probing the conflict between scientific politics and liberalism in post-Reforma Mexico. Halévy's work was a fine blend of the internal and external analysis of ideas. He argued the schematizing and stylizing usefulness of ideas for understanding events. Yet he did not ignore the role of economic and social circumstances in shaping those ideas. Although he was basically an idealist, he was, to quote one perceptive critic, "not a crude idealist." If anything, he was "even less sympathetic to Hegelians than to Marxists." Half-a-century after his death, historians still have much to learn from Halévy, even historians of Latin America.[1]

The following are a few of my many obligations to individuals and

[1] Élie Halévy, *The Growth of Philosophic Radicalism* (London, 1928), 1st ed., 1901–04; "Saint-Simonian Economic Doctrine" (1907–08), in *The Era of Tyrannies* (New York, 1966). For a defense of his method, see Halévy's response to the socialist Max Lazard in 1936 (ibid., pp. 272–77). The quotation is from Charles C. Gillispie, "The Work of Élie Halévy: A Critical Appraisal," *Journal of Modern History* 22 (1950): 234. See also Myrna Chase, *Elie Halévy: An Intellectual Biography* (New York, 1980).

institutions. Throughout my entire scholarly career, Hugh M. Hamill, Jr., has been generous with his encouragement and constructive criticism. Alan B. Spitzer has served as my consultant on Mexico's French connection. Josefina Zoraida Vázquez and Enrique Krauze have taken a keen interest in the project and have aided me in innumerable ways. Sections of the manuscript have been read and ably criticized at various stages by Mitchell G. Ash, Mílada Bazant, Roderic A. Camp, the late Charles Gibson, Joseph L. Love, Florencia E. Mallon, Peter H. Smith, and William B. Taylor. The project has been supported by the American Philosophical Society, the National Endowment for the Humanities, the John Simon Guggenheim Memorial Foundation, the Joint Council on Latin American Studies of the Social Science Research Council and the American Council of Learned Societies, and by the May Brodbeck Award from the University of Iowa. Armand Arriaza and Patrick J. McNamara have provided valuable research assistance. My four children, to whom I dedicate this book, grew up with it and have all contributed greatly in their individual ways. Finally, my wife Lenore has given judicious criticism and constant devotion throughout the two decades it has taken to bring this book to completion.

The Transformation of Liberalism in
Late Nineteenth-Century Mexico

CHAPTER 1

Introduction: The Problem of Liberalism after 1867

THE SUBJECT of this book is liberalism in Mexico from 1867 to 1910, an era that was governed by the experience of midcentury civil war and the heroic struggle against foreign intervention. Nineteenth-century liberalism was a set of political ideas that saw its classic formulation as an ideology in the 1820s and 1830s and its implementation in the Constitution of 1857 and the Laws of Reform. With the victory of Benito Juárez in 1867 over Emperor Maximilian and the native Conservative party, liberalism was triumphant. Thereafter, it became irrevocably identified with the nation itself, a nation that in the words of Juárez had won its second independence. The years following 1867 were ones that saw the establishment of an official liberal tradition, a tradition that was further solidified with the Revolution of 1910. In other words, liberalism after 1867 became transformed from an ideology in combat with an inherited set of institutions, social arrangements, and values into a unifying political myth.

However, liberalism after 1867 also encountered a new intellectual environment, influenced in part by the introduction of the philosophy of positivism. A major characteristic of European positivism at its origin in France in the 1820s was its repudiation of central elements of liberal theory. Though positivism first entered Mexico in the 1860s, its initial impact was not in politics, but rather in the reorganization of higher education. Its effect on political ideas came a decade later in 1878 with the enunciation of scientific politics, a doctrine presented by a self-styled "new generation" of intellectuals in *La Libertad*, a newspaper subsidized by the fledgling government of Porfirio Díaz. Scientific politics came increasingly to provide the intellectual basis of policy assumptions during the long authoritarian Díaz regime, yet ultimately remained in tension with it. Therefore, the focus of this study will be on the definition of this purportedly new and regenerative concept and its complex relationship with liberalism, the dominant political myth.

Whatever Mexican liberalism became after 1867, its ingredients must be sought in the formative years of the previous half-century.[1] At the

---

[1] A definition of liberalism in its formative years was the subject of my earlier work, *Mexican Liberalism in the Age of Mora, 1821–1853* (New Haven, 1968).

heart of the liberal idea was the free individual, unrestrained by government or corporate body and equal to his fellows under the law. In the political sphere this ideal was first to be achieved by placing limits on central government authority through the legal constraints of a written constitution. The protection of civil liberties, representative institutions, the separation of powers, federalism, and municipal autonomy became important liberal goals. These constitutional guarantees and institutions would serve to protect the individual from "despotism." In short, constitutionalism was a major ingredient of the liberal program.

Second, individual freedom could only be realized within a society where traditional corporate entities—church, army, guilds, and Indian communities—would be replaced by a regime of legal uniformity. The principal corporation was of course the church, with its vast wealth, its judicial privileges, and its control over education and the events of life itself. Thus the liberal anticorporate struggle was directed primarily against the temporal power of the church in order to achieve the ends of secularization. The free individual in a modern society must become a citizen whose primary loyalty was to the nation or secular state and not to a corporation under the control of clerics. The supremacy of the secular state was a basic tenet of liberal ideology. Moreover, the secular state must be a republic. Since traditional governmental and corporate restrictions on individual freedom were a legacy of the Spanish monarchical system, Mexican liberals by the mid-1820s were uniformly republicans. The heroic struggle of the 1860s against two emperors and the monarchist conservatives became first of all a struggle to restore the republic.

Liberalism also embraced a vision of social progress and economic development. If enlightened individuals could be left to their natural inclinations, that is, to pursue their own interests freely, the result was supposed to be a spontaneous identification of common interests and social harmony. Individual interest was based on property, the right to which was an extension of the individual's right to life itself. If property, including the property of traditional Indian communities, could be freed from corporate, monopolistic, or governmental restrictions, then individual initiative, a natural division of labor, and free exchange between individuals and nations would flourish, leading ultimately to the general enhancement of wealth. These classic liberal assumptions guided article 27 of the Constitution of 1857, which reaffirmed the inviolability of private property; article 28, which abolished monopolies and prohibitive tariffs; and the many anticlerical decrees issued between 1856 and 1863, which first disentailed and then nationalized ecclesiastical wealth. These socioeconomic measures, even the ones that were extreme because they were issued in a time of armed conflict, became embedded in the Mexican liberal tradition.

The new intellectual environment encountered by triumphant liberalism had scarcely taken form by 1867; there were only scattered indications of the major changes to come within the next decade. One such early indication appeared in what had been a conventional vehicle of the liberal era, an independence day oration delivered on 16 September 1867, in Guanajuato, the fount of Mexican patriotism.[2] The orator was Gabino Barreda, leader of the educational reform commission, newly appointed by President Juárez. Barreda's famous *Oración cívica* repeated all the liberal pieties, putting the most emphasis on the recent war to regain national independence, the conflict between "American civilization" and "European retrogression."

Barreda's address was novel in that he saw Mexico's heroic struggle since 1810 as the culmination of a centuries-long movement toward "mental emancipation," that is, the gradual decline of old doctrines and their replacement by new ones. Political emancipation cannot be separated from religious and scientific emancipation, he said; "for in the domain of the intelligence and in the field of true philosophy nothing is heterogeneous, everything is joined together (*solidario*)." For Barreda the efforts of the great liberators Hidalgo, Morelos, and Juárez were made understandable only by multiple precedents and cumulative influences over three centuries. These included: Galileo's "simple scientific hypothesis"; the Protestant challenge, "whose banner was the right of free inquiry"; the assertion by the Spanish Crown of regalian rights at the expense of the Papacy; and the Dutch, American, and French Revolutions, from which sprang the doctrines of popular sovereignty and equality. Did it not follow, asked Barreda, that just as supernatural explanations were being replaced by natural laws and as human intervention was growing in all the sciences, so "the science of politics would also go forward, freeing itself increasingly from theology?"[3]

However, Barreda emphasized that mental emancipation had also brought with it an anarchy of ideas, "painful collisions" from which great social lessons could be drawn. Moreover, such anarchy would continue until "a truly universal doctrine unites all intellects in a common synthesis." Barreda's acknowledged guide was the philosopher of positivism, Auguste Comte, whom he quoted at the outset and whose influence is apparent throughout the *Oración cívica*.[4] However, this influence is most evident in Barreda's conclusion, the theme of which was "social reconstruction." Because of the sacrifices of two generations, he maintained,

---

[2] Gabino Barreda, "Oración cívica pronunciada en Guanajuato el 16 de septiembre del año de 1867," in *Opúsculos, discusiones y discursos* (Mexico, 1877), pp. 81–105.

[3] Ibid., p. 85.

[4] Barreda identified the epigraph as from Comte's *Cours de philosophie positive*, 6 vols. (Paris, 1842), 6:622. However, I have been unable to locate it.

the obstacles to reconstruction have been cleared and its bases laid—the Laws of Reform and the constitution. "Let our motto henceforth be Liberty, Order, and Progress." Liberty of conscience and expression now reigns and "makes unnecessary and impossible any disturbance that is not purely spiritual, any revolution that is not merely intellectual." Let "material order," he concluded, protected at all cost by the governors and respected by the governed, be the sure road to progress and civilization. Barreda had set the tone for the coming era, but true to his charge, he himself turned away from politics and devoted the next decade to instituting a new system of scientific preparatory education, as we shall see in chapter 5. The full political implications of his message were not formally articulated until 1878. These political implications are the subject of chapter 2.

Although the first appearance of positivism in Mexican politics came with Barreda's dramatic address of 1867, some of its assumptions can be discerned in political writings as early as the 1840s. Positivism was only one of several European intellectual currents that in the aftermath of the French Revolution challenged the validity of the doctrines of natural rights and utility, those two variants of Enlightenment political philosophy that made up classic liberalism. French literary romantics, political conservatives inspired by Burke and De Maistre, legal scholars of the historical school of Savigny, and the early socialists all judged these eighteenth-century doctrines to be abstract, legalistic, and of questionable universal application. Like the contemporary positivists, Henri de Saint-Simon and Auguste Comte, they rejected the notion of the autonomous individual as the root element in society and instead construed him to be · an integral part of the social organism, conditioned by time and place and as ever-changing as society itself.

In Mexico the shift away from classic liberal doctrines can be seen, of course, in Lucas Alamán, who by the early 1830s had become a frank political conservative. It can be seen even more pertinently in Mariano Otero, a young liberal politician and jurist of the turbulent 1840s. In his *Ensayo* of 1842, Otero emphasized historical inevitability, the progress of civilization, and the interrelated nature of all society. Unlike the classical liberal, José María Luis Mora, Otero believed that the method of social science must be historical. He opened his essay with a quotation from Mme. de Stael that asserted that the French Revolution was not an accidental occurrence, the work of specific men, but rather the work of history, the culmination of past events. He criticized the anticlerical reformers of 1833, for whom Mora was the major theorist. Otero maintained that the economic power of the church was being undermined by social changes and the spread of enlightenment, and that the extreme measures of the reformers only caused an unnecessary political schism in the country. He argued that civilization could only triumph if there were a "general change" in society, if "the diverse elements that compose it . . . change in the form necessary for that new state."[5]

Otero combined acute analysis by which he identified property as the "generating principle" of society with a marked optimism about Mexico's future. His optimism, including an apology for federalism, appears to have been inspired by the "associative socialism" of the school of Charles Fourier, which maintained that voluntary association according to a pre-arranged plan was the key to social problems. Otero saw the adoption of federalism in Mexico as a response to a "universal law." From families to nations, men organize, he said, in "diverse associations" to best serve their needs. His philosophical attachment to federalism and his conviction that the power of the church would naturally decline led him to become a political moderate, someone reluctant to seek a strong reformist state acting against corporate privilege. The affinity of Otero's thought with French positivism can be seen in his general approach to the individual and society, in his emphasis on social reconstruction, and in his adoption of the historical method in social analysis, and not in his attitude toward the state. Statism was central to the ideas of both Comte and Saint-Simon. With this significant limitation, Otero may be seen as a precursor of positivism in Mexico.

Mariano Otero (b. 1817) was a precocious and short-lived member of what might be called the "romantic generation" of Mexican liberals, which was also the intellectual generation of the Reforma, including such men as Ponciano Arriaga (b. 1811), Miguel Lerdo de Tejada (b. 1812), Melchor Ocampo (b. 1814), Ignacio Ramírez (b. 1818), and Guillermo Prieto (b. 1818). A study of the intellectual orientation of these men might reveal that they were exposed to many of the same ideas as Otero, and that under other circumstances they might have moved gradually away from classic political liberalism, as did their contemporaries in Argentina and Chile, for example, Domingo F. Sarmiento (b. 1811), Juan Bautista Alberdi (b. 1810), José Victorino Lastarria (b. 1817) and Francisco Bilbao (b. 1823). However, in contrast to Argentina and Chile, political polarization in Mexico after 1846 inhibited the application of the new ideas, such as the organic view of society and the historical approach to social analysis; and the suppositions of classic liberalism continued to hold sway.[6]

[5] Mariano Otero, *Ensayo sobre el verdadero estado de la cuestión social y política que se agita en la república mexicana* (Mexico, 1842), p. 77. See also the detailed study of Otero's ideas by Jesús Reyes Heroles in Mariano Otero, *Obras*, 2 vols. (Mexico, 1967), 1:1–190.

[6] I have argued this point further in "Political and Social Ideas in Latin America, 1870–1930," in *Cambridge History of Latin America*, 5 vols. (Cambridge, 1984–86), 4:373–77.

In Mexico, the dichotomy within earlier political liberalism between doctrinaire constitutionalism and a strong reformist state was perpetuated in the incongruous juxtaposition of the Constitution of 1857 and the Laws of Reform. The Mexican constitution, with its emphasis on natural rights, popular sovereignty, and a limited executive was quite different, for example, from the Argentine Constitution of 1853, which was imbued with the pragmatic and conciliatory spirit of the historical school of law, as espoused by Alberdi. The Argentines regarded all three constitutional doctrines as abstract and radical. Ideological conciliation in midcentury Argentina and Chile was also enhanced by the absence of the church issue that so dominated politics in Mexico. The difference between the situation of Mexico and that of Argentina and Chile was dramatized by the travail of the *moderados* during the Reforma era. Otero might have become one of those tormented political moderates, like for example José María Lafragua or Manuel Siliceo, had he not died prematurely in 1850.[7] Mexico's midcentury civil war not only made political moderation impossible, but it also disrupted the gradual transformation of political and social thought. In Chile and Argentina the grafting of new ideas onto old ones came about more gradually and imperceptibly than it did in Mexico. In Chile, it was Lastarria, Otero's intellectual counterpart and an outspoken political liberal of the 1840s, who introduced positivism in 1868. Whereas in Mexico, positivism found its first champion in Barreda, who, though he was a contemporary of Otero and Lastarria, was an apolitical physician and scientist.

Although Barreda's *Oración cívica* of 1867 introduced positivist concepts that would later be used to attack cherished liberal principles, his address also signaled the beginnings of the official liberal tradition. The elements of this tradition can be found in the public policy of the next two decades; its formal expression came subsequently in the historical writings that flourished from 1888 to 1906, even though most of this historiography revealed an infusion of positivist ideas.

One major policy objective of the years after 1867 (pointed to in Barreda's address) was political reconciliation, which meant both reconciliation of the parties in conflict during the recent civil war and reconciliation of the factions in conflict within the triumphant Liberal party. As we shall see in the chapters that follow, the regime of Benito Juárez (1867–72) dedicated itself particularly to the first task, the regimes of Porfirio Díaz (1877–80, 1884–88) and Manuel González (1880–84) to the second.

---

[7] On Lafragua, see José Miguel Quintana, *Lafragua. Político y romántico* (Mexico, 1958); see also Jan Bazant, *Antonio Haro y Tamariz y sus aventuras políticas, 1811–1869* (Mexico, 1985), which provides insights into the political environment faced by the *moderados*. Siliceo served as minister of *fomento* (development) under Ignacio Comonfort from 1855 to 1857 and later as minister of *instrucción pública y cultos* under Maximilian briefly in 1865.

Within a month of the liberal victory in 1867, Juárez proposed that voting rights be extended to the clergy and that distinctions of degree be made in punishing those who had collaborated with the French or with Maximilian. The proposals caused much controversy, but a broad amnesty law was passed on 10 October 1870. These political measures were supplemented by the efforts of Ignacio M. Altamirano to reunite the Mexican literary community by extending a hand to those writers who had sympathized with the conservative cause. He saw such reconciliation as necessary in order to create a truly national literature, and this became the theme of his weekly periodical, appropriately entitled *El Renacimiento* (1869). Nonetheless, Altamirano made it clear that this national literature was to be based on liberal principles.

It proved less difficult to conciliate former conservatives than to bring together the various liberal factions. The principal division within the liberal ranks was between the followers of Juárez, including his chief lieutenants from wartime days, Sebastián Lerdo de Tejada and José María Iglesias, and the followers of Porfirio Díaz, an ambitious Reforma general. After several unsuccessful challenges, both electoral and military, Díaz finally led a successful rebellion in 1876 against both Lerdo, who had been president since the death of Juárez in 1872, and Iglesias, who as chief justice of the Supreme Court challenged the legality of Lerdo's reelection. Once in power Díaz pardoned and then openly recruited the partisans of his three former opponents, a policy that was continued by Manuel González. The reuniting of the Liberal party was a major theme of the official rhetoric of the early Porfirian years. This policy of reconciliation reached a climax in the second Díaz administration. On 15 February 1885, soon after his inauguration, there appeared *El Partido liberal*, a semiofficial newspaper devoted to liberal "fusion." The glorification of Benito Juárez began during these years, and *El Partido liberal* helped make 28 July 1887, the fifteenth anniversary of Juárez's death, a great ceremonial occasion. Díaz could thus be portrayed as the indispensable perpetuator of national unity within the Liberal party, and the way was cleared for revisions in the constitution to legalize his successive reelections. One of the ironies of Mexican history is that the emergence of Benito Juárez as the central figure in the official liberal tradition was the work of his nemesis, Porfirio Díaz.

The first of the several histories that gave formal expression to the liberal tradition was the monumental *México a través de los siglos*, commissioned by the government and published in 1888–89 after at least a decade of planning and labor. By devoting an entire volume to the pre-Hispanic period, as well as one to the colony, the work became the first major history to identify the roots of the Mexican nation as equally Indian and Spanish. To these two volumes that demonstrated the fusing of ethnic traditions were added three others (*The War for Independence*, *Independent Mexico*, and *The Reforma*), which celebrated the progress of liberal ideas and institutions and their ultimate victory over the forces of reaction.

The five great tomes, all written by prominent men of letters, might be considered a major contribution toward realizing Altamirano's dream of a national literature. In fact, it is possible that the project had its remote origin in Altamirano's literary gatherings of 1868–69: four of its six authors, Vicente Riva Palacio (also the director), Alfredo Chavero, Enrique Olavarría y Ferrari, and José María Vigil had been collaborators on Altamirano's *El Renacimiento*. The work as a whole also provides evidence of the successful efforts to reunite the Liberal party, because the climactic volume 5 was entrusted to Vigil, who, as we shall see later, was philosophically at odds with the positivist intellectuals whose influence was on the increase in governmental circles. In fact, the positivist Justo Sierra, while praising the other authors, found Vigil too passionate, too much an accuser of the reactionary and imperialist party. Sierra would have preferred a treatment of the Reforma that was more "organic and formal" and less like a "polemical pamphlet," a treatment that was more scientific and less purely political.[8]

Sierra's reaction to Vigil's partisan zeal may have guided the writing of his own brilliant and influential history, to be entitled a generation later *Evolución política del pueblo mexicano*. His essay was embedded in the three volumes of another Porfirian monument, *México, su evolución social* (1900–02), whose several authors extolled the elements of Mexican progress. Sierra approached the heroic age more serenely than had Vigil, identifying it as the second of Mexico's two revolutions, or accelerations in the normal process of social evolution, a revolution that freed Mexico from the remnants of the colonial regime. Though Sierra's work generally followed the plan of *México a través de los siglos*, he did add a final chapter on the post-1867 period, which he characterized as an era of peace, when the Mexican nation under Porfirio Díaz had acquired its "international personality." Yet his concluding sentence was disquieting, for it suggested that the Díaz regime despite its material accomplishments and

[8] Justo Sierra, "México a través de los siglos," *Revista nacional de letras y ciencias* 2 (1889): 120–21 (also in Sierra, *Obras completas*, 14 vols. [Mexico, 1948], 9:188–89). On the government's role in the work, see José C. Valadés, *El Porfirismo, historia de un régimen*. *El Nacimiento* (Mexico, 1941), pp. 414–15. See also Daniel Cosío Villegas, *Historia moderna de México*, 9 vols. in 10 (Mexico, 1955–72), 8:660–66, who argues that the work grew out of an invitation by President Manuel González to Riva Palacio to write a history of the war of intervention. Much of Riva Palacio's volume was supposedly written in 1883–84 while he was imprisoned for an attack upon González in the Chamber of Deputies. On Riva Palacio's literary career after 1867, see Clementina Díaz y de Ovando, introduction to Vicente Riva Palacio, *Cuentos del general* (Mexico, 1968), pp. xv–xxiv.

its self-identification with the liberal tradition might be losing sight of underlying ideals. "The entire social evolution of Mexico," wrote Sierra, "will have been vain and fruitless, if it does not lead ultimately to liberty." Sierra's muted criticism revealed mounting disagreement within the Porfirian establishment about the elements of the liberal tradition and the regime's relation to it, but the tradition itself remained unquestioned.

Disagreement turned into outright controversy in the avalanche of publications that accompanied the simultaneous preparations for the sixth reelection of Porfirio Díaz in 1904 and for the celebration in 1906 of the centennial of the birth of Benito Juárez. The controversy was initiated by Francisco Bulnes, a positivist deputy who denounced the "Jacobins" of Mexican history, especially those present-day "false Jacobins" who were promoting the reelection of Díaz in the name of democracy, a democracy that was for them a continuation of the ideals of Juárez. In his dramatic speech of 21 June 1903, Bulnes also called for Díaz's reelection, but as a matter of practicality; and he presented Díaz as a modern Caesar Augustus, who had brought order out of factional strife. He followed up his speech with two lengthy polemical works attacking Jacobinism and denigrating Juárez as the supreme leader of the Reforma, works that provoked an angry and voluminous response.[9]

The polemical writings in defense of Juárez became mingled with the winners of the 1906 centennial contest for the best "sociological study of the Reforma," serious and balanced essays by Ricardo García Granados, Andrés Molina Enríquez, and Porfirio Parra. All three upheld the orthodox view of Juárez, but García Granados went further than the others by identifying within the liberal tradition two distinct elements, the Laws of Reform and the Constitution of 1857. He concluded that the Laws of Reform, which had ushered in the modern secular state, had been a brilliant success. On the other hand, the constitution had been a "partial failure," because its framers had been blind to "the Mexican people's incapacity to adapt to the democratic system." García Granados did not recommend abandoning the constitution, but rather revising it to conform with social reality.[10]

The argument of García Granados was not new. It had been stated

[9] Francisco Bulnes, *Discurso pronunciado por el Sr. ingeniero D. Francisco Bulnes delegado del estado de Morelos, en la sesión del 21 de junio de 1903, presentando y fundando la candidatura del señor general Porfirio Díaz* (Mexico, 1903); idem, *El Verdadero Juárez y la verdad sobre la intervención y el imperio* (Mexico, 1904); idem, *Juárez y las revoluciones de Ayutla y de reforma* (Mexico, 1905). On this entire episode, see Charles A. Weeks, *El Mito de Juárez en México* (Mexico, 1977), chaps. 4–5; also pp. 133–36 of this work.

[10] Ricardo Garcia Granados, *La Constitución de 1857 y las leyes de reforma en México. Estudio histórico–sociológico* (Mexico, 1906), pp. 132–33.

implicitly by the proponents of scientific politics since 1878 and it was embedded in Bulnes's recent diatribe. It constituted an elitist current within Porfirian historiography that reached its climax in *La Constitución y la dictadura* (1912) by Emilio Rabasa. Rabasa argued that unrealistic constitutional limitations on executive authority had been in defiance of "sociological laws" and thus had produced the extralegal but necessary dictatorships of Juárez and Díaz. However, Rabasa did not abandon the liberal tradition; rather he, like Sierra and even Bulnes, optimistically saw authoritarian rule as the prelude to a true liberal regime, one that would entail the revival of institutions and the harmonizing of the written and real constitutions.

The Revolution of 1910 occasioned a strong reaction against these Porfirian views, yet it only served to strengthen the liberal myth. Revolutionary leaders and programs, whatever the differences between them, almost universally sought inspiration in the ideals of the Reforma, which they judged to have been betrayed by the Díaz dictatorship. The anticlerical and secularizing tenets of the Laws of Reform were reaffirmed and made even more extreme, following an era of de facto accommodation with the church. Even stronger was the impulse to restore the constitutional principles of 1857. Not only had Díaz made a mockery of the traditional constitutional restraints on central authority, but his dictatorship had received intellectual support from those like Bulnes and Rabasa who attacked the "Jacobin" constitution-makers. The slogan of Francisco I. Madero, "effective suffrage, no reelection," was constitutionalist, as was the name of Venustiano Carranza's faction, the *constitucionalistas*, which emerged as dominant in the power struggle following Madero's death in 1913. Even the radicals, the Flores Magón group (before 1910), the Zapatistas, and the followers of Pancho Villa sought precedents for their programs in the "popular" midcentury liberal struggle.[11]

The adherence by leaders of the early Revolution to the heroic liberal tradition has been perpetuated as a permanent feature of Mexican public life, integrally related to the official doctrine that the Revolution itself is a continuing affair. This integral relation between the liberal tradition and the Revolution has guided the writing of history in Mexico during the last generation. Most of it is centennial historiography, commissioned by the government to commemorate the heroic anniversaries of the nineteenth century. The output was particularly large during the centennials

[11] On the use of liberal precedent by the Flores Magón group, see Arnaldo Córdova, *La Ideología de la revolución mexicana. La Formación del nuevo régimen* (Mexico, 1973), pp. 87–96; by labor, see Rodney D. Anderson, *Outcasts in Their Own Land: Mexican Industrial Workers, 1906–1911*, pp. 323–26; by the *zapatistas*, see John Womack, Jr., *Zapata and the Mexican Revolution* (New York, 1969), pp. 399–400; by the Villistas, see Robert Quirk, *The Mexican Revolution, 1914–1915* (Bloomington, 1960), pp. 157–58.

(and sesquicentennials) of the mid-1960s, which led Luis González y González to comment that "our present government . . . only recognizes as relatives figures and episodes of the Revolution for Independence and the Reforma."[12] Most centennial historiography is mere patriotic rhetoric, but not all of it, in part because the government recruits distinguished as well as undistinguished historians to write it, but also because the subject itself—the political history of the nation—has wide appeal beyond governmental circles.

The predominance of officially encouraged political history within Mexico (and elsewhere in Latin America) has quite justifiably drawn criticism from foreign professionals. In characterizing professional Latin American history as a "truly international endeavor," Woodrow Borah argues that unlike European history, the leadership in empirical, analytical, and objective scholarship on Latin America has generally not come from within the region but from abroad. Native historians, he adds, are too frequently "caught in the need to create the national legend and strengthen the emerging national state." Or as John Womack, Jr., has recently put it, most Mexican historians "still do *historia patria*. . . . History for them is what it was to the Romans. It's civics."[13] Borah and Womack are suggesting that while a small minority of Mexican historians are sophisticated and innovative by international standards, the majority are "intellectually old-fashioned" (Womack's phrase) and parochial. It should be noted that their criticism applies to topics of study as well as to method, and (one senses) may apply to non-Mexican historians as well as to Mexicans. One of the purposes of this book is to demonstrate, to the contrary, that traditional political themes, approached critically and yet sympathetically, are appropriate for sophisticated modern scholarship.

The continuing attraction of the political history of the nation as a topic of study in Mexico can be demonstrated by the work of two recently deceased historians, very different one from the other, Jesús Reyes Heroles and Daniel Cosío Villegas. Their work reveals the continuing strength of the liberal tradition in Mexican public life and represents a mature commentary on that tradition. The attraction of the topic can also be demonstrated by the work of Arnaldo Córdova, which diverges sharply from the liberal tradition and provides a distinct contrast to that of Reyes Heroles and Cosío Villegas. Let us examine the three briefly, focusing our

[12] Luis González y González (as editor for Mexico) in *Handbook of Latin American Studies*, 48 vols. (Cambridge, Austin, Gainesville, 1936–88), 28:94. See also Robert A. Potash, "Historiography of Mexico Since 1821," *Hispanic American Historical Review* 40 (1960): 395.

[13] Woodrow Borah, "Latin American History in World Perspective," in *The Future of History*, ed. Charles F. Delzell (Nashville, 1977), pp. 151, 153; Womack (interview) in *Visions of History*, eds. Henry Abelove et al. (New York, 1984), pp. 255–56.

attention on their interpretations of the critical era 1867 to 1910, which lies between two landmarks of the heroic liberal tradition, the Reforma and the Revolution. Such an examination can provide a point of departure for my own analysis of the political ideas of the period.

The work of Jesús Reyes Heroles, particularly his magisterial *El Liberalismo mexicano*, is the finest example of official history in contemporary Mexico. The three volumes were published from 1957 to 1961, clearly to celebrate the centennial of the Reforma but also to respond to critics, presumably of the late 1940s and early 1950s, who, according to Reyes Heroles, made it seem that the revolutionary process was coming to an end.[14] Reyes Heroles reaffirmed the continuity of the Revolution by asserting the continuity of liberalism, that is, the rich legacy provided by liberal ideas for contemporary Mexico. Although he studied nineteenth-century theories in detail and identified foreign influences, Reyes Heroles argued that Mexican liberalism ultimately shunned doctrines that were unrelated to Mexican reality. Rather, he argued that liberalism was forged from the specific problems of the country and thus acquired a degree of originality. While including standard doctrines, such as the defense of civil liberties, federalism, and supremacy of the secular state, the legacy of liberalism for the twentieth century also embraced democracy (as opposed to "enlightened" or elitist theories), "economic heterodoxy" (as opposed to laissez-faire), and particularly "social liberalism" (as opposed to rigid adherence to the right of private property). In short, this legacy was the body of doctrines that Reyes Heroles associated with present-day policies. We must remember, he urged his countrymen, that "our generation is not its own offspring." Liberalism for Reyes Heroles provided the basic ideological orientation for the ongoing Revolution.

One of the most notable features of *El Liberalismo mexicano* is that it ignored the years 1867 to 1910, particularly the era of Porfirio Díaz. Reyes Heroles made it clear that he saw no relation between liberalism and the Porfiriato. The latter did not represent "a continuity [of liberalism], but rather a substitution, a veritable discontinuity."[15] As interpreted by Reyes Heroles, liberal ideas developed after 1808, became "integrated" by 1857 (or 1861), then remained in suspension until 1910 when they descended triumphant. What emerges in the three elaborately documented volumes is a sophisticated restatement of the standard

---

[14] Jesús Reyes Heroles, *El Liberalismo mexicano*, 3 vols. (Mexico, 1957–61), 1:xiv. His vague reference may well have been to Daniel Cosío Villegas. Cosío's essay (in 1947) preceded at least three others that were similar by José Iturriaga (1947), Jesús Silva Herzog (1949), and José R. Colin (1950). See Stanley R. Ross ed., *Is the Mexican Revolution Dead?*, 2d ed. (Philadelphia, 1966), pp. 87–114.

[15] Reyes Heroles, *Liberalismo*, 3:xvii. I have pursued this point further in "Liberalismo mexicano," *Historia mexicana* 12 (1963): 457–63.

political ideology advanced after 1910, namely that the Porfiriato was an oppressive old regime that the Revolution destroyed. Moreover, it was a regime that had cast aside the ideals of liberalism, which then were reactivated with the Revolution.

When Reyes Heroles died in March 1985, he was eulogized more as an "ideologist" than as a historian, which reflected his status as the leading intellectual in high government circles for more than twenty years. During this time he directed Petroleos Mexicanos, headed the official Partido Revolucionario Institucional, and was minister of *gobernación* (internal affairs) and of public education. Reyes Heroles was an advocate of the intimate relation between history and action, the necessity for policymakers to look to history for guidance. In his own career, he showed that this conviction could stimulate criticism as well as apology; for in the decade before his death he became the architect of the *"reforma política,"* the now problematic effort to liberalize the rigid structure of politics in Mexico under the PRI. Unfortunately, this critical stance was not reflected in his historical writings. Although as a historian Reyes Heroles dealt primarily with the nineteenth century, Arturo Arnáiz y Freg suggested in 1968 that the reader of several decades hence might find in the writings of Reyes Heroles the best elaborated defense of "the historical significance of the Mexican Revolution."[16] But because his historical writing was essentially ideological, because it perpetuated the official view that the Revolution can only be seen as the antithesis of the Porfiriato, it gives little direct guidance to the analyst of political ideas in post-Reforma Mexico.

Jesús Reyes Heroles would seem to have little in common with Daniel Cosío Villegas, the dean of professional Mexican historians at the time of his death in 1976. The former was the consummate centennial historian and ideologist, the latter the consummate critic, who shunned the centennial impulse. One epitomized the powerful intellectual within the government, the other the powerful intellectual outside the government, constantly at odds with ministers and presidents yet tolerated and respected by both. What Cosío Villegas and Reyes Heroles had in common was their belief that history should serve a public purpose, their adherence to the liberal tradition, and their counsel that policymakers should look to the liberal past for direction and guidance. Following a multifaceted career, Cosío in midlife turned to history out of disillusionment with

---

[16] *Uno más uno*, 20 March 1985; Carlos Monsiváis in *Proceso*, 25 March 1985; Arturo Arnáiz y Freg, "El Liberalismo mexicano y su significación social," *Cuadernos americanos* 27 (1968): 91–92 (a response to Reyes Heroles's lecture "La Historia y la acción," delivered 7 August 1968, on his reception into the Academia Mexicana de la Historia, and reprinted in *Cuadernos americanos* 27 (1968): 65–85); Arnáiz's point was in a sense reemphasized by Enrique Krauze in *Proceso*, 25 March 1985.

the direction of policy in the 1940s. In his famous essay, *La Crisis de México* (1947), he argued that the ideals of the Revolution had been exhausted, that the term "revolution" had lost its meaning, and that the country was entering the "Neo-Porfiriato," that is, it was returning to the characteristics and many of the priorities of the Díaz era.[17] In fact, it might have been primarily in response to Cosío's criticism that Reyes Heroles wrote his study of liberalism.

The result of Cosío's public concern was the massive *Historia moderna de México* (1955–72), a nine-volume, multiauthored work covering the political, diplomatic, social, and economic history of the country from 1867 to 1910, the very years that Reyes Heroles ignored. Cosío's focus was on politics, and he wrote the political volumes of the *Historia moderna* himself. While Cosío was sensitive to the changing economic and social priorities of the 1940s, his attack on current governments emphasized their mounting authoritarianism as revealed in the monolithic revolutionary party, an enhanced executive, a weakened legislature and judiciary, and a general atmosphere of corruption and servility. Cosío Villegas turned to the liberal tradition for inspiration, but not to the protean "integrated" liberalism of Reyes Heroles, which could be used to justify current policies, but rather to the specific liberal principle of constitutional limitations on central authority. He wrote his only centennial essay on the Constitution of 1857, defending its architects against their Porfirian detractors, Sierra and Rabasa.[18] However, Cosío's substantive history began with the Restored Republic, the era from 1867 to 1876 when Juárez, Lerdo, and Iglesias worked against great odds and with only partial success to implement the principles of the constitution. According to Cosío, these constitutional principles became subverted during the regime of Porfirio Díaz, but then they reemerged with Francisco I. Madero in 1910. The "ideals of the Revolution," whose decline Cosío so lamented in 1947, were mainly the constitutional and democratic ideals of Madero, drawn directly from the mid-nineteenth century.

Though Cosío held up the regimes of the Restored Republic as models for his contemporaries, his overall historical vision was balanced and comprehensive. The objective of his project was to treat in detail "modern Mexico," which also included the years 1876 to 1910 when constitutionalism was in decline. To understand the Neo-Porfiriato, he argued, one must know the original Porfiriato. Cosío's conception of using history for a public purpose led him not to ignore the Porfiriato but to investigate it in depth. It is ironic that Cosío Villegas, who began with an opinion of

---

[17] I have considered Cosío's career and historical writing in more detail in "The Liberal Impulse: Daniel Cosío Villegas and the *Historia moderna de México*," *Hispanic American Historical Review* 54 (1974): 479–98.

[18] Daniel Cosío Villegas, *La Constitución de 1857 y sus críticos* (Mexico, 1957).

the Díaz regime that was similar to the official one, ended by making his two volumes on its internal politics his masterpiece. As he immersed himself in the copious and unstudied documentation of the era and sought to unravel its complexities, his appreciation for its leaders and even for Don Porfirio himself increased. In volumes 8 and 9 he explicitly discarded the epithet "tyrannical," used in volume 1 in favor of the milder "authoritarian." Throughout the *Historia moderna*, Cosío's passion for thorough documentation, his attention to detail, and his shrewd observations on political motivation make his work the essential starting point for any analysis of the political ideas of the post-1867 era.

However, we must be wary lest we be mesmerized by Cosío's detail, his documentation, and his objective tone and thus unwittingly take on his interpretation. Moreover, we must remember that Cosío's history is a history of politics and not of ideas, and that therefore he does not subject ideas to severe analysis. Cosío discovered that "political life" (a questioning of arbitrary government by courts, legislatures, and particularly by the press), which was so vibrant during the Restored Republic, persisted during the Porfiriato, even as dictatorship increased. Thus, despite Cosío's appreciation for the Porfirian regime, he put particular emphasis on the opposition, particularly the journalistic opposition, which doggedly defended the constitutional principles of 1857. The opposition press for Cosío was "liberal," "independent," or "democratic"; the press that supported the government "official" or "officialist." This distinction oversimplifies the realities of political debate during this era of ideological consensus. In a period that was governed by the liberal myth in which all those with political aspirations had to be "liberals," Cosío confuses us by applying that term only to a small opposition. Moreover, since Cosío did not focus on ideas, he does not help us understand what the advocates of scientific politics meant when they stoutly maintained that they were both liberals and constitutionalists. It is not useful simply to label their position "officialist."

Cosío's interpretation also raises the problem of continuity, that is, the relation between the ideas and programs of the Porfirian era and those of the Revolution. By bringing into relief the "liberal" and "democratic" opposition to Díaz, Cosío implied that it formed a direct precedent for Madero's program and thus for the ideals that he would see revived in his own day. Yet it is also possible that the assumptions of the constitutionalist movement of the Revolution derived in part from scientific politics and its version of liberalism. The *Historia moderna de México* can be seen as a critique of the official liberal tradition, as put forth in the work of Jesús Reyes Heroles. Cosío and his colleagues broke through the ideological barrier thrown up by the Revolution of 1910 and initiated the serious investigation of the Porfiriato on its own terms. Yet for all of Co-

sío's criticism of the official view, the *Historia moderna* is still very much
a liberal history, guided by the conviction that the ultimate goals for a
modern nation are political, namely constitutional limitations on authority, the functioning of representative institutions, and the exercise of a
free press.

Cosío Villegas and Reyes Heroles seem to be close together (as liberals) when they are compared to Arnaldo Córdova, whose interpretation
of the national political tradition is guided by Marxism and the depen-
dency perspective. Córdova's point of departure in the *La Ideología de
la revolución mexicana* (1973) is a direct attack on the liberal myth. He
exposes the official view that "Mexico's *true past* is its liberal tradition,"
the Porfirian regime "its negation"; and he then goes on to discard 1910
as a critical turning point in Mexican history.[19] The broader theme of his
study, he tells us, is "the ideology of development in dependent societies"; in the case of Mexico this ideology of development had its roots in
the Reforma and became dominant by 1876. This ideology was the set of
ideas that provided the rationale for the promotion of capitalism, which,
Córdova insists, continued with the Revolution, despite the addition of
"*una problemática social.*" Córdova refutes the common view that capitalist economic development began in 1940; on the contrary, he says, it
began in 1867.

Córdova's interpretation is disarming and therefore poses a challenge
for the non-Marxist historian. By laying bare the liberal myth, he clears
the ground for a systematic examination of the ideas of the Porfiriato. He
emphasizes a continuity in ideas between the liberalism of midcentury
and the positivism of the Porfiriato and between the ideas of the Porfirian
intellectuals and those of the revolutionary intellectuals, especially the
constitucionalista group that supported Venustiano Carranza. Moreover,
he is keenly aware of the social context of ideas.

The challenge of Córdova's book arises from his view of liberalism itself. Córdova accords little significance to liberalism as a political idea,
which follows naturally from his deemphasis on political change and his
emphasis on socioeconomic continuity. He regards liberalism as merely
one element in the ideology of capitalist economic development. Moreover, although Córdova's subject is ideology, he fails to subject ideas
themselves to rigorous internal analysis. Córdova tells us that the task of
the historian of ideologies is to reconstruct ideas and the function they
fulfill in society. The Porfirian intellectuals (the advocates of scientific
politics and the later *Científicos*—both of whom will figure prominently
in this book), "prepared the way ideologically for the coming of the [Díaz]
dictatorship" and then provided it with "a consciousness of its mission in

---

[19] Córdova, *Ideología*, pp. 87–88.

history."[20] They clarified this mission by justifying the free accumulation of wealth and the establishment of authoritarian government, both of which were essential to a unified capitalist state. How, might we ask, can ideas be analyzed when they are regarded as essentially derivative and devoid of integrity in themselves? How can they be analyzed when they are construed merely as fulfilling a social function or as providing a justification for the historical mission of a political regime, or indeed when they are construed only as elements in the ideology of capitalist development? Córdova's book does provide insights into the social assumptions of the Porfirian intellectuals and I will turn to these assumptions in chapter 7. However, for the study of political ideas, the value of his work lies primarily in its demolition of the liberal myth.

Therefore, as we begin our inquiry we must be cognizant of the strength of the liberal tradition in Mexico and of its effects on the prevailing interpretations of the post-Reforma era. We can then delineate our own approach to the period, which is to study its ideas, or more precisely the intellectual basis of policy assumptions, on their own terms. We must first of all understand what contemporaries meant or said they meant. Second, we must examine ideas within a broader western intellectual context. We must identify European influences in Mexico, but even more, we must discern the significance of those influences. Why did the Mexicans look to certain European theories, intellectual movements, political models, and individual leaders, and not to others? To answer this question it is necessary to probe the relevant European context of ideas, in short, to make comparisons between Mexico and Europe. We must surmount the sterile controversy as to whether Mexican ideas were imitative or original, whether they were peripheral to Mexican "reality" or properly incorporated and "Mexicanized." I acknowledge at the outset that I am studying the ideas of an elite whose intellectual world was Europe, but also an elite whose ties to government and to policy formation were close. In sum, this book is guided by the conviction that the critical study of ideas in their proper historical and comparative context can aid in understanding the Mexican political process.

I should emphasize at the start that the reader will not find in these pages a coherent political narrative of the post-Reforma years, nor will

[20] Ibid., p. 45. It should be noted that Córdova's notion of "ideology" is quite different from mine. He would probably define it as the set of ideas that provide a rationale for the interests of an ascendant social class. I regard ideology as the propositions or rhetorical positions of a political program that are directed in defense of or in opposition to an institutional or social order. Ideology (as opposed to myth) presupposes conflict in society. I have discussed this matter further in "The Reconstruction of Nineteenth-Century Politics in Spanish America: A Case for the History of Ideas," *Latin American Research Review* 8, 2 (1973): 53–73.

the narrative mode necessarily prevail in the discussion of ideas. Since my objective is analysis, I will frequently depart from chronological order in pursuing the origins or implications of a concept and its relationship to others. However, within the several chapters there are narratives to relate, both large and small, and there are instances in which the establishment of a proper chronology is a key to analysis. The history of ideas, like many other forms of history, can best be approached by a judicious combination of analysis and narrative.

As I have said, the subject of this book is liberalism, but its focus is the contemporary concept of scientific politics first enunciated from 1878 to 1880 in *La Libertad* by a "new generation" of journalist-intellectuals, led by Justo Sierra, Telesforo García, and Francisco Cosmes. In identifying the elements of scientific politics in chapter 2, I will turn first to European positivism, to the ideas of Henri de Saint-Simon and of the young Auguste Comte, and to the historical situation in which they wrote. Even though the *La Libertad* group did not quote Saint-Simon, and quoted Comte only rarely, in their political writings, the intellectual foundations of their argument, their modes of discourse, indeed the very term "scientific politics" itself, were drawn ultimately from French positivism. However, more direct influences came from contemporary political models, the conservative republics of France and Spain under the leadership of Adolphe Thiers, Jules Simon, and Emilio Castelar. These regimes provided an example of strong constitutional governments in the face of "anarchy." They also exemplified "conservative-liberalism," which became for the Mexicans the correlate of scientific politics. For a time *La Libertad* called itself "a liberal-conservative newspaper." The program of *La Libertad* was constitutional reform to strengthen government, in turn the basis of political order and economic progress. Francisco Cosmes even issued a notorious call for "honorable tyranny." In advocating constitutional reform, Sierra and his colleagues attacked the "metaphysical" mentality of the constitution-makers of 1856–57 and called themselves "new liberals." They labeled the defenders of the "pure" constitution, such as José María Vigil, "old liberals."

As we analyze the debates of 1878–79, we are faced with a confusion of political terminology. Scientific politics as a positivist-infused doctrine rejected many classic liberal principles. Yet its advocates were "liberals," albeit it "new" or "conservative" liberals. They attacked the Constitution of 1857 but maintained that they were "constitutionalists," calling for revisions to make the document conform to reality. Were the editors of *La Libertad* mere apologists for dictatorship, that is, for the incipient regime of Porfirio Díaz? Was their program to revise the constitution really an effort to subvert it? These questions provide the point of departure for chapters 3 and 4.

The advocates of scientific politics (and constitutional reform) frequently referred to the *convocatoria* of 1867, the call by Juárez and Lerdo for general elections and their proposals for constitutional change in the aftermath of the liberal victory. In chapter 3 we pursue the relationship between scientific politics and constitutionalism by first turning back to 1867. We discover in the *convocatoria* a clear call for a strengthened executive, in effect a perpetuation of the legal dictatorship exercised by Benito Juárez during the war years. There was also a proposal to reestablish a senate in order to limit the potential excesses of the democratic unicameral legislature and to facilitate central government intervention in the states. The campaign for a senate included one of the nonpositivist elements of scientific politics, namely historical constitutionalism in the tradition of Montesquieu, Benjamin Constant, and more recently Edouard Laboulaye, the French advocate of a senate following the Revolution of 1848.

Next in chapter 3 I will test the constitutionalism of the advocates of scientific politics by examining their political ideas before the founding of *La Libertad* in 1878. We find that they made their entry into politics as strong supporters of Chief Justice Iglesias, who judged Lerdo de Tejada's reelection illegal in 1876 and then claimed his own constitutional succession to the presidency. His cause was legalistic in the extreme, yet it attracted the future positivist critics of legalism. The defeat of Iglesias (and Lerdo) by the "revolutionary" Porfirio Díaz plunged the group, especially Justo Sierra, into political and intellectual crisis during the year 1877. Not only did Sierra turn from constitutional legalism to scientific politics and from Iglesias to Díaz, but (as we shall see in chapters 5 and 6) he also moved from philosophical spiritualism to positivism. In addition, I will examine the development of the notion of "administration" as opposed to "politics" that was present in the *convocatoria* debate of 1867 and reappeared in the crisis of 1877, coming into full flower a year later. A technocratic orientation, that is, the emphasis on administration by an elite who were above politics and unaffected by the play of interests, was central to the emerging concept of scientific politics.

Pursuing further the tangled relationship between scientific politics and constitutionalism, we move ahead in time in chapter 4 to the founding of the National Liberal Union in 1892 and the debate over the irremovability of judges in 1893. We now find Justo Sierra joined by some old and some new colleagues using the same scientific arguments of 1878 to propose a reform of the constitution that would limit, not enhance, the power of Porfirio Díaz. In the course of a complex three-sided debate in late 1893, these advocates of constitutional limitation on authority were dubbed "*científicos*," a label that stuck but whose meaning became much transformed in later decades. By 1893, the advocates of scientific politics (now termed *Científicos*) were still calling for strong constitutional government, but their sense of it had changed with the political situation. The weak executive of 1878 had now become too strong. In sum, from 1878 to 1893 (with precedents dating from 1867) we find a continuing interaction between scientific politics and constitutionalism, despite the theoretical conflict between positivism and liberalism, and we are obliged to take the position of Sierra and his colleagues seriously.

I end chapter 4 with the denouement of the debate of 1893, the calling of a second convention of the National Liberal Union in 1903, again to nominate Díaz for reelection. This subsequent gathering of the "Liberal party" was a final (and weaker) effort by the *Científicos* to introduce "institutions" and governmental continuity and thus to free the country from total dependence on the "personal regime" of a now-aged Porfirio Díaz. The centerpiece of this second effort was the nominating speech of 21 June by Francisco Bulnes, and its concrete result was the constitutional adoption of a separate (though ineffective) vice-presidency in 1904.

Much of the substance of this book involves political debate in an era of consensus. I have noted that with the defeat of the Conservative party in 1867, liberalism ceased to be a combative ideology and became a unifying political myth. Although the debates were often acrimonious, it is important to remember that they were carried on within a wide-reaching liberal establishment. This establishment became increasingly cohesive as the factional conflict of the Restored Republic gave way to the reconciliation of the Porfiriato. Yet despite ideological consensus and political reconciliation, the debates were significant; they were more than mere intellectual shadow-boxing. The ideas at issue became embedded in Mexican politics and would continue to inform policy despite the Revolution and renewed ideological conflict.

In exploring the structure of scientific politics and its relationship to the liberal heritage, I have found it necessary to pursue further the role of positivist philosophy in post-1867 Mexico. This was the subject of a pioneer work by Leopoldo Zea, a leader since the 1940s in the philosophical quest for *lo mexicano*, for Mexican cultural identity.[21] Challenging the view of positivism as a European (or universal) philosophy imposed on Mexican culture, Zea set out to demonstrate its specifically Mexican features, its "circumstantial aspect." Positivism for Zea was the ideology

---

[21] Leopoldo Zea, *El Positivismo en México*, 3d ed. (Mexico, 1968). 1st ed. in 2 vols., 1943–44. For a critique see William D. Raat, "Leopoldo Zea and Mexican Positivism: A Reappraisal," *Hispanic American Historical Review* 48 (1968): 1–18; also my "The History of Ideas: Substantive and Methodological Aspects of the Thought of Leopoldo Zea," *Journal of Latin American Studies* 3 (1971): 59–70. For an alternative approach to the subject of positivism, see William D. Raat, *El Positivismo durante el porfiriato, 1876–1910* (Mexico, 1975).

of the Mexican bourgeoisie in its second stage, that of order, just as French rationalism was its ideology in the earlier combative stage. Zea examined the ideas of many of the same figures to be treated in this book, but because of his philosophical preconceptions, Zea neither penetrated the social and institutional context of ideas ("Mexican bourgeoisie" went undefined), nor did he analyze these ideas in depth. Zea's work opened up a totally neglected area of study and it did point to fundamental themes, such as the relation between liberalism and positivism and the tie between the ideas of the *La Libertad* group of 1878 and those of the *Científicos* of 1893. However, the value of the work for the study of politics is limited not only by Zea's preconceptions, but also because of his focus on positivism. Positivism in Mexico was not a political idea, as Zea seemed to suggest, whatever the effects it had on politics. Therefore, to understand properly the dominant political ideas of the period, my point of departure is liberalism and not positivism.

Earlier I noted an incongruity, namely that while Comtean positivism first appeared in Mexico in the 1860s, it had little effect on political ideas until 1878. Gabino Barreda's *Oración cívica* of 1867 had clear political implications drawn from positivism, but they were not pursued by Barreda or by anyone else. Since the immediate impact of Comtean positivism was on the reorganization of higher education under Barreda's leadership, I turn in chapter 5 to the establishment of the Escuela Nacional Preparatoria (ENP) in 1867, with its Comtean scientific curriculum required of all preprofessional students. The school and its curriculum were the subjects of controversy from the beginning, and I will pursue Barreda's positivist defense of the school against both its practical and philosophical opponents. One of these early opponents was Justo Sierra, who moved from philosophical criticism of positivism and the ENP in 1873–74 to ardent defense of both by 1877. It should be noted that despite the obvious tie between the decade-old positivist educational philosophy and the new doctrine of scientific politics, educational and political ideas followed separate courses until 1880.

The inevitable joining of higher education and politics came with the great debate of 1880 to 1883 over the adoption of logic texts for the ENP, the subject of chapter 6. The controversy was basically philosophical, between idealism (German Krausist and French spiritualist) and positivism; and it engaged the doctrinaire or "old" liberals, particularly José María Vigil, Hilario Gabilondo, and Ignacio Altamirano in combat with the principal advocates of scientific politics, Sierra, García, Jorge Hammeken y Mexía, and Porfirio Parra. In fact, the opposition to positivism and to the ENP reached its peak in the early 1880s with support from key ministers in the government of Manuel González. The defenders of idealist philosophy also became defenders of classic liberal principles, which they saw being threatened by positivism. The debate brought to the surface the theoretical conflict between positivism and liberalism, yet its political implications were muted by the continuing policy of factional reconciliation. Both parties to the debate had a foothold in the González regime. Thus, while educational and philosophical controversy inevitably led back to politics, it did not generate criticism of the regime itself.

Finally in chapter 6, I will trace the reemergence of positivism as the official philosophy of higher education, which resulted from the second National Congress of Public Instruction of 1891 and the subsequent law of 1896. This ascendancy of positivism in education coincided with the apparent ascendancy of scientific politics. However, liberalism was not totally displaced in either establishment politics or higher education, as demonstrated by the constitutional debate of 1893 and its sequel, the renewed Liberal Union movement of 1903, and by the critique of positivist education that began soon thereafter.

I will complete my inquiry by examining positivism as a set of social ideas in chapter 7, in order to identify the social assumptions embedded in scientific politics and their relation to liberalism. I must weigh the relative importance in Mexican social thought of the theories of Auguste Comte and Herbert Spencer. Which vision of society was more pertinent to the Mexicans, Comte's hierarchically organized and noncompetitive collectivism in which state and society were one, or Spencer's industrial society that was individualistic, liberal, and stateless, the product of the evolution and adaptation of all of nature? I shall also discuss the impact of Darwinian biology in Mexico, particularly its application to society, as popularized by Spencer. To what extent did the Mexican liberal establishment absorb the prevailing denigration of the indigenous population and the hostility toward racial mixture? Besides surveying general attitudes of the intellectual and governing elite toward the Indian and toward agrarian rebellion, I will examine two important areas of social policy, obligatory primary education and colonization by foreigners (which included the issue of *terrenos baldíos* or unclaimed public lands). These policy questions engendered controversy and as in previous chapters I will follow the relevant debates and resulting legislation. Finally, since both questions led ultimately to the bases and future of Mexico as a nation, I end the chapter with a consideration of national identity in a climate of rapid economic development.

In probing Mexican social thought in the era of positivism, we must be mindful of the central focus of this study, the concept of scientific politics and its relation to the heritage of liberalism. Let us turn first, then, to scientific politics.

CHAPTER 2

The Structure of Scientific Politics

SCIENTIFIC POLITICS was presented as a new and regenerating doctrine in Mexico by an exceptional group of journalist-intellectuals in their organ, *La Libertad*, a daily newspaper that appeared on 5 January 1878 and ran through 1884. *La Libertad*'s years of great political strength were the first two, which came within the shaky first administration of Porfirio Díaz. Purportedly in concert with the president, the men of *La Libertad* saw themselves as a "new generation" and self-consciously put forth the intellectual bases of a coming era of order and progress. They were a coherent group, bound together by youth, personal ties, and previous political and journalistic collaboration.

The three leaders were Justo Sierra, Francisco G. Cosmes, and Telesforo García. Sierra was twenty-nine in January 1878 and had already established a reputation as a jurist, a poet, and a journalist. As the editorial director of *La Libertad* until his resignation in April 1880, he was clearly the group's intellectual head. Cosmes, only twenty-seven, had been an active journalist since 1874 and served as editorial secretary of *La Libertad* until he received an ill-fated assignment to the Mexican delegation in Paris in late 1880. García was a Spaniard who had lived in Mexico since 1865 and who by age thirty-three was both a publicist and a merchant-entrepreneur. He provided financial backing for the new journalistic enterprise. García and Sierra were close personal friends. Cosmes and Sierra had both accompanied the beleaguered "interim" president José María Iglesias to Guanajuato in late 1876 and served him briefly in official capacities.

The group also included Justo Sierra's talented younger brother Santiago (aged twenty-seven), one of the founders of and leading contributors to *La Libertad* during 1878 before he left the following year to fill a minor diplomatic post in Chile. He returned to the editorial board in October 1879 and remained a member until his untimely death on 27 April 1880 in a duel with Ireneo Paz, the editor of the rival daily, *La Patria*. Justo Sierra temporarily abandoned journalism after the tragic incident, and the political significance of *La Libertad* declined thereafter. Another stalwart was Jorge Hammeken y Mexía (twenty-six years of age), a close friend of García and of the Sierras.[1] Other members of this intellectual constellation were the Spanish-born litterateur Enrique Olavarría y Ferrari (an exact contemporary of García) who joined the editorial board in January 1879, Carlos Olaguíbel y Arista (thirty-one), and scientific editors Porfirio Parra (twenty-four), Manuel Flores (twenty-five), and Luis E. Ruiz (twenty-one). The latter three men were prominent professors and administrators at the National Preparatory School, as was Eduardo Garay (thirty-three), a charter member of the *La Libertad* staff.[2] Three of the youngest collaborators, all later to become leading literary figures, were Agustín F. Cuenca (twenty-eight), Jesús E. Valenzuela (twenty-two), and Manuel Gutiérrez Nájera (nineteen).

Several of the group, Cosmes, Garay, Hammeken, the Sierras, and Olaguíbel had worked together on *El Bien público*, an anti-Lerdo newspaper, from August to October 1876. Other journalistic collaborations by future *La Libertad* editors included *El Federalista* (1872–74), *La Tribuna* (1874), *La Época* (1877), and *El Mundo científico* (1877). *La Época* was directed principally by Olaguíbel, *El Mundo científico* by Santiago Sierra. Thus the appearance of *La Libertad* represented a momentary coalescence of various friends and previous colleagues, a cohort of twenty-five- to thirty-year-old intellectuals drawn together by the prospect of national regeneration under a vigorous leader.[3]

La Libertad openly acknowledged receiving a subsidy from the Díaz regime, while insisting repeatedly that it was not sacrificing its independence in so doing. The presentation of scientific politics was complemented by an "agreement between the president and ourselves" whereby the paper would support Díaz in combating further revolutionary efforts. After the upheaval of 1876, said Sierra, we agreed with the new president that peace was the prerequisite for maintaining our liberties; "the nation . . . solemnly censured civil war, under any guise or for

[1] Hammeken joined *La Libertad* on 3 March 1879, presumably on his return from Europe where he probably had lived since late 1876 and had become converted to positivism (see chap. 3, n. 56). Along with Justo Sierra, he was a witness at the naturalization hearing (14 July 1879) for Telesforo García. See Archivo de la Secretaría de Relaciones Exteriores, 521.23 (46): sección 43, caja 4, expediente 48 [43–4–48]. He stated his age as twenty-eight. Hammeken also served as one of Santiago Sierra's seconds in the above-mentioned fatal duel: Justo Sierra, "Apuntes familiares," *Obras*, 14:14. Hammeken also died young (of a heart ailment), at the age of thirty-two on 15 April 1884. See *La Libertad*, 16, 18 April 1884.

[2] Garay resigned out of disagreement with the newspaper's program (*La Libertad*, 26 September 1878). Such differences did not prevent him from serving as the other second for Santiago Sierra.

[3] The only elder among the *La Libertad* group was León Guzmán, an occasional contributor who was fifty-seven in 1878 (see pp. 57–58). Other more obscure figures listed as on the staff of *La Libertad* were Manuel Martínez de Castro (a novelist whose works are known, but not his biographical data), Gerardo M. Silva, and Benjamin Bolaños.

any reason." While the tie to the regime was implicit from the start, acknowledgment of the subsidy came first in an unusual front-page editorial on 23 April 1879, amid growing disillusionment with the frequent turnover of cabinet officials and with government lethargy in pursuing constructive programs. *La Libertad* continued as a friendly critic, but by late 1879 Sierra and his colleagues were nostalgic for the promises of two years earlier and feared that the campaign for the elections of 1880 meant a return to factionalism. There was no indication, however, that the government was withdrawing its subsidy.[4]

Scientific or positive politics involved the argument that the country's problems should be approached and its policies formed scientifically. Its principal characteristics were an attack on doctrinaire liberalism, or "metaphysical politics," an apology for strong government to counter endemic revolutions and anarchy, and a call for constitutional reform. It drew upon a current of European, particularly French, theories dating back to Henri de Saint-Simon and Auguste Comte in the 1820s, theories that under the name of positivism had become quite generalized in European thought by 1878. Apart from the theoretical origins of their doctrine, the exponents of scientific politics in Mexico found inspiration in the concrete experience of the contemporary conservative republics of France and Spain and in their leaders, Adolphe Thiers, Jules Simon, and Emilio Castelar. The policies of these men were judged to be "scientifically" formulated.

The editors of *La Libertad* in daily articles from 1878 to 1880 saw themselves as systematically interpreting for Mexico the achievements of nineteenth-century science. They argued that the methods of science could be applied to the practical ends of economic development, social regeneration, and political unity. Politics, said Francisco Cosmes, is "an experimental science, based on facts, with a specific goal, the good of the greatest number." It is, moreover, the science of the possible: dogmas, theories, and legal formulas must give way to observation, patient investigation, and experience as the guides to statesmanship. Avoiding universal doctrines, politics now "seeks the particular procedures most appropriate to each situation." We seek relative and not absolute truth, we invite discussion, and we affirm nothing without proof, wrote Jorge Hammeken in outlining "the ideals of the new generation." We esteem liberty, wrote Telesforo García, "but following the road marked by science, we do not love it independent of its results."[5]

---

[4] Justo Sierra in *La Libertad*, 28 December 1879 (*Obras*, 4:267) and 17 February 1880 (*Obras*, 4:275). For other references to the subsidy and agreement, see Sierra in *La Libertad*, 26 September 1879 (*Obras*, 4:242); *La Libertad*, 12 November 1879.

[5] See Cosmes, "Los intransigentes," ibid., 28 December 1878; Hammeken in ibid., 9 September 1879; García in ibid., 12 October 1880 (reprinted with a change of title from

La Libertad contrasted the new politics based on science with the metaphysical politics of the "older generation" of liberals of the Reforma era. Justo Sierra set the tone for this attack on "metaphysics" in his extensive debate in late 1878 with José María Vigil, a defender of the "old" liberalism in *El Monitor republicano*. The old school, said Sierra, like the "men of '93 [in France]," believes that society can and should be molded to conform with the rights of man. This must be done if necessary by violence, by revolution. But, he added, it is a school "that has accomplished its mission"; its day is past.[6]

In referring to the revolutionaries of 1793, Sierra was drawing on the origins of scientific politics, Henri de Saint-Simon's critique of liberal and revolutionary doctrines in France. Writing in 1821, Saint-Simon saw Europe as still in the midst of a thirty-year crisis, which would lead ultimately to the establishment of an industrial and scientific system. With the critical character of the eighteenth century still extant and the organizing character of the nineteenth yet to develop, the bases for policy are in confusion and the "metaphysicians and legists" still predominate. Their role in tearing down the feudal and theological system of the past cannot be denied, but their doctrines are inadequate for the coming age. They "tend to take the framework for the foundation and words for things." Saint-Simon emphasized the distinction between a "metaphysical polity" and a "scientific polity" and appealed to the productive classes in society, *les industriels*, to assume their natural role as leaders in the work of social reorganization.[7]

What came to be major themes of *La Libertad*—the attack upon "metaphysics," the rejection of doctrinaire liberalism, and the application of science to politics and social regeneration—were developed more systematically in 1826 by Auguste Comte, Saint-Simon's former secretary and collaborator. Comte explained at the outset that "positive philosophy" was somewhat analogous to "natural philosophy," the term common in England, or the "philosophy of sciences." Positive philosophy, however, does not limit itself to designating the various "sciences of observation," but emphasizes their interrelationship, "thought of as being subjected to a common method and as forming different parts of a general

---

García's newspaper *El Centinela español*, 10 October). The article was the second of a series, four of which were published with a brief introduction and conclusion as *Polémica filosófica. ¿Garantiza mejor el progreso el sistema metafísico que el sistema experimental?* (Mexico, 1881) and in two subsequent editions (1887 and 1898) as *Política científica y política metafísica*. The focus of these important articles was the conflict over educational ideas in 1880 and they will be treated in more detail in chap. 6.

[6] Sierra in *La Libertad*, 30 August 1878 (*Obras*, 4:157–58).

[7] Henri de Saint-Simon, *Du Système industriel*, 3 vols. (1821), 1:12, 20 in *Oeuvres*, vol. 3 (Paris, 1966).

plan of investigation."[8] Comte stressed that this interrelationship was hierarchical in form. In the study and classification of the sciences, one must move from the simpler, more general, more abstract, and more independent to the more complex and interrelated. This is true not only as between the different sciences, but also within the study of an individual science. Thus the progression is from celestial to terrestial physics, that is, from astronomy to mechanics to chemistry. These sciences Comte termed *corps bruts* as distinguished from *corps organisés*, physiology and social physics or sociology.[9] Social physics, implicitly a part of physiology, merits a special category for study because it is more complicated than the other sciences and conceptions concerning it are less perfected.

In Comte's hierarchy of the sciences, physiology, the study of organic bodies on the individual level, preceded sociology, the study of such bodies as groups. Likewise, the stages of social development were those followed by the individual human mind. Each of our principal conceptions, each branch of our knowledge, passes successively through three stages, the theological (imaginary [*fictif*]), the metaphysical (abstract), and the scientific or positive. These are the three methods of conceptualizing used by the human mind and each has its points of perfection. The principal problem Comte saw in the contemporary state of knowledge was that the theological and metaphysical methods, having largely disappeared in dealing with natural phenomena, "are still, on the contrary, exclusively used . . . in all that concerns social phenomena." We are still plagued, he argued, by an outworn struggle between such concepts as divine right and popular sovereignty.[10]

The necessary point of departure for the human mind in all matters is theological, said Comte, and its definitive and final state is positive. Metaphysical conceptions are transitional and as such are of a "bastard and mobile character," adapting themselves to the gradual decline of the first type or the gradual rise of the third. Like Saint-Simon, Comte saw the present stage of thought as mixed or stationary and intellectual anarchy as the prevailing condition in society. The vigor and clarity of metaphysical conceptions, which reached their peak during the French Revolution in the intellectual struggle against the old regime, have now been lost. The metaphysical spirit, as seen for example in the abstract doc-

---

[8] Auguste Comte, *Cours de philosophie positive*, 5th ed. 6 vols. (Paris, 1907–08), 1:xiv. (The fifth edition was presented as "identical" to the first edition of 1830–42; this presumably meant the same text, but not the same pagination). The six-volume *Cours* was the published version of Comte's lectures, delivered in 1826.

[9] Ibid., pp. 34–60; 4:132n.

[10] Ibid., 1:12. The situation with politics, said Comte, is analogous to the former tendency to substitute astrology for astronomy, alchemy for chemistry, and universal panaceas for systematic medical studies: ibid., 4:153–54.

trines of equality, the rights of man, and freedom of conscience, are now "radically hostile to all true social reorganization."[11] Though the editors of *La Libertad* never reached Comte's extreme antiliberal conclusions, his characterization of the metaphysical spirit, like many of his other themes, was fundamental to their mode of thought.

Comte's rejection of metaphysics and his emphasis on empiricism did not mean he was hostile to the role of theory in social science. On the contrary, he announced that the great need of the modern age was theoretical. Intellectual reorganization must replace intellectual anarchy. The special character of positive philosophy as opposed to earlier modes of thought "consists of regarding theories, in whatever realm of ideas, as having for their objective the coordination of observed facts." In the positive stage, the human mind is no longer concerned with the origin and destiny of the universe or with the search for essences, but instead works "to discover, by a nice combination of reason and observation, the effective laws [of phenomena]." While all positive thought must rest on observation, it is equally true that "to engage in observation, our mind needs some kind of theory."[12] Thus at the heart of positive philosophy is the search for an ever-diminishing number of laws or "general facts," of which all observable phenomena are particular cases. The starting point (and presumably the primary law) of any science of society is "the fundamental notion of progress," which since Descartes has been pointed to by the gradual development of the natural sciences. Comte singled out Montesquieu as the pioneer in establishing that social phenomena are subject to invariable natural laws. Later it was Condorcet who demonstrated, despite his many absurd speculations, "the truly primordial, scientific idea of the social progression of humanity."[13]

Comte frequently emphasized the application of social science. Just as the science of biology is tied to the medical arts, so the science of society must be tied to practical policy. The resolution of "intellectual anarchy" in society leads necessarily to the resolution of "political anarchy," which Comte identified as the "appalling revolutionary constitution of modern society." Social questions, because of their complexity and their entanglement with human passions, must not be left to the arbitrary and blind actions of "an incompetent public," or to the "vagabond liberty" of present-day thinking. Comte called for the intervention of an elite, yet he was distressed by the political indifference of most of the savants of his day, those who should have seen the relation between scientific and po-

[11] Ibid., pp. 370, 38.

[12] Ibid., 4:115; 1:xiii, 3, 5.

[13] Ibid., 4:120–21, 133. Comte said Montesquieu was ahead of his time in seeking a principle of social organization in a period destined for revolution.

litical analysis and who should have provided the leadership for social regeneration.[14]

In adapting to Mexico ideas of which Comte had provided the classic formulation, the writers of *La Libertad* proclaimed the need for more administration and less politics. The editors acknowledged that the phrase had been introduced by former President Sebastián Lerdo de Tejada; now perhaps it could finally be put into effect. They noted the efforts of Matías Romero, the new minister of *hacienda* (finance), and concluded that at least in his domain the government seemed to be entering a new era. Equally promising were the vigorous activities of Vicente Riva Palacio, minister of *fomento* (development). These ministers have moved to recognize the English debt, to initiate new public works, and to expand telegraph lines, railways, and roads. The systematic gathering of statistics has begun. But, warned *La Libertad*, the ultimate success of the Díaz regime will depend on the formation of "a scientific plan of administration and politics, based on the knowledge of the biological, social, and economic conditions of the country."[15]

The idea that society should be administered and not governed was an integral part of scientific politics at its origin. Henri de Saint-Simon in seeking a principle of order for a Europe disorganized by the French Revolution emphasized that the new society should be industrial, that it should be coterminous with the state, and that its basis should be an association of work. In arguing that the *industriels* of his day should be brought into government, he extolled their administrative capabilities, their ability to deal with finance and to draw up a good budget. Administration has now become a "positive science."[16] These views make us forget that Saint-Simon had begun his writing in 1814 as a liberal, reacting to the external conquests and internal despotic administration of the Napoleonic Empire. Like other contemporary liberals such as Charles Comte and Benjamin Constant, Saint-Simon and his secretary Augustin Thierry had idealized England. England represented a government founded on industry, a commercial government, a "liberal government in the true sense of the word."[17]

Saint-Simon broke with Thierry in 1817 and soon came to repudiate the term "liberal." The constitutionalism of a Constant became anathema to him, the tendency to see government as apart from or above society and limited for the protection of its members. Present governmental institutions, in Saint-Simon's view, were to be abolished as far as possible. Managers and administrators, experts performing their functions, were

[14] Ibid., pp. 2–4, 66–67, 111.

[15] *La Libertad*, 4 January 1879; also 9, 12 February, 10 March, 11 April and 13 June 1878.

[16] Saint-Simon, *Du Système industriel*, 1:117–18, 137.

[17] Quoted by Halévy, "Saint-Simonian Economic Doctrine," p. 28.

to replace rulers and governors. Individual liberty, the social goal of the liberals, was to be put aside in favor of association, based on functional specialization. The human race "is destined to pass from governmental or military rule to administrative or industrial rule."[18] These ideas were perpetuated by Saint-Simon's followers after his death in 1827, and especially by Auguste Comte. They came to be the fundamental assumptions of scientific politics. Thus Telesforo García, refuting the liberal constitutionalist Vigil in 1879, asserted that government is not distinct from society, but one of its functional organs. The difference between state and society is the difference between organ and organism, the part and the whole. Government is certainly not the product of a pact between individuals.[19]

The idea of society as an evolving organism to be understood historically was a commonplace of late nineteenth-century thought, and it guided scientific politics in Mexico. Although Justo Sierra questioned how far the "system" of Herbert Spencer could be applied to Mexico, he agreed that certain truths were beyond debate. Like any organism, wrote Sierra, society is subject to the laws of evolution, to the simultaneous action of integration and differentiation. As society becomes more integrated, it moves from the homogeneous to the heterogeneous and its parts become more differentiated and specialized. This dual action leads to the perfection of the organism, or progress. In applying this theory to the political and constitutional problems of the late seventies, Sierra maintained that growing social organization and broader individual activity were merely two intimately connected phases of the same evolutionary process. The great concern of the constitution-maker must be to guarantee the expansion of individual rights and action, but also "to circumscribe [them] within the limits demanded by social development."[20] As we shall see in more detail in chapter 7, unfettered individualism was not part of the evolutionary scheme of scientific politics in Mexico.

The organic view of society was fundamentally historical, a point Sierra demonstrated by his many historical works, the first of which was published in 1878. His government-subsidized *Compendio de la historia de la antigüedad*, which was to serve as a text in the National Preparatory School, gave Sierra the opportunity to affirm the naturalistic origins of civilization and also to present history as a sociological science. Citing the theories of Haeckel and Laplace on the origins of the universe, of Lyell on the origins of the earth, and of Darwin on the origin of species, Sierra

---

[18] Ibid., p. 44. See also Frank Manuel, *The New World of Henri Saint-Simon* (Cambridge, Mass., 1956), p. 74 and passim.

[19] *La Libertad*, 18 October 1879.

[20] Sierra in ibid., 3 September, 3 January 1879 (*Obras*, 4:238–39, 182).

set forth views that occasioned sharp rejoinders in the Catholic press.[21] The mission of the historian, maintained Sierra, is to seek facts and the general laws that govern them. These laws ("general facts" or "higher generalizations") can be reduced to the law of progress and the law of evolution. Comte had written that the historical method is essential to the study of any science, that its "philosophy" is inseparable from its "real history," the relationship between the steps in its development. Though Comte was clearly an organicist in his view of society, he had rejected the idea that sociology was a simple derivation of biology. The direct biologic analogy was in conflict with his principal comparison between the stages of the human mind and the stages of society. However, his emphasis on history as the proper way to study the science of society was an important point of departure for later theorists, including the men of *La Libertad*.[22]

Sierra's reservations about applying the system of Spencer to Mexico pertained to the role of public authority in society. Public order cannot come spontaneously through consensus, by a natural strengthening of the social body. Sierra identified in the development of the organism the gradual dominance of the nervous force over the muscular force. The nervous force would have a directive role analogous to the spiritual power in society envisioned by Auguste Comte. Unfortunately, Mexico was not yet prepared for such a scientific "priesthood." Instead, the country needed a rudimentary strengthening of public authority to forestall the outright disintegration of "one of the weakest, most defenseless social organisms that resides in the orbit of civilization." Sierra had in mind the threat of the United States, that "marvelous collective animal" whose "enormous intestine" has insufficient nourishment. Without stronger public authority, we will perish in the struggle for existence as it was envisioned by Darwin.[23] Despite the impact of Herbert Spencer's evo-

[21] See Sierra, *Historia de la antigüedad* (*Obras*, 10:15–17); also *La Libertad*, 2 November 1878. For Sierra's defense of his history against the attacks of *La Voz de México*, see *La Libertad*, 26 January and 7 February 1878 (*Obras*, 9:80–87); also Santiago Sierra in *La Libertad*, 27 January and 1 February 1878. For evidence that Sierra's *Historia* was really an 1878 publication, see José Ignacio Mantecón Navasal et al., *Bibliografía general de don Justo Sierra* (Mexico, 1969), pp. 54–55. The *Historia* bore the series heading "Biblioteca de 'La Libertad.'" The original subsidy of three hundred pesos was ultimately reduced to two hundred pesos. See letters J. Sierra to M. Romero, 10 December 1877, Archivo Matías Romero, No. 23884; and Protasio P. Tagle to Sierra, 13 February 1878 (Sierra, *Obras*, 14:538).

[22] Sierra, *Historia* (*Obras*, 10:15). Comte, *Cours*, 4:236–37, 241, 257–58, 279. It should be noted that Comte's emphasis on the historical method in sociology was not shared by Spencer (see p. 213).

[23] See Sierra in *La Libertad*, 3 September 1879 (*Obras*, 4:238–40); also "El General Burnside y México," 30 July 1879 (an article not reprinted in *Obras*). See also Santiago

lutionary philosophy on social thought in Mexico, a subject we will examine in detail in chapter 7, Spencer's hostility toward the state placed limits on the relevance of his ideas to emerging scientific politics.

The most dramatic feature of the argument for scientific politics was *La Libertad's* frank appeal for authoritarian government, especially the notorious outburst by Francisco G. Cosmes in the issue of 4 September 1878, in reaction to *El Monitor republicano's* support of the "rights of revolution":

> Rights! Society now rejects them. What it wants is bread, . . . a little less of rights in exchange for a little more of security, order, and peace. We have already enacted innumerable rights, which produce only distress and malaise in society. Now let us try a little tyranny, but honorable tyranny, and see what results it brings.

A month later he spoke of "dictatorship," while reemphasizing that it must be honorable and enlightened, not an end in itself but a means to keep a disorganized society from perishing. Sierra's language was more muted; he rejected "dictatorship" as arbitrary and called instead for a "conservative" or a "strong" government. His general points, however, were the same as those of his colleague: the need for order to replace social disintegration and for peace to replace the proclivity toward revolutions. In countries like Mexico, said Sierra, "weak governments are the sure symptoms of death."[24]

In May 1878 the editors began to call *La Libertad* a "liberal-conservative newspaper," thus adopting a phrase that became central to their political program, just as it was central for their counterparts in France and Spain.[25] In justifying the phrase, Justo Sierra argued that liberal and conservative parties had never really existed in Mexico, only revolutionaries and reactionaries. The "liberals" did not realize that "liberty, considered as a right, cannot be instituted apart from a people's moral development, which is order." The "conservatives" lacked any appreciation for the progress of our era, which meant that their "order" was only "immobility

---

Sierra's argument that a healthy centralism is the natural product of social evolution: *La Libertad*, 22 January 1880.

[24] Cosmes in *La Libertad*, 11 October 1878; Sierra in ibid., 30 October 1878, 7 August 1879, 24 February 1880 (*Obras*, 4:166, 228, 279–81).

[25] From 5 January to 5 May 1878 the paper's subtitle was *Periódico científico y literario*; from 9 May 1878 to 21 March 1879, *Periódico liberal-conservador*; from 22 March to 3 August 1879 there was no subtitle; from 5 August 1879 through 1884 the subtitle was *Orden y progreso*. (The issues for 6–8 May 1878 have been lost.) According to the editors, *liberal-conservador* was merely the translation into politics of Comte's "order and progress" (social statics and social dynamics). They ultimately dropped *liberal-conservador*, maintaining that the term inhibited the fusion of political factions, which they said they were trying to promote in the forthcoming election campaign. See ibid., 27 August 1879; also 2 September.

and death." As Cosmes put it, special privileges (*fueros*), entailed estates (*mayorazgos*), and state religion as defended by the old conservatives are as utopian now as is socialism. For us, argued Sierra, conservatism means "to conserve the social order, the only method of adapting liberty, an exotic plant in our history."[26] Although Cosmes, referring to the famous moderates of English history, the "Trimmers," maintained that moderation and compromise were the only way to heal the country's wounds after sixty years of conflict, Sierra distinguished between the "conservative" or "new" liberals and the old moderates. The *moderados* did not attract youth, whereas we welcome to our banner all youth "educated in the habits of experimentation and in positive methods." For Sierra, experimentation and positive methods entailed a new awareness of the exact conditions of society. Since society is an organism developing according to unchangeable laws, all we can do is to facilitate this development, for example, through material improvements and education. Perhaps "the great national party" will now reject dogmas and metaphysical abstractions and seek a new foundation in science.[27]

Despite *La Libertad*'s generational stance and its appeal to youth, the paper was also presented as the "organ of the conservative interests of an unbalanced society." In terms reminiscent of Saint-Simon, the editors said they hoped to stimulate and to seek the support of "the commercial, industrial, and agricultural elements," the country's "true interests." This was the group that lived in peace and was devoted to work, that sought strong government to combat endemic revolutions, in effect the group that formed the basis of a true liberal-conservative system. Moreover, the "conservative interests" were those most devoted to guaranteeing free institutions in the country. Order and liberty must proceed in concert.[28]

It was of great concern to Justo Sierra and his colleagues that Mexico's rich were not participating in politics, although their withdrawal, even their emigration after years of turmoil, was understandable. Men of wealth, he asserted, are a great potential force in a country that has no nobility and in which the clergy is decimated; yet they only stand by and lament its state of affairs. Hammeken y Mexía pointed to France and England, where the great majority of legislators were from the upper classes: rich proprietors, bankers, industrialists, agriculturalists, notables

[26] Sierra in ibid., 10 May, 23 October 1878 (*Obras*, 4:145, 164); Cosmes in *La Libertad*, 22 January 1879.

[27] Cosmes in ibid., 18 October 1879; Sierra in ibid., 2 July 1878 (*Obras*, 4:154–55); also *La Libertad*, 9 October 1878.

[28] These ideas fill the pages of *La Libertad* during 1878–79. See especially 9–11 May 1878, when the concept *liberal-conservador* was being launched, 13 February 1879, and statements by Sierra, on 12 June, 23 October 1878, and 25 July 1879 (*Obras*, 4:150, 165, 227).

of science. If they didn't fill the chambers, their place would be taken by "butchers, agitators, and communists." The same could happen in Mexico. The focus on conservative interests even led to frank suggestions that former political conservatives be recruited to the liberal-conservative cause. We must "tear from the reactionary party," wrote the editors, those conservatives who are able and who are attuned to the times. Political participation by the wealthy, even by ex-conservatives, would help narrow the existing gulf between government and society.[29] As we have seen, the union of society and government was an important assumption of scientific politics. The marriage of conflicting political terms formed a natural corollary.

The political argument of *La Libertad*, epitomized by the notion of conservative-liberalism itself, might be seen as an exercise in semantics, an ingenious but confusing manipulation of terminology. The "new generation," like its contemporaries in France and Spain, was trying to fill old terms with new meaning, without abandoning them. Because the name "conservative" was identified with clericalism, foreign intervention, and treason, and because Justo Sierra and his colleagues considered themselves heirs to the Reforma, they were, first of all, "liberals." However much they sought to introduce the experimental method into politics, to reject the dogmas and abstractions of their reformist and constitutionalist predecessors, they still had to work within the confines of the traditional term. The exposition and justification of conservative-liberalism in *La Libertad* seems excessive, a kind of doubletalk. However, we must take the argument seriously. The collapse and reconciliation of traditional political positions while preserving the old terms was at the heart of political discourse, not only in 1878 but throughout the entire Porfiriato.

Such considerations provide a perspective for understanding the repeated insistence by *La Libertad* that the Liberal party be transformed into a *partido de gobierno*, a phrase that was to become fixed in the rhetoric of the Díaz era. The Liberal party should be "capable of successfully carrying through the reorganization of the country"; it should be profoundly conservative, yet dedicated to maintaining free institutions. Such a position, added Justo Sierra, is based on the premise that the threat of reaction is over and that a rival party no longer exists.[30] On another occasion, *La Libertad* envisioned the time when the Liberal party would be transformed from a party into the nation. However, for this change to take place, the Liberal party must "create within itself a conservative

---

[29] "Emigración de los ricos," *La Libertad*, 24 January 1879; Hammeken in ibid., 9 August 1879; ibid., 7 January 1879. See also S. Sierra in ibid., 17 January 1880.

[30] Sierra in ibid., 1 January, 7 August 1879 (*Obras*, 4:178, 229–30).

nucleus that can serve as a bond of union with the past and a point of departure for the future." Santiago Sierra, using his customary biological analogy, called for cohesion in the political organism, which like any organism cannot tolerate excessive division without dissolving. For him, a "progressive conservative party" could become the "great Liberal party of the future."[31]

Concern about the Liberal party was stimulated by the forthcoming elections of 1880, and particularly by José María Vigil's scheme for a union of the Liberal party, presumably to support one candidate from among the many that appeared. Although we will examine Vigil's ill-fated political effort in the next chapter, it is worth noting here that it epitomizes the confusion of political discourse in the 1878–80 period. Both opponents in the debate were calling for the union of the Liberal party. Both were using the same phrase, even though they differed sharply on what that phrase signified.[32]

It is difficult to understand conservative-liberalism in Mexico without reference to the contemporary political experience of France and Spain. News from Europe filled the leading Mexico City newspapers after 1867; special lengthy *correspondencias* by European journalists appeared regularly, accompanied by articles and commentaries reprinted from Paris and Madrid dailies. With the laying of the transatlantic cable in 1866, the traditional time-lag in communications was drastically reduced, giving Mexicans a heightened sense of contact with events in Europe. European experience had provided important points of orientation for Mexico's elite at various times earlier in the century; the process increased apace after 1867. By 1878 the men of *La Libertad* were well prepared to reinforce their arguments by frequent references to the continent.

The turbulent and dramatic events of the years 1868 to 1877 in France and Spain were closely watched in the Mexico City press, partly because they were seen to have great relevance to Mexico. The decade began with the abdication of Isabel II, prompted by the September Revolution of 1868 in Spain. It ended with the consolidation of the Third Republic in France after the crisis of 16 May 1877. The two countries became battlegrounds between republicanism and monarchy, just as Mexico had been in the years before 1867. On 17 November 1867, Emilio Castelar, the Spanish republican publicist, paid tribute in *El Monitor republicano* to "that government which has saved democracy" by defeating the forces of Napoleon III. Thus he began his fortnightly commentary, which was

[31] *La Libertad*, 3 October 1879; S. Sierra, "Porvenir del partido reaccionario," ibid., 13 February 1878.

[32] Examples of the response to Vigil can be found in ibid., 18 April, 7–8 May, and 10 July 1879.

to last thirty years. Young America, he added, has solved its problems better than has old Europe.[33]

The decade also witnessed intense conflict over the principles of social and territorial organization, notably the Paris Commune versus the French National Assembly in 1871 and the Spanish revolutionary provinces versus Madrid during the First Republic of 1873. Manuel Payno, the Mexican writer and erstwhile liberal politician, deplored the Commune as "the most brutal, barbarous, and useless of all dictatorships because it contains within it anarchy and weakness." Anyone at all versed in "the positive science and practice of government" will recognize that social order is impossible under such a system.[34] In 1874 Justo Sierra, writing in *La Tribuna*, saw France as epitomizing "the diverse elements that struggle for predominance in the world." Unlike others who refuse to comment on foreign events, he said, we believe there is much to learn from them.[35] The early conclusions of these Mexican observers of Europe, like those of Castelar, were optimistic. Mexico had a constitution, accepted and defended as the law of the land, whereas France (in 1871), though "a thousand years old," had no government and Spain was searching "with a lantern" for a king. In 1874 Sierra could envision the normal and spontaneous progress of liberalism in the New World, unobstructed by the extremes of socialism or absolutism. Both were moral deviations brought about by overpopulation, poverty, or longstanding traditions.[36] Such optimism faded quickly with the political upheavals and the factionalism of 1876.

By the time *La Libertad* was launched, France had weathered the political storms of radical republicanism and socialism on the Left and monarchical restoration on the Right. Jorge Hammeken took note of the

---

[33] Castelar's first "Correspondencia particular" (which customarily occupied the entire front page of *El Monitor*) was datelined Paris, 15 October 1867. The last installment appeared 9–10 December 1896, three weeks before the cessation of the newspaper.

[34] *El Federalista*, 9 August 1871, the first of several articles by Payno on the Commune, placed mostly on page one. News from France, sometimes only a week late, was particularly prominent in *El Federalista* during 1871.

[35] Sierra in *La Tribuna*, 1 January 1874 (*Obras*, 4:367).

[36] See *El Federalista*, 2 January 1871, the initial issue of the newspaper, which explained its title; Sierra in *La Tribuna*, 1 January 1874 (*Obras*, 4:372). Spain's search for a king ended in the brief reign of Amadeo of Savoy (16 November 1870–11 February 1873). News of the new king appeared in *El Federalista* on 20 January 1871, a two-month lag, although General Prim's assassination (27 December 1870) was reported within two weeks (14 January 1871). A recent study of Mexican press reaction to Spanish events points out that news often took three to four weeks to arrive because it traveled by cable to New York and then by telegraph via Matamoros or Vera Cruz: Antonia Pi-Suñer Llorens, *El Sexenio revolucionario español (1868–1874) ante el gobierno y la prensa mexicana durante la república restaurada* (Mexico, 1984), p. 74. On Spain and Mexico during this period, see also her introduction to *México y España durante la república restaurada* (Mexico, 1985).

ninth anniversary of the founding of the Third Republic, now "the model of what common sense and good judgment can do to consolidate a nation." To think, he added, that the republic was first proclaimed by a former "intransigent monarchist," Adolphe Thiers, and that a former "red republican and fierce demagogue," Leon Gambetta, is now saying that a conservative republic is the only one possible. Old utopias and doctrinaire solutions have been put aside in favor of facts to serve the nation. In short, France has witnessed a "peaceful revolution brought about by . . . liberal-conservative ideas."[37]

Repeatedly throughout 1878 and 1879, Justo Sierra, Cosmes, García, and their colleagues put the example of France before their readers. Sierra noted that in France the terms "conservative," "liberal," and "republican" had merged in the service of reason and patriotism. Could not the same happen in Mexico? In response to the "liberals of the old school" who extolled the beneficent influence of the French Revolution, Cosmes maintained that modern French history was nothing more than a reaction by strong but popular governments against "those utopias of absolute rights" bred by the French Revolution. As "documentation substantiating our program," the editors published a selection from Émile Littré defending the conservative republic in the name of historical experience and science against the attacks of the radicals. "If the fortune of radicalism," said the positivist disciple of Auguste Comte, "is linked to metaphysical and absolute politics, the fortune of sociology is linked to the progress of the experimental method in all that pertains to society." France was an example, said La Libertad on another occasion, of where the "liberal party, turning into a party of government, had become conservative."[38]

La Libertad took particular notice of the appearance of Le Gouverne-

[37] La Libertad, 5 September 1879. The Third Republic was proclaimed at the Hôtel de Ville in Paris on 4 September 1870. Speeches by Gambetta were reprinted in La Libertad on 9 October, 27 and 29 November 1878. La Libertad took a lively interest in amnesty measures of the French government toward prisoners from Commune days, in which Gambetta figured prominently: see 3, 11, 13 January 1880.

[38] See Sierra in ibid., 22 December 1878 (Obras, 4:178); Cosmes in La Libertad, 10 January 1879; "El Programa liberal-conservador de M. Littré," ibid., 22 June 1879; ibid., 10 November 1878. See also Sierra in ibid., 18 January 1878 (Obras, 4:135). I have been unable to identify the source of the Littré selection, which from internal evidence appears to have been written in mid-1873. Littré (1801–81) rejected Comte's authoritarian politics after 1848 and became a republican opponent of the Second Empire. His ideas inspired a "positivist generation" of republicans, of which Gambetta was the most notable example. Gambetta was a democrat in 1871, but thereafter he moved toward "opportunism," which he maintained was merely the application of positive science to politics. Like Littré he came to support the party of Thiers and the constitutional laws of 1875, abandoning the principle of a unicameral legislature. See John Eros, "The Positivist Generation of French Republicanism," Sociological Review n.s. 3 (1955): 255–77; also pp. 96–97.

ment de M. Thiers, published in 1878 by Jules Simon. Simon was a philosopher who became minister of instruction during Thiers's presidency from February 1871 through May 1873 and who was briefly premier during 1876–77 under President MacMahon. *La Libertad* particularly admired Simon's consistent moderate position through these troubled years. He emerged in early 1871 as an opponent of Gambetta's radicalism; and yet he aroused the strong antipathy of the monarchical party because of his anticlericalism and policies of educational reform. Under the title of "a great conservative," *La Libertad* printed a fragment of Simon's speech at the Paris Exposition of 1878 in which he condemned the crimes of the Commune as the work of persons alien to the republic. "The republic," said Simon, "is prudent, moderate and conservative."[39]

It would be quite natural that *La Libertad*, which looked to the Third French Republic as a model for political consolidation in Mexico, should be a strong advocate of the renewal of diplomatic relations with France. Mexican policy had been guided by the statement of Benito Juárez on 15 July 1867 that the victory of the republic over European intervention and the empire constituted Mexico's second independence. Juárez considered that relations with Spain, France, and England had been severed by virtue of the London Convention of 1861, and that resumption should only come on terms favorable to Mexico. Though Juárez indicated an interest in restoring relations, Mexican governments came to insist that France take the initiative and be the first to name a minister. Negotiations began seriously only after the fall of the offending government of Napoleon III in 1871, but they were stalled over protocol until the onset of the Díaz regime. Justo Sierra responded to the new, more favorable diplomatic climate in the last lines of a long poem entitled "France," dedicated to the memory of Thiers, who died in May 1877: "The tomb of a monarch separated us; the tomb of a republican unites us."[40]

La Libertad commemorated the victory of 5 May 1862 over the French at Puebla by lauding "the noble French people," now freed from an "impure" government by long and hard suffering. A tyrant's ambition could not break the "natural ties established between the two peoples by common ideas, a common race, and a common destiny." Cosmes carried the theme of Latin solidarity even further by suggesting (despite patriotic protestations) that the French intervention could be viewed as a gener-

[39] See *La Libertad*, 11 November 1878; "Las opiniones de Julio Simon y el credo de 'La Libertad,'" 6 June 1878; also 27 September 1878, 26 September 1879.

[40] For Juárez's cryptic statements on foreign policy of 15 July and 8 December 1867, see Jorge L. Tamayo, ed., *Benito Juárez. Documentos, discursos y correspondencia*, 15 vols. (Mexico, 1967), 12:250, 813. The renewal of relations with France is treated thoroughly by Daniel Cosío Villegas, *Historia moderna*, 6:599–714. Sierra's poem dated October 1877 was printed in *La Libertad*, 3 September 1878 (*Obras*, 1:381–85).

ous effort to block the continual threat of the United States. Strong relations with Europe are vital for "our race," he concluded. Cosmes's fellow editors, especially Carlos Olaguíbel and Santiago Sierra, disputed his benign attitude toward the intervention. At a time when the imprudent truculence of General Edward Ord on the northern border was hindering the efforts of the Díaz regime to secure recognition by the United States, a rift developed among the editors. Olaguíbel and Santiago Sierra argued that France must make further efforts to rectify damages done to the country during the intervention. The firm position initiated by Juárez should be maintained. Cosmes accused Olaguíbel of being an anglophile and even of antipathy toward the Latin race, when it was clear to all that the two civilizers of modern Mexico were Spain and France. Despite dissension in the ranks, *La Libertad*'s conciliatory attitude prevailed, coinciding with actual government policy. With the arrival of Baron Boissy d'Anglas in Mexico City on 26 November 1880 to present his credentials to President Díaz, relations between France and Mexico were finally renewed.[41]

Although the model of the Third French Republic loomed large for the advocates of conservative-liberalism, they found the contemporary political experience of Spain even more relevant to Mexico. The space devoted to Spanish news and commentary in the major newspapers of the capital exceeded that for all other areas. Moreover, the Spanish immigrant colony in Mexico City increased greatly after 1876, a growth accompanied by a flourishing Spanish press and strong personal ties between Spaniards and leading Mexicans. Of all foreigners, it was Emilio Castelar, orator, republican propagandist, prolific publicist, and statesman, who became a kind of demigod in late nineteenth-century Mexico, as he did throughout Spanish America. In addition, Castelar had a special importance for the men of *La Libertad*, which helps elucidate their political ideas.

The fame of Castelar is difficult to summon up today; for our age he is only a relic. A forgotten man of letters, he was primarily an orator and journalist, although he also wrote history, novels, and some poetry. He was the great Hispanic orator in an age of eloquence. His elegant and verbose style was widely admired and imitated, but as Gregorio Marañon has said, "time devours styles."[42] Castelar's publications were ephemeral,

[41] *La Libertad*, 5 May 1878; Cosmes in ibid., 19 November 1879. The debates among the editors over renewal of relations with France can be followed in the issues of 8, 14, 18, 22 November 1879. On General Ord's activities, see Cosío Villegas, *Historia moderna*, 6:1–250.

[42] Gregorio Marañon, "Efemérides y comentarios" (1952), *Obras completas*, 2d ed., 10 vols. (Madrid, 1968–77), 9:588, includes a perceptive comment on Castelar's influence. For examples of estimates by contemporaries see Rubén Darío, *Obras completas*, 22 vols. (Ma-

seized upon like newspapers by an eager public and then as quickly put aside. His complete works have never been published. The great libraries, even in Spain, hold only a scattering of his several score octavo volumes, and no Castelar bibliography has ever been attempted. His cause was republicanism. During the fifties and sixties he became the implacable foe of monarchy and the champion of an inevitable "democracy." Each age has its formula, its idea, he wrote in 1858. "Whether we wish it or not, it is certain that our times are democratic times. Everything tends toward liberty, equality, and the brotherhood of peoples."[43] His version of democracy had no place for demagoguery or social radicalism. His political and humanitarian generalities, devoid of social content or analysis, thrilled republicans in Europe and America but subsequently seemed shallow.

Castelar celebrated the republican spirit in the New World and particularly Mexico's heroic struggle of the sixties, which coincided with his overt attacks on Isabel II at home.[44] He once referred to the independence of America as the "great event of our century," and in the late 1850s he had promoted a benevolent vision of Hispanic solidarity based upon the progress of liberal and republican ideals.[45] Over the years he enjoyed recalling the fall of the Mexican Empire for delighted American readers, as in the following passage of vintage Castelar:

> I still remember, as if I had seen it this very day, the famous gathering . . .
> where the news of the disaster of Maximilian had just reached the ears of his
> protector. It was a great theatre adorned in all the splendor of Babylonian im
> perial luxury . . . the emperor [Napoleon III] seemed a cold cadaver and the

---

drid, 1917), 22:139–67; Sierra, *Obras*, 5:259–68. Darío was present at Castelar's funeral in 1899. Sierra's statement in which he quotes at length from his own enthusiastic appreciation of Castelar in 1869 was a eulogy delivered in the Mexican Chamber of Deputies on 17 June 1899.

[43] Emilio Castelar, *La Fórmula del progreso. Ideas democráticas* (Madrid, 1858), p. 4. This famous tract was not overtly republican, but its attack on monarchy lay just below the surface.

[44] These attacks began with his famous articles in *La Democracia* of Madrid (21, 25 February 1865) scorning "*el razgo*," Isabel's "gallant gesture" of alienating a portion of the royal patrimony to the nation. According to the Constitution of 1812, said Castelar, the royal patrimony already belonged to the nation. On Castelar's role in the developing republican opposition, see C. A. M. Hennessy, *The Federal Republic in Spain* (London, 1962), pp. 14–27; also Carmen Llorca, *Emilio Castelar* (Madrid, 1966), pp. 94–104.

[45] The reference was in a speech to the Constituent Cortes (22 February 1869) in Castelar, *Discursos parlamentarios*, ed. C. Llorca (Madrid, 1973), p. 99. On Hispanic solidarity see "La Unión de España y América" (March 1858) and "Méjico y el gobierno español" (1859?) in *Recuerdos y esperanzas*, 2 vols. (Madrid, n.d.), 1:55–61, 87–104; "El Maquiavelismo de Bonaparte en América" (29 January 1864) and "Juárez y Lincoln" (15 April 1864) in *Cuestiones políticas y sociales*, 2 vols. (Madrid, 1870), 1:51–59, and 3:49–58.

empire a fleeting shadow. What a beautiful and extraordinary spectacle that was!

A champion of republicanism in the nation that Mexicans associated with monarchical despotism had a special appeal for them. Even the hispanophobe Ignacio Ramírez had acknowledged in his famous polemic of 1865 rejecting Castelar's panhispanist overtures that while in Spain Castelar was "only the bastard of public opinion," in Mexico "he is one of our brothers."[46]

Just as Castelar hailed the restoration of the republic in Mexico, so Mexicans eagerly followed the progress of republicanism in Spain. Through Castelar's fortnightly commentary in *El Monitor republicano*, Mexican readers could share in the excitement of the cause as related by one of its leaders. His "letters" were always given "the place of honor," and soon after they began, *El Monitor* announced that their great popularity prompted it to print a much larger edition than usual on the days they appeared.[47] Castelar's contributions continued throughout the years 1868 to 1874, interrupted only during the months of 1873 when he was minister of state and then president of the republic. Apart from Castelar's lengthy commentaries, *El Monitor* carried daily news and documents from Spain during 1873, including speeches by Castelar's fellow republican presidents, Estanislao Figueras, Francisco Pi y Margall, and Nicolás Salmerón. Among the many Mexicans who welcomed the birth of the republic was Justo Sierra in a poem entitled *"España libre. A Emilio Castelar."* Mexico and Spain, "by liberty blessed, we form a single people," he wrote. By the time Castelar had resigned the presidency on 3 January 1874, his stature in Mexico as a political leader was immense.[48]

The experience of the Spanish Republic and of its last president had a new and special significance in Mexico following the upheaval of 1876. During 1878 and 1879 *La Libertad* was saturated with news from Spain and evidences of Castelar, as *El Monitor* had been during the dramatic

[46] Castelar, "prólogo" to Salvador Quevedo y Zubieta, *México. Recuerdos de un emigrado* (Madrid, 1883), p. ix; Ignacio Ramírez, "La Desespañolización," reprinted in *El Federalista*, 1 May 1871, also in his *Obras*, 2 vols. (Mexico, 1889), 1:322. Castelar was in exile in Paris in 1867 following the abortive revolt against the monarchy in mid-1866 led by General Juan Prim.

[47] See the editorial comment in *El Monitor*, 17 January 1868, repeated again the next day.

[48] Castelar's "letters" ceased with the one of 28 February 1873 (*El Monitor*, 1 April 1873) and resumed again with the one of 29 June 1873 (*El Monitor*, 13 August 1873). The second interruption came after his letter dated 7 September 1873 (*El Monitor*, 18 October 1873), resuming 26 February 1874 (*El Monitor*, 31 March 1874). Castelar assumed the presidency on 6 September. Sierra's poem, which does not appear in his *Obras*, was dated 14 February 1873 (three days after the beginning of the republic), and it was printed in *El Monitor* on 30 March 1873.

days of the republic itself. Castelar's fortnightly letters and his speeches were reprinted and commented upon and his comings and goings closely followed. For the editors of *La Libertad*, Castelar, like Thiers and Simon in France, became the very model of a conservative-liberal, a practitioner of scientific politics and the "apostle of liberalism for Latin America." Castelar has captured exactly "the new face of democratic evolution," and we agree completely with his program, they said. Castelar tells us "we are entering a scientific and experimental period. The era of vernal dreams has passed." Like him, we look to the formation of "a great conservative party," more addicted to "practical liberty" than to "liberty declaimed," and "profoundly convinced that positive progress rests on the normal development of a society, that is, on order." Castelar's new "method," in his own words, was "to obtain radical ends through conservative procedures . . . a strong government within the laws placed at the service of the modern spirit." Conservative-liberals in Mexico, noted Justo Sierra, are more fortunate than were the Spanish republicans, because we can pursue these objectives without having to change our form of government. In extolling "conciliation," *La Libertad* referred in July 1879 to Castelar's new (and ephemeral) Possibilist party, comparable to the Opportunist party in France.[49]

Castelar had since the mid-1860s led the conservative wing of the republican movement in Spain. Although he had championed "individualism" against "socialism" in a series of polemics with Francisco Pi y Margall, the issues of the republic were basically political. The prevailing doctrine of the movement was federalism, which Castelar first accepted and then came to repudiate in fact if not in theory during the course of 1873. Federalism, as promoted by Pi y Margall, had roots in medieval regional autonomy, in the sixteenth-century *comunero* revolt against Charles V, and in the War for Independence, when Spain was "virtually a federal republic." Thus federalism was for Pi a native idea, replacing "French" centralist liberalism, which had since 1833 guided the monarchist regimes in Spain. Castelar was the leader in drawing up the draft Constitution of 1873, which was characterized by marked decentralization of authority and separation of powers. Yet he was soon to govern as a strong president of a de facto centralist regime.[50]

[49] These particular examples of Castelariana can be found in *La Libertad*, 14 February 1878 (Sierra, *Obras*, 4:141–42); 9 April 1878; 17 July 1879. The manifesto of the *posibilistas* (Madrid, 1 February 1879) covered an entire page of *La Libertad* on 2 April 1879.

[50] See Hennessy, *Federal Republic*, pp. xii–xiv, 88–93, 247. Hennessy notes the irony of federalist ideology, namely that it was promoted as a native force by intellectuals who were attempting to bring Spain into the mainstream of European thought and politics. Pi, for example, while rejecting "French" liberalism, drew much of his theoretical inspiration for federalism from Proudhon.

Castelar came into office in September 1873 at a time of political crisis. The unsettled years since the 1868 revolution had encouraged a revival of Carlism, the traditionalist movement to restore absolute monarchy and to preserve Spain from the ravages of atheism and liberalism. By June 1873 the republican government was battling the advancing troops of the Bourbon pretender, Don Carlos María. Even more threatening were the revolts in Andalusia to establish "cantonalist" republics, an extreme version of federalism. The basic problem for Madrid was to restore discipline in the army, which was riddled with sympathy for the cantonalists, as well as being weakened in the south by the need for troops to fight the Carlists in the north. The government of Nicolás Salmerón (18 July to 6 September) moved to restore order, but the burden fell principally on Castelar, who came to power vowing to enforce the military *ordenanza,* the death penalty for disobedience. Faced with militant Carlism and the continuing defiance on the part of the cantonalist republic at Cartagena, Castelar suspended constitutional guarantees, closed the Cortes on 21 September, and ruled by decree for three months. Refusing in late December to join formally with the Conservatives under General Serrano in perpetuating the republican dictatorship, Castelar reinstated the Cortes according to his earlier pledge and was promptly voted out of office. The way was cleared for the restoration of the monarchy within a year.[51]

Castelar defended his policies vigorously and at length in his correspondence to *El Monitor,* written in early 1874, as well as in several widely disseminated speeches. He presented familiar liberal-conservative themes not only with the usual Castelarian eloquence, but with a force and immediacy derived from his recent days of embattled leadership. Castelar never formally broke with federalism, even though he saw its extreme implementation at Cartagena as tantamount to demagoguery, anarchy, and even socialism. His cardinal principle was the unity of the nation, "the highest political conception of modern times," and he saw the republic as "a federation that distributes autonomy" among individuals, municipalities, and states. Faced with complete chaos in September, he argued that a "temporary despotism" to meet "combat with combat" was necessary. Under such circumstances it was impossible to consider reforms. By restoring *la ordenanza,* asserted Castelar, "I saved the army and with the army I saved the nation." His goal was to "convert the republican party into a party of government" in order to combat two

[51] The best account of Castelar's presidency is ibid., pp. 220–43, though it is somewhat less sympathetic to Castelar than Joseph A. Brandt, *Toward the New Spain* (Chicago, 1933), pp. 285–326, and Llorca, *Emilio Castelar,* pp. 178–209. The text of the constitutional "project" of 1873 can be found in *Manual of Spanish Constitutions, 1808–1931,* ed. Arnold R. Verduin (Ypsilanti, 1941), pp. 67–76.

utopias—the monarchy and the canton. Either the republic must mean the end of revolutions, both monarchical and anarchical, or it means nothing. All through his defense of specific authoritarian policies ran a characteristic faith in democracy as a historical synthesis of opposing ideas: progress and stability, movement and restraint, liberty and authority, rights and government.[52]

Castelar was the most cosmopolitan of the Spanish republicans. Not only did his historical lectures and his correspondence with American newspapers have a broad European scope, but he was "responsible for linking Spanish federalism to the main current of European republicanism" during its revival of the 1860s.[53] Castelar was drawn particularly to France and to its political conflicts of the seventies, as can be seen in his defense of his presidency. For example, he saw a close parallel between the weaknesses of the French republic of 1848 and those of Spain in 1873; and as he wrote to *El Monitor* in March 1874, he feared Spain would go the way France had in the 1850s. Turning to contemporary analogies, Castelar compared the cantonalist movement with the Paris Commune and argued that only a "conservative republic" on the French model could restrain anarchy, "pass from the monarchical to the democratic regime," and reassure "the permanent interests." In a letter to Adolfo Calzado he commented on the enviable direction of the Third Republic: restoration and demagoguery are in retreat and "order [is] every day more rooted in customs." When Jules Simon became premier in 1876, Castelar wrote him congratulations (in French): You are "republican and conservative at the same time." Three years later Castelar demonstrated his admiration for Thiers in a lengthy introduction to the Spanish edition of Thiers's history of the French Revolution. Castelar's orientation toward French experience formed an important part of his influence in Mexico.[54]

[52] For these arguments see Castelar, the speeches of 8, 11 September 1873 and 2 January 1874 in *Diario de sesiones de las cortes constituyentes de la república española*, 2 vols. (Madrid, 1874), 4:2150–54, 2460–62; "Correspondencias" of 26 February 1874 (*El Monitor*, 31 March 1874) and of n.d. (*El Monitor*, 6 June 1874); also speech of May 1874 at Granada in *Obras escogidas*, 7 vols. (Madrid, 1922–23), 3:9–51. Justo Sierra, on hearing the news of Castelar's fall, was mildly critical of him for indirectly encouraging the military pronunciamiento of January 1874. Such criticism had faded by 1878. See Sierra in *La Tribuna*, 14 January 1874 (*Obras*, 4:378–79).

[53] Hennessy, *Federal Republic*, p. 88.

[54] See particularly Castelar's correspondence appearing in *El Monitor*, 31 March 1874; his speech at Granada, 26 May 1874 (*Obras*, vol. 3); his letter to Simon (20 December 1876) in *Correspondencia de Emilio Castelar, 1868–1899*, ed. A. Calzado (Madrid, 1908), p. 60; "Prólogo" (dated 14 November 1879) to A. Thiers, *Historia de la revolución francesa*, 4 vols. (Barcelona, 1877–79), 1:i–clx. The Calzado collection (of private correspondence as distinct from Castelar's public correspondence to *El Monitor*) contains much commentary on French politics, partly because his friend Calzado was living in Paris. It also contains

As a cosmopolitan publicist and a renowned, but unemployed, republican politician, Emilio Castelar depended for his livelihood on the receipts from his American "letters" and on the patronage of wealthy friends. In his travels through Europe in late 1874, he was often unable to enjoy his status as a celebrity because of the pressure to send off his fortnightly correspondence. He complained to Calzado from Nice that he was confined to his hotel, doing himself the copy work three assistants had done in Madrid. He was at the time sending his commentaries to *El Nacional* of Lima, *La Nueva América* of Buenos Aires, and the *Herald* of New York, in addition to *El Monitor*. He received 250 francs per installment from Mexico, or 500 francs a month, so there was strong incentive to keep up the pace. Since payments were sporadic, he had a persistent cash flow problem, and he relied upon Calzado (a banker) to establish an account in Paris and to make him regular advances against intermittent receipts.[55]

One of Castelar's friends and patrons was Telesforo García of *La Libertad*. Although details are scanty, the two appear to have been close, possibly even relatives. We know that the dining room furniture in Castelar's Madrid residence at the time of his death belonged to García. Castelar's biographer tells us that he had planned to live his last days with García, who spent a great deal of time in Madrid. Castelar dedicated one of his late works (1892) to García and described him in the preface as a "patriot among patriots" and a "profound thinker." Justo Sierra spoke of reading "a hundred or so" letters from Castelar, presumably addressed to García. Perhaps this self-styled leader of the Spanish colony in Mexico City may be regarded as personifying the link between liberal Spain and scientific politics in Porfirian Mexico.[56]

By 1878 Telesforo García and Justo Sierra had solidified a friendship that was to remain intimate throughout their lives, despite the fact that

---

exchanges with Victor Hugo and Edgar Quinet. On Castelar's philosophical orientation, see below, p. 181.

[55] See Castelar, *Correspondencia*, pp. 15–16 (letter from Nice, 12 October 1874) and passim.

[56] T. J. McMahon, author of "The Spanish Immigrant Community in Mexico City During the Porfiriato, 1876–1911" (Ph.D. diss., University of Notre Dame, 1974), reported finding references to García as an "*hijo político*" of Castelar. On Castelar's furniture, see *Blanco y negro. Revista ilustrada* (Madrid), 30 May 1899. This reference was supplied to me by Carmen Llorca. On García, see also her *Emilio Castelar*, p. 313, 316. For Castelar's effusive words on García see *Historia del descubrimiento de América*, 2d ed. 2 vols. (Madrid, 1894), 1:18–20. Louis Lejeune, in his introduction (p. 4) to García's *Considerations sur la guerre européene* (Mexico, 1916), referred to him as Castelar's fellow student and traveling companion. In his eulogy (1899) of Castelar, Sierra mentions Castelar letters to "*un fraternal amigo mío, que fué quizás el último amigo de Castelar*" (*Obras*, 5:266). They await some future scholar who can locate descendants of García.

García was a controversial figure in Mexico. In his flight from the capital with José María Iglesias in late 1876, Sierra sprained his ankle badly in Querétaro and was taken in by García's brothers for several weeks. He wrote his wife in letters delivered personally by Telesforo that he would be "eternally grateful" for their care. García also agreed on that occasion to pay a visit to Sierra's father-in-law, Dr. Martín Mayora, a prominent member of the Spanish community. Mayora took part in the planning and building of the Spanish cemetery in Mexico City and in the reconditioning of the Casino Español (Spanish club), which he administered for many years. When Sierra served as ambassador to Spain during the final days of his life, he resided at a greatly reduced rent in the Madrid house owned by García, "my friend who is like a brother to me."[57]

When García applied for Mexican citizenship in 1879, Sierra along with their colleague Jorge Hammeken y Mexía served as a witness. The application caused some controversy in the press; in fact it appears to have been opposed by the Minister of Foreign Relations, Miguel Ruelas, and perhaps it was ultimately denied, despite the fact that García was married to Luz Castañeda y Nájera of a prominent Mexican family. As a successful and aggressive merchant-entrepreneur as well as a journalist, García had aroused enmity in several quarters.[58] He was a founder of *La Colonia española* in 1873, a newspaper that soon was to engage in an extensive controversy with the *Diario oficial* over the benefits of Spanish colonization; and in 1877 García published a pamphlet defending Spanish immigrants. While still an editor and proprietor of *La Libertad* in 1879, he started another paper, *El Centinela español*, to serve the rapidly expanding Spanish community. He did this even though *La Libertad* always took an extraordinary interest in the activities and fortunes of Spaniards.[59] It seems quite appropriate that at the time of the centennial of

[57] Letters from Sierra to his wife, Luz Mayora y Carpio, 26 November, 7 December 1876, *Obras*, 14:39–43; Sierra, "Apuntes familiares," ibid., p. 13; letter to Amado Nervo, March 1912, ibid., p. 392. See also Agustín Yáñez, *Don Justo Sierra* (Mexico, 1948).

[58] For the documents including newspaper clippings on García's naturalization, see chap. 2, n. 1. Government opposition to García in 1879 may have arisen from his insistence that he be paid properly for grain shipments confiscated by Díaz in 1876 because they were purportedly destined for Iglesias's forces: Letters García to M. Romero, 26 September, 10 October 1877, Archivo Histórico Matías Romero, Nos. 22430, 22737. Luz Castañeda y Nájera's brother was Vidal, director of the National Preparatory School from 1885 to 1901. In 1885 there was a student protest against his appointment because of his relationship with García, who was accused of speculating in the emission of nickel and in the British debt: see Clementina Díaz y de Ovando, *La Escuela nacional preparatoria*, 2 vols. (Mexico, 1972), 1:140.

[59] On García's 1877 pamphlet and on the controversy between *La Colonia española* and the *Diario oficial* initiated in 1875 by García's more aggressive compatriot, Adolfo Llanos Alcaraz, see below, pp. 239–40. The Spanish population in the Federal District grew from about thirteen hundred in 1876 to twelve thousand in 1911. See Manuel Miño Grijalva et

independence in 1910, Justo Sierra should be the one to urge Segismundo Moret, the Spanish statesman and leader of the Liberal party, to attend the festivities in order to promote the "principle of spiritual interdependence among countries of Spanish speech" and to represent liberal Spain. Sierra assured Moret that the Spanish community in Mexico City would do everything possible to make him feel at home, and he particularly mentioned García. Sierra added for good measure that he felt himself "not an old Castilian but a new Spaniard."[60] Thus the forging of a Hispano-Mexican bond became a consistent objective for the men of *La Libertad* and their sympathizers throughout the Porfiriato.

Influenced by the experience of the conservative republics of Europe as well as by positivism, the advocates of scientific politics made their specific target of attack the Constitution of 1857, which they regarded as artificial and in need of reform. Their premise was that a constitution must be a natural expression of the social order. While they acknowledged that the Constitution of 1857 should be respected and obeyed as the supreme law of the land, they emphasized its limitations and defects. For them it was based on abstractions and not on facts. The constitution became the focus of debate between "old" and "new" liberals, especially between José María Vigil and Justo Sierra. Moreover, constitutional reform was an integral aspect of *La Libertad*'s doctrine of conservative-liberalism and its apology for strong government.

The Constitution of 1857, argued Justo Sierra, is a "generous, liberal utopia," but as such "destined . . . for only slow and painful enactment," like all laws designed to "transform customs." The "utopia" was the emphasis on individual rights, which Sierra and his colleagues regarded as an exaggerated, arbitrary, and socially disruptive dogma, based on faith rather than on experience and science. A proper constitution emanates from society, "a reality," said Sierra, "to which individual rights must be molded."[61] Cosmes argued that the "interests of society, order, and peace," not just the rights of the individual, must be guaranteed by the constitution. Some are even concerned with the rights of criminals; what about the rights of the "honorable people" who are their victims? Sierra reminded the readers of *La Libertad* that article 14 of the constitution (prohibiting retroactive laws) was countered by article 29 (giving the

---

al., *Tres Aspectos de la presencia española en México durante el porfiriato* (Mexico, 1981). For other evidence of *hispanofilia* in *La Libertad* see the great attention paid to the death of Anselmo de la Portilla (4–6 March 1879), Hammeken's benign attitude toward Spain on Independence Day 1879, and Cosmes's defense (18 February 1879) of Enrique Olavarría y Ferrari, the Spanish man of letters on *La Libertad*'s staff.

[60] Letter Sierra to Moret, 31 May 1910 (*Obras*, 14:481).

[61] Sierra in *La Libertad*, 23 February, 6 September 1878, 1 January 1879 (*Obras*, 4:143, 160–61, 181); also Cosmes in *La Libertad*, 11 September 1878.

president the power to suspend constitutional guarantees in times of external or internal conflict). Society is an independent fact, concluded Sierra; therefore the rights of man are dependent on the rights of society.[62]

For the men of *La Libertad*, the constitution was the product of a particular historical moment and was the more susceptible to reform. The constitution-makers of 1856 were an embattled faction, obsessed, and appropriately so, with the memory of Antonio López de Santa Anna's dictatorship and the reality of clerical power. In those circumstances they set out to implant liberty, "the revolutionary creed imported from France," which for them was a kind of religion of universal validity. But that moment of struggle has passed, announced Sierra. As admirable and heroic as the constitution-makers were, we now realize that all constitutional precepts "are destined by the fatal exigencies of history to undergo severe revision before the tribunal of new ideas."[63]

At the heart of the movement for constitutional reform was the idea that government must be strengthened. The obsession with "strengthening" accompanied the frequently stated conviction that Mexico, like other Latin societies, had a historical penchant toward disorganization, anarchy, and revolution. These assumptions lay behind the notorious call for "honorable tyranny" by Francisco Cosmes, as they had the establishment of conservative republics in France and Spain. Experience showed that a priori constitutions, the mere imposition of general principles, reinforced these unfortunate Latin tendencies. Are the institutions acquired by the blood of the progressive party to be torn down by "the anathema of the organ of scientific politics [*La Libertad*]?" asked the doctrinaire *La Patria*. No, responded Sierra, we will adhere to the constitution, even though it has been the shield for all manner of pronunciamientos and disorder. But we must introduce reforms, "creating within the law elements of order, of conservation, of vigor for public power." If the "central nucleus" is not fortified, "this country will never become organized."[64] We must, said another editor, "create in the heart of the constitution a government able to smother revolutions and assure tranquillity," or as still another editor put it, we must "reform the constitution in a conservative sense." In reaction to what it saw as the constitution-makers' passion for shackling authority, *La Libertad* declared the state a natural product of social evolution, to be given full legal sanction. It is significant

[62] Cosmes in *La Libertad*, 4 January 1879; ibid., 6 October 1878; Sierra, "El Derecho individual y un opúsculo del Sr. Lancaster Jones," ibid., 29 April 1879 (not in *Obras*). Sierra was responding to a study of article 14 by Alfonso Lancaster Jones of Jalisco, which he took to be critical of *La Libertad*'s stance.

[63] See ibid., 5 February 1879, on the anniversary of the adoption of the constitution; Sierra in ibid., 1 January 1879, 23 February 1878 (*Obras*, 4:178–79, 143).

[64] Sierra in *La Libertad*, 20 August 1879 (*Obras*, 4:233–35).

that concern for the reestablishment of Mexico's international credit frequently accompanied the call for constitutional reform.[65]

The advocates of scientific politics have often been accused, in their day and ours, of working to subvert the constitution, if not overtly attacking it. They of course denied the accusation, a denial we will explore in some detail in chapters 3 and 4. One of their principal arguments was that the constitution had never really functioned because it had never been obeyed, with the result that the political life of the country since independence had alternated between anarchy and dictatorship. Why not reform the constitution, they asked, so that being in conformity with our social reality, it will not be constantly violated? "To eliminate de facto dictatorship . . . we need a practical constitution"; we need "the constitution of an authority whose attributes are at once perfectly defined and very broad." Disillusioning experience has led us to the conviction, said Sierra, that "the way to free ourselves from hypocritical tyranny is to strengthen the administrative power." We simply cannot rely on suspending constitutional guarantees during given moments of crisis. In countries like ours, crises are not the exception, they are the normal state of affairs. *La Libertad*'s argument became part of the standard Porfirian criticism of doctrinaire constitutionalism, which as we have seen had its classic expression in Emilio Rabasa's assertion of 1912 that both Juárez and Díaz had been forced to become extralegal dictators because of the unrealistic limitations placed upon the executive by the Constitution of 1857.[66]

Although the call for constitutional reform was put forth primarily as a general critique of traditional liberalism in Mexico, it did result in several specific proposals. These proposals drew upon important precedents from the Juárez and Lerdo years of the restored republic, and upon recent experiences of political turbulence and constitutional crisis. They appeared in the pages of *La Libertad* and were developed most systematically by Justo Sierra.

As might be expected, the reforms were designed principally "to strengthen the administrative power." First, the presidential term of office should be lengthened from four years to six or seven years. This change, argued Sierra, would increase political stability and exploit the experience gained by an executive in his first years of tenure. Presumably, this measure was regarded as a way of enhancing executive authority while still adhering to the no-reelection principle of the Plan of Tux-

[65] *La Libertad*, 27 December, 3 October, 2 April 1878.

[66] "La Dictadura," signed by "the editors," *La Libertad*, 18 September 1878; Sierra in ibid., 24 January 1879 (*Obras*, 4:191). The principal modern defense of the Constitution of 1857 is Cosío Villegas, *La Constitución de 1857*. His essay was directed particularly against Justo Sierra's articles in *La Libertad* and Rabasa's *La Constitución y la dictadura* (1912).

tepec, the banner of Porfirio Díaz in 1876. Second, the executive should be given a suspensive veto on the American model, the power to suspend legislation of the current session of Congress unless both chambers were to override the veto by a two-thirds vote. The veto power, present in earlier Mexican constitutions, was removed by the constitution-makers of 1856 in their effort to limit executive authority. Sierra said the veto would allow administrators with their special knowledge and practical experience to collaborate in lawmaking with the deputies, whose knowledge was of a more general sort. A third related reform would be to endow the executive with legislative authority, for a specific period and for special purposes. Sierra did not elaborate upon this proposal except to say that it would be a realistic revision of the abstract principle of the absolute separation of powers.[67]

The most complex and confusing of Sierra's proposals, seconded at various times by other *La Libertad* editors, was to establish in the constitution "the political unaccountability [*irresponsibilidad*] of the president." While this measure appears to be an unabashed call for dictatorship, it was advanced with recent experiences in mind precisely to avoid dictatorship and its obverse, revolution. Presidential unaccountability must be accompanied by ministerial accountability, or the establishment of a parliamentary regime in Mexico. Sierra regarded the parliamentary system as "the only way to adapt [*aclimatar*] liberty to countries of Latin blood." The stated objective of the reformers was to revise the presidential system of government as provided for in the Constitution of 1857 by separating the accountability of the president from that of his cabinet, following the practice in constitutional monarchies like England and in the contemporary French republic. By forbidding reelection, said *La Libertad*, the Plan of Tuxtepec emphasized only the limitation of presidential power. It did not provide an outlet short of revolution for opposition to a regime. In short, it did not, as would the adoption of the parliamentary system, provide "the solution to the eternal problem of modern nations, the transformation of liberty into order."[68]

Sierra and his colleagues were advocating increased executive authority, unduly limited, they said, by the constitution, despite the formal provisions of a presidential system. They were also advocating its apparent antithesis, a parliamentary system of government. This paradox needs explanation. The men of *La Libertad* were reacting against what they saw as the excessive executive authority assumed by Benito Juárez

[67] Sierra in *La Libertad*, 24 January, 3 February 1879 (*Obras*, 4:191–94). The principle of no-reelection (for the term immediately following) was adopted as an amendment to article 78 of the constitution on 5 May 1878.

[68] Sierra in *La Libertad*, 24 January 1879 (*Obras*, 4:192); *La Libertad*, 5 April 1878 (an editorial commentary on revised article 78); Sierra in ibid., 13 March 1879 (*Obras*, 4:196).

and particularly by Sebastián Lerdo de Tejada between 1867 and 1876. They identified this excessive authority with the refusal of both presidents to change cabinet officials in response to opposition from the Congress. President Juárez had refused to remove Lerdo (who held two posts, foreign relations and *gobernación* [internal affairs]), and President Lerdo in turn kept the Juárez cabinet intact until 1876. It was impossible, argued *La Libertad*, for Congress to oppose specific ministers without opposing the president himself, an opposition that had only led to armed revolt. If ministers were made accountable for their actions apart from the president, then political conflict could be transferred from the battlefield to the halls of Congress.[69]

Sierra noted that even in the United States, where thanks to "good customs," the presidential system had generally worked, there was mounting concern over the "imperialistic" presidency of Ulysses S. Grant, in which cabinet officials were mere agents of the executive.[70] What Sierra did not make clear (or did not realize) was that the Mexican presidential system (though overtly copied from that of the United States) contained important parliamentary "nuances." In fact, Frank A. Knapp, Jr., has persuasively argued that the country experienced parliamentary government in 1857 and from 1861 to 1863, the only periods during which the constitution was operative prior to the defeat of Maximilian. These parliamentary nuances included the requirement that executive orders be countersigned by the minister in question (article 88), also that each minister (but not the president) must appear before Congress at the beginning of each session to report on the state of his ministry (article 89), and of course the provisions for a unicameral legislature and the absence of the presidential veto. President Juárez, having deferred to the majority in Congress in choosing and dismissing his ministers from 1861 to 1863, tried to recoup his presidential power after 1867. In doing this he was supported by Lerdo de Tejada, an earlier advocate of parliamentarianism. The result was the famous calling of elections (*convocatoria*) on 14 August 1867, which included several constitutional changes to be submitted to popular referendum. The two principal ones were the recreation of a senate to balance the undue power of the single chamber (and indirectly to undercut the parliamentary regime) and the reinstatement of the suspensive or temporary veto. Although these changes were deferred in the face of opposition in 1867, the Senate (but not the veto) was finally adopted during Lerdo's administration in November 1874.[71]

---

[69] *La Libertad*, 5 April, 18 October 1878.

[70] Sierra in ibid., 13 March 1879 (*Obras*, 4:197).

[71] The parliamentary nuances (of the present constitution) are analyzed in detail by Felipe Tena Ramírez, *Derecho constitucional mexicano*, 11th ed. (Mexico, 1972), pp. 249–60. Articles 88 and 89 were perpetuated (under different numbers) in the Constitution of 1917.

Sierra and his colleagues, following the premises of scientific politics, were predisposed to ignore the theoretical paradox of their position and they promoted both parliamentary government and a stronger presidency. Both elements formed part of their notion of "strengthening" government, which in turn was supported by their social assumptions. A parliamentary system, said one editor, would bring into politics those who should be most engaged, the men of substance. A "capitalist or industrialist" is now hesitant to oppose some unappealing measure because to do so would be to challenge the president and not merely a minister. The opponent faces the dilemma of fomenting revolution or doing nothing. "So he folds his arms and yields his place [in Congress] to petty politicians, those who expect everything from disorder."[72]

Popular sovereignty as proclaimed by the Constitution of 1857 was anathema to scientific politics, and restricted suffrage was a natural and important reform proposal. Universal suffrage, said *La Libertad*, makes Mexico "the country of elections," that is, the land of turbulence, corruption, and dictatorship, involving the manipulation of the illiterate masses by cynical politicians. The present system, argued the editors, reflects only the interests of the "official element," as opposed to those of the "merchant, the industrialist, the agriculturalist," or even of the "proletariat." With true popular sovereignty the interests of all are represented. Justo Sierra claimed that although his ideal of government was that "of science, of reason, of the men who make up the spiritual element of a country," he was not an enemy of democracy. Mexico must work toward democracy, but slowly and realistically, with the spread of national education, not starting from an abstract declaration of popular sovereignty. The constitution must be amended to limit the vote to those who are literate and have an "honest profession." Sierra's proposal for electoral reform was accompanied by phrases typical of scientific politics, the need for a "conservative politics" and for the stimulation of an "energetic movement of concentration in society."[73]

Completing the list of proposals were two that were not given great emphasis in 1878–79 but that came to be more important in the course of the Porfiriato. The first was that the chief justice of the Supreme Court should not be in effect the vice-president; the second that judges should have life tenure, irremovable unless they violated their trust. These

---

See also Frank A. Knapp, "Parliamentary Government and the Mexican Constitution of 1857: A Forgotten Phase of Mexican Political History," *Hispanic American Historical Review* 33 (1953): 65–87.

[72] *La Libertad*, 5 April 1878.

[73] See ibid., 11, 12 November and 9 July 1878; 10 January 1879; Sierra in ibid., 24 May 1878 (*Obras*, 4:147–48). Articles 34 and 35 of the constitution gave the vote to all male citizens who were married and eighteen years of age or unmarried and twenty-one.

measures were advanced in the name of political order and judicial responsibility. Jorge Hammeken wrote that the existing system created an inevitable political antagonism between two powers of government that should remain separate, or as Sierra put it, "a worse threat to order and stability in government than ten revolutionary armies." After the experience of 1876, to be examined in chapter 3, and the falling-out between Díaz and Chief Justice Ignacio Vallarta in 1879, this first reform met little opposition and was approved in 1882.[74] The general question of a distinct vice-presidency, however, remained an unsettled issue until 1904. The irremovability of judges was to spark a major political debate in 1893, which is the subject of chapter 4.

The attitude of the advocates of scientific politics toward the first regime of Porfirio Díaz was cordial, but ambivalent. *La Libertad* enjoyed a government subsidy, as we have seen; in exchange it supported many of the policies and actions of the regime and provided a philosophical justification for strong government. However, the men of *La Libertad* were too intelligent and their arguments too penetrating to be regarded as mere apologists for Díaz. If *La Libertad* was less independent than the editors maintained, it did manage to view the regime critically, especially after the newspaper's initial year. Their ambivalent attitude arose from the insecure nature of the regime itself, its questionable legitimacy, and its inner conflicts.

The first presidency of Porfirio Díaz came into being in 1876 through armed rebellion against Sebastián Lerdo de Tejada and José María Iglesias, both of whom could claim to be legitimate presidents within the constitution. Because rebellion, revolution, and disorder were antithetical to scientific politics, Justo Sierra and his colleagues were hard put to justify Díaz. On the other hand, their hostility to doctrinaire constitutionalism made them receptive to a regime that promised social stability and economic progress, a regime whose official organ would commemorate the anniversary of the Constitution of 1857 by the catalogue of "material improvements" it was undertaking. They could speak of Díaz as respecting the "essence" of the constitution, as upholding the "constitutional order," without entering into legal niceties. Sierra wrote frankly that they were prepared to forgive Díaz for rebelling against a legitimate government if he could keep his promise of 1876: "The revolution of Tuxtepec will be the last revolution."[75]

[74] See Hammeken in *La Libertad*, 22 July 1879; Sierra in ibid., 3 February, 20 July, 17 October 1879 (*Obras*, 4:195, 198–200, 202). By reformed article 79, adopted 3 October 1882, the president of the Senate would become president of the republic in case of failure of the latter to perform his duties.

[75] *Diario oficial*, 5 February 1878; *La Libertad*, 21 February, 2 April 1878; Sierra in ibid., 7 June 1879 (*Obras*, 4:223).

As former supporters of Iglesias in 1876, the men of *La Libertad* could hardly condone the revolution of Tuxtepec; in fact, they were delighted to note in 1878 that Díaz himself was breaking from the strict interpreters of the revolution's principles, the *tuxtepecanos netos*, and he was beginning to conciliate former antagonists. The Plan of Tuxtepec was directed primarily against Lerdo and his appointees in office, especially those named in the disrupted elections of June and July 1876. Besides calling for the removal of *lerdista* officials, the plan in its first article upheld the Constitution of 1857 and the anticlerical amendments of 1873, while calling for the additional reforms of no-reelection and municipal freedom. The preamble of the plan spoke of the oppressive Senate, "the work of Lerdo de Tejada and his favorites"; and though abolition of the Senate was not an article of the plan, the constitutional amendment of 1874 creating the Senate was specifically omitted from those amendments recognized in article 1.[76] During the early months of 1878 the *Diario oficial* devoted itself to refuting *El Combate* and *La Bandera negra*, organs of extreme *tuxtepecanismo*, which charged the regime with ignoring the promises of the plan. "The promises were made *revolutionarily*," said the *Diario*. No-reelection is proceeding rapidly, but expansion of municipal autonomy cannot be accomplished overnight. The chief *tuxtepecano* demands, however, were the purge of *lerdista* employees and suppression of the Senate, both of which the *Diario* resisted.[77]

In combating the ultras of the movement, the Díaz regime began to strike the note of continuity, letting it be known that it was prepared to reconcile with former enemies. The *Diario oficial* drew the distinction between refusing to recognize Lerdo's employees (*desconocer* was the term used in article 3 of the plan) and castigating them. Certainly some who are worthy can be rehired (after the initial nonrecognition) without violating the "spirit of the plan." What about those employees carried over from the Juárez regime (which was not mentioned in the plan)?[78] We simply cannot, said the *Diario*, draw only from *tuxtepecanos*. Many of them "do not have the special knowledge or experience sufficient to

[76] The original plan (10 January 1876) and the reformed Palo Blanco version (21 March 1876) can be found in *Archivo del General Porfirio Díaz*, ed. Alberto María Carreño, 30 vols. (Mexico, 1947–61), 12:96–100.

[77] *Diario oficial*, 3 January 1878. For the "constitutional" emphasis see also ibid., 22 February, 11 March 1878. Cosío Villegas argues for the great importance of the *Diario oficial* during these years as a mouthpiece for the regime, a function it had had since 1867 (*Historia moderna*, 8:123). The Tuxtepec rebels tried to eliminate this function (presumably in reaction to its "abuse" by Lerdo), but the effort was short-lived. From 4 December 1876 through 30 March 1877 the *Diario* appeared in small format as a simple register of government acts. On 2 April the traditional large format reappeared, along with a rationale for the change by Juan Sánchez Azcona, the new editor.

[78] *Diario oficial*, 19 February, 4, 7 March 1878.

fill civil posts and even less posts we could call scientific." The *Diario* implied that the new regime would have to enlarge the pool to include *lerdistas, juaristas*, and even "the functionaries who served the reaction, the intervention, and the empire."[79] Díaz is to be commended, said *La Libertad*, for resisting the pressure to regard the public administration as a "Tuxtepec fief." Conservative-liberals had little tolerance for the *tuxtepecanos* and referred to those who "have invaded" the chamber as "hayseeds" (*paletos*), speaking the "coarse language of the hamlet" and lacking the refinement, intelligence, and oratorical skills of past deputies, even those of the Lerdo era.[80]

The *Diario oficial* maintained that regardless of the rhetoric of the Plan of Tuxtepec, the Senate was really the work of the Juárez presidency, dating back to the *convocatoria* of 1867. Actually, as the *Diario* pointed out, the deputies of the seventh Congress had upheld the Senate in 1877, voting down "revolutionary" efforts to adhere strictly to article 1 of the plan. If the Senate is to be abolished, concluded the *Diario*, it must be done by a deliberate constitutional process and not by revolutionary action.[81] Thus reconciliation, continuity, and constitutionality became keynotes of the regime's efforts to discard its revolutionary origin and followers and to acquire legitimacy in the new environment of scientific politics.

The political stance of the *Diario oficial* was remarkably similar to that of *La Libertad* during 1878, except that as a nonofficial newspaper *La Libertad* could attack *tuxtepecanismo* much more openly. Yet the arguments of both *La Libertad* and the *Diario* were subtle and often confusing. They were condemning the punctilious constitutionality of the Plan of Tuxtepec, which *La Libertad* equated with the much despised "revolution," and yet they were calling the regime "constitutional." Such was the message, for example, of an impressive series of articles entitled "El Partido constitucional," by León Guzmán, a distinguished jurist, a deputy

[79] Ibid., 25 March 1878. Perhaps the argument was designed to prepare the way for the appointment of Manuel González as minister of war a few weeks later. González was a former conservative general (see p. 61).

[80] *La Libertad*, 4 April 1878; 22 April 1879. Although there were clear overtones of social conflict within the Tuxtepec movement and the first Díaz administration, the exact dimensions of this conflict are obscure and worthy of further study. Stephen R. Niblo argues that Díaz welcomed support from Mexico's two small labor organizations in 1876 but turned away from it by the end of his first administration: "The Political Economy of the Early Porfiriato: Politics and Economics in Mexico, 1876–1880" (Ph.D. diss., Northern Illinois University, 1972). Another sign of social conflict can be seen in the *tuxtepecano* call for municipal liberty, which was apparently rejected by Díaz (and by *La Libertad*), just as Castelar in Spain had rejected the "utopia" of cantonalism.

[81] *Diario oficial*, 26 January, 1, 23 March 1878. Cosío Villegas treats in detail the debates and votes on the senate issue in 1877: *Historia moderna*, 8:349–61.

to the Constituent Congress of 1856–57, and a Juárez minister during the embattled years 1858 to 1861. Guzmán had developed a hostility toward the "anticonstitutional" influences on Juárez during his wartime dictatorship, and as governor of Guanajuato in 1867 he had refused to proclaim the *convocatoria*, attributing it to Lerdo. Lerdo, said Guzmán, trampled on the constitution and thus opposition to him was legitimate. Guzmán supported Iglesias in 1876 and worked to reconcile Iglesias and Díaz, hoping that Díaz would emerge by election as the constitutional president, following an equally constitutional Iglesias interval. Though he admitted that "the triumph of the revolution of Tuxtepec, such as it was consummated, created a gulf between the new administration and constitutional order," Guzmán also assured his readers that Díaz "is a sincere and genuine constitutionalist." He tried to resolve the contradiction by asserting that the regime was legitimate (if not precisely constitutional) because of the overwhelming popular mandate given Porfirio Díaz in the elections of 1877. The constitutional party can be solidified and constitutional order restored, concluded Guzmán, only if Díaz can resist personalism, by which he meant "despotism" in the style of Lerdo and the job-seeking mania of the *tuxtepecanos*.[82]

As Cosío Villegas has pointed out in detail, Díaz tried to give the impression of "impartiality" in his numerous cabinet appointments for the years 1876 to 1880, balancing off in the first instance political followers with some who were apolitical and administratively oriented. Of the original appointees of 28 November 1876, four (Pedro Ogazón, war; Protasio P. Tagle, *gobernación*, later justice; Vicente Riva Palacio, *fomento*; Justo Benítez, *hacienda*) were leading *tuxtepecanos* and had been loyal *porfiristas* since at least 1872. Tagle continued till November 1879, Riva Palacio till the end of the term, Ogazón till April 1878. Several other shorter-term appointees such as Trinidad García and Eduardo G. Pankhurst (*gobernación*) and Carlos Pacheco (war) were also politically affiliated with the *tuxtepecanos*, though not of Díaz's immediate circle. Less political and more administratively oriented were Miguel Ruelas (briefly in foreign relations), Ignacio Mariscal (justice), José Landero y Cos, and Manuel J. Toro (*hacienda*). All of these, except Ogazón and perhaps Riva Palacio, were "new men" without previous prominence on the national level.

Díaz also made two important "conciliatory" ministerial appointments, Matías Romero and Felipe Berriozábal, strong and able individuals closely identified with his former antagonists. Romero had served four

[82] Guzmán in *La Libertad*, 5 April, 29 March 1878. The series proper ran from 14 March through 21 April, though Guzmán contributed several related articles before and after those dates. On León Guzmán (1821–84), see Cosío Villegas, *Historia moderna*, 8:51–53.

years as Juárez's minister of *hacienda*, and as a deputy had voted extraordinary powers for Lerdo de Tejada; Berriozábal had been Iglesias's minister of war and a leading general in 1876. Other experienced appointees included Ignacio Vallarta and José María Mata (foreign relations, November 1876 to January 1879) and Ignacio Ramírez (justice, November 1876 to May 1877). Although they were supporters of Díaz before 1876, all three were national figures who had served under Juárez. Díaz even selected one known conservative and "imperialist," José Hipólito Ramírez (*hacienda*, April 1879), but the appointment caused such a storm of protest that Ramírez resigned after forty-eight hours. In short, Díaz "tried every formula known" in making the twenty-four appointments for the six cabinet posts of his first administration.[83]

The reconciliation policy of the Díaz regime can be seen not only in its cordial relationship with the editors of *La Libertad*, former *iglesiasistas*, and in the appointment of Romero and Berriozábal to cabinet posts, but also in the return from exile between 1876 and 1880 of three major figures of the Lerdo years, Ignacio Mejía, Manuel Romero Rubio, and Mariano Escobedo. Mejía, the perennial minister of war from 1865 to 1876, had been particularly detested by the *porfiristas* for his efforts to reduce the size of the army, swollen by years of civil war. It is notable that Mejía not only returned to Mexico, but he became one of the many candidates for president in 1880. Romero Rubio had led the Lerdo faction in the Chamber of Deputies and had served as minister of foreign relations in the final days of Lerdo's administration. Escobedo, Lerdo's final minister of war, actually launched a *lerdista* rebellion in May 1878. He was captured in July and the rebellion was crushed. Díaz soon pardoned Escobedo and restored his generalship, leaving only Lerdo himself still in exile, where he remained until his death in 1889.[84]

While first they applauded the president for his policy of reconciliation and his efforts to resist the pressures of *tuxtepecanismo*, the editors of *La Libertad* soon came to express growing concern that the country was returning to politics as usual. This concern focused first on the numerous cabinet changes made in early and mid-1879 and then shifted to the forthcoming presidential election of 1880. The editors claimed to be nonpolitical in their criticism of the cabinet, which they said should be "homogeneous," filled "with men capable of developing *una política científica*," the only safeguard against anarchy. The president must shake off

[83] See ibid., pp. 255–93. We have no reliable list of cabinet officials and their dates of tenure from 1867 to 1910. A recent list in the *Encyclopedia de México*, 12 vols. (Mexico, 1966–77), 5:43–62 is useful, but far from exact. A list should be compiled from the *Diario oficial* and the *Memorias* of the several ministries.

[84] On Mejía's candidacy in 1880, see Cosío Villegas, *Historia moderna*, 8:558–59; on Escobedo's conspiracy, ibid., pp. 165–82.

the influence of Benítez and Tagle and draw in men of stature like Ramón Corona, Eduardo Ruiz, Francisco Gómez del Palacio, and Ignacio Vallarta, instead of nonentities like Pankhurst and Ruelas.[85] Besides quality, *La Libertad's* list had a balance of its own: Corona and Ruiz had strong *reformista* credentials and had served Juárez and Lerdo. Gómez de Palacio had been an Iglesias stalwart. Vallarta, for whom *La Libertad* claimed great respect despite differences over constitutional reform, had been Díaz's initial minister of foreign relations and was presently on the Supreme Court. "Conciliation" was always a watchword of the men of *La Libertad,* as long as those reconciled did not include the *tuxtepecanos.*

Other standard themes of conservative-liberalism came forth in the context of this ministerial critique. Government should be no more than an "organ of society," acting "in accord with social interests and necessities." The party of Porfirio Díaz should "abandon the revolutionary tradition and become a party of government." The old divisions are obsolete in "our political world"; from now on "there will be only men of order and men of disorder." Though referring in May 1879 to "the deplorable tendencies in present-day politics," Justo Sierra reaffirmed *La Libertad's* "solemn commitment" to support Díaz through the course of his "mandate as legal president." This commitment, said Sierra, is born of "the scientific principles which form the base of any political conception that aspires to be called positive," such as the repudiation of revolutions and the linking of conservatism with liberalism, order with progress. Our opposition to the president, concluded Sierra, could never be "revolutionary," only "governmental."[86]

In its early phase, the presidential campaign of 1879–80 was out of tune with the premises of scientific politics and caused anxiety among Justo Sierra and his colleagues. The reelection of the president had been ruled out by the adoption of reformed article 78 in May 1878. Moreover, Díaz did not intervene in the election process until late in the campaign, with the result that no less than eight candidates emerged, several strong ones being in contention for almost a year-and-a-half. The political atmosphere was charged with confusion, intrigue, and speculation, which only reinforced *La Libertad's* fear of coming revolution and anarchy and solidified its call for strong government. The men of *La Libertad* did not openly favor any one of the candidates, but they strongly opposed Justo Benítez, the major focus of intrigue and speculation. Benítez departed for a stay in Europe from December 1878 to October 1879, first renouncing and then later reviving his candidacy. This leading *tuxtepecano* and Díaz in-

---

[85] *La Libertad*, 4 January, 22 February, 19 April 1879.

[86] Ibid., 28 November 1878, 17 July 1879; Sierra in ibid., 21 May 1879 (*Obras*, 4:215–17).

timate of 1876 epitomized for the editors the evils of personalism and government by clique. Closer to home, they believed it was Benítez who had persuaded Díaz not to reach a compromise with Iglesias in late 1876, and they charged that his candidacy was directed particularly against those who like themselves had been former adherents of Iglesias.[87]

The men of *La Libertad* had no more sympathy for the president's hands-off policy through the course of 1879 than they had for the "heterogeneous" cabinet he was creating. His conduct was "vacillating and mysterious," they said. The president should not hesitate to intervene, at least subtly, in the choice of a successor. Cosmes spoke of a "fusion" of the many candidates to avoid anarchy; Justo Sierra suggested a "compromise." If he could bring his influence to bear upon the coming campaign, added Sierra, "[Díaz] the caudillo of the revolution will give way to [Díaz] the conqueror of anarchy, all to the glory of [Díaz] the president." Although the writers of *La Libertad*, perhaps out of political necessity, claimed to admire the president for adhering to the principle of no-re-election, it is clear they were not totally convinced that he should step down. León Guzmán suggested as much on 1 May 1878; Sierra did the same a year-and-a-half later. Another editorialist stated that more than four years would be needed to produce stability, attract foreign capital, and promote the material progress of the country. The only solution was for Díaz to continue in office. Such sentiments were of course consistent with both *La Libertad*'s general argument for strong government and its specific advocacy of a six- or seven-year presidency.[88]

By the end of 1879 there were indications that Díaz would finally intervene and that General Manuel González would emerge as the favored candidate. González was not from the ranks of the *tuxtepecanos netos*. As a candidate he carried the burden of having fought on the conservative side in the Three Years War (1858–61). However, he switched to the republican cause with the intervention of the French, became Díaz's chief subordinate in the Army of the East, and a Díaz follower after 1867. He served as governor of Michoacán in 1877 and as minister of war in 1878–79. On 15 November 1879, González resigned the ministry and was appointed head of the Army of the West. Justo Sierra, who feared anarchy above all else, welcomed the move. Now in control of half the army, González was in a good position to contain potential revolutionary fac-

---

[87] On Benítez see *La Libertad*, 6, 10 October 1878; 2 April 1879; Sierra in ibid., 16 May, 27 December 1879 (*Obras*, 4:213–14, 266). The *Diario oficial* (8 January 1878) refuted a charge by *El Federalista* that *La Libertad* was founded by order of Díaz to promote the candidacy of Ignacio Vallarta. I have found no evidence to substantiate the charge. For the details of the election campaign see Cosío Villegas, *Historia moderna*, 8:515–71.

[88] See *La Libertad*, 22 February 1879; Cosmes in ibid., 28 August 1879; Sierra, "Un Consejo al presidente," ibid., 6 September 1879 (not in *Obras*).

tions. In his review of the candidates in late December 1879, Sierra seemed to favor González, though he did fear the possibility of a revival of militarism.[89] When it became clear in the spring of 1880 that González was to be the official candidate, *La Libertad*'s criticism of the president and its fear of anarchy subsided. Perhaps Porfirio Díaz was beginning to show the strength and authority that were essential to the realization of scientific politics.

The new doctrine, therefore, emerged in a political regime born of rebellion and pronunciamiento and tainted with illegitimacy. There seemed to be a mutual attraction between the weak and divided administration, struggling for stability, and the group of young journalist-intellectuals, disillusioned with the mounting factionalism of the Restored Republic and ultimately frustrated by the failure to find a "legal" solution to the political crisis. *La Libertad* became the vehicle for a set of ideas that would bring together concrete political aspirations for the consolidation of power and intellectual aspirations for an era of peace, economic development, and social stability. For many reasons scientific politics cannot be regarded as a mere rationalization of dictatorship; the most obvious of these reasons is that the first administration of Porfirio Díaz was insecure and its prospects limited. The years 1878 to 1880 did demonstrate, however, a remarkable marriage of politicians and intellectuals, both groping for a principle of authority in the wake of upheaval.

The significance of scientific politics or its correlate conservative-liberalism derived from the specific political context in which it developed, but also from the relevance of its theoretical bases to post-Reforma Mexico. As in France, the doctrine responded to the search for reconstruction in the wake of ideological conflict and civil war. The application of "science" to society, however vaguely defined, was supposed to provide the answer. As was the case with the liberals of the 1820s and 1830s, the recent political experiences of France and Spain had guided the men of *La Libertad* in their formulation of a doctrine that would apply to Mexico. To understand the ideas they put forth we must understand the European world they observed.

There remains a nagging problem that I have alluded to throughout this chapter and that is central to the study as a whole. The advocates of the new ideas were all self-consciously liberals, heirs to the heroic age of the Reforma. As we have seen, "liberal" became an official term that was universally adhered to after 1867. Justo Sierra and his colleagues spoke

[89] Sierra in *La Libertad*, 25, 27, 28 December 1879 (*Obras*, 4:259–70). Although Sierra's review was generally impartial, González was the last candidate he discussed (see especially his remarks on 28 December [p. 270]). On González's candidacy see Cosío Villegas, *Historia moderna*, 8:563–71.

of a "new" liberalism, but they also enunciated ideas theoretically hostile to the term itself. More specifically, they attacked the Constitution of 1857, the symbol of the liberal heritage and a badge of patriotism. But they did so as constitutionalists. The relation between liberal constitutionalism and scientific politics is the subject of chapters 3 and 4.

CHAPTER 3

Scientific Politics and Constitutionalism

THE ATTEMPT BY *La Libertad* to reorient the course of liberal thought and policy in Mexico did not go unchallenged. The Mexico City press, while less vociferous than before 1876, still retained much of its earlier vitality. There was little evidence of government encroachment on free political expression until the 1880s. Besides the *Diario oficial* and prestigious and longstanding dailies such as *El Siglo XIX*, *El Monitor republicano*, and *El Federalista*, there were many short-lived papers that sprang up in support of specific issues, and particularly in support of the several candidates for president in 1879–80. Newspapers had not yet become as they would after 1896 organs primarily for dispensing news and occasional commentary; they still served as the vehicles for political and philosophical expression by the country's intellectual elite. The contents of many significant pamphlets and books appeared originally in the newspapers. If *La Libertad* was a prime example of a newspaper that became a vehicle for intellectuals, another was certainly *El Monitor republicano*. It was *El Monitor*'s José María Vigil who challenged Justo Sierra in 1878 and who in the next two years solidified the paper's reputation as the chief defender of Mexico's democratic and constitutional tradition.

The debate between Sierra and Vigil was touched off by Vigil's attack on recent Supreme Court decisions that he saw as infringements on individual rights, notably the right (in article 5 of the constitution) to be free from having to perform personal services without consent and just remuneration. Vigil regarded the abuses of article 5, now upheld by the court, as evidence that "the habits of tyranny handed down by our [colonial] forefathers are being perpetuated among us."[1] When he asserted that Mexico's "democratic revolution," like that of France, had sought above all to establish individual guarantees, Sierra's retort was that Vigil represented the "old liberal school, which, as the French say, *a fait son*

---

[1] Vigil in *El Monitor*, 22 August 1878. The juridical issue was the conflict between article 5 and article 31, which specified public obligations of citizens, such as doing military service and jury duty, paying taxes, and serving on municipal councils (*cargos concejiles*). Vigil was particularly concerned about abuses of enforced military service (*la leva*). In one case (28 June 1878) involving article 5, Chief Justice Ignacio Vallarta made the basic distinction between public services, which were not included under article 5, and personal services, which were. See Vallarta, *Cuestiones constitucionales. Votos . . .*, 4 vols. (Mexico, 1894–96), 1:91.

temps." Vigil preferred to read the phrase as "out of fashion" and accepted with pride the epithet "old." Vigil proceeded to champion the doctrine of popular sovereignty and even defended the "school of Rousseau, parent of unconditional democracy." In doing so he quoted at length from the French spiritualist philosopher Elme-Marie Caro's recent eloquent defense of innate individual rights against the naturalistic theories of the "scientific school," particularly Darwin and Spencer.[2] Vigil said he was not basing his arguments on metaphysical abstractions, as Sierra claimed, but on the experience of fifty-six years of struggle, which proved "that the republican, representative, democratic, and federal system was the only one possible in our country." The challenge for Mexico, concluded Vigil, was to enact this system without reservations, putting aside all "spurious elements that might discredit the [democratic] idea and bastardize its practice."[3]

Vigil regarded the "new liberalism" of Sierra and his colleagues as the old conservatism in disguise. The call by Cosmes for "honorable tyranny" was preposterous, as was Sierra's argument that government should be strengthened as a way of preparing the people for the eventual practice of constitutional liberties. Sierra's contention that "the best way to avoid the violation of guarantees and the abuse of the law is to suppress law and guarantees" was for Vigil not only contradictory but reactionary. By spreading the notion that the constitution is unworkable, that democracy is a farce, and that the people are not ready for liberty, *La Libertad* is simply preparing the way for dictatorship. Vigil acknowledged that he shared Sierra's concern for preserving social order, but not at the expense of public liberty; and he concluded that *La Libertad*'s effort at compromise was illusory, just as that of Ignacio Comonfort had been in 1856–57. "Between conservative reaction . . . and constitutional liberalism there is no middle ground." Vigil did not distinguish between the guarantees of the constitution and the anticlerical measures of the Reforma. Both formed part of Mexico's democratic tradition.[4]

[2] Vigil in *El Monitor*, 21 December 1878. The quoted passage was taken from Elme-Marie Caro (1826–84), "La Démocratie devant la morale de l'avenir. Les nouvelles théories sur le droit naturel," *Revue des deux mondes*, 1 November 1875, pp. 5–36. Caro's point of departure was the appearance of Spencer's *Study of Sociology* (1873) in French translation as *Introduction à la science sociale* (1874) and several publications that formed part of a debate in France on Darwin's *Origin of Species*. Vigil translated other segments from Caro in his *Revista filosófica* (1882): see p. 179.

[3] Vigil in *El Monitor*, 28 November 1878. Vigil drew back (10 September) from total acceptance of Rousseau, especially the "idea of the state" dominant during the French Revolution, which he saw as derived from the *Social Contract*. Vigil must have sensed the contradiction between Jacobin centralism and constitutional guarantees.

[4] See especially *El Monitor*, 27 August, 27 September, 22, 26 October 1878; also 12 December, for a good example of Vigil's identification of the constitution and the Reforma. *La*

Vigil feared that behind *La Libertad*'s subversive campaign against Mexico's institutions was a growing alliance between President Díaz and the "conservative band." In the course of 1879 and 1880 Vigil shifted the target of his attack from *La Libertad* to the leading Catholic newspapers, *La Voz de México* and *La Ilustración católica*. He now accused the conservatives of promoting dictatorship, of undermining the constitution, and especially of fostering noncompliance with the Laws of Reform. Whether or not Vigil's failure to mention *La Libertad* after mid-1879 was by design, he certainly conveyed the impression that he equated scientific politics with the threat of insurgent conservatism.[5]

José María Vigil's adherence to doctrinaire liberalism may be explained in part by his age, but perhaps even more by the peculiarities of his career. Born in 1829, he literally was an "old" liberal, twenty years older than most of the editors of *La Libertad*. More significant is the fact that his education and career until age forty were totally provincial. Between 1855 and 1867 he had established himself in his native Guadalajara as a man of letters, a professor of philosophy, and a political journalist. Among other activities, Vigil served ten years as chief editor of *El País*, the official liberal newspaper of the state of Jalisco. When he went to Mexico City as a deputy and journalist in 1869, it is fair to assume that his philosophical and political ideas were fixed, making him resistant to the new scientific doctrines. Vigil provides a good example of the oft-repeated generalization that the seat of classic nineteenth-century liberalism was the provinces and not the capital.[6]

One of the marks of political discourse during the Porfiriato was an obsession with the "union" or "reconstruction" of the "Liberal party." Both "old" and "new" liberals called for it, though their conceptions differed significantly. "Reconstruction" was put forth as an effort to recapture the political unity among liberals that had been achieved despite many obstacles during the course of the Reforma and the Intervention, a unity that faded after 1867 and disappeared in the three-sided conflict of 1876. The advocates of scientific politics sought to transform the Liberal party from a party of revolution based on abstract doctrines or metaphysics into a party of government based on practical experience or science.

Libertad's call for "honorable tyranny" came in the midst of the Sierra-Vigil debate on 5 September. A complete list of Vigil's writings can be found in Gabriel Agraz García de Alba, *Biobibliografía general de don José María Vigil* (Mexico, 1981).

[5] On Díaz and the conservatives see *El Monitor*, 27 September 1878. One can follow Vigil's polemic with the conservative press particularly between October 1879 and March 1880.

[6] For an account of Vigil's early career focusing on his journalism, see Carlos J. Sierra, ed., *José María Vigil* (Mexico, 1963), pp. 7–59; also Agraz García de Alba, *Biobibliografía*. During the French occupation of Guadalajara Vigil did spend the year 1864–65 abroad in San Francisco, where he edited a liberal periodical.

On the contrary, for José María Vigil those very doctrines of the heroic age must become the rallying cry for a new unity among liberals.

Vigil's call for reconstruction was overtly a response to the threat of resurgent conservatism and thus it often appeared in his polemical arguments with the clerical press. On another level, it was prompted by the growing factionalism of the presidential election campaign, which of course called up memories of 1876. Day after day throughout late 1879 and 1880, Vigil contrasted the liberal and democratic ideals and achievements of the Mexican "revolution" with the shabby spectacle of present-day political contention. He feared that the struggle to institute the anticlerical reform laws, universal suffrage, and constitutional guarantees such as the separation of powers and federalism had been in vain and that Mexico had merely changed rulers, "the political castes" for "the privileged classes." His editorials invariably concluded that the only solution to the country's political woes was that "movement of [Liberal party] organization which will complete the work that was begun by the liberators and was sealed with the blood and sacrifices of the Mexican people."[7]

Liberal party union went beyond rhetoric to become an eleventh-hour organizational effort, led by the editors of El Monitor, "to see that in the coming elections popular suffrage is truly free." The effort produced at least three meetings and a proclamation on 2 June 1880. The document voiced the customary lament that "the lack of organization of the Liberal party has led to divisions within it of a purely accidental and personal nature because of the several candidacies that have been announced." The immediate objective of the organizers was apparently a "fusion" of the presidential candidates opposed to General Manuel González, who by then clearly had official backing. One of these opposition candidates was Manuel María Zamacona, whom El Monitor had proclaimed as its choice beginning on 20 February. Zamacona was elected president of the executive committee of the Liberal party, a committee that also included Ignacio Vallarta, Justo Benítez, Ignacio Mejía, Trinidad García de la Cadena, and Juan N. Méndez, in short, all of the candidates except González.

The Liberal party proclamation designated 15 October (that is, three months after the presidential election) as the date for a national convention of the party, to be made up of delegates who were to emerge from a three-stage election process on the municipal, district, and state levels. The original organizing committee, which included Vicente García Torres, the proprietor of El Monitor, acknowledged that the model was

---

[7] The quoted phrases, drawn from El Monitor of 21 October 1879 and 16 July 1880, are typical of Vigil's generalized argument over a period of thirteen months. For a sympathetic summary of Vigil's ideas, see Cosío Villegas, Historia moderna, 8:419–28. On Cosío's interpretation, see pp. 15–18.

North American. Because our constitution is taken from that of the United States, said the statement, it is logical that we should also "accept the means by which our neighboring country puts these same institutions into practice." The organization came to nothing and there is no evidence of Liberal party activity beyond the initial meetings.[8]

Though some might be tempted to dismiss this abortive organizational effort altogether, it is significant for two reasons. First, it demonstrates the attraction of the idea of Liberal party union, implemented as a political convention of the North American type, an idea that was to recur in the coming years. Second, the effort reveals the confusion inherent in post-Reforma liberalism and the weaknesses in the doctrinaire position. Whereas *La Libertad* could adhere to the principles of scientific politics in supporting Díaz, in rejecting Benítez, Tagle, and the *tuxtepecanos*, and ultimately in favoring González as the official candidate in 1880, *El Monitor* had to eschew its principles in advocating a diverse anti-official coalition. It is true that Zamacona, *El Monitor*'s candidate, had been a consistent constitutionalist, opposed first (as a *porfirista* journalist and deputy) to the "authoritarian" *convocatoria* of 1867 and later to the Lerdo regime. By 1880 he also found Díaz to be authoritarian.[9] But the Liberal party coalition promoted by *El Monitor* included not only Zamacona, but also Benítez and Tagle, whom *El Monitor* (like *La Libertad*) had earlier condemned as epitomizing "personalism."[10] We are forced to conclude that *El Monitor*'s call for the reconstruction of the Liberal party based on classic liberal principles turned out in practice to be a confusing and ineffectual maneuver.

The political experience of José María Vigil himself reinforces this impression of doctrinaire liberal confusion. As a journalist, deputy, and supreme court justice before 1876, Vigil had been a Lerdo partisan but he

---

[8] The minutes of the organizational meetings of the Liberal party (26, 30 May, 2 June) appeared in *El Monitor*, 1, 4, 5 June 1880. At the first meeting García Torres agreed that *El Monitor* would publish the minutes and "would dedicate every effort to promoting the development of the concept and to strive for its realization." The proclamation appeared 5 June. On the Liberal party convention see also Cosío Villegas, *Historia moderna*, 8:565–68.

[9] On Zamacona's career see F. A. Knapp, *The Life of Sebastián Lerdo de Tejada, 1823–1889* (Austin, 1951), pp. 68–74, 140–41; on his candidacy see Cosío Villegas, *Historia moderna*, 8:546–51. *La Libertad* (16 January 1880) printed his letter from Washington, dated 30 December 1879, which presented his program as a candidate. On 17 January, Santiago Sierra expressed admiration for Zamacona but commented that events had passed him by. It should be noted that Zamacona's hostility toward Lerdo began when the latter was minister of foreign relations in 1861. Lerdo was the leader of the congressional opposition to the Wyke-Zamacona treaty with Great Britain; when the treaty was defeated, Zamacona was forced to resign. Zamacona attacked the *convocatoria* of 1867 as editor of *El Globo* (see below, p. 71).

[10] See *El Monitor*, 12, 26 December 1879.

broke with him over the issue of reelection. Vigil supported Iglesias briefly in December 1876 in *La Legalidad*, and with the victory of Díaz he left journalism and lost his supreme court post. He was "politically displaced," to use Cosío Villegas's phrase, until he joined *El Monitor* in August 1878. Following the election of 1880, Vigil's militant constitutionalism subsided. On 1 December he resigned from *El Monitor*, after receiving appointments as director of the National Library and as professor of logic at the National Preparatory School. He was also reelected to the Chamber of Deputies. Though Vigil remained a vigorous opponent of positivism in the educational and philosophical controversies of the early 1880s, he was no longer a political opponent of the regime. His regular editorials in the progovernment newspaper *La Patria* during 1883 presented an optimistic vision of factional reconciliation and material progress.[11] Had Vigil, deprived by the *tuxtepecanos* of public employment in 1876, now been coopted by the González regime? Perhaps. But Vigil also represented the travail of doctrinaire liberalism in the growing ideological consensus of the Porfiriato.

The editors of *El Monitor*, Vicente García Torres ("Tancredo") and Enrique Chávarri ("Juvenal"), continued to speak out after the departure of Vigil. They were joined in 1882 by Federico Mendoza y Vizcaino. Yet the passion for economic development, the continuing politics of reconciliation, and the growing centralization of the González regime had a dampening effect on the opposition press.[12] *El Monitor* lamented the passivity of the legislature, the loss of autonomy by the states, and the growing accommodation with the church. Mendoza y Vizcaino warned in a typical statement that the loss of liberties and the drift toward reactionary political ideas would eventually undermine material progress, now so highly prized. The wisdom of the ages has proved, he concluded, that "liberty is the only base upon which the edifice of popular prosperity and greatness can be built."[13] Despite frequent general pronouncements, *El Monitor's* rejoinders on specific issues, for example on the reform of article 7 of the constitution to limit freedom of the press, were remarkably mild. Throughout late 1882 and early 1883, the editors seemed resigned to the fact that a passive Congress and docile state governments would ratify the measures that did violence to the system of constitutional guarantees.

[11] On Vigil's career after 1869 see C. Sierra, ed., *José María Vigil*, pp. 31–59; Cosío, *Historia moderna*, 8:670–74. Vigil wrote over one hundred editorials in *La Patria* between January 1883 and January 1884. For a list, see Agraz García de Alba, *Biobibliografía*, pp. 117–23. See particularly "México en 1882" (1 January 1883), "La Paz pública" (18 January), and "La Constitución de 1857" (4 February).

[12] For a good statement on this process see Cosío Villegas, *Historia moderna*, 8:710–11 and passim.

[13] Mendoza y Vizcaino in *El Monitor*, 29 May 1883.

Because of the climate of opinion in the country, they saw resistance as fruitless.[14]

Our examination of José María Vigil's response to Justo Sierra, and in more general terms doctrinaire liberal opposition to the regimes of Díaz and González, leads us to the central problem of chapters 3 and 4. *El Monitor* clearly had the defense of the constitution and the constitutional system as its main concern. How then do we interpret the efforts of *La Libertad* to reform the constitution? Was scientific politics merely a rhetorical cloak, a rationale for dictatorship? Was the debate between Sierra and Vigil in effect one between an opponent and a defender of the constitution? Or can we identify scientific politics itself as a variety of constitutionalism? To probe this question we must gain historical perspective and turn first to the *convocatoria* of 14 August 1867.

Justo Sierra and his colleagues were of two minds about the *convocatoria*. They acknowledged that the initiatives of 1867 "form a part of the [constitutional reform] program of *La Libertad*."[15] And yet their complex proposal for a parliamentary regime was designed to correct the pattern of excessive executive authority that they saw embodied in the *convocatoria* and that came to characterize the administrations of Juárez and Lerdo.

The document itself was overtly a "call for elections of higher authorities," that is, for president, for chief justice of the Supreme Court, and for deputies to the national parliament. As such it comprised the long-awaited reactivation of the constitutional separation of powers following the wartime dictatorship of Benito Juárez.[16] The unexpected came in article 9, which included a list of five constitutional reforms to be in effect approved or rejected by popular vote.[17] Approval would mean dispensing

[14] The reform of article 7 transferred "crimes of the press" from the jurisdiction of juries to the jurisdiction of federal and state courts that would administer penalties under the criminal code. The measure was passed by Congress in October 1882 and ratified on 15 May 1883. For typical though infrequent comments by *El Monitor* see 3, 9 January, 14 February, 22 June 1883. *La Libertad* supported the measure, and in fact it lamented journalistic excesses as early as 12 February 1879. The press should have the "freedom to discuss" but not the "license to insult," said Cosmes. On the article 7 episode, see Don M. Coerver, *The Porfirian Interregnum: The Presidency of Manuel González of Mexico, 1880–1884* (Ft. Worth, 1979), pp. 96–100. See also Cosío Villegas, *Historia moderna*, 8:726–40, a detailed discussion of government encroachment on the opposition press.

[15] Sierra in *La Libertad*, 22 December 1878 (*Obras*, 4:177).

[16] See editorial by Alfredo Chavero in *El Siglo XIX*, 29 July 1867. Chavero said Juárez was well aware of the need to reinstate the separation of powers following the supreme authority he exercised during the French intervention. As if foreseeing what was to come, Chavero also criticized Rousseau's theory of the general will.

[17] Besides (1), the addition of a senate and (2), the institution of a suspensive presidential veto, these reforms were: (3), that communications between the executive and legislative branches be in writing and not verbal; (4), that the congressional deputation functioning

with the normal procedure for amending the constitution (ratification by two-thirds of the state legislatures) and would allow instead for the reforms to be decided by majority vote in the Chamber of Deputies.

The reaction by the press to this part of the *convocatoria* was immediate and overwhelmingly hostile, a fact acknowledged by the *Diario oficial*. A few journalists like Manuel María de Zamacona, editor of *El Globo*, opposed the reforms themselves, while most, like Pantaleón Tovar of *El Siglo XIX*, objected more to the way in which they were presented to the people. Zamacona announced his rigid adherence to the constitution and called the proposals a "plot against the sovereignty of the nation, an artful conspiracy against our institutions." Tovar emphasized the unconstitutionality of the proposed referendum. In an editorial accompanying the text of the lengthy circular presented by Lerdo to the state governors justifying the decree, Tovar added that the states did not want constitutional changes, particularly by ministers; they wanted the constitution itself. Ever suspicious of Lerdo, Zamacona asserted that the *convocatoria* "was not [Juárez's] idea." In fact, opposition was so strong that President Juárez had to issue a "manifesto," claiming full responsibility for the decree and defending his ministers against public attack. However, the government apparently had expected some public opposition to the *convocatoria*, for Lerdo's circular was unusually elaborate and skillfully argued.[18]

"Now that the Reforma is completed, our greatest concern is good administration," announced Lerdo in sounding the keynote for the government's proposals. The term "administration" appeared repeatedly in the circular, and the changes were presented as having been added to correct the 1857 system, in which, according to Lerdo, the unicameral legislature was everything and the executive nothing. The constitution-makers, disillusioned by the experience of dictators, sought to create a "convention" as a vehicle of "social reform." Under the stressful circumstances of 1857 or 1861–63, convention government might have been justified, but

---

during recesses be limited in its power to call Congress into extraordinary session; (5), that a means be provided for provisional replacement of the executive in the absence of both the president and the chief justice. For a clear explanation of the referendum procedure, see Friedrich Katz, "Mexico: Restored Republic and Porfiriato, 1867–1910," *Cambridge History of Latin America*, 5:8.

[18] See *Diario oficial*, 20 August 1867; also 17 October 1867; Zamacona in *El Globo*, 13 September 1867, and as quoted in *El Siglo*, 20 August; also *El Siglo*, 19, 22 August. The "*Convocatoria para la elección de los supremos poderes*" and the "*Circular de la ley de convocatoria*" (both 14 August) can be found in Manuel Dublán and José María Lozano, *Legislación mexicana*, 34 vols. (Mexico, 1876–1904), 10:44–56; the Juárez manifesto of 22 August in ibid., pp. 67–68. There is a good discussion of Lerdo's role in the *convocatoria* episode in Knapp, *Lerdo*, pp. 122–30. See also Cosío Villegas, *Historia moderna*, 1:141–72.

"in normal times the despotism of a convention can be as bad as the despotism of a dictator, or worse." It is now the moment, concluded Lerdo, to restore balance to the system. "Constitutional balance" and "administration" became complementary concepts in Lerdo's argument for the five points of reform, concepts that were to reappear in *La Libertad*'s program to "strengthen" government in 1878.

Given his emphasis on Mexico's return to "normal times," Minister Lerdo found it difficult to justify submitting the reforms to a referendum instead of following the ordinary amendment procedure. In deciding to submit it, he shifted his ground and now claimed that the "terrible and painful crisis" from which the nation was just emerging demanded a "direct appeal to the people." Such an appeal can be based, he said, on article 39 of the constitution: "National sovereignty resides essentially in the people. . . . The people has at all times the inalienable right of changing or modifying its form of government." Lerdo distinguished between constitutional amendment by referendum and amendment by decree, for example the anticlerical measures of 1859–60. Though the nation "has approved" these measures, he continued, and has thus set a precedent for constitutional reform by decree, the government does not intend to exploit the precedent. In referring to the "precedent" of the anticlerical "amendments," which were issued under the extraordinary wartime powers of the president, Lerdo was apparently reminding the citizens that these powers were still in force by virtue of the most recent extension of 8 November 1865. Under these circumstances, his distinction between the prior submission of a decree to a "yes" or "no" vote and a subsequent national "approval" for extraordinary wartime measures was a dubious one. For those who now sought a return to the regime of the constitution, both procedures seemed equally arbitrary.

The *convocatoria* revived the classic conflict within Mexican political liberalism between constitutionalism and strong reformist government. Should individual liberty, the goal of liberalism, be attained by strengthening government (an instrument of the people) to eliminate corporate privilege and legal inequality, or should it be attained by limiting government through a system of constitutional guarantees? José Díaz Covarrubias in the *Diario oficial* frankly acknowledged this conflict when, in defending the *convocatoria*, he referred to "that coup d'etat known as the Reforma," which "not only attacked the letter of the constitution but also its spirit." For Díaz Covarrubias, as for Lerdo, the "coup d'etat" was sanctioned by the "national will."[19] The liberal triumph of 1867, however, placed the dichotomy between constitutionalism and strong government in a new context, one only partially reflected in Lerdo's circular. The

[19] *Diario oficial*, 22 August 1867.

victory over corporate, particularly clerical, privilege removed the grounds for arguing for strong government as a means of attaining classic liberal goals of individual freedom and legal equality. Presumably these goals had now been achieved. Lerdo's pragmatic concepts of "good administration" and "constitutional balance" responded to the imperatives of the new context; his appeal to popular sovereignty in the referendum did not. Thus in 1878 Justo Sierra and his colleagues rejected the latter as essentially an appeal to metaphysics. For them, popular sovereignty was a "dogma" contrary to the principles of science.

The problem presented by the new political imperatives of the immediate postwar period can perhaps most clearly be demonstrated by the response of Francisco Zarco to the actions of the Juárez government. Zarco was among the giants of the heroic liberal era. At the age of twenty in 1849 he became director of *El Siglo XIX*, a position he held intermittently until his death. Zarco was a principal liberal spokesman following the war with the United States; he led the way in drawing up the Constitution of 1857; and he was the chronicler of the Constitutional Congress. He served Juárez as minister of foreign relations in early 1861, accompanied him north in 1863, and then left for the United States where he defended the republican cause in the Hispanic press. He returned to Mexico on 15 October 1867, and he resumed his directorship of *El Siglo* on 1 December. Announcing *El Siglo*'s "political program" that very day, Zarco stated that "we yearn for the complete restoration of constitutional order." Our answer to the question whether we will be "spokesmen for the ministry or for the opposition" is that we will be forever constitutionalists.[20]

Because he had been a major participant in both the constitutionalist and the reformist phases of the liberal movement, Zarco's attitude toward the present regime was distinctly ambivalent. Zarco returned too late to express an immediate reaction to the *convocatoria*, but he asserted on 4 December that "the *convocatoria* is not a crime, nor a coup d'etat, nor a betrayal of our institutions, as has been said in the heated polemics of the press." Moreover, Zarco went out of his way to defend the wartime powers of Juárez, which he saw as responsible for national salvation and social reform without destroying the constitution. Yet, his comment on the reelection of the president was guarded. The people, he said, have shown their confidence in Juárez as the personification of our nationality and of republican resistance, but they do not believe he is infallible. In delaying their approval of the constitutional reforms, they have "declared in an

[20] For Zarco's career see Francisco Sosa, *Biografías de mexicanos distinguidos* (Mexico, 1884), pp. 1097–1101; Raymond C. Wheat, *Francisco Zarco. El Portavoz liberal de la reforma* (Mexico, 1957).

unequivocal manner that they reprove all violation of the constitution" and that "strict legality" must not be sacrificed to "considerations of public convenience."[21]

Zarco saw the advance of "administration" as the chief threat to the reestablishment of constitutional liberty. Repeatedly he referred to the "men of administration," to the "false liberals" or the "timid minds" who "consider politics [only] as a source of upheaval" or who call for a continuation of the wartime dictatorship. They have, he declared, "begun to form a kind of political sect that preaches enlightened despotism." These men prize "administrative order over the constitution; they find it more interesting to reorganize a bureau of stamped paper or of [ecclesiastical] disentailment than to give back to the states their liberties and to the citizens their guarantees." On occasion, Zarco would identify these "men of administration" as "government employees who are notable for their particular accomplishments." Moreover, he added, they are committed to "material improvements," irrespective of political principles. Zarco was undoubtedly responding to an infusion of personnel, "from the highest positions to the doormen of the offices," which took place in the early postwar months.[22] Despite the vagueness of Zarco's characterizations, it is apparent that he was identifying an incipient corps of apolitical experts, a group somewhat different from the pre-Reforma officeholders who had been the frequent target of attacks by earlier liberal reformers.[23]

Zarco went on to place this new administrative cadre in historical and comparative perspective. The Constitutional Congress of 1856–57 contained a group devoted to "government" and "order," who in their zeal to avoid "tumult (*agitaciones*)" were responsible for omitting certain libertarian items from the constitution, such as freedom of worship, abolition of the death penalty, and total freedom of the press. To include these provisions would have been, in their view, "contrary to good administra-

[21] Zarco's defense of Juárez's wartime powers can be seen in *El Siglo*, 1, 4, 6, 22 December 1867 and 1 April 1868. The congressional decree of 20 December 1867 declaring the reelection of Juárez can be found in Dublán and Lozano, *Legislación*, 11:219. For Zarco's commentary, see *El Siglo*, 22 December 1867. In his speech at the opening of Congress on 8 December 1867, Juárez abandoned the referendum as the means of amending the constitution and submitted the reforms instead "to the wisdom of Congress," as set out in the constitution. See Tamayo, *Benito Juárez*, 12:814–15. José Fuentes Mares has studied (from the Juárez correspondence) the resistance of the state governors to the *convocatoria*, an important factor in the government's decision to retreat: see his "La Convocatoria de 1867," *Historia mexicana* 14 (1964): 423–44.

[22] See comments of Alfredo Chavero in *El Siglo*, 23 July 1867; also 14 August. Chavero applauded an announcement by Juárez that ability would be the criterion for appointments.

[23] Zarco's principal statements on this theme, "Orden administrativo," and "Se puede gobernar con la constitución" appeared in *El Siglo* on 16 December 1867 and 14 June 1868. Other similar editorials appeared on 23, 24, 25 December 1867, and 8 January, 5 February, 4, 5 April 1868.

tion." Ignacio Comonfort's "coup d'etat" against the constitution in 1857 was in large part a product of such ideas, as was internal opposition to the Juárez government in 1861.[24] Here Zarco appeared to be singling out the political moderates of the Reforma era as the precursors of the new bureaucracy, though elsewhere he suggested it was made up of crypto-conservatives, "perpetuators of the work of Zuloaga and Miramón, of Bonaparte and Maximilian." His reference to Bonaparte, however, placed the issue in a context broader than the bounds of Mexican politics. "The one who most stands out among the men of administration is Napoleon III," said Zarco, despite his supposed adherence to the principles of 1789. Zarco also mentioned Leopoldo O'Donnell, Ramón María Narváez, and Candido Nocedal in Spain, leaders of the Moderate and Liberal Union governments of the 1850s and 1860s.[25] Though he was still groping for definitions, Zarco sensed the entry into Mexico of a new set of assumptions about government, ones that would come to fruition in the scientific politics of 1878.[26]

In defending the constitutional order against this encroaching administrative mentality, Zarco contended that the Constitution of 1857 had eschewed the "Latin principle of the omnipotence of the state" for the "Saxon or Germanic principle of individual liberty." The principle of state omnipotence, even if it is supported by the "vague invocation of popular sovereignty," only degenerates into Caesarism.[27] Inspired by the "administrative law" of the French Second Empire, the advocates of this principle seek to destroy federalism, that is, "to centralize everything, and to extinguish the liberties of the states." He cited particularly the movement to impose uniform codes and regulations throughout the country, as drawn up by "erudite Mexico City jurists."[28] Zarco was referring to the

[24] See Zarco in ibid., 16 December 1867 and June 1868. Richard N. Sinkin's analysis of voting in the Constituent Congress reveals that concern with "law and order" was high among the delegates, even among those traditionally thought of as "radicals": see Richard N. Sinkin, "The Mexican Constitutional Congress 1856–1857: A Statistical Analysis," *Hispanic American Historical Review* 53 (1973): 1–26; also idem, *The Mexican Reform, 1855–1876. A Study in Liberal Nation-Building* (Austin, 1979).

[25] Zarco in *El Siglo*, 5 April, 16 December 1867. On French administration as set out by Louis Napoleon on 2 December 1851, see Félix Ponteil, *Les Institutions de la France de 1814 à 1870* (Paris, 1966), pp. 356–58, 372.

[26] I would not of course argue the novelty at this time of a bureaucratic or administrative cadre in Mexico or of a mentality peculiar to bureaucrats. These were all entrenched prior to the Reforma and had a venerable history in the Spanish imperial system. What did seem to be new (with the Reforma) was the conceptualization of a political conflict between the objectives of "administrative order" and the objectives of "constitutional order." The term "administrative order" appeared in article 86 of the Constitution of 1857, which set out the powers of the executive.

[27] Zarco in *El Siglo*, 14 June 1868.

[28] Zarco, "La Soberanía de los estados," ibid., 8 January 1868.

judicial commissions appointed by Juárez to complete the work of legal codification begun in 1859 and continued under Maximilian. Codification progressed rapidly; the civil code was issued in 1871, followed by numerous others in the coming decades.[29] Accompanying the codes was the appearance in 1873 of *El Foro*, a learned and long-lived newspaper dedicated to promoting and explicating a uniform and specialized jurisprudence. Avowedly nonpolitical, *El Foro* claimed that its principal object was "to smooth the way for the practical application of the codes." An editor and frequent contributor during its initial year was the young lawyer and jurist, Justo Sierra Méndez, whose father, the liberal Justo Sierra O'Reilly, and whose uncle, the conservative Luis Méndez, had been pioneers in the codification movement. As a natural advocate of the uniform and nonideological jurisprudence that Francisco Zarco had resisted, Sierra was adding another block to the edifice of scientific politics.[30]

Behind Zarco's fear of advancing administration was the frequently expressed conviction that "it is possible to govern with the constitution" and that "true administrative order can only proceed from the adherence to constitutional order." He urged Congress to use its constitutional powers (as set out in article 72, section 7) to approve budgets, fix taxes, and review the accounts of public expenditures. Separation of powers would

---

[29] See Cosío Villegas, *Historia moderna*, 1:15. The civil code (1871), the penal code (1872), the codes of civil and criminal procedures (1872, 1880), the postal code (1883), the commercial code (1884), and the mining code (1884) can be found in Dublán and Lozano, *Legislación*, vols. 11, 12, and 15. The postwar commission to prepare the civil code was made up of Mariano Yáñez, José María Lafragua, Isidro Montiel, and Rafael Dondé (ibid., 11:201). All were members of the interim Supreme Court as appointed on 1 August 1867 (ibid., 10:32–33).

[30] See the article by José Linares in *El Foro. Periódico de jurisprudencia y de legislación*, 1 June 1873 (the initial issue). Editors listed were Sierra and Pablo Macedo. For Sierra's contributions (1873) see Mantecón Navasal et al., *Bibliografía general*, pp. 28–39. Work on the civil code had proceeded despite political conflict. In 1859 Benito Juárez in Veracruz commissioned Justo Sierra O'Reilly to prepare a draft civil code, three books of which were adopted by the state of Veracruz in 1861 and published (but not adopted) in Mexico City. Juárez then appointed a new commission (which included Luis Méndez) to revise the draft. After the flight of the liberals from Mexico City in 1863, the same code commission continued to function under the regency and the empire, producing an incomplete civil code for the empire, published in 1866. In 1867 Luis Méndez passed the imperial commission's files on to the newly appointed republican body. Méndez himself, a former imperial councillor, formed part of another commission for the code of civil procedure. He was Justo Sierra's godfather and had brought the thirteen-year-old Justo to Mexico City immediately following the elder Justo's death in 1861. He presided over the boy's education in the Liceo-Franco Mexicano and San Ildefonso and later in 1871 helped him establish a law office adjacent to his own. See Helen L. Claggett and David M. Valderrama, *A Revised Guide to the Law and Legal Literature of Mexico* (Washington, 1973), pp. 63–66; Yáñez, *Don Justo Sierra*, p. 30, 44; Claude Dumas, "Justo Sierra y el liceo franco-mexicano. Sobre la educación en México, 1861–1862," *Historia mexicana* 16 (1967): 531–40.

thus be maintained and arbitrary executive actions curtailed.[31] He repeatedly called for the issuance of organic laws detailing the structure and function of the various organs of government as essential to restoring constitutional guarantees in the country.[32] After the first postwar Congress had completed its work, Zarco expressed general optimism. As one of its leaders, he concluded with pride that the difficult "transition from dictatorship to legal order" had been accomplished and that congressional opposition to the executive had not degenerated into factiousness and obstructionism. We are now all defenders of the constitution, he said optimistically, and "we have no intention of sacrificing [it] for the sake of administrative order."[33]

Perhaps the real target of Zarco's attacks on administration was Sebastián Lerdo's circular accompanying the *convocatoria*, for it revealed the very emphases that he deplored. However, Zarco never mentioned Lerdo or the *convocatoria* in these discussions. His comments on Lerdo were limited to the question of the Juárez cabinet, a question that showed Zarco's ambivalence toward the regime. Though he claimed to have more confidence than did some in the ministers held over from wartime days (Lerdo, Iglesias, and Mejía), he questioned the wisdom of perpetuating these men in office. "The policies of the [wartime] dictatorship cannot be the policies of the constitutional order," he said. Since Zarco was an advocate of the parliamentary responsibility of ministers, he condoned only with reluctance the government's request for permission from the Congress to allow Lerdo and Blas Balcárcel (*fomento*), when elected as deputies in December 1867, to remain in the cabinet. He strongly supported, moreover, the refusal of the Supreme Court to permit Lerdo, its elected chief justice, to continue as foreign minister. Following the December elections, Lerdo had briefly held positions in all three branches of government, but he was soon forced by constitutionalist opposition to keep only his ministry post. Though Zarco's general stance could certainly be termed constitutionalist, his response to the cabinet question was remarkably restrained.[34]

---

[31] Zarco in *El Siglo*, 16 December 1867.

[32] See Zarco in ibid., 3, 27 December 1867; 5 February, 1, 5 March 1868. The only legislation referred to as *leyes orgánicas* during the period pertained to notaries (29 November 1867) and to education (1 December 1867). Zarco also referred to a *ley orgánica* on the press, the *decreto* of 11 January 1868 (reinstating another of 2 February 1861), in which freedom of the press according to article 7 of the constitution was restored. See Dublán and Lozano, *Legislación*, 10:228. These laws may all have been technically *leyes reglamentarias*. On the confusing issue of terminology, see Tena Ramírez, *Derecho constitucional*, p. 329.

[33] Zarco in *El Siglo*, 14 June 1868, 16 December 1867.

[34] Zarco in ibid., 2 January 1868; also 11, 12 January, 16 April, 21 June. For a thorough treatment of the cabinet issue, see Knapp, *Lerdo*, pp. 129–32. Under articles 57 and 58 of the constitution, deputies could not hold salaried offices in the government without the

Zarco's inclination toward doctrinaire constitutionalism was undermined decisively by the struggle of the Juárez government after August 1867 to maintain law and order in the face of regional rebellions, military insubordination, and increased banditry—the heritage of the de facto decentralization of power during the civil war years. Open defiance of the regime by the governors of Guanajuato and Puebla, who refused to publish the *convocatoria*, was followed by other challenges in Guerrero, Sinaloa, and Yucatán in December 1867 and January 1868. Immediately after relinquishing his extraordinary wartime powers on 8 December, President Juárez began pressing for the reinstatement of those powers in order to meet disorder in specific situations and for limited periods. This pattern of regional and military challenges and strong governmental responses continued throughout the Restored Republic, culminating in the unsuccessful revolt of La Noria (1871) and the successful revolt of Tuxtepec (1876), both led by General Porfirio Díaz.[35] In requesting the restoration of extraordinary powers in early 1868, the government contended that the constitution should be "practical" and not just "theoretical," that it embodied "social" as well as "individual" guarantees. Should a poorly organized country that faces professional revolutionaries and criminals, asked the *Diario oficial*, "remain in the upper regions of idealism or tread the firm ground of reality?" Material progress and national reconstruction is vain rhetoric unless public order can be upheld.[36]

Convinced that "we have reached an era in which the people know that peace is our prime need," Francisco Zarco was compelled to sympathize with the official position. He supported taking firm action in Guerrero, where neither state nor federal elections had taken place. The problems of that isolated state—communications, port development, "the civilizing of the indigenous race, and the existence of the last of the *cacicazgos*"— are national problems justifying federal intervention. Zarco's response to disorder in Yucatán, declared by Congress to be in a state of siege, was similar.[37] Throughout early 1868 Zarco weighed the problem of maintain-

---

previous permission of Congress. The *Diario oficial* argued at length (mostly in response to Zamacona) that the constitutional restriction did not apply to a position such as minister: see 21, 26, 28 June 1868.

[35] The challenges to the regime and the resulting "constitutional relaxation" are treated in detail by Cosío Villegas, *Historia moderna*, vol. 1. In defense of the regimes of Juárez and Lerdo, Cosío emphasizes that during the ten years of the Restored Republic the nation lived more than half the time within the constitution: suspension of constitutional guarantees was in effect in only forty–nine of the one hundred twenty months (p. 348).

[36] See *Diario oficial*, 16 March, 2 April 1868.

[37] On Guerrero see Zarco in *El Siglo*, 9 December 1867; on Yucatán, see 21 March 1868. The state of siege law for Yucatán (4 January 1868) can be found in Dublán and Lozano, *Legislación*, 10:225–26. It reinstated the regime of military tribunals as provided for in a law of 21 January 1860 (ibid., 8:733–34). The wartime laws of the Reforma decade provided

ing constitutional guarantees in the face of mounting disorder and concluded that it was impossible "to separate the cause of order from that of liberty." The nation need not fear "coup d'etats" by Juárez, "who twice restored our institutions." Though declaring himself "neutral" regarding the president's request to reinstate the broad powers granted in the notorious law of 25 January 1862, his support was apparent. Not only was Zarco's name attached (as president of the Chamber of Deputies) to the congressional decree of consent on 8 May 1868, but several of his editorials on the question were reprinted approvingly in the *Diario oficial*. Francisco Zarco, "that colossus of maturity and good judgment," as Cosío Villegas has described him, was succumbing to the political imperatives of the postwar era, just as his spiritual colleague and exact contemporary, José María Vigil, did later.[38]

Francisco Zarco's writings elucidate the problem of political liberalism in post-Reforma Mexico. As both a constitutionalist and an anticlerical reformer, both an antistatist and a statist during the previous decade, Zarco was bound to be ambivalent toward the Juárez government. As a constitutionalist, he resisted the perpetuation of the wartime dictatorship and he was sensitive to the threat of a burgeoning administrative apparatus. Yet as a *reformista*, he was prepared to accept strong government and an abridgment of constitutional liberties to meet the even greater threat of public disorder. Moreover, he came increasingly to emphasize the need for economic development and social reconstruction, even though these objectives demanded an ever more active bureaucracy.[39] Zarco's health was poor; he resigned the directorship of *El Siglo* on 1 September 1869, and he died on 22 December. In the editorials of his final months, he stressed that public opinion "demands peace, liberty, and great material improvements." Although he did not abandon his hope for further constitutional and political evolution, he asserted that

---

convenient precedents for postwar governments seeking strong powers within the liberal tradition.

[38] See Zarco in *El Siglo*, 2, 27 April 1868; also 16, 29 March. The congressional decree authorizing the president to suspend specified guarantees until 31 December 1868 can be found in Dublán and Lozano, *Legislación*, 10:319–20. It actually fell far short of a reinstatement of the 1862 law, the *ley Doblado* (ibid., 9:367–71), which was a detailed and comprehensive grant of powers to "punish crimes against the nation, order, public peace, and individual guarantees." This decree had been judged by the minister of justice on 13 January 1868 to be "incompatible with the constitutional regime" (ibid., 10:229). Zarco's editorials from *El Siglo* were reprinted in the *Diario oficial* on 23, 31 March and 19 April. His approval of the congressional measure of 8 May can be seen in *El Siglo*, 20 May 1868. For Cosío Villegas's comment on Zarco, see *Historia moderna*, 1:249.

[39] Manuel Payno, later to become director of *El Siglo XIX*, recognized this fact in a series of articles during November 1867 entitled "Cuestiones administrativas." It dealt primarily with railroad development, but also with a wide range of social and economic problems: see particularly 7 November 1867.

"in Mexico, as in other countries, the time of merely abstract questions has passed; the hour of practical questions has come." Foreshadowing the rise of scientific politics, Zarco's views also placed in doubt the survival of doctrinaire constitutionalism, a doubt that was even greater by the early eighties.[40]

The most successful of the 1867 proposals for constitutional reform and the one most vigorously defended later by the writers of La Libertad was the reinstitution of the Senate. Epitomizing Lerdo's complementary concepts of "good administration" and "constitutional balance," the Senate reform helps us further to understand the relation between constitutionalism and emerging scientific politics in the Restored Republic. Though first introduced into Congress on 13 December 1867, the proposal was not debated until April 1870, following a committee report of 24 December 1869. In 1867 Lerdo had argued that while a convention-type unicameral legislature might have been necessary to carry out basic social reforms, the present priority was "to consolidate our institutions." After 1867, the government recognized that mounting regional and military challenges made imperative some means of strengthening control short of a general suspension of guarantees and establishment of martial law by executive decree. Such actions could easily be branded "dictatorial" by Congress and the press. When urging the state governors in March 1870 to support the reforms about to be debated in Congress, President Juárez emphasized recent "disgraceful upheavals" in Zacatecas and San Luis Potosí. Direct and equal representation by the states in a second chamber, he added, could give them more authority in creating legislation and thus allow them to participate more effectively in curbing local disorder. The creation of a senate, therefore, was frankly presented as a means of "consolidation," which meant in part the strengthening of central authority.[41]

In promoting the adoption of a senate, the government published a

[40] Cosío Villegas in his broad review of the press of the Restored Republic emphasized an "anxiety for peace" as one of the great themes of the era. Zarco's statements were made in September 1869 and quoted in Cosío Villegas, Historia moderna, 1:377. Zarco apparently suffered from a respiratory ailment. He wrote a few editorials after 1 September, the last on 11 October. Before his death (at age forty) he was reelected to the Chamber of Deputies and to important committee posts therein. See Wheat, Francisco Zarco, pp. 310–14.

[41] The government's proposal of 13 December 1867 followed Juárez's decision of 8 December to abandon the referendum method of constitutional reform. This document, along with the Juárez circular to the governors of 3 March 1870 and the "Dictamen de la comisión de puntos constitucionales" of 24 December 1869, can be found in Tamayo, Benito Juárez, 14:403–39. The dictamen was also incorporated into Agapito Piza's "Historia parlamentaria de la cámara de senadores," in Diario de los debates. Senado, 8th congress, 3 vols. (Mexico, 1882), 1:7–32. These volumes constitute the initial record of Senate debates (1875–76). The members of the 1869 committee were Ezequiel Montes, Rafael Dondé, and Joaquín M. Alcalde.

Spanish-language edition of Edouard Laboulaye's *Histoire des États-Unis*, translated by Manuel Dublán, a prominent deputy and jurist and a stalwart in the work of codification.[42] Without making direct reference to a senate, Dublán's introduction did evoke suggestive themes. Laboulaye's work can provide us, said Dublán, with valuable lessons on the "instability of power"; it can introduce us to the spirit behind the North American institutions we have imitated; it can teach us about "liberty without revolution" (a phrase Dublán repeated several times). The committee recommendation of December 1869 was more explicit. Approximately half of it consisted of sections from Laboulaye's discussion of the Senate in the United States Constitution, a discussion its authors deemed particularly relevant to Mexico.

Laboulaye (1811–83) was a French constitutional liberal, supporter of the Orleans monarchy before 1848, a leader of the liberal opposition to Napoleon III, and after 1870 a strong adherent of Adolphe Thiers and the conservative republic. Laboulaye's history consisted of three series of lectures delivered at the Collège de France begun in 1849 in the wake of democratic revolution and the adoption of a republic and a unicameral legislature and continued in 1863 and 1864. In his preface to the first series, Laboulaye said that the United States, where "customs uphold the laws," had been a kind of "revelation" to him "in a moment of crisis and danger." Its experience might demonstrate "what the lasting conditions of liberty were and how a country [like France] that suffers from anarchy can reform its institutions."[43]

Laboulaye saw the French Constitution of 1848 as abstract and unworkable, one that had inevitably led to Caesarism because a single chamber could provide no resistance to tyranny. Its creation, he reiterated in 1866, was the constitution's "capital error."[44] "In France," wrote Laboulaye in a passage cited in the Mexican committee report of 1869,

[42] Laboulaye, *Historia de los Estados Unidos*, 2 vols. (Mexico, 1870). Dublán (1830–91) was a relative of Juárez (they both married Maza sisters) and had been his adherent in Veracruz, in the 1861 Congress, and in the Supreme Court before defecting to the empire in 1864. He was director of the Oaxaca Institute in 1865 and served in 1866–67 as Maximilian's *procurador general*. After 1867, Dublán was a member of the committee that drafted the codes of civil and criminal procedure. One biographer said Dublán's father was French, which might explain his facility with the language and in part his defection to the empire: Ireneo Paz, *Los Hombres prominentes de Mexico* (Mexico, 1888), p. 25.

[43] Laboulaye, preface (dated 15 July 1855) to vol. 1 of *Histoire des États-Unis*, 6th ed., 3 vols. (Paris, 1877), pp. ii–xiii. Vol. 1 was first published in 1855, vols. 2 and 3 in 1866. Vol. 3 (vol. 2 of the Mexican edition) was a study of the formation of the American Constitution of 1787.

[44] Laboulaye, *Histoire*, 3:27. The lapse of time from 1849 when Laboulaye initiated his lectures to 1866 when he wrote his preface to vol. 3 seems to have had no major effect on his ideas, particularly with regard to the importance of a senate.

"we have always confused the nation with its representation. Since the nation is sovereign, [we assume] its representatives must be also." The result is "usurpation and anarchy," which can be prevented only by dividing the legislature so that "the spirit of consequence and moderation" may reign. Pointing to the frequent violation of individual guarantees since 1861 in Mexico, the constitutional reform committee maintained that the nation's history fully confirmed the theories of Laboulaye. If a senate is adopted, said the authors, "dictatorship will be less frequent among us."[45]

Although Laboulaye was a constitutionalist in the tradition of Montesquieu, Constant, and Tocqueville, he also adhered to the German historical and comparative school of law derived from Savigny, and thus he was not in principle hostile to the state, which he termed the "greatest and most august of human institutions."[46] His concern was to set limits to its authority, to avoid tyranny through constitutional restraints and through civic education and participation. He equated this state tyranny with the revolutionary doctrine of popular sovereignty and its sequel, the Caesarism of the two Napoleons. Thus, like the Mexicans who cited him, he distinguished between dictatorship and strong government. The Senate was an important part of his vision, because through it men of merit, moderation, and substance could complement as well as limit administrative authority. Laboulaye was less legalistic than Benjamin Constant, who had been so important to Mexican constitutional liberals in the 1820s, though he did publish two editions of Constant's writings in 1861 and 1872 and referred to him as the great master of liberty. In introducing the Constant edition of 1872, Laboulaye wrote that France "wants to found a government which will assure public peace, while providing a solid guarantee for every interest and every right."[47] Such phraseology,

[45] Tamayo, *Benito Juárez*, 14:419–20 (quoted from Laboulaye, *Histoire*, 3:375); also p. 426. The wording of the lengthy passages translated from Laboulaye in the committee report of 24 December 1869 differs from those in the Dublán translation (1870) and from those in *Estudios sobre la constitución de los Estados Unidos*, 2 vols. (Sevilla, 1869), a translation of vol. 3 by Joaquín Guichot. Thus presumably the committee did its own translating, unless it used an earlier Spanish version by Manuel R. García (Paris, 1867), which I have been unable to locate. For an interesting critique of the committee's reliance on Laboulaye, see León Guzmán, *Cuestiones constitucionales. El Sistema de dos cámaras y sus consecuencias* (Mexico, 1870). Guzmán, a leader in the adoption of a unicameral legislature in 1856–57, admitted to ambivalence on the question. On Guzmán see pp. 57–58.

[46] Quoted by Guido de Ruggiero, *History of European Liberalism* (Oxford, 1927), p. 199, from Laboulaye, *L'État et ses limites* (1863). Frederich Carl Von Savigny (1779–1861), the founder of the German historical school of jurisprudence, said that every nation's law, like its language, was an emanation of the *Volksgeist* and thus corresponded to national needs. Laboulaye published a study on Savigny in 1842.

[47] Laboulaye, preface to Benjamin Constant de Rébeque, *Cours de politique constitutionnelle ou collection des ouvrages publiés sur le gouvernement représentatif*, 2d ed., 2

joining interests, guarantees, and the authority of the state, struck a responsive chord among post-Reforma liberals in Mexico. Thus it was quite natural that the editors of *La Libertad* should cite Laboulaye in 1878 to support their contention that Mexico needed strong government and constitutional reform. Following his example, they said, they could call themselves "liberals," and yet be "in favor of reforming the constitution in a conservative sense."[48]

The Senate proposal in general was passed by Congress on 26 April 1870, but not in its particulars until 9 April 1874. The first Senate did not convene until September 1875. The measure in its final form allied the Senate even more closely with centralized authority than the original committee had intended. In provisions added after 1869, the Senate was given the power to declare, upon the "disappearance" of a constitutional state government, that the president (with Senate approval) could name a provisional governor, who in turn would call new elections. Also, the Senate could act to resolve conflicts between branches of a state government.[49] The Senate was repudiated by the Tuxtepec rebels in 1876 because they regarded it as an arm of the executive, President Lerdo; though as we have seen, it was preserved by Porfirio Díaz once in power. The adoption of the Senate in Mexico was clearly a sign of the times. A bicameral legislature was one of the principal features of the republican "constitution" of 1875 in France and of the monarchical constitution of 1876 in Spain, thus becoming an integral part of the liberal-conservative system on both continents.[50]

---

vols. (Paris, 1872). On Constant's influence in Mexico, see my *Mexican Liberalism*, pp. 76–78 and passim.

[48] *La Libertad*, 17 October 1878.

[49] The progress of the Senate proposal is summarized in Piza, "Historia," pp. 32–36; Tamayo, *Benito Juárez*, 14:383–402; and Knapp, *Lerdo*, pp. 189–91. For the lengthy debates of 16–26 April 1870, see *Diario de los debates. Cámara de diputados*, 5th congress, 4 vols. (Mexico, 1871), 2:104–227, passim. Two subsequent committee reports (25 October 1871 and 7 October 1873), modifying the original proposal of 1869, can be found in ibid., 6th congress, 4 vols. (Mexico, 1871–73), 2:167–71, and ibid., 7th congress, 4 vols. (Mexico, 1873–75), 1:254–58. Manuel Dublán was a member of the 1871 committee. The provisions commented on appeared in rudimentary form in the 1871 and 1873 reports, assuming their final wording in the course of debate (ibid., pp. 405–99). They appeared ultimately as article 72, sec. iii, B, v–vi of the constitutional amendment of 13 November 1874 (Dublán and Lozano, *Legislación*, 12:635–41). For the decree of 15 December regulating Senate elections, see ibid., pp. 692–93. Two senators from each state were to be chosen by the same district juntas that elected deputies. Senators had to be thirty years of age instead of twenty-five; otherwise the qualifications were the same as for deputies.

[50] For the French constitutional law of 24 February 1875 establishing a senate, see Leon Duguit and Henri Monnier, *Les Constitutions et les principales lois politiques de la France* (Paris, 1925), pp. 321–22; for the Spanish Constitution of 1876, see Verduin, *Manual*, pp. 77–84. The movement to create a senate in France is discussed by Louis Girard, "Political

Francisco Zarco's ambivalence toward the Juárez regime and the adoption of the Senate provide an introduction to the tangled relationship between scientific politics and constitutional liberalism. More direct evidence must be sought in the early ideas and political allegiances of the seven or eight men, twenty years or so younger than Zarco, who came together in 1878 to found *La Libertad*. Though biographical information is scarce, as a composite they appear to have entered the literary and journalistic world after 1870, in part under the tutelage of the older Ignacio M. Altamirano (1834–93), and to have held minor posts in the Lerdo administration from 1872 to 1876. Though we can find some indications of embryonic scientific politics in their pre-1876 writings, the group's ideas and political activities are notable for their adherence to generalized liberal and constitutional precepts and for their support of the Juárez and Lerdo regimes.[51]

Let us take the example of *La Tribuna*, a short-lived paper whose founders included the two Sierras and Hammeken y Mexía. The editors announced in the first issue of 1 January 1874, that "as progressivists in the broadest sense of the word, we will uphold not only the principles of liberty and reform . . . but all the corollaries that inevitably follow." They then cited peace, progress, and the democratic system and vowed "not a step backward" from the victories won over obscurantism in the previous decade. Their intellectual orientation was further revealed by the inclusion of Hammeken's translation of a recent article by the French spiritualist philosopher Paul Janet (1823–93), which defended the rights of man and other principles of the Revolution of 1789.[52] Julio Zárate, another

---

Liberalism in France, 1840–1875," in *French Society and Culture Since the Old Regime*, eds. E. M. Acomb and M. L. Brown, Jr. (New York, 1966), pp. 126–29.

[51] In addition to *La Tribuna* members of the group also collaborated on *El Artista* (1874–75), a literary monthly directed by Jorge Hammeken y Mexía, and on the weekly *El Precursor* (1874–76). *El Precursor*'s message was generally rationalist and anticlerical: see the introduction by Telesforo García, 8 October 1874. Altamirano and Justo Sierra were also listed as editors, but apparently Sierra did not contribute. Altamirano had founded the Sociedad de Libres Pensadores in 1870: see Ignacio M. Altamirano, *Discursos* (Mexico, 1934), pp. 199–203. Inspiration for the group in its early days also came from Emilio Castelar, especially from his speeches in the Spanish Constituent Assembly of 1869–70 on standard liberal themes such as republicanism, individual liberty, the abolition of slavery, and the separation of church and state. See Sierra's testimony of 1899 (*Obras*, 5:262) in which he quoted from his article of 1869 in *El Renacimiento*, 1:481–82.

[52] Janet, "La Filosofía de la revolución francesa," *La Tribuna*, 14–24 February 1874. The article was a translation of part one (of three) of Janet's "La Philosophie de la révolution," which appeared in the *Revue des deux mondes*, 1 January 1872, pp. 42–73. It was an examination of the several schools of thought on the French Revolution from Burke and De Maistre to Louis Blanc. After his conversion to positivism, Hammeken recalled his early days as one of a group of "raging (*furieux*) spiritualists" in "La Philosophie positive au Mex-

editor and a *lerdista* deputy, extolled the Constitution of 1857, but he did interject the unsettling thought that it should not be regarded as "the final expression of the needs, desires, and legitimate aspirations of the people." Justo Sierra introduced the standard problem of discord within the Liberal party, for example the hostility by some former *juaristas* toward President Lerdo, and reiterated the need for unity and vigilance against the ever-present "reactionary" threat. The hope for the nation, he continued, resides in a new group of leaders, offspring of the "virile generation" of the Reforma, who utilizing "modern ideas" will put aside factionalism and turn to the "sacred work of reconstruction of our country." Such statements as those by Zárate and Sierra were scarcely in conflict with the official rhetoric of the Lerdo administration.[53]

Although it is difficult to separate incipient scientific politics from classic liberalism in the early ideas of Justo Sierra and his colleagues, their political stance became increasingly clear amidst the mounting factionalism of 1875–76. The future editors of *La Libertad* at first supported Lerdo against the armed rebellion of Porfirio Díaz, which began in January 1876, but then they abandoned the president as governmental authority hardened. On 2 August they launched *El Bien público*, branding as anarchical and extraconstitutional both the movement to reelect Lerdo and the Plan of Tuxtepec. Their concern, they said, went beyond the struggle between "despotic and demagogic elements" to social organization and the creation of national prosperity. In short, concluded the editors, our causes are liberty and order.[54]

While resisting Lerdo, Sierra and his colleagues revealed the same ambivalence toward centralized authority as had Zarco earlier. In the complex constitutional debate over the Morelos tax case, the *amparo de Morelos*, Sierra had attacked excessive executive power while at the same

---

ique. Lettre . . . à M. Littré," *La Philosophie positive*, 20 (1878): 210. For further discussion of spiritualism in France and Mexico, see chap. 6.

[53] See Julio Zárate in *La Tribuna*, 4 February 1874; Justo Sierra in ibid., 30 January (*Obras*, 4:54–55). *La Tribuna* ran from 1 January through 28 February 1874 and also included Altamirano as an editor. Zárate (1844–1917), most prominent for his later historical writing, managed to support as deputy and journalist all the regimes from 1867 through 1910, including that of José María Iglesias. He even served as Díaz's minister of foreign relations from December 1879 to September 1880. For information on his activities from 1867–76, see Cosío Villegas, *Historia moderna*, vols. 1 and 8. One can compare *La Tribuna*'s rhetoric with that of Lerdo's program presented in July 1872: see Knapp, *Lerdo*, p. 174. Also cf. Zárate's contribution, "Episodios históricos. La Convención (1792–95)," in *El Artista* 1 (1874): 230–40. Dedicated to Justo Sierra, it was a benign appreciation of French radicalism, including the doctrine of popular sovereignty.

[54] For support of Lerdo, see J. Sierra in *El Federalista*, 15 March 1876 (*Obras*, 4:81–82). The Sierras and Cosmes explained the break from *El Federalista* and Lerdo in *La Libertad*, 10 January 1878 (Sierra, *Obras*, 4:129–31). Founding editors of *El Bien público* included Cosmes, Garay, Hammeken y Mexía, and the Sierras.

time condoning centralization. Certain landowners from the state of Morelos appealed in 1873 to the Supreme Court for an *amparo* or stay against taxes levied by the state regime, which they claimed had been illegitimately imposed by presidential influence. Chief Justice José María Iglesias ruled in favor of the landowners, because the state government was "incompetent by origin." Sierra defended the *incompetencia de origen* doctrine of Iglesias, asserting that individual rights were above the rights of the states and that it was the duty of the federal courts to intervene if necessary to protect these rights. The constitutional issue, which arose again in Puebla and Tamaulipas, is impossible to separate from the burgeoning conflict between the chief justice and the president. Whether we regard Sierra's arguments of 1874–75 as basically juridical or political, it is manifest that his position was not hostile to centralism, that is, to intervention in the states by the judiciary if not by the executive. The fact that the constitutionalist opponents of the clearly centralist Lerdo did not challenge him using federalist arguments is evidence of the weakness of federalism as an element of constitutional liberalism by 1876.[55]

El Bien público was founded as a response to the midsummer voting of 1876 in which Lerdo was reelected president. The editors regarded the reelection as a coup d'etat, illegal because several states were officially under siege at the time the voting took place. The full force of their constitutional case against the president, however, had to await the congressional confirmation of reelection, which did not come until 26 October. In the meantime, *El Bien público* joined the growing opposition press with incessant attacks upon presidential "despotism."

There was evidence, however, that the editors' attacks were more *antilerdismo* than opposition to "despotism" per se. Francisco Cosmes, seconded by Jorge Hammeken and Justo Sierra, characterized the regime as "Caesarism without Caesar," entailing the evils of authoritarianism without the benefits. They pointed out that though the regime of Napoleon III in France had been a blow to liberty, at least it had had the support of the great majority of property-holders, who saw socialism as a threat.

[55] For Sierra's arguments see *El Federalista*, 15, 22 April, 15, 7 May 1874; 8 January, 1, 7 September 1875 (*Obras*, 4:9–28, 30–32, 36–41). Iglesias defended his judgment in *Estudio constitucional sobre facultades de la corte de justicia* (Mexico, 1874). On the *amparo* question, see Cosío Villegas, *Historia moderna*, 8:16–23; Laurens B. Perry, *Juárez and Díaz: Machine Politics in Mexico* (De Kalb, 1978), pp. 285–88; Knapp, *Lerdo*, pp. 194–95. Knapp, though a strong defender of Lerdo against Iglesias, emphasizes Lerdo's intervention in the states and his centralism in general. It might be noted that Justo Sierra and his colleagues were curiously silent on the adoption of the Senate in 1874. There was one article in *La Tribuna* by Julio Zárate (14 January 1874) justifying the Senate in terms similar to those used by the government and applauding its progress through Congress. We might infer that *La Tribuna*'s editors did not oppose the centralist implications of the measure.

"The French people felt the need of strong administration . . . that would make industry and commerce prosper, that would organize public finance, and that would put a stop to anarchy." The implication of the argument was that Lerdo's "Caesarism" might have been more palatable if it had not been so narrowly political, if it had promoted material progress and had not levied excessive taxes on property. Though such sentiments appear to be an undercurrent to the flood of constitutionalist rhetoric, they do reveal the further encroachment of the administrative mentality that so troubled Francisco Zarco in 1867.[56]

Whatever contrary assumptions can be discovered below the surface of their writings, the dogged adherence by Justo Sierra and his colleagues to the legalistic cause of Chief Justice Iglesias is impressive. In its final three issues (10–12 October), El Bien público ran a front-page proclamation entitled "The Constitutional Solution." Summarizing assertions repeated ad nauseam since August, it declared that as soon as Congress in collusion with Lerdo had confirmed his reelection, his presidential powers would legally cease and Iglesias would become interim president under the constitution. "From that moment, resistance to all measures of the so-called government of Lerdo will be a right, obedience to the constitutional authority a sacred duty, struggle against the usurpation an act of high patriotism." The editors rejected the label of decembrista, given to the Iglesias party because of his previous pronouncement that in the absence of legal elections and thus with Lerdo's term legally ending on 30 November, he, the vice-president, would become constitutional president on 1 December. The editors of El Bien público said that the label downgraded their cause, making it that of a political faction. In point of fact, they were doing decembrismo one better by asserting that Lerdo's presidency was illegal and thus terminated not on 30 November, but at the moment the reelection was confirmed. "We are not decembristas," declared Justo Sierra, "we are purely and simply constitutionalists."[57]

The constitutionalist cause of the young adherents of Iglesias reached a political dead end in the swiftly moving events of the next three months. By mid-January 1877 both Iglesias and Lerdo had embarked for

[56] See Cosmes in El Bien público, 1, 17 August; Hammeken on 3 August; and J. Sierra, 27 August 1876. El Bien público published a list of opposition and "ministerial" papers on 10 September. Of the major dailies only El Federalista and the Diario oficial continued to support Lerdo. Hammeken left El Bien público on 9 September, presumably for Europe. The next trace of him is his article "Philosophie positive" (see chap. 3, n. 52), datelined Naples, 1 January 1878.

[57] J. Sierra in El Bien público, 7 September 1876 (Obras, 4:99). On decembrismo see also El Bien público, 18 August, 14 September (S. Sierra), 27 September. After Iglesias established his government at Guanajuato, his spokesmen no longer rejected the term: see Francisco Sosa in Boletín oficial del gobierno interino de los Estados Unidos Mexicanos (Guanajuato), 19 November.

exile, and Porfirio Díaz, after several decisive military victories, had assumed power in Mexico City. Those who had taken posts with the Iglesias government in Guanajuato after the cessation of *El Bien público*, including the Sierras, Garay, Cosmes, and Olaguíbel were now forced to seek other pursuits and to contemplate the fate of legalism in the face of new political realities.[58] Justo Sierra on returning to Mexico City from Querétaro began writing his history of the ancient world and was appointed professor at the National Preparatory School in April. Garay returned to the school in February where he had begun teaching in 1873. Santiago Sierra opened a printing establishment and in June began editing and publishing a weekly scientific journal, *El Mundo científico*. We know less about Francisco Cosmes, who apparently had been closer to Iglesias than had any of the others and who was perhaps more shaken than they were by the failure of his cause. Carlos Olaguíbel launched *La Época*, a newspaper that ran from May through December and that provides our main source for the reflections of the group during the critical year 1877. In fact there was some validity in *La Libertad*'s acknowledgment two years later that *La Época* had been its precursor as a champion of "scientific philosophy."[59]

In its reformulation of political ideas *La Época* emphasized the changed conditions since the days of *El Bien público*. The task now was to "build a new order of things" rather than to tear down "a rot-infested edifice." Mexican society is disillusioned by the experience of recent years; it no longer "places any hope whatever upon unrealizable theo-

[58] Díaz assumed executive power in Mexico City on 28 November and named Juan N. Méndez provisional president on 6 December, while he campaigned against Iglesias. He reassumed power on 17 February 1877. Detailed accounts of the events of late 1876 can be found in Cosío Villegas, *Historia moderna*, 1:871–925; 8:1–252; Perry, *Juárez and Díaz*, pp. 285–337; Knapp, *Lerdo*, pp. 235–54. Knapp's account is exceedingly hostile to Iglesias, the accounts of the others more balanced. Justo Sierra was editor of Iglesias's *Boletín oficial* from 2 November until 1 December 1876, when he was confined in Querétaro with a badly sprained ankle. Garay was minister of *fomento* until 1 December; Olaguíbel, administrator of the stamp tax; Cosmes, personal secretary to Iglesias. Cosmes was also sent to New Orleans to discuss with Ignacio Mejía, Lerdo's minister of war who was dismissed on 30 August, the possibility of Mejía's collaboration in the Iglesias movement. Cosmes remained with Iglesias until the latter embarked from Mazatlán on 29 January 1877. See José María Iglesias, *La Cuestión presidencial en 1876* (Mexico, 1892), pp. 303, 322–26.

[59] *La Época* was printed in Santiago Sierra's shop and he was listed as co-editor, but he seems not to have contributed any of the articles. *La Libertad*'s acknowledgment appeared on 27 August 1879 in response to an enthusiastic comment by the student publication *La Escuela de jurisprudencia* on *La Libertad*'s adoption of "order and progress" as its subtitle. The editors went on to claim that from the time they were writing in *El Federalista* and *El Bien público* they had upheld "the need for adopting the scientific bases of the evolutionist school as a point of departure to judge our social and political state." The assertion seems in part to be true, in part to be colored by hindsight.

ries," but rather seeks its solutions through "practical means, through truth." *La Época* stressed the "defense of social interests" and their reconciliation with "the principle of authority." We ask the "support of the laboring classes, the useful ones, for government," wrote Olaguíbel; "we ask [in turn] that government focus its attention on the needs of work, in order to satisfy them." All efforts, all wills must be bent toward the realization of peace, justice, work—*La Época*'s oft-repeated watchwords. Like its successor, *La Época* proclaimed its support for the Díaz regime and also its independence. "We will not be the echo of some opposition interest, nor will we carry a ministerial banner to the press."[60]

Olaguíbel introduced many of the themes that became more systematically developed by *La Libertad*, the merging of conservatives and liberals, the need for administration instead of political contention, the pursuit of practical solutions rather than abstract principles, and the consolidation of order as opposed to anarchy. Within the old Conservative party, argued Olaguíbel, there is a segment that "now accepts accomplished facts and respects the advance of the liberal idea." Within the Liberal party, there are those who see that exclusive domination by the majority "is equivalent to erecting a throne to the despotism of ignorance, or establishing the turbulent reign of demagoguery." Some are even admitting the need to sacrifice democracy if we are "to secure our institutions." Olaguíbel appeared here to be articulating the resistance that was mounting against the extreme *tuxtepecanos*; he spoke, for example, of the need to return to constitutional rule, which he equated with "harmony in the Liberal party, and not [with] the revolutionary suppression of the Senate." Telesforo García also pursued these themes in one of his few contributions to *La Época*, expressing the overt elitism that was to become a hallmark of conservative-liberalism in *La Libertad*.[61]

Olaguíbel's special cause was the primacy of economics over politics, "the protection of labor and national industry," and his enthusiasm for the regime rose and fell on the issue of protectionism. For example, he was jubilant over the replacement of José Landero y Cos by Matías Romero as minister of *hacienda*. He saw in Romero one who would actively support *La Época*'s policy:

To promote the identification of social interests with politics, such that politics, descending from the regions of theory and abstraction, becomes not an end,

[60] *La Época*, 1 May 1877; Olaguíbel in ibid., 9 May. The newspaper had all the marks of a one-man enterprise, with occasional signed contributions by others. Thus all the unsigned editorials were probably written by Olaguíbel.

[61] Olaguíbel in *La Época*, 1, 9, 18 May 1877; García in ibid., 7 July. On the Senate, see also 22 May 1877.

but a *means*, an *instrument* put at the disposition of the intelligent and industrious classes, to serve the interests of agriculture, industry, and commerce in the country.[62]

Romero must have responded favorably to this enthusiasm, for soon afterward Olaguíbel was appointed to a good position in the ministry, which he held for nearly a year. In the final issue of *La Época*, Olaguíbel found it necessary to defend himself against the charge that the newspaper had been a "speculation" to get a "crust (*mendrugo*)" in exchange for flattery. His only concern, he insisted, had been "to promote the solution of the economic question upon which the future of the country depends."[63]

Though Carlos Olaguíbel's protectionist mission dominated the pages of *La Época*, these pages also provided an outlet for articles by Justo Sierra and Francisco Cosmes from which we get a unique insight into the immediate impact of the crisis of 1876. Sierra was challenged by the *tuxtepecano* newspaper *El Combate* to give his reasons for supporting José María Iglesias and specifically to explain how, if he regarded the Plan of Tuxtepec as anticonstitutional, he could accept an appointment in the regime of Porfirio Díaz. To do so he had had to take an oath to uphold both the plan and the constitution. Sierra's explanations and a reaction by Cosmes reveal mental turmoil and a heightened tension in their thinking between the assumptions of constitutionalism and those of scientific politics.[64]

Sierra emphasized his veneration for Iglesias and his continuing belief in the legitimacy of the Iglesias cause, which sprang from the manifest illegality of Lerdo's reelection. To accept Iglesias required of Sierra no "subtle interpretations of the constitution." To accept the legitimacy of Díaz was more difficult. Sierra said he considered Iglesias president until

[62] Olaguíbel, "El Gobierno y los intereses agrícolas, industriales y mercantiles de México. El Sr. Romero y las indicaciones de 'La Época.' Primeros triunfos a las clases laboriosas, honor al presidente y a sus consejeros," *La Época*, 30 May 1877. See also Olaguíbel, ibid., 25 May. Romero served as minister from 24 May 1877 to 4 April 1879.

[63] Olaguíbel in *La Época*, 20 December 1877. Olaguíbel served as deputy *oficial mayor* of *hacienda* sometime during the period 1 July 1877 and 1 July 1878: see *Memoria de hacienda y credito público, 1877–78* (Mexico, 1879), p. 109. After resigning, Olaguíbel joined *La Libertad* on 25 August 1878. Olaguíbel's relations with Romero go back to the period from September 1869 to May 1872 when he wrote to him frequently and appeared to hold posts in *hacienda* and in foreign relations: Guadalupe Monroy, ed., *Archivo histórico de Matías Romero*, 2 vols. (Mexico, 1965), vol. 1.

[64] These heretofore–unknown articles, all in *La Época*, are Sierra, "A Carlos Olaguíbel" (24 June 1877),"La Protesta del plan de Tuxtepec" (27 June), and "La Constitución y el plan de Tuxtepec" (29 June), which includes a letter from Cosmes (dated 25 June) to Sierra and his response. Sierra's appointment was presumably that of professor in the National Preparatory School (April 1877).

"the people, or all that can be called people in our country, respecting the *convocatoria* [of 1876] that emanated from a de facto power," elected Díaz.[65] Though Sierra regarded this "popular sanction of a usurpation" as an evil, he maintained that "there was no possible preventative against it in a radically democratic constitution like ours." The popularity of Díaz was beyond question; unlike Lerdo, he was "the true candidate of the masses." Sierra also suggested a precedent, the Juárez "usurpation" at Paso del Norte in 1865, which was sanctioned by the people and supported by Lerdo and Iglesias and even agreed to (reluctantly) by the then–chief justice, Jesús González Ortega. Sierra justified at length his oath to the Plan of Tuxtepec with a legalistic examination of its several articles.[66] Those that were anticonstitutional, he argued, had either been reformed, such as article 1 that now included the Senate, or had been converted into "facts" (articles 3 through 6) by popular sanction, thus making them "dead articles." All that is left of the plan is article 2, proclaiming no-reelection, an incontrovertible principle also advanced by Iglesias.[67]

Sierra's defense of his actions on legal grounds is not convincing. It was based primarily on the popular sovereignty argument, namely that the essentially unconstitutional assumption of power by General Díaz was given legitimacy by subsequent popular vote. Cosmes revealed himself as a diehard, still regarding Iglesias as the legitimate president in June 1877; he challenged Sierra's view, saying that the 1877 election of Díaz was no different from that of Lerdo in 1876.[68] Sierra was then forced, as we have seen, to advance the manifest popularity of Díaz and the manifest unpopularity of Lerdo, hardly a compelling legal argument. More damaging to Sierra's constitutionalism was his obvious distaste for this "popular sanction for a usurpation" and his oblique attack on Mexico's "radically democratic" constitution. Most revealing of all, however, was

[65] Sierra's argument to justify Díaz was similar to the one used by León Guzmán the next year in *La Libertad* (see pp. 57–58). The referred-to *convocatoria* was issued by General Méndez on 23 December, 1876. It set primary elections for 28 January 1877 and district elections for 11–13 February. The new congress was to be installed on 12 March. See Dublán and Lozano, *Legislación*, 13:120–22.

[66] Sierra in *La Época*, 24 June. The Plan of Tuxtepec Sierra mentioned was of course the Palo Blanco version.

[67] The plan also had an article 7, calling for municipal independence, which Sierra regarded as "entirely within the literal spirit of the constitution."

[68] Cosmes's position, expressed with emotion and commitment (*La Época*, 29 June 1877), is puzzling because it is in strong contrast with his later views and even with those expressed in *El Bien público*. One can only surmise that either his disillusionment with legalism came later or that he submerged it in 1878 for reasons of expediency. Given his forthright call for "honorable tyranny," the latter seems improbable.

the pragmatic and nondoctrinaire tone of his articles, which undercut his legalistic points.

Sierra prefaced his first article by declaring himself an "enemy of political revolutions" that only tend to change administrative personnel, and by condemning "dull" orations on liberty and democracy. "All that verbal display of the liberalism of petty journalists and kangaroo-courts (*de gacetilla y de guillotina*) is not worth in my opinion a single penny of solid and positive liberty." Later, in defending the popular election of Díaz as opposed to that of Lerdo, he concluded that politics was "the science of the possible," a phrase he attributed to Iglesias himself. Once constitutional principles have been subverted, he mused, there is no legal way to return to them. Pursuing its "supreme right to existence," society recovers its "normal life" by giving power to a governor; and thus "necessity becomes the source of a transient but manifest right." The distance was short from these views to Sierra's opening statement in *La Libertad* six months later in which he referred to the existence of the Díaz regime as "an undeniable fact, despite the entire constitutional liturgy." However, there followed in *La Libertad* a general query that would have seemed out of place in *La Época*: "Have not all legalities had their origin in the same way?"[69] The men of *La Libertad* could then proceed to recant their legalism of 1876 as youthful inexperience and idealism, to draw their conclusions on politics from "the severe study of social science," and to "consider societies as organisms whose state must be analyzed experimentally to determine the means necessary to their development."[70] Their transition from constitutional legalism to scientific politics was complete.

We have seen that Justo Sierra and his colleagues either before or after 1878 were not detached intellectuals, observing politics from afar. Like most men of ideas in Mexico, they had a personal stake in the system, either as elected officials or as governmental appointees. Their extreme hostility to President Lerdo de Tejada can only be explained in part by ideology. A major complaint against Lerdo was that he refused to replace the Juárez cabinet, and presumably this refusal included subcabinet officials as well. It is quite possible that by so doing Lerdo was blocking young, ambitious, and intelligent men from access to higher government posts. The generational theme that became so prominent in *La Libertad* also appeared in *El Bien público*, for instance when Santiago Sierra spoke for the disillusioned youth of the nation in the face of the administrative corruption of the Lerdo regime. "Let us proclaim energetically our de-

[69] Sierra in *La Libertad*, 5 January 1878 (*Obras*, 4:125).

[70] These sentiments were expressed anonymously in *La Libertad*, 28 December 1878, and by Santiago Sierra in ibid., 16 January 1880, two of many retrospective articles on the group's change of views since 1876.

termination to redeem Mexico," he wrote; "the salvation of Mexico is in her youth."[71] Was this "youth" perhaps a new generation of aspiring but frustrated government officials? Could part of the appeal of the Iglesias cause have been that it offered this group major offices within a respectable regime, the legitimate heir to those of Juárez and Lerdo? On at least two occasions Justo Sierra characterized the Iglesias movement as a "refuge" from the despotic Lerdo and the revolutionary Díaz.[72] With the collapse of Iglesias, the group was forced to turn (in the manner of Carlos Olaguíbel) to the less respectable Díaz as an outlet for their personal aspirations as well as for their ideas of national regeneration.

Earlier in the chapter we posed the general problem of interpreting, in the context of the Sierra-Vigil debate, the constitutional reform proposals advanced by *La Libertad*. Scientific politics theoretically repudiated basic liberal tenets, such as the rights of man and popular sovereignty, which Vigil said formed the basis of the Constitution of 1857. The advocates of the new doctrine characterized the constitution as abstract, utopian, and a stimulus to revolutions. At best, their reform proposals seemed aimed at subversion, particularly when juxtaposed to their call for "honorable tyranny."

In reviewing the questions raised by the *convocatoria* of 1867, by the response of Francisco Zarco to the government of Benito Juárez, by the addition of a senate, and by the pre-1878 ideas and politics of the men of *La Libertad*, we can conclude that constitutional liberalism and assumptions foreshadowing scientific politics were thoroughly intertwined during the years of the Restored Republic. The post-Reforma era, indeed the entire period from the liberal triumph of 1867 until at least 1900, was one of consensus, during which political debate, open political contention, and even the rise of a significant new political doctrine took place within the confines of a single liberal establishment. Even Porfirio Díaz, despite his several rebellions and despite some radical overtones in the Tuxtepec movement, formed part of this establishment, and indeed came to preside over it. Once in power, Díaz moved immediately to conciliate former antagonists at the expense of his ultra followers, the *tuxtepecanos netos*. Thus our analysis of political ideas from 1867 to 1877 reveals am-

[71] S. Sierra, "A La Juventud," *El Bien público*, 1 August 1876. Sierra apparently was dismissed at this time from a position he held in the Ministry of Foreign Relations (see *El Bien público*, 6, 8, 12 August 1876). Justo Sierra also advanced the generational idea by reference to theories of the Italian philosopher, J. Ferrari (1812–76), in ibid., 3 October (*Obras*, 4:111–15). In the final issue of 12 October (*Obras*, 4:115–16), he used scientific terminology to describe the struggle between a dying organism (the Lerdo regime) and an organism that is to be born.

[72] See J. Sierra in *El Bien público*, 22 August 1876; and in *La Época*, 24 June 1877. Sierra's notion of "refuge" was couched, of course, in legal and constitutional terms.

bivalence and inconsistency at every turn. It also reveals a universal attachment to the Constitution of 1857, even and especially among the future advocates of scientific politics. In fact, they moved to the new doctrine in 1878 from the seemingly antithetical position of exaggerated constitutional legalism in 1876.

The political and social ideas that underlay the post-Reforma consensus were comparable to those that guided Emilio Castelar's republican presidency in Spain and the incipient Third Republic in France. In fact, as we have seen, both served as models for the advocates of scientific politics and for their predecessors. Of particular relevance to the Mexicans was the confluence in the Europe of the 1870s of formerly antagonistic elements of political liberalism, the system of constitutional guarantees and the centralized state. We have just noted the example of Edouard Laboulaye, who in promoting the conservative republic in France combined the constitutionalist doctrines of Benjamin Constant with Savigny's reverence for the state as a natural product of historical growth. Another example of this confluence of ideas can be seen in the École Libre de Sciences Politiques.

It was no accident that Laboulaye was one of the founders of the École Libre, a private institution established in 1872 to train an elite cadre to administer the French state in the modern world. The École Libre's founders, men such as François Guizot, Émile de Girardin, Auguste Casimir-Périer, Laboulaye, and their leader Émile Boutmy were anglophiles, Orleanists or former Orleanists addicted to English constitutionalism and to a higher education independent of the state. And yet they had a close working relationship with the traditional French *grands corps de l'état*, so that the École Libre promoted statist values from the start. Moreover, its founders, teachers, and graduates were thoroughly elitist and hostile to "democracy." As a mirror of the infant republic itself, the École Libre "system" was also guided by the assumptions of a generalized positivism, what Paul Janet later called the "experimental school" of philosophy led by Hippolyte Taine. These assumptions included an antipathy toward theoreticians, toward abstraction, toward doctrines of rights, and a fondness for practitioners, for "social facts," and particularly for history. The historical method was seen at the École as the scientific way of approaching any subject. Taine was a founder of the École, a longtime board member, and a close friend of Boutmy. The cast of mind, indeed the vocabulary and phraseology, of the École Libre group closely resembled those of Justo Sierra and his colleagues. It was the language of an intellectual and social elite that infused "science" into traditional liberal discourse, producing an amalgam of formerly conflicting concepts.[73]

---

[73] See the excellent study by Thomas R. Osborne, "The Recruitment of the Administra-

As in France in the 1870s, one theme that comes forth clearly in the confusing debates over the Mexican Constitution of 1857 is the growing disrepute of the doctrine of popular sovereignty, the basis of political democracy. Lerdo resorted to the doctrine in submitting his constitutional reforms to a referendum in 1867 and suggested as a precedent the popular sanction for the Juárez dictatorship of 1865. However, his main justification for a strong executive and a weakened legislature was the more pragmatic needs of "administration," a justification that foreshadowed the "scientific" position of 1878. Lerdo's constitutional reform proposals were set aside in part because of the postwar resurgence of constitutionalism, that is, the tendency within classic political liberalism to limit executive authority (whether that authority was justified by popular sovereignty or by pragmatic considerations) through a system of constitutional guarantees. However, the heritage of strong government was too deep-rooted and the problems of reconstruction (including the many regional challenges) were too pressing for such limitations on the executive to make much headway—witness the ambivalence of Francisco Zarco toward the Juárez regime.

The adherents of Iglesias based their constitutional case in part on popular sovereignty, namely, their contention that the reelection of Lerdo was illegitimate because "the people had not voted"; but the doctrine lost its appeal in the upheaval to follow. When Justo Sierra tried in 1877 to justify Díaz's "usurpation" by saying it had popular sanction (again, like Lerdo, he referred to the Juárez precedent of 1865), his case lacked conviction. Justification of revolution by an argument from popular sovereignty, he regretted, was inevitable as long as Mexico retained a "radically democratic" constitution. We can see in 1877 the germ of his proposals for constitutional reform to "strengthen" government and society as a way of curtailing dangerous democracy and extralegal dictatorship. In the era of the Reforma, executive authority (the Juárez dictatorship) and popular sovereignty had been in harmony; by 1878 they were discordant. Justo Sierra now justified strong government (and constitutional reform) on positive and scientific grounds and he condemned popular sovereignty as anarchical. The defense of popular sovereignty, "the school of Rousseau," was relegated to the beleaguered doctrinaire liberals, as exemplified by José María Vigil who equated it with constitutionalism. The democratic ideal was clearly out of tune with the new theories and the new political realities, in Mexico as well as in France and Spain.

One confusing feature of the doctrinaire liberal position was its incli-

---

tive Elite in the Third French Republic, 1870–1905: the System of the École Libre des Sciences Politiques," Ph.D. diss., University of Connecticut, 1974. Janet's comments can be found in *Histoire de la science politique dans ses rapports avec la morale*, 3d ed., 2 vols. (Paris, 1887), 1:viii. For an example of the ties between founders of the École Libre, see Émile Boutmy, *Taine, Scherer, Laboulaye* (Paris, 1901).

nation to identify scientific politics with traditional conservatism. For José María Vigil, *La Libertad*'s appeal for "honorable tyranny," its argument that the constitution should be altered to conform to Mexican social reality, and its criticism of the rigidities of the reform laws were all "reactionary" tendencies, designed to subvert the constitutional system. Vigil's attacks on *La Voz de México* or *La Ilustración católica* and those on *La Libertad* often seemed interchangeable. In short, from the doctrinaire liberal viewpoint it is not always clear which group, old conservatives or new liberals, was the true antagonist. The confusion of the doctrinaires was of course abetted by the tendency of those who advocated scientific politics to merge conflicting terms and to proclaim the advent of a liberal-conservative order. To understand further the complexities of constitutional debate in the ideological consensus of the post-Reforma era, let us review briefly the relationship between scientific politics and traditional conservatism. Was it as close as Vigil and his colleagues maintained?

At the heart of scientific politics was the effort to reconcile in theory and practice conflicting concepts of man, society, and government. The motto "order and progress," later implemented politically as conservative-liberalism, was derived from Auguste Comte's attempt to surmount through science and thus to reconcile the sterile conflict between the theological and the metaphysical mentalities. Although Comte lamented that the "doctrines of order" of his day were drawn from the "theological school," he openly acknowledged his own debt to "Catholic philosophy," particularly to De Maistre's *Du Pape* (1819). De Maistre helped me, wrote Comte, develop a healthy appreciation for the Middle Ages. In this context Comte also affirmed that "positive philosophy is able to do full justice to both retrograde and revolutionary politics."[74] Saint-Simon's conception of the high administration of an organic society was drawn from the *Essai analytique* (2d ed. 1817) of Bonald, another theoretician of the Catholic reaction against the French Revolution. Since scientific politics at its origin included such traditionalist affinities as these, it is not surprising to find an occasional approving reference to conservative theory in the pages of *La Libertad*.[75]

This traditionalist strain in early positivism came to the surface with Comte's "second career" following the Revolution of 1848, the occasion of the great schism in the movement. Comte then began to elaborate his "positive polity," including the religion of humanity and the establish-

---

[74] See Comte, *Cours*, 4:13–14, 96–97n.

[75] On the influence of Bonald and de Maistre on Saint-Simon and Comte, see Halévy, "Saint-Simonian Economic Doctrine," pp. 38–40; Manuel, *Saint-Simon*, p. 320. J. Sierra cited De Maistre in *La Libertad*, 1 January 1879 (*Obras*, 4:180); Hammeken cited Burke in his article "Política positiva" in *La Libertad*, 16 October 1879; also T. García in ibid., 18 October 1879.

ment of a corporate spiritual power. Positive philosophers would direct the mental and moral regeneration of society from which political regeneration was to follow. According to his republican and freethinking disciple, Émile Littré, Comte's schemes resembled the traditional Catholic order and did violence to the "progressive" character of his earlier thought. Moreover, Comte embraced Louis Napoleon's coup d'etat in 1851 and before his death in 1857 came to regard the Catholic church and especially the Jesuits as allies against a common enemy. Orthodox Comtism continued to have appeal among French political movements of the Right, most notably Charles Maurras's Action Française. In breaking away from Comte and repudiating his sociological system, Littré nevertheless clung to the positivist method, which he interpreted for liberal republicans and freethinkers in France and elsewhere. We will recall that this method included an approach to history as a process of gradual mental emancipation from theological and metaphysical ideas, a concept of modern society as guided by scientific thought and industrial pursuits, and an analysis of society based on descriptive and factual techniques. Thus the tendency toward reconciliation in Mexican scientific politics had intellectual roots in the dual legacy of classic positivism.[76]

Perhaps the best evidence of this tendency toward reconciliation comes from La Libertad's ambivalent attitude toward the church. The editors first of all proclaimed their allegiance to the secular state, the most significant principle of the Reforma, and they reaffirmed their commitment to its continued realization. For Justo Sierra, "the cause of civilization" was tantamount to "the preponderance of the civil element," as the words themselves revealed. The attacks by the editors on clerical obscurantism, brought out for example in Telesforo García's debate with La Voz de México over the Syllabus of Errors, rivaled those by El Monitor. The writers of La Libertad distinguished, as we have seen, between conservatism and the clerical reactionary party, and they also disassociated themselves from the old moderados whose position on church and state they regarded as timid. Inhibited by their Catholic conscience, wrote Sierra, the moderados always "moved fearfully toward progress." Sierra spoke of the new terrain of "scientific method" on which the strug-

[76] Comte's major work of his second career was Système de politique positive (1851–54). The transmission of Positivism (i.e., Comte's system as a whole) and the schisms within the movement are treated in detail by W. M. Simon, European Positivism in the Nineteenth Century (Ithaca, 1963). Also valuable is D. G. Charlton, Positivist Thought in France During the Second Empire, 1852–1870 (London, 1959). Charlton elucidates the positivist method but does not delve into politics. He and Simon differ on the definition of the term. Also useful on positivism and politics are John A. Scott, Republican Ideas and the Liberal Tradition in France, 1870–1914 (New York, 1951), pp. 87–118 (on Littré) and Eros, "Positivist Generation." A famous (and lucid) contemporary critique of the "two" Comtes is John Stuart Mill's Auguste Comte and Positivism (Ann Arbor, 1961), first published in 1865.

gle for "the radical conversion of the Mexican nation to a secular state" should now take place, and he referred particularly to education. The passions engendered by "metaphysics," whether "ultramontane" or "revolutionary," would be left behind.[77]

Despite *La Libertad*'s adherence to the ideal of secularization, its anticlericalism was muted. The editors frequently debated with *El Monitor*, *El Combate*, and even with the *Diario oficial* the prudence of rigidly enforcing the reform laws. Was it so alarming that an Indian in Tonalá, Chiapas, paraded through the streets during Holy Week festivals dressed as a Roman centurion? Was it necessary to imprison five women for teaching children in a house on the Calle Montón, which they had supposedly turned into a surreptitious convent? The prohibitory measures on religious behavior, argued the editors, were "decreed in moments of revolutionary fervor"; they "cannot be justified in the eyes of reason and the law"; in short, they are illiberal.[78] Justo Sierra had applauded the elevation of the reform laws to constitutional status in September 1873 and the subsequent enabling legislation, just as he had supported President Lerdo's expulsion of several foreign Jesuits. By late 1876, however, his mounting hostility to Lerdo included a rejection of official anticlericalism; and the way was prepared for his moderation of 1878.[79] "Clericalism has never perished by persecution," affirmed *La Libertad*, "but rather by the universal penetration of the spirit of the century." Thanks to the progress of science, "revolutionary liberalism" is yielding to "rational liberalism."[80]

La Libertad's conciliatory attitude toward political conservatism and its ambivalence toward the church in a sense merely confirmed the policy of the Díaz regime itself. We have seen the efforts by President Díaz to cast off his *tuxtepecano* followers and to embrace groups that were more socially and constitutionally conservative. Yet the regime, like *La Liber-*

[77] Sierra's arguments appeared in *La Libertad* on 2 July 1878 and 29 October 1879 (*Obras*, 4:154–55, 207), García's on 27 March 1878 and 11 July 1879. See also unsigned articles in *La Libertad*, 11 April, 29 November 1878; 7 January, 3 October 1879.

[78] On the Tonalá incident see *La Libertad*, 21, 25 May 1878, on the incident at the Calle Montón, see 27, 29 November. The quoted passages are from 21 May.

[79] On the Jesuits, see Sierra in *El Siglo*, 16 August 1873, as quoted in Knapp, *Lerdo*, p. 218. On the reform laws, see Sierra in *El Federalista*, 14, 25 January, 24 February 1875 (*Obras*, 4:60–62, 64–69). His change in outlook appeared in *El Bien público*, 3 October 1876 (*Obras*, 4:113–14). The constitutional amendments incorporating the reform laws (25 September 1873) can be found in Dublán and Lozano, *Legislación*, 12:502–04, the detailed enabling act (14 December 1874) in ibid., pp. 683–88. Knapp discusses church-state tensions during Lerdo's administration in *Lerdo*, pp. 214–22.

[80] *La Libertad*, 9 June 1878. It is interesting to note that during Holy Week 1878 religious subjects predominated. The 18 April issue (Maundy Thursday) was devoted entirely to religion and the paper did not appear again until Easter Sunday.

tad, reaffirmed the principles of ecclesiastical reform. Perhaps because of the enthusiasm shown by the conservative and clerical press for the Díaz movement, the new government felt obliged to issue statements in early 1877 assuring the nation "that the revolution of Tuxtepec is not a reaction against the Laws of Reform and that the present government will not protect or lend its support to the tendencies of retrogression." The statements, significantly enough, were signed by Minister of Justice Protasio Tagle, himself accused of conservative sympathies because of his family background. A year later the *Diario oficial* insisted that Tagle was a good liberal, though it openly admitted that he had given jobs to intelligent and honorable members of the Conservative party.[81]

The accommodation policies of the Porfiriato both toward the church specifically and toward political conservatives generally are well known; it is worth recalling their less well-known precedents in the Restored Republic. The temper of the Juárez regime was manifest in two proposals of the *convocatoria* of 1867; one, that voting and political rights be extended to the clergy, and two, that distinctions of degree be made in punishing those who collaborated with Intervention governments. These issues were much debated in the press along with publication of episcopal and imperial documents revealing widespread treason. The *Diario oficial* argued that clerical rights followed naturally from the separation of church and state, but it could not persuade *El Siglo XIX* of its view. The best clerics, wrote Zarco, have always withdrawn from political activity to the sanctuary, quietly "ministering to the salvation of souls and giving spiritual bread to their parishoners."[82] It appears that anticlerical resistance was strong enough to forestall implementation of the govern-

---

[81] There were two circulars issued by Tagle on 15 January and 16 February 1877. The first (Dublán and Lozano, *Legislación*, 13:134–35) reaffirmed that the Plan of Tuxtepec would respect the Laws of Reform, the constitutional amendments of 25 September 1873, and the enabling legislation of 14 December 1874. The second was the more general statement quoted (ibid., pp. 159–60). The *Diario oficial* statement appeared on 8 May 1878. On the conservative press and Díaz, see Robert Case, "Resurgimiento de los conservadores en Mexico—1876–1877," *Historia mexicana* 25 (1975): 204–31.

[82] Zarco in *El Siglo*, 4 December 1867. The proposal on clerical rights appeared in article 15 of the *convocatoria* and was based on a wartime election decree of 16 July 1864 (Dublán and Lozano, *Legislación*, 9:689–90); the conditions for amnesty were set out in articles 22–26. For the government's argument see *Diario oficial*, 22 August 1867, also Lerdo's circular of 14 August (Dublán and Lozano, *Legislación*, 10:50). For further examples of opposition to the extension of rights to clergy see *El Siglo*, 21, 28 August, 3, 21 September 1867. *El Siglo*'s campaign included the printing (6–7 October 1867) of a *representación* against freedom of worship issued in 1865 by Bishops Labastida (México) and Munguía (Michoacán): "*Los Traidores pintados por si mismos. Libro secreto de Maximiliano en que aparece la idea que tenía de sus servidores.*" It appeared in the *Diario oficial* daily beginning on 26 December 1867 and received extensive commentary by Zarco in *El Siglo* on 3–4 January 1868.

ment's proposal, for in 1878 *La Libertad* was still campaigning for the extension of political rights to the clergy. Why should we single out the clergy as enemies? asked Telesforo García; it is merely one of the many groups making up "the social organism."[83] We might also note that the Juárez regime showed marked restraint in the enforcement of the reform laws, a long-term tendency that was temporarily reversed under the presidency of Lerdo de Tejada.[84]

The elaborate amnesty proposals of 1867 met with a more favorable response. *El Siglo XIX*, for example, agreed with the government that while those who had actively served Maximilian or had expressly recognized the foreign intervention should be denied rights, this denial should not be extended to the large number who had passively accepted the enemy. After considerable debate in the press and the introduction of several draft proposals in Congress, a broad amnesty law was passed on 10 October 1870. The measure excluded only those who had held the highest military and civil posts in the empire, and even in these cases the executive could make exceptions.[85] The government's conciliatory policy was also demonstrated, as we have seen, by the appointment of erstwhile imperialists to the postwar codification commissions, men such as Justo Sierra's uncle, Luis Méndez, Juárez's relative Manuel Dublán, and Manuel Siliceo.[86]

Evidence of the spirit of reconciliation engendered by the Juárez regime comes from still another quarter, the exceptional effort by Ignacio Altamirano to reunite the Mexican literary community after years of civil

[83] T. García in *La Libertad*, 1 June 1878; also 3 May.

[84] See Karl M. Schmitt, "Catholic Adjustment to the Secular State: the Case of Mexico, 1867–1911," *Catholic Historical Review* 48 (1962): 183. One of the few measures pertaining to the reform laws issued by the Juárez regime was a circular (Dublán and Lozano, *Legislación*, 10:396–98) of 20 July 1868, reminding the governors that they must enforce compliance. On the enforcement of the reform laws during the Porfiriato, see Robert J. Knowlton, *Church Property and the Mexican Reform, 1856–1910* (De Kalb, 1976); Karl M. Schmitt, "The Díaz Conciliation Policy on State and Local Levels, 1876–1911," *Hispanic American Historical Review* 40 (1960): 513–32.

[85] For *El Siglo's* position on amnesty, see especially 13, 14 December 1867 and 18 February 1868. There is a good discussion of the amnesty question drawn from the contemporary press: *Índices de El Renacimiento*, ed. Huberto Batis (Mexico, 1963), pp. 21–25. The 10 October 1870 law can be found in Dublán and Lozano, *Legislación*, 11:184–85.

[86] On Méndez, see p. 76n. Dublán (see chap. 3, n. 42) was also an active deputy during the Juárez regime. Emilio Rabasa maintained, however, that Dublán's imperial service did block him from gaining a cabinet post until 1884, when Díaz appointed him to *hacienda*: see Emilio Rabasa, *Evolución histórica de México*, 2d ed. (Mexico, 1956), pp. 98–100. Virtually all biographical accounts, including elaborate newspaper obituaries (*El Siglo*, 1, 6 June 1891), scrupulously avoided (and continue to this day to avoid) mention of Dublán's imperial service, which can be verified in Charles R. Berry, *The Reform in Oaxaca, 1856–76* (Lincoln, 1981), pp. 94–95, 107.

war. The principal product of this effort was the appearance in January 1869 of the weekly literary journal, *El Renacimiento*. Its stated purpose was to "restore in the country the love of letters, so much abandoned in recent times." Following a tribute to the literary and scholarly contributions made during the war years by conservatives such as Manuel Orozco y Berra, José Fernando Ramírez, and José María Roa Barcena, Altamirano invited "to our ranks those from every political persuasion who cherish belles lettres."[87] In July of the same year Altamirano made another conciliatory gesture in an oration commissioned by the government on the occasion of depositing the ashes of two liberal martyrs, Generals José María Arteaga and Carlos Salazar, in the cemetery of San Fernando. After extolling at length the sacrifice of these men for the heroic liberal and republican cause, he concluded with an eloquent plea that the nation abandon the vindictiveness and rancour of recent years: "Let us extend our hand and make all sons of this poor and unfortunate country into a single family of brothers, which will command the world's respect for its unity and its culture."[88]

Our brief review of the relationship between scientific politics and traditional conservatism demonstrates that points of intellectual compatibility derived from classic positivism were reinforced by an official reconciliation policy having roots in the early Restored Republic. The policies of the Juárez regime toward the church and toward secular collaborators were designed to restore national unity by surmounting the conflicts of the Reforma and the Intervention. Policy statements and their implementation were in turn fortified by case histories of the reincorporation of political conservatives of the war years into the life of the Restored Republic. The result was that the formulation in 1878 of a doctrine of conservative-liberalism, the correlate of scientific politics, had a firm social basis as well as a basis in ideas and in policy. Increasingly after 1867 ideological conflict gave way to a unifying liberal myth that affected constitutional debate and produced confusion and frustration among the doctrinaire defenders of the Constitution of 1857.

[87] Altamirano, introduction to *El Renacimiento*, 1:3, 6. See Batis, *Índices*, for a thorough study of *El Renacimiento* and its background. It might be noted that the twenty-one-year-old Justo Sierra contributed frequently to the journal and was listed as one of its editors.

[88] Altamirano, "Discurso pronunciado . . . en el Panteón de San Fernando de México . . . el día 17 de julio de 1869," in *Discursos*, p. 179. Arteaga and Salazar were captured in Michoacán in 1865 and shot at Uruapan.

CHAPTER 4

The *Científicos* as Constitutionalists

THE GENERAL THEME of chapters 3 and 4 is the complex and tangled relationship between scientific politics and constitutionalism, their specific point of departure the problem of assessing *La Libertad*'s reform proposals in the light of the Sierra-Vigil debate of 1878. I have contended that Sierra and his colleagues' claim to being constitutionalists must be taken seriously, despite their apparent support for authoritarian government. To pursue the argument further, let us turn to another significant episode of ferment within the liberal establishment, the formation of the National Liberal Union in 1892 and the ensuing constitutional debate of 1893. Here we encounter similar reform proposals, familiar general arguments, and even some of the same parties to the debate as participated in 1878. The political context, however, had changed markedly in fifteen years, adding further complexity to the relationship between liberalism and scientific politics. We shall then turn briefly to the denouement of the debate of 1893, the program of the second convention of the Liberal Union in 1903.

The first Liberal Union grew out of the Central Porfirista Council, organized in January 1892 to promote the third reelection of Porfirio Díaz. The Liberal Union was described in the statement of the organizing committee as a "political league" for the purpose of "transforming the Liberal party into a great electoral force" to "combat absenteeism" and to "defend at all costs the freedom of suffrage." The result was to be the formation of a national Liberal convention, built upon municipal and state conventions, for the sole purpose of designating a presidential candidate. Since article 78 of the constitution had been amended a year earlier (on 20 December 1890) to remove all limitations on presidential reelections, the committee maintained that now for the first time the Mexican people had the opportunity to exercise the vote, without fear that "the statesman . . . who is the symbol of order and progress the people do not wish to renounce" would be forced to leave his post. The Liberal Union seemed, therefore, a routine election-year organization to arouse an apathetic populace to hail yet another term for a now perpetual president.[1]

---

[1] The *proyecto* of the Comisión del Comité Central Porfirista (23 January 1892), of which Justo Sierra was one of the five signers, appeared in *El Siglo XIX* on 29 January. Other meetings of the *comité* were reported on 9 January and 25 February.

However, the Liberal Union manifesto of 23 April, signed by a committee of eleven plus the seventy delegates to the first National Liberal Convention included more than reelectionist rhetoric. Written by Justo Sierra and clearly drawn from his recent luminous essay on Mexican political history, the manifesto presented a program that might be seen as epitomizing the principles of scientific politics.[2] Following the customary tribute to peace and prosperity achieved under President Díaz, the manifesto called for further "severe application" of the "program of administrative integrity." With an eye to economy, some branches of government should be reorganized, especially the Ministry of War. The tax system should be placed on a more scientific basis. The final steps should be taken to remove barriers to free internal commerce. In order to capitalize on the amazing expansion of communications, moral and intellectual progress should now be brought up to the level of material progress by expanding popular education and by making known "the value of that mental force that is transformed into the measureless physical force called *science*." If this transformation is not accomplished, said the manifesto, the spirit of Mexican democracy will be degraded "to a low utilitarianism lacking ideals," and civic virtues will atrophy.[3]

The references to education remind us that the National Liberal Union began its activities immediately following the two National Congresses of Public Instruction (1889–91), which Justo Sierra also led and in which several future Liberal Union members participated. As we will see in chapters 6 and 7, the first congress urged that free obligatory primary education, adopted for the Federal District in 1888, be expanded to encompass the entire republic. The second congress reaffirmed the classic scientific curriculum of the National Preparatory School, established in 1867 as the prerequisite for all higher education. By the 1890s this curriculum had become an integral component of scientific politics.

Despite the emphasis on "administration" and "science," the most notable feature of the Liberal Union program was political and constitutional. Sierra depicted the Liberal party as entering a new period in its history. The struggle to defend its political creed against internal and external enemies and to "consolidate order" against revolts and revolutions is over. Its "directive groups" have been transformed into "organs of government." In short, the Liberal party has become a *partido de gobierno*. In his 1889 essay Sierra interpreted this process as having begun

[2] The essay was the final section of Justo Sierra, "México social y político," *Revista nacional* 1 (1889): 328–36, 371–80 (*Obras*, 9:151–69). Sierra was director of the three-volume *Revista* (1889–90).

[3] The "*Manifiesto a la nación*" of the Primera Convención Nacional Liberal appeared in *El Siglo*, 26 April 1892. Justo Sierra was elected president of the *mesa directiva* of the convention (ibid., 7 April).

with the admirable program of the *convocatoria* of 1867, designed to check the reappearance of "revolutionary" elements within the postwar Liberal party. After abandoning the *convocatoria*, "the chiefs of the republic proposed to convert the party of innovation into a party of government." Anarchy threatened again in 1876, but fortunately those who triumphed, "men of civic spirit and real political instincts," pursued a policy of political tolerance and material progress. In effect, concluded Sierra, "they continued the same policy of conservation and order, indeed the authoritarian policy, begun by Juárez."[4]

The climax of the Liberal Union manifesto was Sierra's reflection that if "effective peace has been acquired by the strengthening of authority, definitive peace will be acquired by its assimilation with liberty." The Liberal party, he suggested, should pursue this latter objective through certain constitutional changes, the irremovability (as opposed to the recurrent popular election) of judges, the creation of a distinct vice-presidency, and the modification of penal legislation pertaining to the press so that infractions might be brought before a common jury. The nomination of President Díaz for reelection came almost as an anticlimax following this emphasis on liberty and the call for specific constitutional reforms. A democratic people, argued Sierra, must hold fast to the "right of renewal [of its officials]," and not merely pursue the "constant exercise of renewal"; reelection should be the exception and not the rule. Thus, in the tradition of earlier scientific politics, the Liberal Union program juxtaposed economic progress through "administration" under a strong executive with points of constitutional reform. In fact, the first two reform measures, the vice-presidency and irremovability of judges, had formed part of Sierra's proposal of 1878.[5] However, the program of 1892 revealed a dramatic shift in emphasis, reflecting political changes in the intervening years. The thrust of scientific politics was no longer "the strengthening of authority," but rather "its assimilation with liberty."[6]

There were numerous precedents for the Liberal Union and its first national convention. The restoration of the republic in 1867 was seen officially as the victory of a unified Liberal party over the forces of internal reaction and foreign intervention. After 1867 Liberal party unity was tantamount to national unity, which had to be upheld against the imagined resurgence of political conservatism and the real and constant threat

[4] Sierra, "México social," *Revista nacional*, 1:376–77 (*Obras*, 9:163–65).

[5] See p. 54. The third item can be seen as a call for freedom of the press, and in effect it would have restored article 7 of the Constitution to its original form. Article 7 had been amended (with the support of *La Libertad*) in 1882. See p. 69.

[6] Sierra struck this same theme in the conclusion of his 1889 essay and said that the irremovability of judges "must be an obligatory clause in the program of a liberal party of government": Sierra, "México social," *Revista nacional*, 1:379 (*Obras*, 9:168).

of liberal factionalism and civil strife. We will recall that following the upheaval of 1876, "reconstruction" of the Liberal party became an obsession of both "new" and "old" liberals, of both *La Libertad* and *El Monitor republicano*, even though their conceptions of that reconstruction differed significantly. The eleventh-hour effort in 1880 by the editors of *El Monitor* to organize a coalition of candidates to oppose Manuel González took the form of a projected national convention of the Liberal party. This abortive organizational effort, including the overt reference to North American practices, might be regarded as a precedent for 1892. However, the character of the two movements was different; the first was antiofficial and the second developed within the official circle. Given this difference, it is ironic that the president of the National Liberal Convention of 1892 was Manuel María Zamacona, the same man promoted by *El Monitor* as the Liberal party candidate for president of the republic in 1880.[7]

The National Liberal Convention of 1892 can be interpreted as the culmination of the reconciliation policies of the Porfiriato, initiated in the first Díaz administration, continued under González, and maturing in the second Díaz administration from December 1884 through November 1888. Though Porfirio Díaz and Manuel González remained individually on good terms during the latter's presidency, conflicts between their followers did develop, posing the threat of an open clash, for example, in the event of a Díaz reelection movement in 1888.[8] The new administration, through *El Partido liberal*, a semiofficial newspaper launched 15 February 1885, seemed to play a double game, discrediting the scandal-ridden González regime for its encouragement of unbridled economic gain and yet urging the reconciliation of *gonzalistas* and *porfiristas*. It depicted the new administration as pursuing "a policy of moralization," the "consolidation of liberal institutions" and the enhancement of public and national interests as opposed to dictatorship and the reign of narrow private interests. Yet *El Partido liberal* also spoke of "the need for a newspaper like ours to serve as a nucleus or common center for the diverse factions of the Liberal party." It responded in familiar terms to the attacks on the *gonzalista* daily, *El Pacto federal.* "We need to convince these monomaniac combatants that the eras of struggle have gone by, never to return, and that fortunately we are now in a purely administra-

---

[7] The organizers of the Liberal Union made an effort to enhance the respectability of their enterprise by recruiting a number of older but now inactive political and military figures. Besides Zamacona, these included Mariano Escobedo, Sóstenes Rocha, Trinidad García, and Ignacio R. Alatorre.

[8] On the conflict between *gonzalistas* and *porfiristas*, see Coerver, *Porfirian Interregnum*, pp. 47–55. According to Cosío Villegas, a distinct *gonzalista* faction only developed toward the end of the 1884–88 regime: *Historia moderna*, 9:12–13.

tive period," one that demands liberal "fusion" and "a scientific politics, based on reality and experience."[9] The new regime backed up its rhetoric by deeds. Three of the six cabinet posts, foreign relations, justice, and *fomento*, were filled by men who had served a considerable time under González, and González himself was elected governor of the important state of Guanajuato.[10]

There were two further manifestations of the policy of "fusion" in which *El Partido liberal* had an important role. Through its director, José Vicente Villada, the paper championed the official effort to establish Benito Juárez as a symbol of national unity. The fifteenth anniversary of Juárez's death, 28 July 1887, became a great ceremonial occasion with orations by Ignacio Mariscal and Manuel Dublán, who as close collaborators of Juárez and as Oaxacan contemporaries of Díaz were living testimony to the continuity of liberalism since the Reforma.[11] Because of Dublán's now-carefully-concealed service under Maximilian, for which he had narrowly escaped being executed by General Díaz in 1867, his presence at the Juárez ceremony was ironic; and yet it served as potent evidence of the administration's policy. As president, Díaz is said to have remarked, "in politics, I have no feelings of love or hate," words which summarized his policy of liberal union.[12] Besides espousing the Juárez myth, *El Partido liberal* became a leading promoter of the constitutional amendment of 1887 to provide for the reelection of Díaz. Commenting on the lengthy collection of articles, documents, and speeches that he compiled on the subject, Villada wrote that "they constitute an incontrovertible sign of our social regeneration and a sure guarantee of our liberal

[9] *El Partido liberal*, 15, 25, 28 February, 4 March 1885. Much of *El Partido's* polemic with *El Pacto federal* focused on the nature of the clerical and conservative menace (see e.g., *El Partido liberal*, 19, 20 February). *El Pacto's* chief target was Manuel Romero Rubio, the new minister of *gobernación*, who was suspected of backsliding on the enforcement of the reform laws. The appointment of Dublán as minister of *hacienda* would also have been a logical target, but his name did not appear.

[10] Ignacio Mariscal, named minister of foreign relations in January 1885, had served González in that position from December 1880 through May 1883. Joaquín Baranda was named minister of justice by González in September 1882 and continued in the post until April 1901. Carlos Pacheco replaced Díaz as González's minister of *fomento* in June 1881 and continued on until March 1891. However, only Baranda might be regarded as a true *gonzalista*. Mariscal had been Díaz's minister of justice and public instruction until December 1880, and he held the foreign relations post under Díaz from 1885 to 1910. For his important role in the educational controversy of 1880, see chap. 6. On the new Díaz ministry, see Cosío Villegas, *Historia moderna*, 9:11–27.

[11] See Weeks, *Mito de Juárez*, pp. 41–42. Mariscal (1829–1910) had been a Supreme Court justice, an ambassador, and a ministry official during the Reforma and had served as minister of justice and public instruction in 1871–72.

[12] Attributed to Díaz by Rabasa in *Evolución histórica*, p. 101.

institutions."[13] Villada was preparing the way for still another reelection movement, the National Liberal Convention of 1892.

Much of the partisan controversy during the second Díaz administration centered on Manuel Romero Rubio, the new minister of *gobernación* who had been a Lerdo stalwart and who in 1881 became the president's father-in-law. Romero Rubio might be regarded as the éminence grise of the Díaz regime, at least from 1884 through 1892. He appeared to have guided the policy of reconciliation, both toward conservatives and toward former *lerdista* and *gonzalista* liberals. He may have been the silent partner of *El Partido liberal*. Before the constitutional reform and reelection movements of 1887 developed, the *gonzalista* press attributed presidential ambitions to Romero Rubio, placing him in competition with the former president.[14] More significant, there is strong evidence that beginning in the González regime, Romero Rubio became the catalyst for a group of young lawyers, intellectuals, and men of technical accomplishment who sought a new order in the return of Porfirio Díaz. José Yves Limantour, one of their number, recalled that Romero Rubio's law office, opened in 1881, became the meeting place for talk and planning. Several of the group, said Limantour, were oriented toward administration, others toward politics, "but the separation [between the two] was not very pronounced."[15]

The Romero Rubio group believed that by firm direction the country could emerge from its period of disordered economic growth; its credit could be established abroad and its administration could be reformed and strengthened at home. Through political consensus, that is, through a strong, homogeneous Liberal party, Mexico could achieve mature constitutional government. These were to be the suppositions of the Liberal Union that, according to Limantour, sprang from the discussions stimulated by Romero Rubio. Of the eight lawyers mentioned by Limantour— Rosendo Pineda, Justo Sierra, Joaquín Casasús, Roberto Núñez, Emilio Pimentel, José María Gamboa, Fernando Duret, and himself—at least six overtly supported the Liberal Union and the constitutional reform move-

[13] José V. Villada, introduction to *La Reelección del presidente de la república y gobernadores de los estados. Memorandum acerca de la reforma de los artículos 78 y 109 de la constitución mexicana* (Mexico, n.d. [1887?]), pp. iii–iv. The volume ran to 646 pages. The reformed articles were ratified on 21 October 1887 and made possible the reelection of a president and governors for the term immediately following. Villada served as governor of Mexico state from 1889 until his death in 1904.

[14] See Ricardo García Granados, *Historia de México desde la restauración de la república en 1867, hasta la caída de Porfirio Díaz*, 4 vols. (Mexico, 1923–28), 2:118–29; Villada and Romero Rubio had been fellow partisans of Lerdo in the Congresses of 1872–76. On the politics of the 1884–88 era, see also Cosío Villegas, *Historia moderna*, 9:3–316.

[15] Limantour, *Apuntes sobre mi vida política* (Mexico, 1965), p. 15 (1st ed. of a MS dated 1921). On Romero Rubio's role, see also Cosío Villegas, *Historia moderna*, 9:524, 648.

ment of 1893. Sierra and Limantour were acknowledged leaders in both efforts, though Limantour's active participation ceased when he was appointed minister of *hacienda* in May 1893. Pineda, private secretary to Romero Rubio and a Díaz confidant, was the organizer of the reelection campaign and of the National Liberal Convention of 1892. These men were among the small group to be labeled *"científicos"* by their opponents in 1893.

The "legislative program" of the Liberal Union was brought to the Chamber of Deputies by Justo Sierra on 30 October 1893 as a bill to amend the constitution.[16] Though Sierra's introductory comments made reference to all three reforms proposed in the manifesto, jury trials for crimes of the press, the creation of a vice-presidency, and the irremovability of judges, the measure itself included only the third. Involving changes in several articles of the constitution, it provided that no federal judge could be removed from office unless he was derelict in his duty, and that Supreme Court magistrates be appointed by the president (and confirmed by the Senate), while district and circuit judges be appointed by the Supreme Court. The revised bill that emerged from committee on 4 December comprised a change in article 92 only and applied only to Supreme Court magistrates. They would be irremovable once they were in office but they would continue to be popularly elected as at present. In submitting its revisions, the committee acknowledged that it was influenced by "serious differences of opinion among the deputies" and "heated discussions in the press."[17] Debate on the revised measure in the chamber, though spirited, lasted only two days, 11 and 12 December. However, the formal debate was merely the culmination of a major controversy conducted in the Mexico City press during the preceding weeks.

The conflict of ideas in 1893 recalled the Sierra-Vigil exchange of 1878. Both episodes were touched off by an apparently technical constitutional issue. Both led to a debate on the nature of the Constitution of 1857 and the liberal heritage and on the value and implications of applying scientific principles to politics. In both instances, Justo Sierra and his colleagues called for constitutional reforms in the name of science, while their opponents defended the integrity of the document against subversion, if not frontal attack. The debate of 1893, however, was more com-

---

[16] Ramón Prida y Arteaga asserted in 1918 that when Limantour was appointed minister of *hacienda* in May 1893, Pineda, Sierra, Macedo, and Emilio Pimentel presented him with a reform proposal in accord with the principles of the Liberal Union manifesto: Ramón Prida y Arteaga, ¡*De La Dictadura a la anarquía!* 2d ed. (Mexico, 1958), p. 101. I have found no other documentation of this action.

[17] The Sierra *proyecto de ley* of 30 October (and the accompanying speech) can be found in *El Universal*, 1 November 1893; also in *Diario de los debates*, 16th congress, 4 vols. (Mexico, 1892–1905), 3:218–23. The committee report appeared in ibid., pp. 411–12.

plex than its predecessor in two respects. The first, was that Sierra's current proposal was directed toward limiting as opposed to strengthening executive authority. The second was that with its submission a split developed among the adherents of scientific politics, which produced a third party to the controversy. Let us examine some of the features of this new complexity.[18]

The advocates of irremovable or life tenure magistrates presented the elements of traditional or historical constitutionalism in the language of the new sociology, along with occasional references to the doctrines of Herbert Spencer. Sierra saw "an increasingly more elevated and comprehensive formula of justice" as a product of social evolution. Apologizing to his fellow deputies for using the "technical terminology of the sociologists," he argued that the effective separation of powers was no more than the creation of a healthy autonomy among the interdependent vital organs of a vigorous social body. For Francisco Bulnes, liberty, the object of an independent judiciary, was "a moral need of human beings, as powerful and demonstrative as the need for nourishment and reproduction." Or, as Sierra put it in his famous biblical paraphrase, "the Mexican people hunger and thirst after justice." *El Universal*, the chief journalistic advocate of the reform, refuted the doctrinaire defenders of the constitution by evoking the exigencies of the law of progress. "In sociological matters, yesterday's truth is today's error, just as today's truth is tomorrow's error." These "new reactionaries" want to stop evolution, as if they were zoological organisms trying to retain their rudimentary members. Liberty can never result from declarations, continued *El Universal*, but only from the needs experienced by society after a long and painful struggle to surmount obstacles. In short, liberty is the product of "positive facts," not of "metaphysics."[19]

The proponents of irremovability were quick to point out that an independent judiciary, their real objective, had long been regarded in civilized nations as a prime guarantee of individual liberty against tyranny. Despotic regimes have always feared independent magistrates, main-

[18] There is a useful introduction to the debate, but it is viewed there as pertaining only to two parties, *Científicos* and Jacobins, in García Granados, *Historia*, 2:251–61. See also the pioneer studies by Walter N. Breymann, "The *Científicos*: Critics of the Díaz Regime, 1892–1903," and "The *Científicos* and the Collapse of the Díaz Regime. A Study in the Origins of Mexican Revolutionary Sentiment, 1903–1910," in *Proceedings of the Arkansas Academy of Sciences* 7 (1955): 91–97, and ibid. 8 (1955): 92–97.

[19] Sierra, speech of 30 October 1893, *Diario de los debates*, 16th congress, 3:220; Bulnes, speech of 12 December 1893, in ibid., p. 495; *El Universal*, 22 November 1893. Beginning 21 November, *El Universal* was under the directorship of Ramón Prida, one of the chief supporters of the measure in the chamber. The unsigned editorials on irremovability may have been written by him or by Bulnes, former editor of *El Siglo XIX*, who joined *El Universal* on 4 November.

tained Sierra, as he proceeded to highlight the epic struggle for a free judiciary.[20] When Philip II moved to implant the Inquisition, "the most absolute of despotisms," the obstacle in his path was "an irremovable judge," Juan de Lanuza, the *justicia mayór* of Aragón. Lanuza's execution meant the ruin of judicial independence, in effect the destruction of "the liberty of the Spanish people." The English Revolution, culminating in the Bill of Rights of 1689 that included judicial irremovability, was the people's response to the "venal judges" who had approved the illegal taxes imposed by Charles I. In France, continued Sierra, it has taken a century to surmount the ravages of Jacobin and Napoleonic tyranny that laid waste the independent judiciary. In Mexico, conservative centralist regimes, especially those of the dictator Santa Anna, had made a mockery of the independent Supreme Court provided for in the Constitution of 1824. *El Universal* mentioned that Mexico now had the dubious distinction, along with Venezuela, Honduras, Costa Rica, and the Dominican Republic, of being the only nations of some twenty-five that had not instituted permanent magistrates.[21]

For adherents of scientific politics as for traditional constitutionalists tyranny could come from below as well as from above, a point implied by Sierra's reference to the French Jacobins. The argument for irremovability was built upon a hostility toward the doctrine of popular sovereignty and a suspicion of democracy. In fact, this hostility and suspicion was so great that Francisco Bulnes and Emilio Pardo, Jr., continued to refute the popular election of judges just as if Sierra's proposal of 30 October had not undergone revision. We do not commit the error of our adversaries, said Bulnes in his eloquent remarks to the Congress, "the same one committed by the Jacobins of 1793, that is, believing that liberty and democracy are the same thing, or that liberty necessarily emanates from democracy."[22] Bulnes was repeating the charges of 1878, linking his opponents' adherence to popular sovereignty to their defense of the Constitution of 1857. Now, however, the former label of "metaphysician" was giving way to a new label, "Jacobin." Hippolyte Taine's passionate attack on France's revolutionary tradition, written in reaction to the Commune of 1871, had appeared in the intervening years. His trenchant character-

---

[20] Sierra, speech of 11 December 1893 in *Diario de los debates*, 16th congress, 3:470–72 (*Obras*, 5:175–76). See also Bulnes, speech of 12 December, *Diario de los debates*, 16th congress, 3:495; and Sierra, speech of 30 October, ibid., p. 220. Due to a printer's error in the *Diario de los debates*, both sessions in which the irremovability measure was debated are listed as 12 December. Thus Sierra's speech of 11 December is often dated as 12 December.

[21] *El Universal*, 15 November 1893.

[22] Bulnes, speech of 12 December 1893, *Diario de los debates*, 16th congress, 3:495. See also Pardo, speech of 11 December, ibid., pp. 462–63.

ization of the Jacobin mentality had now become thoroughly integrated into the vocabulary of scientific politics in Mexico, and Taine was frequently cited in the press and in the chamber.[23] Oblique and disparaging comments about "our Jacobins" could be counted on to bring applause. These were men who followed "absolute principles," who had no respect for the past, who looked for immediate transformation instead of introducing reforms by careful scientific study in accord with evolving customs and social relations. Manuel Flores ridiculed the doctrinaire stance of *El Monitor republicano* as a "Jacobin symphony."[24]

Since Justo Sierra had justified the reelection of President Díaz in 1892 as the triumph of expanded popular suffrage, he was necessarily more receptive to "democracy" than were some of his colleagues. Democracy must be educated, not by mere schooling, "but by exercise, like any organ." A free judiciary could serve as protection for this process, or as he put it in another passage, as a shield for liberty, that is, the practice of free institutions. Democracy for Sierra (perhaps following Taine) pursued a dual impulse toward "absolute sovereignty" and toward anarchy. He saw the judicial power as both promoting "the conciliation of liberty with democracy" and providing democracy its "element of stability" against the disintegration of the "social organism."[25]

Sierra asserted that judicial irremovability was not antidemocratic, not a step backward, but a "restoration." The constitution-makers have "dragged down all the institutions of conservation." Following different principles and methods, "we believe it necessary to restore them to life in a full organic and normal period." More specifically, Sierra argued that judicial irremovability, which had been established in the Constitution of 1824, was sacrificed in 1856 in order that the vice-presidency could be rooted in the Supreme Court, making rotation of magistrates through popular election essential. This was merely another example of the "ab-

---

[23] H. A. Taine, *Origines de la France contemporaine*, 6 vols. (Paris, 1876–94). The first volume, *L'Ancien Régime* (1876), was referred to occasionally by the editors of *La Libertad* in 1878–79. Successive volumes were: *L'Anarchie* (1878), *La Conquête jacobine* (1881), *Le Gouvernement révolutionnaire* (1885), *Napoléon Bonaparte* (1891), and *L'Église, l'école* (1894). The famous section "Psychologie du jacobin" appeared first in the *Revue des deux mondes*, 1 April 1881, pp. 536–59, as did several other sections. Taine (and several other French writers) were probably known best in Mexico from that source (see p. 180). For examples of specific references to Taine see *El Universal*, 29 November 1893; Pardo, speech of 11 December, *Diario de los debates*, 16th congress, 3:456–57. *El Siglo XIX* (25 November), opposing the measure, referred to Taine as "the master of our adversaries."

[24] See particularly Sierra, speech of 11 December 1893 in *Diario de los debates*, 16th congress, 3:471 (*Obras*, 5:175); Pardo, *Diario de los debates*, 16th congress, 3:456; *El Universal*, 29 November 1893; Flores in ibid., 23 November.

[25] Sierra, speeches of 30 October and 11 December, 1893, *Diario de los debates*, 16th congress, 3:222 and 470 (*Obras*, 5:174).

solute dogmas" followed by the constitution-makers, justifiable perhaps in 1856 but not today.

In fact, judicial irremovability, along with the separation of the vice-presidency from the Supreme Court, had been one of the less emphasized features of *La Libertad*'s reform program of 1878–79 and had been formally introduced at least once in the intervening years.[26] The Senate was of course another of the "institutions of conservation" dismantled by the constitution-makers, the restoration of which Sierra regarded as a precedent, an integral part of the long-term program of constitutional reform initiated with the abortive *convocatoria* of 1867.[27] Resorting to religious imagery in the conclusion of his second speech to Congress, Sierra urged his opponents to abandon their cramped and poorly lighted "chapel of absolute and pure constitutionalism" and enter "our more spacious church, where candles are not needed because the light of science suffices."[28] As in 1878, Sierra saw the adaptation of the constitution to changing conditions as the task of science.

Permeating the critique of democracy was a naturalistic view of the political process in which the true force at work was the struggle of interests—corporate, group, and individual interests. Bulnes, who presented this view more explicitly than did Sierra, maintained that although these interests operating in parliament or in the electoral colleges were always "despotic," the "conflict of despotisms" often produced gains for liberty and social betterment. However, judges should be above or apart from these interests and thus they should be appointed, not elected. "The people as a single and absolute entity never elected anyone, here or elsewhere," affirmed Bulnes.[29] *El Universal* maintained that "the ideal of any scientific institution" must be the reign of law, which meant judicial intervention in the battle of interests; but it was never clear from the ar-

[26] For *La Libertad*'s proposal, see p. 54. Irremovability was introduced by an opposition group in Congress in 1885: see Cosío Villegas, *Historia moderna*, 9:35; also Bulnes in *El Universal*, 17 November 1893 and in his speech of 12 December 1893, *Diario de los debates*, 16th congress, 3:489. Alberto Lombardo speaking for the measure said he used the same arguments in an article for *El Foro* in 1880: ibid., p. 485. Ignacio Vallarta asserted in 1881 that he had been promoting a separate vice-presidency since 1876, when he accepted the appointment as chief justice of the Supreme Court. In 1881 a measure to amend the constitution was pending in the Senate: *Acta de las audiencias [de la suprema corte de justicia] en que se trató del proyecto de la reforma constitucional sobre la vicepresidencia de la república* (Mexico, 1881).

[27] Sierra, speech of 30 October 1893, *Diario de los debates*, 16th congress, 3:222. Cf. "México social," *Revista mexicana*, 1:375 (*Obras*, 9:163–64).

[28] Sierra, speech of 11 December 1893, *Diario de los debates*, 16th congress, 3:475 (*Obras*, 5:180–81).

[29] Bulnes, speech of 12 December 1893, *Diario de los debates*, 16th congress, 3:492–93. Note that Bulnes persisted in arguing that judges should be appointed, despite the revised version of the bill.

guments whose interests the judges would intervene to protect. There was some talk of protecting the weak against the strong; yet on one occasion at least, Manuel Flores, in discussing the imperatives of "economic evolution," suggested that a reorganized European-type judiciary might serve to extend guarantees to "the foreign capitalist and worker." Several of the proponents of the measure implied that the progress of the country was not in the hands of the people, but rather in the hands of its minorities.[30] The elitist assumptions of scientific politics, always compatible with traditional or historical constitutionalism, came into full flower in 1893.

The rhetorical and polemical strands of scientific politics were brought together by *El Universal* on 25 November in its vigorous attack on the "new reactionaries," those defenders of the inviolable constitution who would deny the "constant evolution" of the universe and who would negate progress "in its diverse manifestations." They are arguing, it was said, as if change had ceased in 1857, as if Edison had not invented the phonograph, Pasteur had not discovered the bacillus, Taine had not exposed Jacobinism, as if Leo XIII had not recognized the French republic. The "new reactionaries" have destroyed the infallibility of the church but have substituted for it the infallibility of the constitution; they have stripped away the priest's tunic, only to replace it with the Phrygian cap of the French Revolution. Moreover, the constitution was not the "work of democracy," as the "new reactionaries" maintain; it was imposed "against the will of the people who were howling in the gallery."[31] Progress in the country, continued *El Universal*, juxtaposing the formation of the constitution with the recognition of the English debt in 1885 and the construction of railroads, has always been "imposed by an advanced group, by *una minoría científica*—now that this phrase has been used [by our opponents]—against democratic opinion, against the desires of the great mass of the citizens." The advocates of constitutional reform were taking on with pride the epithet thrown at them in the course of debate.

A few days after Justo Sierra introduced the reform bill of 30 October, *El Monitor republicano* announced that "there is a group conspiring in the name of scientific politics against the constitution and democratic principles."[32] *El Monitor*'s response followed the familiar lines established by José María Vigil in 1878 and carried on into the González ad-

---

[30] *El Universal*, 19 December 1893; Manuel Flores in *El Universal*, 7 December 1893; see also ibid., 28 November, 1, 6, 9 December. On 8 November *El Universal* suggested that "the most numerous professions, those that have the most considerable interests" (agriculturalists, industrialists, merchants) should be most heavily represented in Congress.

[31] The editorialist cited specifically the sessions of 29, 30 June, and 1 July 1856 and the speeches of Ezequiel Montes, Guillermo Prieto, and Joaquín Villalobos.

[32] Dr. Luis Alva in *El Monitor*, 4 November 1893.

ministration. The editors, Luis and Ramón L. Alva, regarded themselves as defenders of "institutions" against dictatorial and "militaristic" encroachment. They described the evils of Mexican politics as resulting from personal ambition and not from the model document of 1857. Since it recognizes the full range of basic human rights, how can our constitution be regarded as impossible to put into practice? On the contrary, its adoption gave the country "the opportunity of molding the character of the people to new institutions." Though *El Monitor* identified the political degeneration of the country as chiefly a post-Tuxtepec phenomena, it acknowledged that the evils of "perpetualism" went back to Lerdo and even to the wartime dictatorship of Juárez.[33] Ramón Alva was particularly sensitive to Sierra's aphorism that the Liberal party had become a party of government. He saw the two as antithetical. Ours is the Liberal party, said Alva, the one that has always upheld the reign of the constitution. The other is the personal party of one man, which pursues "the illustrious task of destroying institutions that cost the Mexican people so much bloodshed."[34]

El Monitor's position was less categorical than it appeared. In debating the reform measure itself, the editors did not oppose judicial irremovability, only the appointment of magistrates by the executive. They maintained that appointment of judges would merely reinforce existing official corruption and do violence to the principle of popular sovereignty, which "is universally recognized as an indisputable truth in modern political science."[35] *El Monitor* rejected the model of the United States, so openly referred to by the proponents of the reform, because of the difference in political practice between the two countries. It may be appropriate for the president of the United States to appoint judges, since he is elected by the people and truly responsible to them; but in Mexico "the president nominates, elects, and then reelects himself." Therefore, concluded the editors, "the independent judiciary has to be sought in a different manner [here] than in the United States," namely by popular election.[36] After the appearance of the revised measure on 4 December with the appointment provision deleted, *El Monitor* had little more to contribute to the debate.[37]

[33] *El Monitor*, 25, 29, 30 November, 1 December 1893; also 24 November.

[34] Ramón L. Alva in *El Monitor*, 3, 25 November 1893.

[35] Luis Alva in *El Monitor*, 11 November; Ramón L. Alva, 2 December 1893. On popular sovereignty see also 3 November.

[36] Ramón L. Alva in *El Monitor*, 17 November; Luis Alva, 18 November. Although both Sierra and Bulnes referred to North American judicial practice, the Alvas were refuting Pablo Macedo, another important supporter of the measure.

[37] It should be added that one reason (though probably not the principal one) for *El Monitor*'s silence after 4 December was the death on 1 December of Luis Alva, "former cham-

The doctrinaire position of 1893, as voiced by *El Monitor*, was flawed by the tendency we noted earlier to equate constitutionalism with popular sovereignty or democracy in opposition to the new ideas. Luis Alva, for example, contrasted the errors of "scientific politics," based on the misguided evolutionary doctrines of Comte and Spencer, with the ideas of "Constant, Fritot, Tocqueville, Laboulaye, Wheaton, and others who sought democracy as the origin and foundation of modern constitutions."[38] The latter group cited by Alva were all traditional constitutionalists, who with the possible exception of Wheaton had opposed the popular sovereignty that loomed so large in the 1857 document. Laboulaye, for instance, was the key theorist referred to in the movement to reestablish the Senate, a movement clearly in violation of the integrity of the constitution. Moreover, we have noted that Laboulaye's constitutionalism, built upon that of Constant and Tocqueville, was compatible with the positivism of Émile Littré and of the founders of the French Third Republic. Claiming for their own a man like Laboulaye only confused *El Monitor*'s stand. In viewing scientific politics as a conspiracy against the constitution and democratic principles, and yet in concurring with constitutional change (the independent judiciary), the doctrinaires were left without a clear position of their own and thus were vulnerable to the parliamentary maneuvering of their adversaries.[39]

The main opposition to Sierra's proposal did not come from the doctrinaire liberals but rather from the venerable newspaper, *El Siglo XIX*, which had been a principal advocate of the Liberal Union in 1892. On 4 November 1893, Francisco Bulnes, a co-director of the paper, resigned in disagreement with his colleague Luis Pombo on the issue of judicial irremovability.[40] The departure of Bulnes to join *El Universal* was accompanied by a general shake-up in the staff of *El Siglo*, and beginning 10 November the new editors under Pombo's direction joined battle against

---

pion of democracy and liberal institutions." See comments by Ramón L. Alva, 3, 5 December 1893.

[38] Luis Alva in *El Monitor*, 8 November 1893; also 30 November. On Constant, Tocqueville, and Laboulaye, see pp. 81–83. Albert Fritot (1783–1843) was a minor French publicist of constitutionalist persuasion who was cited frequently by Mexican liberals throughout the century. Henry Wheaton (1785–1848) was an American jurist known particularly for his treatises on international law. In politics he was a Republican.

[39] The other important Mexico City newspapers expressing the doctrinaire liberal position in 1893 were the much-persecuted *El Diario del hogar* and *El Demócrata*: see Cosío Villegas, *Historia moderna*, 9:557–64. The most consistent point in the doctrinaire argument was opposition to the perpetual reelection of Díaz, expressed with particular force by Emilio Vázquez in two pamphlets, *La Reelección indefinida* (Mexico, 1890) and *La Reelección* (Mexico, 1892). Cosío refers to Vázquez as "one of the first, if not the first, of the precursors of the Mexican Revolution" (*Historia moderna*, 9:644).

[40] Bulnes's letter of resignation was printed in *El Universal* on 7 November.

the bill before Congress.[41] *El Monitor* saw the turn of events as a conflict within "the president's party" between the advocates of scientific politics and those who at least gave lip service to democratic principles. In a curiously analogous interpretation, the Catholic newspaper *El Nacional* identified an ideological division within the "Liberal party" between "positivist politics" and "the revolutionary metaphysics born in the French Revolution of the last century." *El Siglo*, said *El Nacional*, was abandoning the one for the other, and its new program constituted a "true declaration of war on positivism." For Bulnes, now writing in *El Universal*, the new opponents of the measure were merely promoting a "mechanical peace," that is, absolute power for Porfirio Díaz.[42] All three observers were probably correct in part: *El Siglo's* shift of position had both an ideological and a personal aspect.

It seems clear that the president himself was opposed to the reform measure and that he had made his opposition known to *El Siglo's* co-director, Luis Pombo. Pombo was a lawyer and judge from Oaxaca and a longtime deputy, regarded as "an unconditional friend" of the president. The other three known *El Siglo* contributors to the debate constituted a mixed group. One was Hilarión Frías y Soto, a doctrinaire liberal from the era of the Reforma and a prominent journalist of the Restored Republic, who had not been active since 1876.[43] The other two were Justo Sierra's colleagues from the 1876–79 period, Francisco Cosmes and Carlos Olaguíbel y Arista. All four may have had personal or careerist reasons for courting presidential favor and thus for entering the great debate. Yet, the novelty and force of some of *El Siglo's* arguments go beyond those of a manipulated press and suggest that there existed a latent conflict of ideas within the official circle that was activated by the initiatives of the Liberal Union.

The most significant contribution by the writers of *El Siglo XIX* was historical and polemical, namely to introduce "*científico*" as a epithet in Mexican politics. The terms "science," "scientific," and "scientific poli-

[41] Beginning 9 November the list of editors of *El Siglo* was omitted and only Luis Pombo was named. Carlos Díaz Dufoo's letter of resignation appeared 13 November; another from Francisco Javier Osorno appeared on 17 November.

[42] Ramón L. Alva in *El Monitor*, 25 November 1893; *El Nacional*, 14 November, also 2 December; Bulnes in *El Universal*, 19 November.

[43] See the article from *El Diario del hogar*, reprinted in *El Siglo*, 13 November 1893; also *El Nacional*, 14 November, which described Frías y Soto as "a former journalist faithful to the political traditions of 1857." Biographical information on Frías y Soto is scanty, though he did return to the fray against Francisco Bulnes in 1903. Luis Pombo was born in 1838; his brother Ignacio had been director of *El Siglo* in 1891 and an intimate friend of Manuel Dublán. Most of the articles published in *El Siglo* during the debate were signed "the editorial board." Both Rabasa (*Evolución histórica*, pp. 115–17) and Limantour (*Apuntes*, pp. 19–21) emphasized the hostility of the president to the reform program.

tics" had of course been a part of political discourse since the seventies, but the systematic use of such phrases as *"la escuela científica," "el grupo científico," "el partido científico,"* and *"los científicos"* dates from *El Siglo*'s editorial of 10 November, which initiated its campaign against judicial irremovability.[44] The polemical component in *El Siglo*'s argument can be seen, for example, in its attempt to identify its adversaries as "the reactionary *científico* party," that is, to associate them with the old conservatives.[45] The editors portrayed themselves as defending "the most radical principles of modern democracy," and yet they were careful to refute *El Nacional*'s suggestion that they were new revolutionaries, pursuing "metaphysical" doctrines of 1793. On this occasion they also tried to minimize the political significance of the split between Luis Pombo and the former editors and even had kind words for the Liberal Union.[46] After all, two of the leaders of the Liberal Union movement, at least at its inception, José Yves Limantour and Manuel Romero Rubio, were ministers. The strategy of *El Siglo XIX* was to discredit the constitutional reform measure without alienating its advocates, the *Científicos*, from the regime. In pursuing this strategy, the writers of *El Siglo* also made a major substantive contribution to the great debate.

In his initial speech of 11 December favoring the revised irremovability measure, Emilio Pardo, Jr., summed up the opposing arguments. For some, he said, we are mutilating the constitution, for others we are allowing political and juridical reforms to take precedence over the social and economic redemption of the people.[47] Pardo, it seems, was referring first to the doctrinaire liberals and second to the forceful position of *El Siglo XIX*, as expressed particularly by Carlos Olaguíbel y Arista in two open letters to Justo Sierra. Olaguíbel began by taking issue with the standard criticism of the constitution-makers as metaphysicians who proceeded from abstractions rather than from reality. Their great accomplishment, said Olaguíbel, which gave meaning to Mexico's political independence, was "to gain the supremacy of the civil power." The entrenchment of the church had made imperative their pursuit of "advanced ideas," as opposed to the "positivists" of the day, the moderates, who had favored institutions that conformed to the country's character. If the *moderados* had prevailed, clerical domination would have continued and the Liberal

---

[44] The various phrases are used continuously after 10 November, though the noun *"los científicos,"* which came later to be most common, appeared less frequently at first than the others. As nearly as I can determine it first appeared in *El Siglo* on 25 November 1893.

[45] Ibid., 14, 27 November 1893. There was nothing new, of course, in identifying advocates of scientific politics with the old conservatives; José María Vigil and his colleagues on *El Monitor* had done this in 1878.

[46] *El Siglo*, 10, 17 November 1893.

[47] Pardo, speech of 11 December, *Diario de los debates*, 16th congress, 3:459.

party of today would never have come into being. Our mission, now being pursued by President Díaz, is to advance the work begun by the reformers, "the creation of our nationality" through policies of "economic organization." Since future liberty can be achieved only through economic transformation, why, asked Olaguíbel, "should we complicate [this work] by projects that are strictly political," ones that are rejected by public opinion?[48]

Olaguíbel's emphasis on the primacy of economics over politics was an important premise of scientific politics and was reminiscent of his message of 1877 in *La Época*. However, Olaguíbel's argument of 1893 went further, as Pardo's summary suggested. It identified social problems whose solution demanded the "action of the government," even "the use of authoritarian means." The problems were peasant servitude, "the intellectual oppression of women," and entire classes still alienated from work, undisciplined and demoralized, side by side with "groups that could be called castes." Just as our forefathers struggled against the monopolists of the church, so our children will have to struggle against the monopolists of the banks and railroads. These challenging assertions by Olaguíbel were developed by Francisco Cosmes into a full-blown assault not only upon judicial irremovability but also upon several cherished assumptions of scientific politics.[49] It is significant that this attack came not from "Jacobins" or "old liberals" but from two former stalwarts of *La Libertad*, two members of the "new generation" itself.

El Siglo's position, as elaborated by Cosmes, was presented as thoroughly scientific, that is, as starting from an appreciation of Mexican reality and of the integrity of Mexican society as a unique and evolving organism. His position was also reformist in the sense that it looked to the power of the state to redress social inequities. Finally, it showed respect for the Constitution of 1857 and accepted popular suffrage as the base of government. Thus it drew from both scientific politics and doctrinaire liberalism while adding a novel concern for the social question. Since this position was also in effect an apology for the authoritarian regime of Porfirio Díaz, it might be categorized as "democratic Caesarism," or in more modern terminology, "populism." In developing the argu-

[48] Olaguíbel's letters to Sierra appeared in *El Siglo* on 24 November and 4 December 1893. Sierra responded to the first by reprinting a letter he had written to Altamirano on 9 October 1880 and had published in *La Libertad* on 13 October. In it Sierra expressed reverence for the *reformista* generation (including Altamirano), but he reaffirmed the inadequacy of "revolutionary formulas" for the new generation (see pp. 189–90). For arguments analogous to those of Olaguíbel, see *El Siglo*, 27, 28 November 1893.

[49] Cosmes, "Un Poeta extraviado entre los positivistas. El Sr. Sierra y su discurso sobre inamobilidad del poder judicial," *El Siglo*, 14, 15, 19, 27, 30 December 1893. These articles appeared after the measure was debated and approved by the Chamber of Deputies.

ment, Cosmes also cleverly manipulated the epithets of the debate, labeling his erstwhile colleague a "poet" and a "Jacobin," separated from reality and in pursuit of abstractions and unrealizable ideals.

The "reality" ignored by Sierra and his colleagues, said Cosmes, is the centuries-long heritage of exploitation of the people by the "privileged castes." Under such conditions it is useless to talk of justice, it is useless to look to an irremovable judiciary as the protector of the rights and interests of the people, as one might in a more advanced society like the United States. In Mexico the state is the "only barrier protecting the people (*pueblo bajo*) from the tyranny of the upper classes"; moreover, "only the state is concerned with the interests of the community." Ultimately, only work and education stimulated by the government can improve the condition of the people, making them independent and thus able to exert their rights. But Cosmes went further, asserting that irremovable magistrates would inevitably be tied to "the interests of an oligarchy determined to keep the country in backwardness and the people in slavery." Another writer in *El Siglo* maintained that the "restoration" Sierra called for was really "the restoration of the colonial regime with its tribunals at the command of the rich." Two orators in the Chamber of Deputies saw in Sierra's measure "a dictatorship of the toga"; irremovable judges themselves becoming a "privileged caste," immune from "the vigilance exercised by the public power."[50]

Francisco Cosmes attributed to Sierra's speech of 11 December "the major liability of dressing up in the formulations of positivism the principles of pure constitutional metaphysics." Sierra, continued Cosmes, has set law and justice up as abstractions above society, whereas according to "the teachings of the scientific school" the relationship should be reversed. Justice should be "the humble servant of society." Sierra also seeks to impose an alien institution, the irremovable judiciary, on Mexico. The *Científicos* are enamored of North American models, just as Robespierre and Saint-Just were enamored of models from Greece and Rome. For Cosmes, each society was a complicated and unique organism to which an institution such as the permanent judiciary could be introduced only after careful "experimentation" and not by "artificial means." Otherwise, it would become a "devisive force," or in the phrase of another writer, it would "introduce static elements that will hold up [society's] development." Society and the state were the supreme realities for Cosmes. The rights of the state are above those of the individual, he

[50] Cosmes, "Un Poeta"; *El Siglo*, 5 December 1893; Guillermo Prieto and Agustín Arroyo de Anda in *Diario de los debates*, 16th congress, 3:465, 479. Prieto and Arroyo de Anda appeared to be arguing from the doctrinaire position, which at points was compatible with that of *El Siglo*. For other statements analogous to those of Cosmes, see *El Siglo*, 30 November and 14 December 1893.

argued, because "the state performs a high mission, a sacred duty: the conservation and development of the social organism it has in its care."[51]

The attack by Francisco Cosmes on the elitism of the *Científicos* reached its climax with a strong affirmation of "popular suffrage." Although he conceded that suffrage was not a natural right and that its exercise by an unevenly educated populace was ineffective, Cosmes nevertheless insisted that it "is a real and positive fact that obtains in all civilized societies." He went on to cite Johann Kaspar Bluntschli and Émile Louis Victor de Laveleye, two recent theorists who saw the modern state as resting on a popular base.[52] The Cosmes argument might be interpreted as an effort to reestablish with the support of new theories the harmony between popular sovereignty and strong executive authority. As we have seen, popular sovereignty, which had provided the rationale for the wartime dictatorship of Benito Juárez, became discredited after 1867 and particularly after 1876 because it was not compatible with the assumptions of scientific politics. Its reassertion by Cosmes, already hinted at in the reelection rhetoric of 1892, formed part of the recent official effort to cultivate the Juárez myth and to portray Porfirio Díaz as perpetuating the work of the great reformer and democrat. A corollary to this effort at mythmaking was the critique by Cosmes of his own former hero, José María Iglesias. Cosmes accused the supporters of judicial irremovability of "falling into Iglesias's error of placing individual rights above those of society."[53] The legalism of the Iglesias movement of 1876 was antithetical to the new democratic Caesarism of 1893.

The revised irremovability measure, which occasioned the wide-ranging debate we have just examined, passed the Chamber of Deputies on 23 December by a margin of 108 to 42. Negative votes included those of

---

[51] Cosmes, "Un Poeta"; *El Siglo*, 5 December 1893. The latter's term "static element" was a response to Sierra's contention (see p. 111) that a permanent judiciary could provide democracy "its element of stability."

[52] Cosmes, "Un Poeta" (30 December 1893). Bluntschli (1808–81), a Swiss-German disciple of Savigny, was perhaps the leading exponent of the state as a living organism. His much read *Lehre vom Modernen Stat* (1875–76) appeared in French translation in 1877, in Spanish in 1880. See F. W. Coker, *Organismic Theories of the State* (New York, 1910), pp. 104–14. Laveleye (1822–92) was a prolific Belgian publicist of the social democratic persuasion and a regular contributor to the *Revue des deux mondes*. He argued for the social responsibility of property and the necessity of its wide distribution as a base for political democracy, topics referred to by Cosmes.

[53] Cosmes, "Un Poeta" (27 December 1893). It is possible that the appearance of Iglesias's *La Cuestión presidencial en 1876* in December 1892, a year after his death, served as a stimulus to the constitutional reform movement; but direct evidence is lacking. Cosío Villegas concluded that the book was not much noticed in the press except for a series of articles on it in *El Monitor* (March and April 1893): see *Historia moderna*, 8:104–08. On 10 November 1893 *El Siglo* referred to the Sierra proposal as a new "Plan of Salamanca" in the Congress, but it did not pursue the comparison.

Luis Pombo, Carlos Olaguíbel, and Francisco Cosmes, while all of the leading *Científicos* who were deputies voted in the affirmative. The bill was then sent to the Senate where on 14 December it was referred to committee, from which it never emerged. The president's opposition to judicial irremovability, an opposition supported by the potent arguments of *El Siglo XIX*, clearly had an effect on the senators; and the constitutional reform movement that had begun with the founding of the Liberal Union collapsed.[54] Although the movement was revived in 1903 with the convening of the second National Liberal Union, its main force was spent. The intervention of Díaz himself in 1893 does not diminish the significance of the ideas put forth by *El Siglo*. In the face of such a clear challenge to authoritarian government by those they called *Científicos*, that is, by men within the official circle itself, the supporters of the president were forced to justify his extraordinary power. In doing so they did more than refashion doctrines that were current in Mexico; they also struck upon novel ideas that represented a departure from the apparent ideological consensus of the post-Reforma liberal establishment.

Despite the failure of the constitutional reform movement, the principal casualty of the great debate was not the *Científicos*, but rather the Jacobins, that is, the doctrinaire liberals represented by *El Monitor republicano*. They had inherited Francisco Zarco's ambivalence toward strong government and José María Vigil's confusion of the constitutionalist and the democratic traditions of the Reforma. The advocates of judicial irremovability encroached upon the doctrinaires' opposition to the authoritarian presidency, while the apologists for the president and the fashioners of the Juárez myth appropriated their defense of democracy and reform. It is no coincidence that by the end of 1896 *El Monitor* had ceased publication and that the Jacobins were left without a forum within the liberal establishment. Doctrinaire liberalism had a history after 1893, but, as we shall see, it was an increasingly underground and ultimately revolutionary history in which classic liberal precepts became infused with new doctrines of social radicalism.

The opposition to the irremovability measure both by the vigorous advocates of democratic Caesarism and by the less effective doctrinaire liberals brought into relief the constitutionalism of the *Científicos*. Their constitutionalism was not based on the inviolability of the 1857 document, but rather on the "scientific" premise that its precepts should be adapted to changing conditions. This was the same premise that guided the constitutional reform proposals put forth by Justo Sierra and his colleagues of *La Libertad* in 1878. Moreover, the major proposal of 1892–93

---

[54] *Diario de los debates*, 16th congress, 3:498–513; *Diario de los debates. Senado*, 16th congress, 2 vols. (Mexico, 1893–94), 2:257–60.

itself, the permanency of judges, had also been one of those suggested in 1878. The major change that had taken place over fifteen years was that of context. Whereas the reforms of 1878 were advanced in the wake of political "anarchy," the later proposals came in a period of political stability. In 1878 constitutional reform was presented as part of the program to "strengthen" government. In 1892 the effort was rather to place limits on government, now thoroughly strengthened. In both cases, the reformers pursued the goals of historical constitutionalism, social order through institutional guarantees for individual liberty and for the advance of individual interests. In both cases they held elitist social assumptions and were suspicious of democracy. In 1878 constitutional reform as a part of the strengthening of authority was called conservative-liberalism by its advocates. It is significant that in the new political context of 1892, the term had disappeared from reformist rhetoric. Now that the Liberal party had become a *partido de gobierno,* "conservative" liberalism had lost its relevance.[55]

In pursuing the origins and details of the great debate of 1893 we must not forget that proposals for constitutional reform made up only part of the program of the Liberal Union. This program also included specific recommendations for fiscal, economic, and educational improvements through technical administrative action. The program was further strengthened by the reaffirmation in 1891 of the scientific curriculum of the National Preparatory School in the second National Congress of Public Instruction. Moreover, the overt purpose of the Liberal Union and of its offshoot, the first National Liberal Convention, was to nominate President Díaz as the Liberal party candidate for reelection. In its several dimensions, administration through science, strong and continuous executive authority, and constitutional order, the program of the Liberal Union may be seen as the fulfillment of scientific politics as pointed to by the *convocatoria* of 1867 and as formulated by *La Libertad.* It represented the fusion of statism and constitutionalism and of liberalism and positivism in the assumptions of the governing elite of post-Reforma Mexico. However, the great debate of 1893 also introduced new ideas and a division within this elite, indicating that the ideological consensus, finally achieved, would eventually break down.

To add precision to our discussion of the constitutional reform ideas of 1892–93 and their precedents, we should identify the men who expressed them, those who were called *Científicos.* We must also explore some continuities and discontinuities of individuals. Were the *Científicos* of 1893

[55] In 1889, without using the term "liberal-conservative," Sierra described the characteristics of an ideal conservative party that "would personify the doctrine that regards progress as the evolution of order," "México social," *Revista nacional,* 1:333 (*Obras,* 9:156). The matter of a conservative party was taken up again by Bulnes in 1903 (see p. 136).

in effect a later version of the *La Libertad* group, as Leopoldo Zea argued in 1944? If not, how can we characterize them? What happened to the earlier exponents of scientific politics who did not participate in the events of 1892–93? Among those who did participate, how do we explain the appearance of two stalwarts of *La Libertad*, Carlos Olaguíbel y Arista and Francisco Cosmes, as vigorous opponents of the *Científicos* in the great debate? Let us turn first to what Daniel Cosío Villegas has called "the *Científico* mystery," to the group that has been much discussed but little understood in Mexican historiography. Our understanding of the *Científicos* is clouded by the three different perspectives from which they have been viewed, and particularly by the political emotions aroused by the term after 1910.

From the first or post-1910 revolutionary perspective, the *Científicos* were a group of highly intelligent men of technical accomplishment who formed an informal advisory elite within the late Díaz dictatorship. As financiers, lawyers, and entrepreneurs, some of whom held high government posts, they saw themselves as guiding the nation's progress. In their public or quasi-public roles they also advanced their own interests; they won lucrative contracts and were often closely tied to foreign capitalists. They were frequently exploiters and monopolists, an oligarchy scornful of the interests of the people and the nation. In this view, the *Científicos* came to be equated with the evils of the Díaz dictatorship and revolutionary opposition to *cientificismo* and to *porfirismo* were one. From this first perspective, almost any political enemy who was wealthy and who had connections in high places before 1910 could be considered a *Científico*.[56]

A second perspective on the *Científicos* was provided by the political ferment of the years 1908–10 (with precedents dating back to 1900), which culminated in the seventh and final reelection of Porfirio Díaz. Contemporaries disagreed as to whether a *"Científico* party" actually existed, but all did define an active political grouping within the dictatorship, one that began to coalesce about 1900, was based in Mexico City and hostile to the power of the regional governors, particularly to General Bernardo Reyes. Reyes was the longtime governor of Nuevo León who served as minister of war from 1900 to 1902 and who then returned to his regional seat of power. Reyes was widely perceived to be a possible successor to Díaz and thus was seen as a threat to *Científico* influence in the regime. From this pre-1910 perspective, the *Científicos* had many of the characteristics, construed less negatively, which were attributed to them in later revolutionary rhetoric. The best discussion of the *Científi-*

[56] See Anthony T. Bryan, "Political Power in Porfirio Díaz's Mexico: A Review and Commentary," *The Historian* 38 (1976): 661.

cos, by Daniel Cosío Villegas, proceeds from this second perspective. Cosío sees them as the country's first technocrats, dedicated to the idea that the nation should be guided by a scientifically oriented apolitical elite. In Cosío's treatment the make-up of the group was broad and imprecise and it numbered possibly as many as fifty individuals.[57]

A third perspective comes from the events of 1893, when the term *Científico* actually entered the vocabulary of Mexican politics. It is necessarily narrower than the others and leads to a more precise definition of the *Científicos* as a group. It also happens to be the perspective from which later sympathetic observers viewed the *Científicos* and from which they viewed themselves (both in 1893 and later).[58] As such it is a useful corrective to the others. Finally, this third perspective furnishes a definition of the *Científicos* that is relevant to our discussion. In effect, we come to the *Científicos* from an earlier point in time, relating the men and ideas of 1893 to the past rather than to the future. While our approach cannot (nor does it attempt to) provide a full understanding of the *Científicos* in Mexican history, it does set down a firm base freed of the spongy substance of revolutionary mythology from which to begin a more general inquiry.

From this third perspective, the *Científicos* can be identified simply as those men to whom the label was attached in the course of the great debate of 1893, essentially the ones most closely associated with the constitutional reform movement. The *Científicos* then would be drawn from three categories: first, the leaders of the Liberal Union, that is, the members of the executive board elected 5 April 1892, the eleven original signers of the Liberal Union manifesto of 23 April, and the seventy who signed as delegates to the National Liberal Convention;[59] second, those deputies who signed Justo Sierra's constitutional reform proposal of 30

[57] See Cosío Villegas, *Historia moderna*, 9:840–62. Cosío's treatment rests on contemporary observers of the 1908–10 period, such as Juan Sánchez Azcona, Manuel Calero, José López Portillo y Rojas, and Luis Cabrera. Cabrera's list of about fifty *Científicos*, quoted by Cosío (p. 858), is the one referred to in table 1.

[58] See, for example, Limantour, *Apuntes*, pp. 16–22; Rabasa, *Evolución histórica*, pp. 111–16; Antonio Manero, *El Antiguo régimen y la revolución* (Mexico, 1911), pp. 287–307, 409–10; U.S. Congress, Senate, *Investigation on Mexican Affairs, Preliminary Report and Hearing of the Committee on Foreign Relations*, 66th Cong., 2d Sess., on S. Res. 106 (Washington, 1920), 1:771–73 (testimony by William F. Buckley, 6 December 1919). These accounts presented the *Científicos* as reformers who tried to liberalize the dictatorship from within. See also Breymann, "The *Científicos*."

[59] The members of the *mesa directiva* were listed in *El Siglo XIX*, 7 April 1892; for the eleven original signers of the manifesto, see Manero, *Antiguo régimen*, p. 297; for the list of delegates, see *El Siglo XIX*, 26 April 1893. See also the valuable prosopographical study of the seventy Liberal Union delegates by Jacqueline Ann Rice, "The Mexican Political Elite: Life Patterns of the Delegates to the 1892 Union Liberal Convention" (Ph.D. diss., University of California at Los Angeles, 1979).

October 1893 and those who ultimately voted in favor of the revised measure in the chamber;[60] third, those who defended the irremovability measure openly in the chamber and in the press. Pursuing this analysis, the principal *Científicos* would logically be those who appeared most frequently in the three categories. Those selected can be compared with contemporary lists of *Científicos* compiled from the same perspective (where such lists exist), and discrepancies can be explained and accounted for.[61] The group can then profitably be compared with those identified as *Científicos* in contemporary lists drawn up from the first two perspectives.[62]

The results in tabular form suggest three echelons: nine principal *Científicos*; four others just outside the nuclear group; and a few others whose identification as *Científicos* is more questionable. The measure of who is and who is not a *Científico* must of course be qualitative as well as quantitative, according to the above criteria.

There is little dispute about six of the nine men identified above as the principal *Científicos*, Sierra, Pineda, Bulnes, Pablo Macedo, Casasús, and Limantour. They are virtually always regarded as having made up the nucleus of the group. There are special reasons for including the other three. Flores was a leading spokesman for the irremovability measure in *El Universal* as well as being both a Liberal Union delegate and a deputy. Pimentel appears on all three sample lists. Pardo, though appearing on no list, was secretary of the executive board of the Liberal Union and was a principal spokesman for irremovability in Congress. Several individuals in the second and third echelons deserve comment. Prida should be included because of his role in the press. Núñez is a special case, a Liberal Union delegate who appears on all three lists and who was appointed subsecretary of *hacienda* in May 1893 under Limantour. Miguel S. Macedo is often mentioned as a *Científico*, but his activity in the first reform movement was limited. Castañeda y Nájera, direc-

---

[60] The list of the thirty-six men who signed the 30 October proposal can be found in *Diario de los debates*, 16th congress, 3:223; the vote was recorded in ibid., pp. 499–500.

[61] The two lists selected were by Limantour in *Apuntes*, p. 15, and by Buckley. I have referred to the latter as "Buckley (Rabasa)" because Buckley's interpretation of the *Científicos* (1919) closely approximates that of Rabasa (1920). Buckley was counsel to the Mexican (Huerta) delegation to the Niagara Falls Conference in 1914, of which Rabasa was a member. Since Buckley testified that he had kept in close touch with the delegation and since Rabasa was in exile in New York from 1914 to 1920, I have inferred that Buckley's list of *Científicos* and Rabasa's would be similar. Unfortunately, Rabasa did not mention names. Rabasa himself was governor of Chiapas from December 1891 to February 1894 and took no part in the first Liberal Union. However, he did participate in the second Liberal Union movement in 1903.

[62] The list in [Luis Cabrera], *Obras políticas del Lic. Blas Urrea* (Mexico, 1921), pp. 6–7 and cited by Cosío Villegas has been chosen as a sample in this category.

TABLE 1
The *Científicos*, 1893

Name (age: Nov. 1893)	Category I Liberal Union 1892			Category II Chamber Deputy 1893			Category III Spokesman		Listed as Científico		
	Mesa Directiva 15 Apr. 1892/office	Signed Manifesto 1 of 11	Signed Manifesto as Delegate 1 of 70	Deputy 1893	Signed Sierra Proposal 30 Oct.	Voted for Revised 13 Dec. Measure	In Chamber	In Press	Limantour[a]	Buckley (Rabasa)[b]	Cabrera[c]
Sierra, Justo (45)	+/Pres	+	+	+	+	+	+	+	+	+	+
Pineda, Rosendo (38)	+	+	+	+	+	+	+	−	+	+	+
Bulnes, Francisco (46)	−	+	+	+	+	+	+	+	−	+	+
Macedo, Pablo (42)	+	+	+	+	+	+	+	−	−	+	+
Casasús Joaquín (35)	−	−	+	+	+	+	−	−	+	+	+
Limantour, José (39)	−	+	+	−	0	0	0	−	+	+	+
Flores, Manuel (40)	−	−	+	+	+	+	−	+	−	−	+
Pimentel, Emilio (36)	−	−	+	+	+	+	−	−	+	+	+
Pardo, Emilio, Jr. (43)	+/Sec	−	+	+	+	+	+	−	−	−	−
Nicoli, José P. (58)	+	−	+	+	+	+	−	−	−	−	−
Gamboa, José M. (37)	−	−	+	+	+	+	−	−	+	−	−
Prida, Ramón (31)	−	−	−	+	+	+	−	+	−	−	+
Núñez, Roberto (35)	−	−	−	0	0	0	0	−	+	+	+
Macedo, Miguel S. (47)	−	−	+	−	0	0	0	−	−	+	+
Castillo, Apolinar (53)	+	−	+	−	0	0	0	−	−	−	−
Duret, Fernando (?)	−	−	−	−	0	0	0	−	+	−	+
Castañeda Y Nájera, V. (60)	−	+	+	−	0	0	0	−	−	−	−

Key: + = Yes; − = No; 0 = Not Relevant
[a] Limantour, *Apuntes*, p. 15. See n. 15.
[b] For explanation of "Buckley (Rabasa)" see nn. 58 and 61.
[c] [Luis Cabrera], *Obras políticas del Lic. Blas Urrea* (Mexico, 1921), pp. 6–7. See also n. 57.

tor of the National Preparatory School, was important in the Liberal Union but is usually not mentioned as a *Científico*. It should be noted that I have attached significance to the Limantour and Buckley (Rabasa) lists, drawn up from the same perspective as my analysis, despite their obvious sympathy toward the group.

The points of continuity and comparison between the men of *La Libertad* and the *Científicos* are suggestive.[63] The intellectual leader of both groups was Justo Sierra, who provided much of the continuity of ideas from 1878 to 1893. Two other *Científicos* of 1893, Manuel Flores and Francisco Bulnes, had been on the staff of *La Libertad*, but their contributions were minor.[64] There were other points of contact between individuals of the two groups that might be expected since the *Científicos* (of the first two echelons) were on the average only three years younger (in absolute terms) than the men of *La Libertad* would have been on the average in 1893. For example, Pablo Macedo and Justo Sierra were the first co-editors of *El Foro* in 1873, a post also held by Limantour from 1877 to 1882. Limantour, along with Sierra who was six years his elder, was an apprentice in the law office of Sierra's uncle, Luis Méndez, in 1874–75. Since the *Científicos* (of the first two echelons) were twelve years older in 1893 than the editors of *La Libertad* were in 1878 (forty years of age on the average as opposed to twenty-eight), they were by that time men of greater accomplishment. In 1878 the editors of *La Libertad* had barely begun their careers. Sierra, for example, was a fledgling lawyer and jurist in 1878 and only later achieved prominence as an educator. In one sense, then, the *Científicos* were men of the same age generation as those of *La Libertad*, having matured over time like the political regime to which they were attached.

However, the differences of professional and career orientations between the two groups are more than a matter of age. The early experience and associations of the *La Libertad* group were literary and journalistic, whereas typically the *Científicos* developed technical specialties as young men. Bulnes was an engineer, Casasús an expert in monetary problems. Flores pursued medicine and science; Limantour specialized early in economics and finance.[65] Of course, the principal training and

[63] Leopoldo Zea argued in 1944 the direct continuity of men and ideas from 1878 to 1893: see Zea, *Positivismo* (1968), pp. 397–406. For further biographical information on the *Científicos* of 1893, see Alfonso de María y Campos, "Porfirianos prominentes: Orígenes y años de juventud de ocho integrantes del grupo de los científicos, 1846–1876," *Historia mexicana* 34 (1985): 610–61.

[64] Flores was a science editor from 1878 through 1880, Bulnes a general editor from 4 January 1881 to 7 December 1884.

[65] Bulnes taught at the Escuela Nacional de Ingeniería, at the Colegio de Minas, and at the Escuela Nacional Preparatoria. In 1874 he was a member of the Mexican commission sent to Japan to transcribe the path of the planet Venus. Casasús published the detailed and

profession of all the *Científicos*, except for Bulnes and Flores, was law, and the early association of most of the group was as lawyers in the office of Manuel Romero Rubio. One key to this qualitative difference between the orientations of the two groups may well have been the rapid development of scientific and professional education after 1867, with its base in the National Preparatory School, the subject of chapters 5 and 6. In summary, the *Científicos* represent in ideas and personnel more than the evolution of the *La Libertad* group under the continuous leadership of Justo Sierra. They also were a distinct cohort, older in a relative sense and more professionally and technically oriented than the editors of *La Libertad*.

The political ties between each group and the respective Díaz administration was perhaps the most important point of differentiation between them. The men of *La Libertad* came together as journalist-intellectuals in support of a new presidency that promised stability and progress after years of contention. They were seekers, politically as well as intellectually. They had been frustrated by the lack of mobility under Lerdo, disillusioned after achieving high posts in the ephemeral government of Iglesias, and that were now waiting to be drawn into the Díaz regime as it gained respectability. By 1880 Justo Sierra and Hammeken had become deputies. Cosmes, Olaguíbel, and Santiago Sierra all received government appointments, but they were short-lived or of minor importance. The *Científicos*, on the other hand, were virtually all either deputies or appointees to high government posts in 1893. Moreover, they were defined as a group first by their participation in the Liberal Union, the overt purpose of which was to organize the third reelection of the president. As we have noted, the *Científicos* were well within the official circle from the outset of their reform campaign. By comparison, the men of *La Libertad*, despite their intellectual support for the government, were still outsiders in 1878.

The most striking fact about the careers of the principal editors of *La Libertad* in the years from 1878 to 1893 is their obscurity. Apart from Justo Sierra they achieved neither political nor professional eminence and even their journalistic contributions were modest. As political seekers their success was uneven at best. Two of the group, Santiago Sierra and Jorge Hammeken y Mexía, died at an early age, Sierra in 1880 and Hammeken in 1884. Besides being a deputy, Hammeken was a confidant of Porfirio Díaz during the González administration, so it is possible in

---

technical *Historia de la deuda contraída en Londres* (Mexico, 1885) at the age of twenty-seven. Flores received a medical degree, also at age twenty-seven, and became a professor in the National Preparatory School. Limantour taught economics as early as 1876 (at the age of twenty-two) and the next year was named secretary of a commission studying a possible commercial treaty with the United States.

his case that death cut short a bright political future.[66] The González era "awakened in Telesforo García the Spanish merchant that had lain dormant," and he amassed a great fortune. However, García was so closely identified with the sordid business activities of the regime that he failed to receive a post under Díaz.[67] After 1885 he appears to have withdrawn from the national scene into a position of leadership in the Spanish community, while spending much time in Madrid. Eduardo Garay was somewhat more successful politically, becoming a senator, the subsecretary of foreign relations in 1885, and thereafter a diplomat in Central America and Italy.

The careers of the two *La Libertad* stalwarts who entered the 1893 debate against Sierra were no more prosperous than those of the others. Carlos Olaguíbel served as a deputy in the early eighties, was appointed to an *alcabala* commission in 1882, and then became a customs inspector at Matamoros. He left Mexico City in 1885 to serve Governor Manuel González in Guanajuato, probably until the latter's death in May 1893. He was a deputy at the time of the great debate. Francisco Cosmes was appointed to the Mexican delegation in Paris in December 1880 but he resigned under a cloud of scandal and intrigue the following May.[68] He was a deputy intermittently thereafter, a post he also held in 1893. Thus, the *La Libertad* group, seemingly so coherent in the years 1876 to 1880, was ravaged by death and by political crossfire in the transfer of power from González to Díaz; its remnants emerged divided in 1893.

The defection of Cosmes and Olaguíbel in 1893 might be interpreted as their attempts to rehabilitate their careers by currying presidential favor. However, there is no evidence that political rewards went to those who countered so vigorously the reform proposals of the *Científicos*. Moreover, the forceful statements of Cosmes and Olaguíbel, despite their novel features, did maintain a certain consistency with those of earlier days. Olaguíbel had always stressed the primacy of economics over politics and had been an advocate of artisan interests in 1876–77, attempting to muster that group's support for Porfirio Díaz. Cosmes, we will remember, had been (except for his unexplainable aberration as a fervent supporter of Iglesias) a more overt advocate of authoritarian government than Sierra. He had described the Lerdo regime as "Caesarism

---

[66] On S. Sierra, see chap. 2, n. 1. Hammeken acted as Díaz's representative in Mexico City after the latter had returned to Oaxaca in 1881: Coerver, *Porfirian Interregnum*, pp. 45, 54.

[67] Cosío Villegas, *Historia moderna*, 9:25. See also p. 48.

[68] The voluminous documentation on the Cosmes affair in Paris, including accusations and counteraccusations from Emilio Velasco, the Mexican ambassador to France, and Alberto García Granados, the secretary of the delegation, can be found in Archivo de la Secretaría de Relaciones Exteriores, L–E–1910, expediente H/131 "884–903"/7192.

without Caesar" in 1876 and had called for "honorable tyranny" in 1878. Thus his formulation of democratic Caesarism in 1893, justified by arguments from science, was not a total departure from his earlier views. Since scientific politics contained the seemingly incompatible elements of statism and constitutionalism, we should not be surprised that the earlier advocates of the doctrine might ultimately divide over the limits of presidential power, particularly with the emergence of the social question by the 1890s.[69]

Let us turn briefly to the sequel to the great debate, the second convention of the National Liberal Union of 1903. During the intervening decade, the ties between the *Científicos* and the regime of Porfirio Díaz grew even closer. Limantour as minister of *hacienda* emerged as the central figure in the development-oriented administration. His subsecretary was another *Científico*, Roberto Núñez. Justo Sierra was elevated to the Supreme Court in late 1894 and in 1901 was appointed the nation's first sub-secretary for public instruction within the Ministry of Justice. That same year Manuel Flores became director of the National Preparatory School. Miguel S. Macedo served as subsecretary of *gobernación*. Other *Científicos* continued in the Congress, held minor government posts, or were recruited for special assignments. Nonetheless, the reform impulse of 1893 remained alive, particularly in the Mexico City press during its major transformation of the mid-1890s. *El Universal*, the *Científico* organ of 1893 directed by Ramón Prida, continued on till 1901, despite the demise in late 1896 of its two venerable opponents, *El Siglo XIX* and *El Monitor republicano*. More important, the *Científico* position also found expression in the mass-circulation, low-priced *El Imparcial* of Rafael Reyes Spíndola, whose appearance that same year constituted a journalistic watershed. After 1901 *El Imparcial* and its afternoon edition *El Mundo* dominated the establishment press of Mexico City and became the principal forums for the *Científicos*.[70]

---

[69] On Olaguíbel's ties with the Gran Círculo de Obreros, see David W. Walker, "Porfirian Labor Politics: Working Class Organizations in Mexico City and Porfirio Díaz, 1876–1902," *The Americas* 37 (1981): 261–62. It should be noted that Cosmes's penchant toward statism can also be seen in his history of the 1867–77 period, published in 1901–02. He regarded the "new conception of the higher rights of the state [i.e., above individual rights]" as a product of the Reforma, "gradually becoming spread throughout the ranks of liberalism." Although he still saw nobility in the Iglesias cause of 1876, he made no effort to reconcile statism and constitutional legalism. History was on the side of Díaz in 1877, he concluded. See Francisco G. Cosmes, *Historia general de Méjico, continuación de la de Don Niceto de Zamacois*, 4 vols. (Barcelona and Mexico, 1901–02), 1:xxi, xxxii; 4:1047–59.

[70] *El Siglo*'s last issue appeared on 15 October, *El Monitor*'s on 31 December. On the restructuring of the press see Cosío Villegas, *Historia moderna*, 9:525–31. By 1903 *El Imparcial*, which sold for one *centavo*, had runs of sixty to seventy thousand copies per day, compared with a maximum of five thousand (at five *centavos*) for newspapers before 1896.

Although Justo Sierra took no direct part in the second reform effort of 1903, he did reveal the continuity of his ideas during the preceding years. In 1899 he wrote to Don Porfirio reiterating the opposition he had expressed in the Liberal Union manifesto of 1892 to further reelections. Such a declaration may well have been premature then, he acknowledged, but "now reelection signifies a lifetime presidency, in other words, elective monarchy in republican dress." Sierra pointed to the increasingly acute problem of succession; the absence of Díaz might lead to internal chaos and international humiliation. The perception exists abroad, he said, that "in the Mexican republic there are no institutions, there is only a man; on his life depends peace, productive work, and credit."[71] Thus Sierra broached privately to Díaz the themes that were soon to be expressed publicly by his *Científico* colleagues. A year prior to the convention of 1903, Sierra put the matter more generally by drawing the distinction between Mexico's political and its social evolution: the first had been sacrificed to the second. Moreover, he concluded, "the entire social evolution of Mexico will have been vain and fruitless, if it does not lead ultimately to liberty." The founding father of the *Científicos*, though now a virtual minister and perhaps for that reason absent from the proceedings of 1903, clearly remained a guiding spirit.[72]

The second convention of the National Liberal Union met amid growing political tensions both inside and outside the establishment. The related problems of presidential succession and the vice-presidency were still unresolved, despite efforts made by the advocates of scientific politics since 1878. A constitutional amendment of 1896 had provided for the president to be succeeded by the minister of foreign relations, followed by the minister of *gobernación*. While this solution seemed to be an improvement over the earlier amendment of 1882, which had designated the president of the Senate as the successor, there was still alarm when Díaz suffered a brief illness in 1901. The president's response to the issue of succession was to recruit General Reyes into the cabinet in 1900, at the same time that he lavished favor on Limantour. Both ministers seemed likely successors or vice-presidents and, as we have seen, they emerged as rivals. Díaz apparently desired a reconciliation, with Liman-

---

[71] Sierra to Porfirio Díaz, [2] November 1899, *Obras*, 14:96–97. Sierra was even more outspoken on "the absurdity of the last two reelections" in a letter to his wife from Paris dated 2 April 1901 (ibid., p. 218). His comment was prompted by the news of the president's illness.

[72] Justo Sierra, "Historia política. La Era actual," in *México, su evolución social*, ed. Sierra, 2 vols in 3 (Mexico, 1900–02), 2:434 (*Obras*, 12:399). Sierra's entire essay was first published as a separate volume in 1940 under the now-famous title, *Evolución política del pueblo mexicano*. For a wealth of detail on Sierra's activities from 1894 to 1903, see Claude Dumas, *Justo Sierra et le Mexique de son temps, 1848–1912*, 3 vols. (Lille, 1975), 1–2:353–671.

tour the designated successor, supported militarily by Reyes. When this scheme failed, Reyes was forced to resign from the cabinet and return to Nuevo León in late 1902.[73] Thus by 1903 the vaunted peace and order of the regime were being threatened by a potential conflict between the Mexico City *Científico* and the provincial military challenger.

The year 1900 also saw the beginnings of a dissident "liberal" movement that directly attacked the Díaz regime. It sprang from two provincial sources, soon to merge. One was the clandestine newspaper *Regeneración*, published by Jesús and Ricardo Flores Magón, who had come from Oaxaca to Mexico City to study law. The second was a call by Camilo Arriaga, a mining engineer from San Luis Potosí, for the formation of Liberal clubs throughout the country and for a convention of a national Liberal party to meet in his home city. Arriaga's particular concern was the revival of the church and the laxity of the government in enforcing the constitutional Laws of Reform, while the focus of the Flores Magón brothers was more broadly on the antidemocratic character of the regime. As their pronouncements grew more radical, leaders of both groups were arrested several times between 1901 and 1904. They finally fled the country and in 1905 founded the Partido Liberal Mexicano in St. Louis, Missouri. Although historiographical attention has been lavished on the rebellious Liberals as the "precursors" of the Revolution of 1910, the impact of the movement on the establishment Liberals of Mexico City was modest.[74]

Despite the political changes of the intervening decade, the second National Liberal Union of 1903 presented itself as following directly in the path of its predecessor. Continuity was the theme of Pablo Macedo's welcome to the convention delegates on 19 June. Our mission is the mission of 1892, he said, namely, to demonstrate that the Liberal party can no longer be accused of exaggerated individualism, of sowing the spirit of anarchy. Rather we must demonstrate that "liberty is closely compatible with organization and discipline," a point also made by Joaquín Casasús, elected to host (*ofrecer*) the convention banquet. Organization and discipline clearly suggested economic priorities, now being spelled out in detail by Macedo in three chapters of *México, su evolución social*,

---

[73] On Reyes, see E. V. Niemeyer, Jr., *El General Bernardo Reyes* (Monterrey, 1966); Anthony T. Bryan, "Mexican Politics in Transition, 1900–1913: the Role of General Bernardo Reyes," Ph.D. diss., University of Nebraska, 1970.

[74] Of the many works on the dissident Liberals, see particularly Florencio Barrera Fuentes, *Historia de la revolución mexicana. La Etapa precursora*, 2d ed. (Mexico, 1970); James D. Cockcroft, *Intellectual Precursors of the Mexican Revolution, 1910–1913* (Austin, 1968). For further dimensions of the anti-*Científico* press during this period, see William D. Raat, "The Antipositivist Movement in Prerevolutionary Mexico, 1892–1911," *Journal of Inter-American Studies and World Affairs* 19 (1977): 83–98.

which celebrated the country's progress in communications and public works, commerce, and public finance. For his part Casasús was heading a government commission studying the question of foreign exchange in preparation for Mexico's return to the gold standard in 1905.[75]

The social base of the Liberal Union was revealed by *El Imparcial*, editorializing that the convention was "drawn from very diverse groups"—merchants, agriculturalists, industrialists, and the professions—and thus had a "double interest in national politics." These traditional themes of scientific politics, economic development, sound fiscal administration, and the tie of government to "interests," formed the contextual backdrop for the principal message of the Liberal Union, the need to provide institutional continuity against the threat of anarchy, of "extralegal political agitation," or of improvised institutions or caudillos. We must prepare for the fateful day, said Rosendo Pineda, when the unprecedented authority that is guiding the destiny of the country "slips from the sure hands of its present trustee." With rotund phrases, the Liberal Union spokesmen were calling for the revival of political parties, specifically "the great Liberal party, the only party that is truly national." Only through the Liberal party can citizens actively exercise their electoral rights.[76]

The occasion for the second convention of the National Liberal Union, as for the first, was the nomination of President Díaz for reelection. Unlike the first convention, however, which was a direct outgrowth of the election-year *porfirista* organization, the second convention remained separate from the start, reflecting the independent and antipersonalist stance established by the *Científicos* in 1893. The climax of the 1903 convention was the notorious speech by Francisco Bulnes on 21 June nominating Díaz as the Liberal Union candidate. His message was not novel; much of it had been stated before either by the *Científicos* of 1893, by Sierra (and even by Bulnes himself) in the intervening years, or by the other leaders of the Liberal Union since March 1903. But Bulnes now spoke more boldly, directly, and elaborately than the others, unafraid of whom he might offend, always accentuating rather than muting points of controversy. The 1903 speech solidified his reputation as a polemicist and

[75] Macedo's speech appeared in *El Imparcial*, 20 June 1903, that of Casasús on 24 June. Macedo's three chapters, "La Evolución mercantil" (dated 31 August 1903), "Comunicaciones y obras públicas" (12 April 1903), and "La Hacienda pública" (27 December 1903) appeared in Sierra, *México*, 2:250–415. They were also reprinted as a separate volume in 1905. The various reports of the Casasús commission dated from 1 August to 5 December 1903, can be found in Joaquín Casasús ed., *La Reforma monetaria en México* (Mexico, 1905). Other commission members active in the Liberal Union included Francisco Bulnes and Fernando Pimentel y Fagoaga. See Alfonso de María y Campos, "Los Científicos y la reforma monetaria de 1905," *Estudios políticos* 5 (1979): 157–87.

[76] See *El Imparcial*, 19 June, 23 March, 15 April.

served as a kind of preface to his controversial books of 1905, designed to diminish the heroic stature of Benito Juárez in his centennial year.[77] Bulnes began his speech by asserting that the only effective argument for reelection was the argument from practicality. To be for or against reelection on the basis of democracy is specious, since we are not a democratic people. In practical terms, Porfirio Díaz has given the country stability and peace, which have inspired the confidence of foreign bankers, investors, and entrepreneurs. Thus our international credit and continued economic progress depend directly on Díaz. These are the only grounds for reelection, said Bulnes.

However, the talk of practicality was only a foil for the main message of the Liberal Union, reiterated by Bulnes, namely that the accomplishments of Díaz and Mexico's international standing could only be perpetuated through institutions. Foreigners would be alarmed if they realized that without Díaz there would be chaos. The "political disorganization" of the country has amply justified the personal rule of Díaz, as the factionalism of the Roman republic justified the rule of Caesar Augustus. But personal rule is no longer justifiable; "magnificent as an exception, the personal regime as a system is detestable." Turning polemical, Bulnes claimed that Mexico's "political disorganization" was the work of the Jacobins, who, "if they have been impressive in demolishing, have been unimpressive in governing." They did not settle for instituting the Laws of Reform and defeating the French, but went on to impose through "the omnipotence of a popular assembly" the "false equation" between individual rights and equality. Bulnes's attack upon Jacobinism brought forth an impassioned response by Hilarión Frías y Soto, a self-proclaimed "pure (*neto*) Jacobin," who defended the reelection of Díaz as an expression of democracy, just as he had defended the president's pursuit of democratic goals in 1893. Bulnes in turn refuted Frías y Soto, expanding upon his earlier points, calling reelection on grounds of democracy "false Jacobinism" and identifying the epoch of Juárez as "legal anarchy." Bulnes had set the stage for the grand polemic over Juárez to take place two years later.[78]

Continuing to press the need for institutions, Bulnes argued that the

[77] Bulnes, *Discurso*. In a wide-ranging sociological essay of 1899, Bulnes had expressed concern that Mexico's peace was quite so dependent on "the personal action of a [single] statesman": *Porvenir de las naciones hispano americanas ante las conquistas recientes de Europa y los Estados Unidos* (Mexico, 1899), p. 281. The *convocatoria* for the Juárez centennial was on 21 March 1903, a day before the initial gathering to plan the Liberal Union convention and three days after the first meeting of the Círculo Nacional Porfirista. The text of each of these contiguous events appeared in *El Imparcial* one or two days later.

[78] Hilarión Frías y Soto, *Carta de . . . al Sr. diputado Francisco Bulnes* (Mexico, 1903); Bulnes, *Defensa y ampliación de mi discurso pronunciado el 21 de junio de 1903 ante la convención nacional liberal* (Mexico, 1903).

nation now recognized that Jacobinism had failed. It fears a recurrence of disorganization and the inevitable sequel, personal government. Instead, the country desires that "law" be the successor to Porfirio Díaz. Which law is not important, "provided it is not the most perfect (*hermosa*) law, but rather the positive, the true law, the one that best fits us." Institutions "that suit Mexico," concluded Bulnes later in his rebuttal to Frías y Soto, is what "we *Científicos*" want. As in 1893, Bulnes and his Liberal Union colleagues framed their appeal for institutions in sociological terms. Whereas peace in a personalist state is "mechanical," said Bulnes, in a modern state it is "organic," which as in all of nature involves incessant struggle, in turn a sign of health and inevitable progress. "The nation desires political parties; it desires institutions; it desires the struggle of ideas, interests, and passions." Bulnes made no specific political references, though he did call upon Díaz to provide for the continuation of civil government, which Frías y Soto took to refer to the threat of General Reyes as a possible successor. It seems clear that the conflict between Limantour and Reyes lay behind the generalized rhetoric of the Liberal Union.[79]

Though the overt message of the Liberal Union of 1903 was a restatement of the *Científico* position of 1892–93, subtle changes had taken place. The principal theme continued to be the need for limitations on personal executive authority, moving from irremovable magistrates to functioning political parties. Also, there continued the less explicit call for a separate vice-presidency. The Liberal Union of 1903 continued to support reelection, but it now put more emphasis than it had in 1892 on active nomination by the Liberal party as opposed to mere passive acceptance of reelection.

A more significant change was the new conception of the nature of the Liberal party and particularly its relation to other political parties. In justifying the personal power of Díaz, Bulnes cited a "sociological law," namely that a single party, once triumphant, inevitably breaks into factions, forcing the people to turn to a personal leader, in the case of Rome to Augustus, in the case of Mexico to Díaz. According to Bulnes, the Liberal party ceased to exist in 1867 at the very moment of its triumph. Having entrusted its destiny to Díaz, the nation's challenge now was to reconstitute the Liberal party, to "search inwards to see if liberals still remain. If it finds them, it is saved."[80] Although reconstruction of the Liberal party was a persistent theme of political discourse after 1867, the notion that it had ceased to exist was novel. The argument of 1892 was that the Liberal party had finally become a *partido de gobierno*, led by

[79] Bulnes, *Discurso*, p. 17, 19; *Defensa*, p. 49; Frías y Soto, *Carta*, p. 25.
[80] Bulnes, *Discurso*, p. 23.

Porfirio Díaz. Now faced with the perpetuation of Don Porfirio's personal rule, more precarious each year, the *Científicos* found it increasingly difficult to make the connection between the personal regime of Díaz and the supposed Liberal party.

Bulnes's exhortation to the nation to search for liberals led directly to the climax of his *Discurso* of 1903, the need to search also for "modern conservatives." Since the existence of a single party is impossible, the reorganization of the Liberal party demands a comparable reorganization of the Conservative party. The result will be a beneficial "organic struggle" between at least two political parties. Bulnes went no further in defining a new conservative party, except to assert that "a new Mexican, be he liberal or conservative," is taking form. This new Mexican "profoundly detests militarism; he has a passion for independence, a yearning for progress, and a striving for institutions." Could Bulnes have been suggesting that the *Científicos*, whom he often characterized in similar terms, epitomized this "new Mexican," and that the Liberal Union might be in effect the beginnings of a new Conservative party? In summing up the work of the Liberal Union convention, *El Imparcial* took up again the question of a conservative party but failed to present as promised its potential characteristics. Instead, it merely attacked the conservatives of mid-century and said that their attachment to old ideas of monarchism, privilege, and clericalism was too strong to allow for change. Seeming to rule out the possibility of a new conservative party, *El Imparcial* concluded that the political stuggle of the future would be between the Liberal party and some other, "perhaps one of more advanced ideas, perhaps one that diverges from it only in a few details."[81]

The only concrete result of the Liberal Union movement, in effect the culmination of three decades of effort by the advocates of scientific politics, was the constitutional amendment of 6 May 1904 extending the presidential term to six years and establishing a separate vice-presidency to coincide with the sixth reelection of Porfirio Díaz. But the action hardly fitted the prescription of the Liberal Union. Instead of choosing a strong vice-president and possible successor like Limantour, Díaz turned to Ramón Corral, his dependent, lackluster minister of *gobernación*, thus solidifying further his "personal regime."[82]

[81] See editorials of 25 and 27 June (the final ones pertaining to the Liberal Union) in *El Imparcial*. The editorial of 27 June was entitled "El Programa conservador. Sus Viejos Ideales no pueden servirle ya de bandera." It is quite possible that these editorials were written by Rafael Reyes Spíndola, the director of *El Imparcial*.

[82] Limantour maintained that he strongly supported the *Científicos*' call for a separate vice-presidency and that he personally took up the matter with the president. He also insisted that he steadfastly refused to become the candidate, despite persuasion by Díaz, and instead he supported Corral. See Limantour, *Apuntes*, pp. 137–44. His interpretation was supported by José López-Portillo y Rojas, *Elevación y caída de Porfirio Díaz*, 2d ed. (Mex-

The Liberal Union campaign failed in its effort to establish political parties. There was no reorganization of the Liberal party and no new conservative party emerged. Despite the notorious speech by Bulnes, the reformist vigor that had characterized the *Científicos* as constitutionalists in 1893 was clearly in decline by 1903, as they were drawn increasingly into the regime. There was no leader to replace Sierra, though the other principal *Científicos* of 1892–93, Pineda, Bulnes, Pablo Macedo, and Casasús, were also central figures in 1903, along with Miguel S. Macedo, who had been less active earlier.[83] The 1903 Liberal Union movement did not involve a major debate on national issues like that of 1893. The doctrinaire liberal defenders of the 1857 Constitution had been forced out of the establishment. A populist defense of the president as social reformer may have been embedded in the confused and discursive rhetoric of Hilarión Frías y Soto, but if so, it is hard to detect.[84] The Liberal Union of 1903 was essentially an effort by the *Científicos* to influence the president directly, and like the first more broadly conceived effort, it failed.

The ill-fated attempt by the *Científicos* to bring about "organic peace" in the form of a competitive party system points up a major dilemma of Mexican politics during the Porfiriato. How was it possible to implant a regime of peacefully contending parties in a country dominated by an all-embracing liberal myth, in which "conservatism" signified treason and the perpetuation of an outmoded colonial system? The advocates of scientific politics of 1878 and their successors the *Científicos* of 1893 had sought to break the bonds of the liberal myth, to differentiate their positivist position from the classic or "metaphysical" liberalism of mid-century. But they were always forced to do so as liberals. In their efforts of 1878 to reform the constitution they spoke of a "conservative-liberalism," but by 1890 they had abandoned the label, arguing that the Liberal party had finally become "a party of government."[85]

As constitutional reformers the advocates of scientific politics had

---

ico, 1975), p. 255 (1st ed. 1921). Cosío Villegas favored the view that Corral was a compromise candidate in the impasse that developed between Limantour and Reyes: *Historia moderna*, 9:346–48, 846–47.

[83] Other signers of the *convocatoria* of the Liberal Union of 14 April, who have often been identified as *Científicos* but who were not active in 1892–93, included Fernando Pimentel y Fagoaga, Porfirio Parra, Emilio Rabasa, Rafael Reyes Spíndola, and Enrique C. Creel. See *El Imparcial*, 15 April 1903.

[84] Francisco Cosmes and Carlos Olaguíbel, who articulated the populist position so forcefully in 1893, were now silent. Antonio Manero identified the group who supported reelection on democratic grounds as "red Jacobins," led by Joaquín Baranda, minister of justice until he resigned in 1901, in apparent conflict with Limantour: *Antiguo régimen*, p. 298; also Limantour, *Apuntes*, p. 145; Prida, *Dictadura*, pp. 138–39.

[85] Sierra mused about an ideal conservative party in 1889, but did not pursue the question further. See chap. 4, n. 55.

moved from a program to strengthen weak executive authority to one that would impose limitations on a now overly strong executive. By 1903 the realities of the "personal regime" of Porfirio Díaz were more apparent to them, and they sought reform through a vice-presidency and particularly through functioning political parties. They even hinted that they might become the new conservatives. But the hold of the liberal myth was too strong and the suggestion for a new conservative party came to naught. The only viable "party" in Mexico between 1867 and 1910 was a "liberal" party. And so as the personal regime of Porfirio Díaz reached its climax, Mexico was left with two so-called liberal parties, the Gran Partido Liberal of the *Científicos* of 1903, ever-more-closely identified with the aged Díaz, and the new Partido Liberal Mexicano of 1905, in rebellion against the regime. Party conservatism, taking form elsewhere in Latin America by 1905, had little success in Mexico, then or now.

Despite the apparent demise of its constitutionalist component, the doctrine of scientific politics in many ways had achieved by the 1890s the official status sought by its advocates in 1878. As it acquired this status, positivist assumptions increasingly affected general thought and policy on social questions. However, before examining social thought, we must turn first to education, for the refashioning of the system of higher education after 1867 was an integral part of the rise of scientific politics.

CHAPTER 5

Positivism and the National Preparatory School

THE YEAR 1867 was as decisive in Mexican higher education as it was in politics. Within three months of the collapse of the empire and the restoration of the republic, an educational reform commission appointed by President Benito Juárez had presented a new plan of studies for the Federal District, at the heart of which was a uniform preparatory curriculum to be taught in a single school for all students ultimately seeking a professional education. The civil war of the previous decade had finally killed the ancient Royal and Pontifical University, moribund since the Revolution for Independence when its buildings had served briefly as a military barracks. So low was the level of student preparation that in 1851 the faculty decided to forego the traditional *acto literario* honoring the new archbishop of Mexico. Indeed, the university was formally abolished by liberal regimes in 1833, 1857, and again in 1861, only to be reinstated in each instance when conservatives returned to power. The institution became a pawn in the ideological conflict of the postindependence years, a symbol for liberals of clericalism and the colonial tradition. University reform, still possible elsewhere in Spanish America, was no longer an option in Mexico, a fact recognized by Emperor Maximilian when he issued the final decree of abolition on 30 November 1865. "What was called university in the Middle Ages," he said, "has become today a word without meaning."[1]

The novelty of the 1867 plan was in the uniformity of the preparatory curriculum and in the philosophy that guided it. The general notion of preparatory studies, followed by professional training in "special" schools, had evolved gradually from the late colonial era, despite ideological conflicts over secularization and despite the several efforts to abolish and to reinstate the university. In 1833 the government of Valentín Gómez Farías divided higher education into six "establishments," one of which would be devoted to preparatory studies and two others that would essentially perpetuate the most important of the colonial *colegios*,

---

[1] Letter to Manuel Siliceo, *Diario del imperio*, 14 June 1865. The decree can be found in Alberto María Carreño, *La Real y Pontificia Universidad de México, 1536–1865* (Mexico, 1961) p. 453. Maximilian's decree formally reaffirmed the liberal decree of 14 September 1857.

San Ildefonso and Minería, under more neutral designations. Schools of arts and trades and of agriculture were introduced in 1843 and 1853 respectively, and a school of commerce was begun in 1854. The most direct precedent for the 1867 program emerged naturally enough from the Juárez government of 1861. It was a plan that thoroughly secularized higher education and established a single preparatory school in the former Colegio de San Juan de Letrán, along with the full range of special or professional schools. However, in the plan of 1861 preparatory studies were not made uniform, but they varied for each profession. Some were to be taken at San Juan, some at the respective professional schools themselves. The educational program of the Maximilian regime, apart from delivering the university its death blow, was brief and general and did little to contradict the liberal legislation of 1861.[2] Thus the Juárez commission of 1867 could introduce its novel plan in an educational vacuum, while at the same time having ample precedents upon which to base it.

The philosophy that guided the educational program of 1867 was the positivism of Auguste Comte, championed principally by Gabino Barreda who headed the Juárez commission. In fact, it was in the reorganization of higher education that Comtean positivism had its most direct influence in Mexico, as it had in the rest of Latin America. The doctrine of scientific politics, first espoused by the *La Libertad* group in 1878, drew upon many positivist assumptions, ones that can be traced back to the ideas of Saint-Simon and Comte in the early 1820s and that later became generalized in European thought. Nonetheless, positivism was only one element in scientific politics, and indeed the explicit references by its advocates to Comte and especially to Saint-Simon were rare. The dominant set of political ideas in Mexico after 1867 can be characterized as an official liberalism that was gradually transformed by the infusion of positivist assumptions. Scientific politics and liberalism were theoretically in conflict, but despite periods of intense debate, they tended toward reconciliation in an era of political consensus. Thus in the realm of political ideas it is a mistake to regard positivism as having achieved "official" status in late nineteenth-century Mexico. However, Comtean positivism did achieve that status in higher education a decade earlier than its influence was manifest in politics.

The introduction of Comtean positivism to Mexico is an obscure subject. Though Gabino Barreda was its generally acknowledged progenitor

---

[2] The best account of initiatives in higher education before 1867 appears in Edmundo O'Gorman, "Justo Sierra y los orígenes de la universidad de México, 1910" (1949), *Seis Estudios históricos de tema mexicano* (Xalapa, 1960), pp. 145–71. See also Hale, *Mexican Liberalism*, pp. 171–75 (for the 1833 plan) and Guadalupe Monroy, "Instrucción pública," in Cosío Villegas, *Historia moderna*, 3:633–50. The educational law of 15 April 1861, issued by Minister Ignacio Ramírez, can be found in Dublán y Lozano, *Legislación*, 9:150–58.

and major advocate, the first Mexican positivist appears to have been Pedro Contreras Elizalde. A native Spaniard whose mother was Yucatecan, Contreras studied medicine in Paris with two of Comte's disciples, knew Comte personally, and was a charter member of the Société Positiviste in 1848. He returned to Mexico in 1855 and became close to Juárez, marrying one of his daughters and serving in the Ministry of Justice and Public Instruction from 1861 to 1863 and again from 1867 until 1872. It was probably through Contreras that Barreda, who had gone to Paris in 1848 (like Contreras to study medicine), was exposed to positivism. Barreda attended Comte's famous Palais Royal lectures on the general evolution of humanity before returning home in 1851. During the Reforma and Intervention he practiced, wrote on medical subjects, and held chairs of medicine, physics, and natural history in the capital and in Guanajuato. His eulogist Agustín Aragón assures us that during these years he reeducated himself in the Comtean manner, "completely assimilating" the 150 volumes of Comte's *Bibliotheque positiviste*.[3] In 1863 Barreda published *De La Educación moral*, Mexico's first positivist essay, and in September 1867 he delivered his famous *Oración cívica*, the independence day speech in which was embedded a Comtean interpretation of Mexican history. Completing the cadre of major pioneer positivists were Barreda's brothers-in-law, Francisco and José Díaz Covarrubias, Juárez intimates who held ministry posts and who along with Contreras and Barreda were members of the educational reform commission. Thus by 1867 Comtean positivism had permeated the official circle of President Juárez.[4]

The product of the Juárez commission was the law of 2 December 1867 (supplemented by detailed regulations in 1868 and revised in 1869), which created the Escuela Nacional Preparatoria (ENP) and its positivist curriculum.[5] The new school, which occupied the stately eighteenth-century quarters of the former Colegio de San Ildefonso, opened its doors on 3 February 1868 to nine hundred students. Gabino Barreda was the

[3] Agustín Aragón's *Essai sur l'histoire de positivisme au Mexique. Le Docteur Gabino Barreda* (Mexico and Paris, [1898?]) is the principal source for biographical information on Barreda and Contreras Elizalde before 1867. See also Moisés González Navarro, "Los Positivistas mexicanos en Francia," *Historia mexicana* 9 (1959): 119–29, and William D. Raat, "Agustín Aragón and Mexico's Religion of Humanity," *Journal of Inter-American Studies and World Affairs* 11 (1969): 441–57. The imposing list of Comte's recommended volumes (including his own) can be found in Comte, *Système*, 4:557–61.

[4] See Ernesto Lemoine, *La Escuela nacional preparatoria en el período de Gabino Barreda, 1867–1878* (Mexico, 1970), pp. 15–21; Díaz y de Ovando, *Escuela*, 1:9–16. Another positivist member of the commission was Ignacio Alvarado (1829–1904), a distinguished physiologist.

[5] The legislation in question can be found in Dublán and Lozano, *Legislación*, 10:193–205, 242–54, 515, 560–66, 591–601, 753–63.

director from the start and he remained so for a decade. The early success of the ENP, despite the problems of limited space and equipment, continual student resistance to discipline, and public and political opposition to the curriculum, was due in large measure to Barreda. He was a firm administrator; he assembled a cadre of talented teachers; he provided philosophical guidance and inspiration in the critical formative years. Though a forceful defender of the institution, he was unable personally to weather the political storms of the mid-1870s. The followers of Porfirio Díaz regarded Barreda as too closely associated with Juárez and Lerdo and they forced him to leave his post in 1878.[6] Between 1880 and 1883 the Preparatoria faced its most severe test, an official effort to abolish it and a public debate over a part of its curriculum that grew into a major philosophical controversy. That the institution survived and indeed by the 1890s had regained its former preeminence in national life is a tribute to its founder and to the effectiveness with which he implanted there positivist educational philosophy.

It has been argued that the positive philosophy of Auguste Comte constituted a system of "universal education." Comte never published a treatise on education, yet pronouncements on pedagogy permeated his writings and he presented his philosophy in a form that reflected the habits of teaching.[7] Positivism in its strictly philosophic sense as opposed to positivism as a plan for social regeneration is a theory of knowledge in which the scientific method represents man's only way of knowing. The elements of this method are first, the primacy of observation and experiment, and second, a search for the laws of phenomena or the relations between them. In the positivist view, we can know only phenomena (or "facts") and their laws, but not their essential nature or ultimate causes. These were Barreda's assumptions when he emphasized in his most systematic justification of the ENP curriculum that "good method" was fun-

---

[6] For the early history of the ENP in detail including the transition from San Ildefonso, see Lemoine, *Escuela*; also Monroy, "Instrucción pública." Articles from the press pertaining to the school have been collected in Díaz y de Ovando, *Escuela*, vol. 2. For a colorful description of the first days of the Preparatoria by an entering student of 1868, see Juan de Díos Peza, *Memorias, reliquias y retratos* (Paris, 1901), pp. 112–16. Overall enrollment, which in 1868 included all students from other *colegios*, dropped in 1869 to 568, and then crept back upward to 782 in 1877. San Ildefonso formerly had about three hundred students. For a thorough analysis of ENP enrollment through 1875, see Geralda Dias, "Conformación social y política de la escuela nacional preparatoria," Ph.D diss., El Colegio de México, 1979, chap. 6. For the chronology of Barreda's career from 28 February, when he was given leave from the ENP, till 19 April, when he sailed for Europe as minister to Germany, see Díaz y de Ovando, *Escuela*, 1:72–77; also Josephine Schulte, "Gabino Barreda y su misión diplomática en Alemania, 1878–1879," *Historia mexicana* 24 (1974): 230.

[7] Paul Arbousse-Bastide, *La Doctrine de l'éducation universelle dans la philosophie d'Auguste Comte*, 2 vols. (Paris, 1957).

damental in education, as opposed to mere instruction.[8] The distinction between education and instruction was frequently made by positivists. By "method" Barreda meant the procedures of the "positive sciences," those "most appropriate, sure, and proven for seeking the truth." Comte's central construct, the classification or hierarchy of the sciences, was in a sense a demonstration of the way a student would logically go about learning, that is, by moving from simpler to more complex subjects.

Mathematics, beginning with arithmetic and ending with calculus, was the cornerstone of the preparatory school curriculum. In its simplicity mathematics is the best way to learn deduction and the syllogism, wrote Barreda; its "rigorous logical method" is the best preparation for later "more complicated speculations." From mathematics in the first and second years, the students moved in the third year via mechanics to elementary astronomy (cosmography), which treats the simplest of the "real phenomena in nature," and to physics. In the process they passed from deduction to simple observation (in astronomy), to observation and experiment in physics. The fourth year was devoted to chemistry, in which the "experimental method acquires its fullest development" and in which "induction is the predominant logical procedure." In the fifth and final preparatory year, the student would pursue natural history (botany and zoology), applying the methods learned in the simpler sciences to complex living beings as well as perfecting the procedures of classification and hypothesis.

The fifth year was also devoted to logic, in Barreda's view a vital (though controversial) part of the curriculum. There can be no better preparation, Barreda argued, for this "abstract and theoretical course in logic" than the "practical course in logic" students actually take in passing naturally from one science to the next. Logic as a subject was controversial, as we shall examine later in detail, because it was now moved from the beginning to the end of the curriculum. Dislodged from its traditional place as an introduction to philosophy, it now became a synthesis of the sciences. In positivist educational terminology, "logic" essentially replaced "philosophy" and "metaphysics"; neither of the latter two terms appeared in the revised curriculum of 1869. Barreda was the professor of logic and the text he adopted was the treatise by John Stuart Mill that had won the praise of Comte himself.[9]

---

[8] Barreda, "Carta dirigida al C. Mariano Riva Palacio, gobernador del estado de México, en la cual se tocan varios puntos relativos a la instrucción pública" (10 October 1870), *Opúsculos*, pp. 31ff.; also idem, "Instrucción pública" (1872), *Revista positiva* 1 (1901): 291, where he inserted the same quotation from Comte as in "Carta . . . a Riva Palacio."

[9] John Stuart Mill, *A System of Logic, Ratiocinative and Inductive, Being a Connected View of the Principles of Evidence, and Methods of Scientific Investigation*, 2 vols. (Lon-

The systematic study of the sciences, then, was the core of the curriculum. Nonscientific subjects were interspersed throughout the five years, but Barreda's rationale for their placement was brief, even casual.[10] In his view, the study of languages should be guided by utility. The student began with French in the first year and then took up English in the next two years. The third year was also devoted to the elements of Greek, in addition to Spanish grammar. Latin was relegated to the last two years, along with geography and history in the fourth year and literature in the fifth. Barreda justified teaching French because it was the language of so many of the texts used in the school and the principal language students brought with them from primary school. The same was true to a lesser degree with English.[11] Barreda acknowledged that the major change from previous educational plans was the deferral of Latin to the fourth year; the reason was simply that "scientific" texts were no longer written in Latin, except for a few in law and medicine. Latin in the final two years would be quite sufficient for future lawyers and physicians. As for the deferral of Spanish grammar, Barreda argued that its "abstruse and highly analytical character" demanded prior development of mental skills if its study was to be a truly intellectual exercise. The elements of Greek were best studied in the year least burdened with other subjects. Geography was placed to follow cosmography, to which it was related; history would be "more agreeable" if studied along with geography. Barreda omitted entirely a rationale for the study of literature. As we shall see, neither Barreda nor Comte intended to neglect the affective, artistic, and humanistic side of education. However, they regarded it as "spontaneous" rather than "systematic" and thus more appropriate for the early years, particularly under maternal direction. In practice, such a theory diminished the cumulative humanistic preparation acquired by students by the time they entered professional schools.

Education in the Preparatoria, according to its advocates, was necessarily "homogeneous." It was designed to fill what José Díaz Covarrubias identified as the traditional void that existed between primary and professional training; "cultivation of the mind" would replace the early im-

---

don, 1843). On the complex relationship between Comte and Mill, see Simon, *European Positivism*, pp. 180–86. Barreda expanded his justification of the new course in logic in "Instrucción pública," pp. 322–31. The article first appeared as a series in the *Diario oficial* beginning 22 September 1872.

[10] See Barreda, "Carta . . . a Riva Palacio," *Opúsculos*, pp. 24–26, 35.

[11] For example, Mill's *Logic* was read in French (presumably easier for the students than English); no complete Spanish translation existed. As one of the few departures from a totally uniform curriculum, German was substituted for Latin in the fourth and fifth years for those preparing to study engineering and architecture. Barreda said the elimination of Latin was a mistake (though he did not deny the usefulness of German): "Carta . . . Riva Palacio," *Opúsculos*, p. 63.

mersion in specialties.[12] Those who oppose parts of the uniform curriculum as useless for this or that profession, said Barreda, often do so in the name of "freedom of teaching [enseñanza]," as specified in article 3 of the constitution. But their progressivism is misguided. In effect they are reverting to the benighted attitudes of a "theocratic" age, when "secret knowledge" for a career was perpetuated within a narrow caste. The modern lawyer must be involved in administration and business, unlike his ancestor who "was always buried in voluminous dossiers and weighty parchments." Solid geometry, chemistry, botany, and zoology are are all part of a homogeneous system of studies based on observation and experiment to discern the relations between phenomena and ultimately "to understand the effective laws of society." In short, the positivist premise was that because all of nature was one, "preparatory studies should be uniform for everyone and at the same time complete."[13]

In defending the uniform curriculum of the ENP, Barreda found himself drawn to the educational achievements of the Jesuits. In Renaissance Europe they were the first to teach coherently the scientific knowledge of the day. "They always understood," wrote an admiring Barreda, "the immense advantages [that] a perfectly homogeneous education under their direction" could have in molding "the influential classes of society." In sum, their objective was "to take control of education and make it identical for everyone." The Jesuit plan failed because of the "retrograde motive that inspired it," by which Barreda meant not so much the urge to exert intellectual and moral sway over students but the omission of crucial sciences, the findings of which conflicted with theological dogma. The result was an incomplete, insufficiently "encyclopedic" program. Barreda made it clear, however, that general education under the Jesuits was superior to the narrow and exclusive professional training of the colony. Perhaps Barreda also had the Jesuits in mind when, in addressing the question of poor pay for teachers, he referred to the profession as a "social ministry."[14]

[12] Díaz Covarrubias, *La Instrucción pública en México* (Mexico, 1875), p. ccxx. This was a comprehensive report on education by the minister of justice and public instruction under President Lerdo, not a standard ministerial *memoria*.

[13] Barreda, "Instrucción pública," pp. 284–336, and passim; idem, "Carta . . . a Riva Palacio," *Opúsculos*, p. 62. Barreda singled out San Ildefonso and Minería as "theocratic" schools. However, when Minería was defended by Eduardo Garay, a former student and a math professor at the ENP, Barreda admitted he was referring to Minería of an earlier era: Barreda, "Instrucción pública," pp. 332–40.

[14] For Barreda's assessment of Jesuit education see "Carta . . . a Riva Palacio," *Opúsculos*, pp. 28–30, 60–61; "Instrucción pública," p. 285. On *"sacerdocio social"* see "Invitación a los ciudadanos profesores de las escuelas nacionales" (1877), ibid., p. 242. Barreda's admiration for the Jesuits brings to mind Ernest Renan's famous comment that the Jesuit colleges both killed the old universities in France and provided an important model for the

Barreda's emphasis on the professor's social ministry and his allusions to the Jesuits remind us that the aims of positivist education went beyond inculcating a new generation of leaders with a mastery of the methods of science. Intellectual education of the individual must lead to the reconstruction of society. Barreda's first exposure to Comte was in 1849, when the philosopher was beginning what he called his "second career," that is, his application of positive philosophy to social and religious ends. Although the lectures that Barreda presumably heard were never published, they were a summary, according to Littré, of what came to be the final three volumes of Comte's *Système de politique positive* (1853–54) in which he set out his theory of social evolution and the bases of the religion of humanity. Comte sounded the keynote of this second phase of his thought, which became an important premise of positivist education in Mexico, when he asserted in 1848: "Positivism consists essentially of a philosophy and a polity, which are necessarily inseparable. The former is the basis and the latter the end of one universal system, in which intellect and social reconciliation (*l'intelligence et la sociabilité*) become intimately connected." Comte insisted that his two careers were in "perfect harmony." The objective of the first, realized in his *Cours de philosophie positive* (1830–42), was to lay the theoretical philosophical foundation, "out of materials supplied by the sciences," for carrying out the "social objective" of the second career, namely, the creation of a "universal religion."[15]

For positivists the major obstacle to achieving order or social reconstruction through scientific education was anarchy, a condition that prevailed in the difficult transition to the third and positive stage of mental and social evolution. Resulting from the "corrosive action of negativism," the legacy of the "disintegrating doctrines of the eighteenth century," anarchy was all-pervasive, intellectual and moral anarchy as well as political and social anarchy. Díaz Covarrubias saw intellectual anarchy as the "origin of all social and political evils." Anarchy can only be surmounted, insisted Barreda as he began his educational labors, by instituting a "truly universal doctrine that brings together all minds (*todas las inteligencias*)

---

new so-called university, created by Napoleon: See Ernest Renan, "L'Instruction supérieure en France" (1864), *Oeuvres completes*, 10 vols. (Paris, 1947), 1:76.

[15] On Comte's lectures, see Émile Littré, *Auguste Comte et la philosophie positive*, 2d ed. (Paris, 1864), pp. 619–23. The quotation opened Comte's "Discours préliminaire sur l'ensemble du positivisme," first published in 1848 and then included as an introduction to *Système*, vol. 1 (1851). (The "Discours" is the most accessible Comtean text in English: Auguste Comte, *General View of Positivism* [New York, 1957].) I have retranslated the quoted passage. Comte argued for the harmony of his two careers in the preface to *Système*, vol. 1, and in the appendix to vol. 4 where he included as proof several of his early essays (1819–28). Comte said (ibid., 1:2) that his *Cours* should have been titled *Système de philosophie positive*.

in a common synthesis." The philosopher-educator must lead the way by identifying the "painful conflicts" produced by the prevailing anarchy and the social lessons that can be drawn from them.[16] Because of the positivist insistence on the interrelation of all phenomena, surmounting anarchy through science had strong political implications, ones that Comte pursued and ones that were clearly present in Barreda's thought. However, Barreda and his fellow educators did not choose to apply their theories to the specifics of Mexican politics.

There is no better example of unpursued political implications of the positivist educational mission than the activities and philosophic discussions of the short-lived Asociación Metodófila "Gabino Barreda." The group was formed early in the critical year 1877 by twenty-five student disciples of Barreda, mostly in medicine. Many were graduates of the Preparatoria. Their purpose, as stated by Porfirio Parra who had entered the ENP in 1870, was to apply the rigorous logic of scientific method to "every kind of phenomena," as a contribution "to the raising of the great edifice of reconstruction." Parra's optimism was extreme. For him, the scientific method could be a lever of Archimedes to move the world; it could solve all problems, no matter how complex. As applied to social phenomena, the scientific method was the only "sure panacea for the present troubles." This was as close as Parra came to a specific reference to politics. Besides pursuing their own discussions, which we will examine later, these "friends of method" published Barreda's writings as the best example of their purpose. Not only had Barreda brought positive philosophy to Mexico, but he had fought a titan's battle for ten years to implant a system of education, which Parra was confident would create a spiritual bond among the educated.[17] The decade-old positivist educational mission and the doctrine of scientific politics of 1878 had an obvious intellectual affinity and they were bound to intersect. But until 1880 educational philosophy and political ideas followed essentially separate courses.

Gabino Barreda was not an orthodox positivist. He never became a

---

[16] See Barreda, "Discurso leído en la distribución de recompensas escolares" (1877), *Opúsculos*, p. 247; "De La Educación moral" (1863), *Opúsculos*, p. 117; Díaz Covarrubias, *Instrucción pública*, p. ccxxx; Barreda, "Oración cívica" (1867), *Opúsculos*, p. 82. Particularly revealing is the epigraph from Comte, quoted and interpreted by Barreda (see p. 5). See also "La Ley de instrucción pública," *Diario oficial*, 20 January 1868, a positivist statement by José María Bustamante, one of the initial contingent of math professors in the ENP.

[17] See Parra's introduction to *Anales de la asociación metodófila "Gabino Barreda"* (Mexico, 1877), pp. 1–11. He may also have been the author of the anonymous preface to Barreda, *Opúsculos* (1877), pp. i–iv, published by the Asociación. The list of twenty-five student members of the Asociación, plus Barreda as president, includes twenty-one men in medicine, two men in law, and one man each in engineering and pharmacy (*Anales*, p. 12). The group presumably disbanded when Barreda left Mexico in early 1878.

follower of Pierre Lafitte, the self-appointed guardian and perpetuator of Auguste Comte's total philosophical and religious system. Barreda did not attempt to establish a positivist church in Mexico nor did he embrace the idiosyncratic details of Comte's religion of humanity. Nonetheless, the premises or essentials of Comte's creed permeated Barreda's writing and guided his educational philosophy. He accepted implicitly the idea of replacing revealed religion with a proven or positive religion, based on the worship of a real God, humanity, rather than an imaginary one. Like Comte, Barreda envisioned love, that is, altruism or social feeling, as the principle of morality. This social love is innate in men and if properly educated it can prevail over self-love, or egoism. Love is not its own reward, as it is in Christianity, but it can be utilized for human betterment or progress. Besides these assumptions, Barreda also took on the Comtean cult of the holy dead, the great men of the past who were the true servants of humanity.[18]

Barreda devoted his earliest nonmedical essay to "moral education" or ethics, a theme to which he returned frequently during the decade he directed the Preparatoria. Writing first in 1863 at the height of liberal anticlericalism and ideological conflict, Barreda argued the need for a "radical reform," even a "regeneration," in order to instill in future citizens an awareness of their moral as well as their political duties. While recognizing the necessity of separating ethics from Christian theology, Barreda nevertheless lamented the current ascendancy of an "anarchical and immoral skepticism." This skepticism could only cease, he continued, if ethics were made systematic, that is, placed on a basis that was evident, positive, and thus universal. Or, as Díaz Covarrubias put it, ethics should be reduced "to a practical science, with the application of principles or laws scientifically deduced" from "the nature of man and society." Barreda went on to explain that Saint Paul, the founder of Catholicism, identified a perpetual struggle between man's evil nature and God's redeeming grace, thus locating "benevolent inclinations" outside mankind. Such a conclusion, said Barreda, was appropriate to a theological age. Now, however, after eighteen centuries of progress, especially after the recent physiological research of Gall, Broussais, and Bichat, science has located "good" (altruistic) as well as "evil" (egoistic) inclinations within human beings. True moral education should aim to repress egoism

---

[18] In addition to works cited above in chap. 3, n. 76, see D. G. Charlton, *Secular Religions in France, 1815–1870* (London, 1963), pp. 87–95; L. Lévy-Bruhl, *The Philosophy of Auguste Comte* (London, 1903), pp. 303–42. The most convenient brief exposition by Comte of his religion appears in "Discours," *Système*, 1:321–99 (*General View*, chap. 6). On Barreda and the Religion of Humanity, see Aragón, *Essai*, pp. 37–38; González Navarro, "Los Positivistas mexicanos," p. 121. Barreda apparently met Lafitte in France just before his death in 1881.

and to encourage altruism instead of exploiting the former, as all previous religions (including atheism, deism, and pantheism) have done.[19]

Barreda's special hostility was reserved for a liberal and anticlerical text on ethics written by Nicolas Pizarro and presented for use in the Preparatoria.[20] According to Barreda, the book was based on a "vague and incoherent deism," which was one more religious sect, intolerant of all others; and thus the text was inappropriate in a country where the separation of church and state had precluded religious teaching in state schools. From his attack on Pizarro's book it is clear that Barreda, like Comte, had less sympathy for liberal anticlericalism, a product of the age of metaphysics and intellectual anarchy, than he did for traditional Catholicism.[21] Though Barreda was able to prevent the adoption of Pizarro's text, there is no evidence that he tried to substitute a positivist text on ethics in its place. He was probably content to teach his version of ethics orally as a part of his course in logic. After Barreda's departure from the ENP in 1878, the issue of moral education emerged as a part of the major philosophical controversy over the teaching of logic.[22]

"I am only in part a Benthamite," wrote Barreda, responding to the charge in 1875 that the system of ethics he taught was utilitarian and epicurean, that is, predicated on the exclusive pursuit of individual interest and sensual pleasure. Barreda's ambivalence toward Bentham reflected the complex relationship that existed between positivism and utilitarianism. On this occasion Barreda defended the social concern implicit in Bentham's principle of the greatest good for the greatest number, and he rejected the association of utilitarianism with epicurean pursuits. At

[19] Barreda, "De La Educación moral," Opúsculos, pp. 109–17 (first published in El Siglo XIX, 3 May 1863); Díaz Covarrubias, "Plan de estudios," Diario oficial, 11 October 1867 (Díaz y de Ovando, Escuela, 2:9). Barreda also discussed moral education in "Carta dirigida al editor del 'Seminario ilustrado' " (21 October 1868), Opúsculos, pp. 133–42, and in "Discurso . . . recompensas escolares," Opúsculos, pp. 245–48. Franz Joseph Gall (1758–1828), Marie François Xavier Bichat (1771–1802), and François Joseph Victor Broussais (1772–1838), were all physicians who in Comte's view contributed to establishing physiology as a "positive" science, that is, establishing those of its truths that could form the connecting link to the other sciences: see Comte, "Examen du traité de Broussais sur l'irritation" (1828), in Système, 4: 216–28 (appendix).

[20] Nicolás Pizarro, Catecismo de moral (Méjico, 1868). Pizarro (1830–91) was a novelist and prolific propagandist for the liberal cause during the Reforma. His ideas also revealed an infusion of utopian socialism. See Luis Reyes de la Maza, "Nicolás Pizarro, novelista y pensador liberal," Historia mexicana 6 (1957): 572–87. See also p. 215.

[21] Barreda, "Informe presentado a la junta directiva de estudios" (1868?), Opúsculos, pp. 119–21; also "Carta . . . 'seminario ilustrado,' " ibid.

[22] I have frequently translated the terms "la moral" (Spanish) or "la morale" (French) as "ethics," which in nontechnical usage is virtually synonymous with "moral science," "moral philosophy," or "morals," and is often more meaningful than those terms in English. The Spanish and French cognates of "ethics" were rarely used in the nineteenth century.

the same time, Barreda, following Comte, did not accept the utilitarian premise that there was an identification, either natural or artificial, between enlightened self-interest and the general interest. Utilitarian ethics was based on rationally deduced laws of human nature that were independent of historical development ("sheer metaphysics," said the positivists). Comte's system of ethics was historically conditioned, that is, it was derived from the discoveries of science in the positive era. Thus Barreda could take a relativist or tolerant view of past ethical systems as being appropriate to their age, while vigorously rejecting the charge that he was fostering immorality or disbelief. On the contrary, said Barreda, we seek to reawaken belief and moral values where none exist in the present transitional or anarchical stage of history. Barreda implicitly saw utilitarian ethics as giving way to positivist ethics, to a system that took social feeling or sentiment as its universal principle.[23]

In an apparent reaction against utilitarianism, positivist educational and ethical theory accorded a special place to aesthetics. Yet there remained the tendency in practice to subordinate the arts to the sciences in the preparatory school curriculum. In dedicating a highly academic and allegorical mural painted for the school by Juan Cordero, Barreda insisted that it symbolized the "voluntary subjection of science to love," the obedience of the mind to the heart. It was a "glorification of art by science in its own temple." Yet, as Barreda acknowledged, the painting itself idealized "the spirit of science and industry, that is, the peaceful activity of man, both mental and practical." Barreda was following Comte's definition of art as "an ideal representation of fact or reality (ce qui est)." Whereas science "appraises the whole of reality," wrote Comte, art "embellishes it." The painting also bore the Comtean motto "know in order to forsee" (beneath the figure representing science), "forsee in order to work" (beneath the figure representing industry).[24] Clearly the values of utility and practicality did not lose ground in the artistic implementation of positivist theories.

An integral part of the positivist system of ethics and of its foundation in scientific education was the worship of humanity, carried out most tangibly by celebrating the great servants of mankind, "the resurrection of the dead in the soul of the living," as Barreda put it. On numerous oc-

---

[23] Barreda, "Carta dirigida a los redactores de la "revista universal" (1875), *Opúsculos*, pp. 192–94; "Discurso . . . recompensas escolares," *Opúsculos*, pp. 247–48; Parra, introduction to *Anales*, p. 9. Cf. Comte, "Discours," *Système*, 1:91–101 (*General View*, pp. 101–11), a brief exposition of his ethical system.

[24] Barreda, "Discurso . . . laureando al eminente artista, Sr. Juan Cordero" (November 1874), *Opúsculos*, pp. 153–57; Comte, "Discours," *Système*, 1:282–83 (*General View*, p. 314). Cordero's mural was later removed. An illustration can be found in Lemoine, *Escuela*, p. 231.

casions, some of which were officially sponsored by the Preparatoria, Barreda evoked with grandiloquence the accomplishments of these heroes of the past, both national and universal. The short-lived Asociación Metodófila was to devote a meeting every three months to a student paper on a benefactor of humanity; two were actually given, one on Galileo and the other on Dante.[25] *La Libertad* ran biographies of great men periodically beginning in late 1879. In his oration on Alexander Von Humboldt, Barreda said mankind was now sufficiently advanced to relegate military heroes to their proper (subordinate) place. Peace guides our "modern apotheoses," which are frankly human; in them "the present comes to glorify the past in order to improve the future." How different are these servants of humanity, added Barreda on another occasion, from the "egoists of all breeds, whether materialists, theologians, or atheists." Barreda himself became an object of reverence by his students even before his death. On Barreda's birthday in 1878, Parra said that because of his "blessed doctrines," ethics could now be based on "profound conviction, the offspring of vigorous proof," rather than on "blind faith." The cult of Barreda was carried on throughout the century by positivists and then became a persistent theme of Agustín Aragón's *Revista positiva* (1900–14).[26]

Let us review briefly the elements of the positivist system of higher education, espoused by Gabino Barreda and his followers and in large part implemented in the Escuela Nacional Preparatoria during its first decade. The ENP instituted a uniform curriculum for all preprofessional students consisting principally of encyclopedic learning of the sciences in an ordered hierarchy. Such learning was intended to create intellectual order, to surmount anarchy in all its forms, and to provide the key to the reconstruction and ultimately the moral regeneration of society. Throughout the program and its rationale ran an authoritarian strain that was also manifest in the scientific politics of the late 1870s. Barreda extolled the virtues of "homogeneity," of control, even of indoctrination. He evoked the Jesuits as model educators, despite their imperfect mastery of the sciences. Barreda's attack on the ethics text by Pizarro re-

[25] Barreda, "Discurso pronunciado . . . en honor del Barón de Humboldt" (14 September 1869), *Opúsculos*, p. 145; *Anales*, pp. 231–37, 303–15 (6 May and 5 August 1877). See also Barreda, "Discurso . . . en la apoteosis de Don Leopoldo Río de la Loza" (15 November 1877), *Boletín de la instrucción pública* 8 (1907): 447–69 (also in Lemoine, *Escuela*, pp. 215–34); Barreda, "En Los Funerales del Sr. Dr. Miguel Jiménez" (21 May 1876), *Opúsculos*, pp. 231–39. Río de la Loza was a chemistry professor at both San Ildefonso and the Preparatoria; Jiménez was a professor of medicine and Barreda's teacher. Barreda depicted both as pioneers of the scientific method in Mexico.

[26] Barreda, "Discurso . . . Humboldt," *Opúsculos*, p. 146; "Discurso . . . Río de la Loza"; Parra in *La Libertad*, 3 March 1878. Aragón's *Essai* is an excellent example of the Barreda cult.

vealed more tolerance toward traditional Catholicism than toward liberal anticlericalism. Catholicism represented an "organic" and universal system that in a sense Comteans were trying to recreate in the new and positive stage of history. Liberalism represented a "critical" and negative system, a necessary phase, perhaps, in the overall scheme of evolution, but at present one that was only productive of disorganization and anarchy. Order and progress—the compatibility of mental and social order and scientific progress—was the frequently enunciated Comtean motto of the positivist educational enterprise.

Besides being authoritarian, the system of the Preparatoria was clearly oriented toward educating a new elite to guide Mexico in the positive era. Although both Barreda and Díaz Covarrubias maintained that the ENP would break down traditional barriers in Mexican society, it was not democracy that they envisioned but rather a kind of meritocracy that would be consistent with Mexican mores. For Barreda, the "fusion" of all preparatory students in a single school would erase "all distinction of race and origin among Mexicans," create "intimate fraternal ties" among the students, and promote "new connections among families." Díaz Covarrubias argued that the traditional division between those trained in professional specialities and those who were ignorant of them would give way to the spreading of science "to all those who aspire to cultivate their minds and enter the select of society."[27] This select group, drawn from various traditional sectors, would emerge as the technocratic managers of the new social order, "capitalists" in Comte's terminology, *industriels* in Saint-Simon's. This positivist vision of social organization was more hinted at than explicitly developed by the Mexicans. Nonetheless, it formed an important element in the ENP system.

It is important to recall that the educational program of the Preparatory School was government-directed and -controlled. As such it was a departure from the Comtean ideal of the disestablishment of education from the state. Comte's "positive polity" envisioned coextensive but separate temporal and spiritual powers. The latter was to consist of positive philosophers, who as priests of the religion of humanity had sole authority over education. Barreda revealed some inclination toward Comte's ideal in his reference to the professor's "social priesthood," in his use of the Jesuit model, in his defense of the Junta Directiva de Instrucción Pública (see below), and in his generally benign attitude toward Catholicism. However, the imperatives of Mexican politics, particularly the cardinal reform principle of secularization, made positivists (despite their muted anticlericalism) champions of "the state as educator (*el estado do-*

[27] Barreda, "Carta . . . a Riva Palacio," *Opúsculos*, p. 65; Díaz Covarrubias, *Instrucción pública*, p. cxcvi–viii.

cente)." In his 1863 essay Barreda emphasized that while the government should not intervene in the religion of its subjects, "it can and must intervene in their moral education, appropriate to the demands of society and civilization."[28] Although the precise relationship between the government and higher education became a subject of continual debate and controversy after 1867, the principle of state control won general acceptance within the liberal establishment.

The ENP completed its first decade in a national climate of heightened scientific awareness, an awareness in large part stimulated by Barreda and his followers themselves. A generation later, Porfirio Parra characterized the decade in Comtean terms as the onset of the "epoch of general scientific culture" in Mexico, when "specialization" or isolated scientific work by lone investigators gave way to "synthesis," or a bringing together of "science and philosophy."[29] He could have been recalling the sessions of the Asociación Metodófila, in which he himself had been a leader. Besides producing papers on astronomy, chemistry, or the conservation of energy, the meetings provided a forum for the first major discussion in Mexico of Charles Darwin's biological theories. The rigor of the debate, which found Barreda opposed to Darwinism in contrast to several of his students, was testimony to the impact of the new biology.[30]

Further evidence of the changing scientific climate in Mexico was the appearance of numerous scientific and technical journals. One prominent example was Santiago Sierra's *El Mundo científico* (1877), a serious weekly devoted to the "popularization of the sciences," which Sierra maintained was virtually nonexistent in Mexico.[31] Though it only ran for six months, *El Mundo*'s range was wide. Its articles covered subjects both theoretical and applied written by Mexicans and by Europeans. Sierra himself was a principal contributor, noting in one article the need for better sanitary conditions in Mexico City, deploring in another official indifference to a typhus epidemic, calling in still others for a national observatory and for the creation of an official polytechnic institute that would consolidate existing scientific associations and academies. He also wrote profiles of leading European geologists and he presented an enrap-

[28] Díaz Covarrubias defended *el estado docente* in ibid., pp. cxlix–cl. Barreda's statement appeared in "De La Educación moral," *Opúsculos*, p. 115.

[29] Parra, "La Ciencia en México" (1902), in Sierra, *México*, 1:458.

[30] See Roberto Moreno, introduction to *La Polémica del darwinismo en México. Siglo XIX* (Mexico, 1984), pp. 17–42, an essay first published in 1975 (also in English in *The Comparative Reception of Darwinism*, ed. Thomas F. Glick [Austin, 1974], pp. 346–74). We will examine this debate, recorded in *Anales*, pp. 97–186, in chap. 7. On general scientific activity, see also Eli de Gortari, *La Ciencia en la historia de México* (Mexico, 1963), pp. 316ff.

[31] *El Mundo científico. Revista de las ciencias y de sus aplicaciones a las artes y a la industria* (2 June 1877–26 January 1878).

tured monthly description of the night sky. In January 1878 Sierra brought his scientific enthusiasm to the board of the newly founded *La Libertad*, whose mission was broader and more ambitious—the explicit application of science to national politics. Nonetheless, *El Mundo's* more specific agenda was perpetuated in *La Libertad's* "scientific section," directed by the young leaders of the Asociación Metodófila, Luis E. Ruiz, Manuel Flores, and Parra. The culture of science had now taken center stage in Mexico City.

The institution that did the most to promote this new scientific culture became a focus of controversy from its earliest days. The resistance to the ENP came from Catholics and liberals, from outside the government and within, and from students and parents. The grounds for this resistance were both theoretical and practical. Although the critical years for the ENP and for its educational philosophy were the early 1880s when opposition reached its height, we can nonetheless find in the previous decade the elements of controversy.

Catholic hostility to the positivist system of education was fundamental, though not loudly articulated before 1883. The triumph of the liberal and republican cause in 1867 and its identification with *la patria* left political conservatism powerless. The official culture that emerged during the Restored Republic was secular and anticlerical, despite the conciliatory efforts of the Juárez government to heal the wounds of civil war. What had earlier been a comprehensive ideology of political conservatism combining reverence for the Spanish colonial system, the promotion of monarchy, and the defense of the church's traditional role in society became after 1867 a more limited espousal of traditional social and educational values in the name of religion. The new National Preparatory School and its philosophy was clearly anathema to the church hierarchy: "Positivism is not only a blasphemy," wrote an outspoken ecclesiastic from Puebla, "[it is] the most atrocious calumny that can be launched against Catholicism." Science, in the atheistic scheme of Auguste Comte, has become a religion, complete with its priesthood and its sacramental system. But, concluded the cleric, the history of civilization has demonstrated that true "positive science" must spring from the word of the gospel.[32]

Such sentiments were also present in Mexico City, but were muted in two newspapers that sprang from the Sociedad Católica, founded in December 1868. One of the papers, *La Voz de México*, became the bulwark of the Catholic press for a generation. The early issues of *La Voz* bemoaned "the excesses and disasters which accompany liberalism,"

[32] F. N. V., "El Positivismo" and "La Ciencia positiva," *La Revista eclesiástica* (Puebla), 25 July, 1 August 1868.

namely the threat of "social dissolution"; and they called for a revival of authority ultimately "subject to moral and divine law." Though the ENP was not the direct target of Catholic rhetoric in 1870, the society did establish a competing Escuela Preparatoria Católica. By 1878, the school (and the Sociedad Católica) had ceased to exist, but *La Voz* was attacking the ENP more openly. The paper refuted what it called the pedagogical pretentions of the Preparatoria to fill the place "abandoned" by Catholicism. There has been no such abandonment, said *La Voz*; belief in redemption by the crucified Lord "still lives on in Mexican hearts" and continues to be the basis of education. The paper consistently claimed that it was abstaining from politics, that its only concern was to defend the church and *la patria*, the one our guide in the "spiritual order," the other in the "social."[33] Catholics found positivist educational philosophy particularly insidious because its advocates appeared to be more tolerant toward the Catholic heritage than toward liberal anticlericalism (that is, than toward "anarchy"), while at the same time promoting a secular religion based on humanity and an ethical system based on science. Catholic opposition to the ENP and its philosophy increased in the early 1880s, and, ironically, even found some common ground with the opposition from the liberals.

The objections from within the governing group to the curriculum of the Preparatoria were most often made in the name of the constitutional principle of freedom of teaching, as stated in article 3, and they took the form of parliamentary efforts to "reform" the educational law of 1867–69. Among their objections, it is difficult to distinguish the theoretical from the practical, that is, the opposition to the official imposition of a uniform curriculum, guided by a single philosophy of education, from the opposition to the requiring of subjects deemed unnecessary as preparation for one or another career. The notion of higher education exclusively as preparation for a career was deeply rooted, and resistance to a burdensome and costly prolonging of that preparation was intense. The interests of many were adversely affected by the new plan of studies.

The first attempt to modify the plan came in a proposal of 1872, two of whose sponsors, Manuel Dublán and Guillermo Prieto, were stalwarts of

[33] *La Voz de México. Diario político, religioso, científico y literario de la 'Soc. Católica,'* 17 April 1870 (the initial issue); 1, 24 January 1878. *La Voz* ceased as organ of the Sociedad in 1875 when it became more political; but it ran until 1908. The other paper, the fortnightly *La Sociedad católica*, ran from 1869 to 1873. The initial issue of *La Voz* carried an ad for the Catholic Preparatory School, directed by Tomás Sierra y Rosso. On the Catholic press and the Sociedad Católica, see Jorge Adame Goddard, *El Pensamiento político y social de los católicos mexicanos, 1867–1914* (Mexico, 1981), pp. 19–27. See also Emeterio Valverde Téllez, *Apuntaciones históricas sobre la filosofía en México* (Mexico, 1896), pp. 301–06, and his *Bibliografía filosófica mexicana* (León, 1913), 1:212–18.

the Juárez regime. The proposal, which aroused, as we have seen, a major defense of the ENP system by Gabino Barreda, set "absolute" freedom of teaching as the basis for public instruction. According to the proposal, this principle should mean that the only requirement for a license to practice a profession would be "proof of competence," and not "the study of unrelated sciences." The interpretation of article 3 was at the root of much of the controversy over education and especially over the curriculum of the Preparatoria. On the one hand, the article upheld academic freedom and the freedom of expression, cardinal principles of the liberal system. On the other hand, the article inhibited state surveillance or control of education, which was central to secularization, the major goal of the Reforma. The problem of interpretation had been revealed in the debate on article 3 in the constituent congress, but in the libertarian climate of 1856 the measure, deemed one of the "rights of man," passed readily. The constitution-makers generally regarded the second sentence of the article giving the government power to set requirements for professional licenses (*títulos*) as sufficient control against "charlatanism," whether lay or clerical.[34]

The direct inspiration for article 3 was probably article 9 of the French republican constitution of 1848. In the French case, however, teaching was made "free" but also subject to the "surveillance of the state," which was to extend without exception to all educational establishments. The French republicans were at once conceding the important role of the church in French education while at the same time explicitly affirming the principle of state supremacy. The article, taken together with the Falloux Law of 1849, recognized a basic partnership between church and state in the educational process. Such recognition could never be made by liberals in Mexico, where the state's role in education was traditionally weak and the church's strong. Nonetheless, the constitution-makers avoided confronting "the clerical monopoly" (as they called it) directly, relying optimistically instead on the free flow of ideas to undermine it. This laissez-faire attitude soon gave way to the liberal drive for state supremacy inherent in the Laws of Reform; but article 3 remained unchanged. Thus, the educational debates of the seventies and eighties incorporated both sides of the classic liberal program, the guarantee of constitutional liberties of 1856–57 and the state-directed reform of 1859

[34] The text of the brief proposal can be found in *Revista positiva* 1 (1901): 257, reprinted from the *Diario oficial*, 22 September 1872; it is followed by Barreda's "Instrucción pública." The text of article 3 (article 18 of the draft constitution) was: "Teaching is free. The law will determine which professions need a license to be practiced and the requirements to be set." The debate on the article took place on 11 August 1856 and is summarized in Zarco, *Historia del congreso extraordinario constituyente, 1856–1857*, 3d ed. (Mexico, 1956), pp. 713–25.

to 1863. However, because of what appeared to be the complete triumph of the Liberal party in 1867, the governmental debate over freedom of teaching in Mexico, unlike France, was essentially secular and did not involve the church.[35]

The efforts of the 1870s to introduce a new law of public instruction were vigorous but ultimately ineffective, and the National Preparatory School, the principal target of legislative change, managed to survive. The proposal of 1872 won support; for example, it got the strong approval of *El Monitor republicano*, which attacked the "encyclopedic system" of the Preparatoria.[36] The formal bill, which first appeared in the Chamber of Deputies in November 1874, began with a reaffirmation of article 3, stating that professors were free to teach any doctrines whatsoever as long as they were not contrary to "universal morality." This statement was followed by an article abolishing the ENP. In the second, modified, version of the bill introduced a year later, no provision was made for a separate preparatory school; yet the subjects of its scientific curriculum were termed "indispensable," that is, required for all professional schools. History, literature, and elements of Greek were termed "voluntary." The portions of the bill pertaining to higher education never reached the floor for debate, probably because of the political upheaval of 1876–77.[37] The first Díaz regime modified some ENP requirements in 1877 (for example, future lawyers needed only to take zoology and not biology; lawyers, doctors, and pharmacists needed only to take linear and not spherical trigonometry), but these modifications were minor. Basically, Ministers Ignacio Ramírez and Protasio Tagle were sympathetic toward the school and its philosophy, if not toward its director.[38]

[35] On the French experience, see Joseph N. Moody, *French Education Since Napoleon* (Syracuse, 1978), pp. 49–57.

[36] "Juvenal" (Enrique Chávarri) in *El Monitor*, 24 September 1872 (Díaz y de Ovando, *Escuela*, 1:34).

[37] The first reading of the "Proyecto de ley de instrucción pública" was on 16 November 1874: *Diario de los debates*, 7th congress, 3:570–80. Four days later two of the bill's sponsors, Juan Palacios and Guillermo Prieto, proposed an interim measure abolishing the ENP immediately (p. 607). The second version of the bill was introduced on 9 October 1875 (*Diario de los debates*, 8th congress, 1st ser., 2 vols. (Mexico, 1875–85), 1:154–62). Debate began on 25 October (p. 267) and ended on 11 December, when the part pertaining to primary education was approved and sent to the Senate (pp. 675–77). See chap. 7, n. 42. The part on secondary and professional education apparently was not debated further.

[38] The various regulations issued by Ramírez and Tagle can be found in Dublán and Lozano, *Legislación*, 13:127–48, 153–54, 721–27; the one reorganizing the math courses can be found in *Revista de la instrucción pública mexicana*, 1:100–01 (1 May 1896). Note particularly the positivist statement by Ramírez on 6 January 1877 (Dublán and Lozano, *Legislación*, 13:130). These regulations both confirmed and rescinded changes that had been made in a congressional decree of 22 October 1873. See *Revista de la instrucción pública*,

Gabino Barreda became the indirect target of another provision of the proposal of 1872 and the subsequent bills, namely the weakening and ultimately the abolition of the Junta Directiva de Instrucción Pública, the governing board established in the 1867 law. The junta had broad administrative powers and was to make recommendations to the minister of justice on a variety of policy questions, including textbooks, budgets, professional titles, scholarships, and internal regulations for the various schools. Though the minister was ex-officio chairman, the junta was composed of elected professors and the directors of the national schools, one of whom was to serve as vice-chairman. Though Barreda apparently never held this post, his influence on the junta was strong, in part because of the central place of the ENP in the educational system. This influence was revealed, for example, in a recommendation by the junta in 1870 that ENP regulations be tightened so that students would be obliged to pass exams in all preparatory subjects, whatever their future professional studies might be. The report complained that the ENP program was being undermined by student and parental resistance to the uniform curriculum.[39]

The educational bill of 1874 identified the Junta Directiva as "the obstacle to the development and advance of education" and transferred its functions directly to the minister of justice. By doing this, higher education could be made more directly responsive to public (that is, student and parent) interests. The junta in effect insulated the ENP and its uniform positivist curriculum from such pressure. The advocates of the change proposed it in the name of the freedom of teaching versus monopoly, even though their action would bring higher education more directly under governmental control. For positivists having the Junta Directiva under their influence may have represented, as Leopoldo Zea has argued, Comte's spiritual power in society.[40] Again, it should be noted, however, that in the debate over the Junta Directiva the principle of state control of higher education was not at issue, only the precise definition

---

1:68 (15 April 1896). Most notably the 1877 decrees restored required chemistry for lawyers.

[39] See articles 53–58 of the law of 2 December 1867: Dublán and Lozano, *Legislación*, 10:201–02. The recommendation appeared in a report (dated 5 February 1870) by Ramón I. Alcaraz, vice-chairman of the Junta Directiva, in *Memoria . . . de justicia y instrucción pública . . . 1869* (Mexico, 1870), pp. 218–19. Alcaraz (1823–85) was a man of letters and close collaborator of Juárez from pre-1867 days who served as director of the School of Fine Arts and the National Museum, *oficial mayor* of the ministry, and interim minister in 1872–73. There is no evidence that he opposed the ENP or Barreda.

[40] See the prologue to the 1874 bill: *Diario de los debates*, 7th congress, 3:572, plus articles 97–99 (p. 580). Barreda had made a strong defense of the Junta Directiva in response to the milder proposal of 1872 that teaching faculty be eliminated from the junta: "Instrucción pública," pp. 268–74. For Zea's argument, see *Positivismo*, pp. 140–42.

of that control. This subtle question also guided the suggestions for an autonomous university, which had their origin in this era, as we will see below. Though the "reformers" of the seventies failed in their efforts to abolish the ENP or the Junta Directiva, they did manage to influence the removal of Barreda, who resigned from the ENP and accepted a diplomatic post to Germany in February 1878.

To understand more clearly the early opposition to the positivist system of higher education, let us examine the case of Justo Sierra. Between 1874 and 1878 Sierra turned from being a friendly critic of the National Preparatory School to becoming one of its leading apologists. His lifelong engagement in the theory and practice of education began during these years, an engagement that ultimately made him *El Maestro*, the universally respected statesman of the nation's educational system. The change in his ideas on higher education during the 1870s ran parallel to the change in his political ideas examined in chapter 3. He embraced positivist education as he embraced scientific politics, not as an unquestioning devotee but always with a good measure of ambivalence. In education, as in politics, the ideas of Justo Sierra exemplify the complex relationship between positivism and liberalism during the years 1867 to 1910.

Sierra's principal criticism of the Preparatoria in his early writings was directed against the elimination of philosophy, that is, metaphysics, from the curriculum and its replacement by logic. For him, this change revealed "the spirit of positivist exclusivism that reigns in the development of the plan of studies." It constitutes a "monopoly," the exercise of a "despotic pressure" on the minds of students that is contrary to "the spirit of our institutions." Such teaching, he added, is enough to call into rebellion "all that there is of dignity and independence in the soul."[41] These were strong words, ones that were taken up in the early 1880s by the enemies of the Preparatoria and of positivism. But Sierra was no enemy. He did point readily to this philosophic exclusivism and to other defects in the curriculum: Mill's *Logic* was simply too heavy going for teenagers; the math course was too fast and too demanding; Latin and Greek were minimal; literary studies were "exceedingly slack and slipshod"; history as a subject hardly existed. At the same time, Sierra defended against Catholics and against traditional careerists what he construed as the basic objective of the ENP system: to establish a scientific education that was abreast of modern progress; or as he repeatedly put it, an education that before forming lawyers, physicians, and engineers would form men.

---

[41] Sierra, "Un Plan de estudios en ruina," *La Tribuna*, 9 January 1874 (*Obras*, 8:14). Sierra's colleague on *La Tribuna*, Jorge Hammeken alluded in 1878 to their "spiritualist" critique of positivism, which culminated in the successful effort to introduce the history of philosophy into the curriculum: "La Philosophie positive au Mexique," p. 210 (see also pp. 84–85).

Soon after his attack upon positivist exclusivism, Sierra paid a visit to the Preparatoria, now housed in San Ildefonso, his old school. Though the visit evoked nostalgia and some pain at finding familiar haunts eliminated, he left generally impressed by the changes. He reported on the well-appointed and outfitted laboratories, the expanded gymnasium, and on the decorum kept by four hundred students in contrast to the turbulence of a hundred in his own day. He interpreted the change in behavior as a dedication to study and to science in the new generation of students. Later that same month he reported with enthusiasm on "an intimate fiesta" given by professors and students of the ENP for Gabino Barreda, and he summarized sympathetically speeches by Eduardo Garay and José Díaz Covarrubias and by Barreda himself. He agreed with Barreda that instruction would benefit greatly by "the adoption of a method founded on facts, that is to say, on the truth, instead of on the stale and arbitrary systems of the past."[42]

Despite Sierra's admiration for the pedagogical objectives of the ENP and for the systematic teaching of the sciences in its curriculum, he continued to express reservations about what he called its "philosophy." He emphasized his belief in "liberty" and "human personality," which he said had a place among "the positive truths." He cited Claude Bernard, Marcelin Berthelot, and Émile Littré, eminent men of science (and positivists) who had identified a realm of the spirit beyond the reaches of the experimental method. His clear implication was that this basic truth was not being recognized by the zealous and even dogmatic Mexican disciples of Auguste Comte. Sierra's solution for this defect in the ENP system was to urge a course in the history of philosophy, so that "those who are going to be men can learn what other men have thought and what influence they have had on the destiny of societies."[43] Guillermo Prieto, the liberal author of the several measures to abolish the ENP, took up Sierra's proposal and successfully had a professorship in the history of philosophy written into the 1875 budget. He found it difficult to understand, he said, how Congress could have authorized the "official" teaching of "this positivist school [of Comte and Mill] which is so tyrannical." The new course was duly incorporated into the curriculum, but without apparently disturbing its positivist "homogeneity"; for the first instructor appointed for

[42] Sierra, "Una Visita a la escuela preparatoria," *La Tribuna*, 7 February 1874 (*Obras*, 8:14–18); "Una Fiesta íntima," *La Tribuna*, 26 February 1874 (*Obras*, 8:23).

[43] Sierra, "El Nuevo Plan de estudios" [i.e., the bill of 9 October, discussed above], *El Federalista*, 19 October 1875 (*Obras*, 8:42); "Una fiesta," (ibid., p. 23), in which he quoted (but did not identify) a passage from Littré, that began: "What is beyond is absolutely inaccessible to the human mind, but inaccessible does not mean null or non-existent." Its source was Littré, *Auguste Comte*, p. 519. See also Sierra, "Un Plan de estudios," *La Tribuna*, 9 January 1874 (*Obras*, 8:14).

it was the young physician Adrián Segura, a member of the Asociación Metodófila "Gabino Barreda"![44] Sierra's proposal revealed one of his basic intellectual characteristics, a flexibility of thought and a resistance to doctrinal rigidity, which he had acquired through the study of history.

The debate over the organization and objectives of secondary and professional education in which Justo Sierra became an increasingly active participant was sharpened in the year 1875 by a brief student rebellion. It began as a protest by a few students in the School of Medicine against the teaching methods of Dr. Rafael Lavista, and it resulted in a general strike by students in most of the schools (including the ENP) from 26 April through 8 May. The strike was precipitated by the expulsion of the top three boarding students (*internados*) in medicine and the removal of their scholarships. During the strike the students set up a "free university" in the Alameda, taught many courses themselves, and found sympathetic professors to teach others. Although the rebellion did not directly involve the National Preparatory School and its positivist curriculum, it did serve as a catalyst for the discussion of three subsidiary issues that were related to the controversy: the institution of the *internado* and its place in the schools; education versus instruction; and the overall relation between higher education and the state. Sierra became engaged in each of these issues and like many other liberal and positivist intellectuals of the day he supported the students' cause.[45]

One reason why the students of 1875 elicited such broad support was that it was difficult to oppose their slogan, "*la enseñanza libre,*" that is, their interpretation of article 3 to mean generally a greater degree of curricular and extracurricular freedom for themselves as students. Their manifestos attacked outworn pedagogy and heavy-handed intervention in the schools. The government, they said, "adheres only to ancient practices, the dismal legacy of Spanish domination." Their impulse to strike "arose from profound and intimate convictions, studied in the works of Stuart Mill and H. Abrens [sic], and from the redeeming principles of [17]93." They would push on without turning back, "taking as their motto that sociological and positive law: progress and order."[46] This eclectic

---

[44] Prieto's successful proposal can be found in the discussion of the ENP budget in the Chamber of Deputies on 17 May 1875 (*Diario de los debates*, 7th congress, 4:360). Press coverage on the new course is documented in Díaz y de Ovando, *Escuela*, 1:57–59; 2:65–66.

[45] For further details on the strike and documents from the press, see María del Carmen Ruiz Castañeda, "La Universidad libre (1875), antecedente de la universidad autónoma," *Deslinde* 110 (1979): 1–35. I am grateful to Maestra Ruiz Castañeda for providing me copies of additional documents from the press on this episode. See also Díaz y de Ovando, *Escuela*, 1:50–59; 2:61–65.

[46] "Manifiesto" of 29 April 1875, cited in Ruiz Castañeda, "La Universidad libre," p. 13; "El Porvenir es nuestro" (3 May 1875), in ibid., p. 18 (originally in *La Enseñanza libre*, a

"ideology" (like their leadership and outside support) seemed drawn equally from positivists and liberals, from positive philosophy and metaphysics. Several student leaders were from Barreda's circle; yet one of their articulate champions was Ignacio M. Altamirano, the quintessential "old" liberal. In fact it is difficult to identify opponents of the students' cause, further evidence that the movement was tangential to the controversy over the ENP, and that it was directed toward educational practice and not toward theory.

The movement's most concrete objective was the abolition of the *internado*, a symbol of traditionalism and oppression for post-Reforma students. Those who defended the institution, which created a group of state-subsidized and regimented boarding students in each school, argued that many parents indeed wanted to "confine" (*encerrar*) their children and should be allowed to do so, that students learned more effectively under discipline without distractions, and that the *internado* provided an opportunity for poor students to better themselves (socially and educationally). For the opponents, such as Manuel Rocha, leader of the student rebels, the *internado* inhibited healthy social interaction and relations between the sexes, which could only come about as a result of normal family life during adolescence. Moreover, the *internado* was reminiscent of the Jesuits and thus out of tune with the times. The institution had been partially abolished in article 91 of the law of 2 December 1867, by which boarding students were limited to those without relatives in the capital; but it was reinstated by Congress on 27 December (by rescinding article 91), over the vigorous objections of deputies Barreda and Díaz Covarrubias. The educational bills of 1874–75 called for the abolition of the *internado*, which was accomplished finally by special decree in 1877 except in the ENP and the School of Agriculture. The confusing positions taken on the issue of the *internado* suggest that they involved attitudes toward mores and social values rather than formal educational philosophy.[47]

The concrete question of the *internado* led into the broader issue of education versus instruction. The issue is a difficult one to grasp, particularly for the Anglo-American observer. First of all, it is a dated issue, less compelling today than it was in the nineteenth century. Secondly, it involves terms that carry more significant differences of meaning in Span-

---

now-lost student publication). Heinrich Ahrens (1808–74) was a German popularizer of the philosophy of K.C.F. Krause (see p. 174).

[47] See Rocha, "El Porqué de la abolición del internado," *La Universidad libre*, 26 May and 2 June 1875. The short-lived student weekly ran from 26 May to 30 June. For the debate on the measure to rescind article 91, see *Diario de los debates*, 4th congress, 4 vols. (Mexico, 1872–74), 1:111–14; for the subsequent decree, dated 2 January 1868, see Dublán and Lozano, *Legislación*, 10:224. For the decree of 1 February 1877, see ibid., 13:153–54.

ish (and in French) than do their cognates in English, reflecting of course the fact that the issue itself has been more compelling in Hispanic countries and in France than in the United States and England.[48] Like the question of the *internado*, this tangled issue did not pertain directly to the controversy over the National Preparatory School and its positivist curriculum. Nonetheless, that controversy did lie just below the surface of the discussion. It is significant that the issue of education versus instruction was of considerable importance to Barreda, Díaz Covarrubias, and Sierra, the leading educational spokesmen of the day.

In Mexico the issue was a product of the anticlerical program of secularization initiated during the Reforma, the replacement of the church by the state as principal educator. Was the role of the state to educate, that is, to form character and values, or merely to instruct, that is, to train the mind? "The clergy," said Sierra, "does not instruct, it educates," and traditionally the most effective clerical educators were the Jesuits, especially through the institution of the *internado*. Could the state replace the clergy (especially the Jesuits) as educators without contradicting article 3 and thus the cardinal liberal principle of *enseñanza libre*? Díaz Covarrubias in attacking the *internado* said that it continued to exist because of a "lamentable confusion between education and instruction, . . . principally in the nations of Latin race." For him, the state should instruct the mind, whereas education (even for students of ages twelve to twenty-two) should be left to parents. Otherwise, the state would be trying to perpetuate the work of the Jesuits. As we have seen, Díaz Covarrubias did refer to *el estado docente*, but for him this role was synonymous with "public instruction," not education.[49]

Sierra was more ambivalent. He initially agreed with the students (and with Díaz Covarrubias) that the *internado* should be abolished and for the same reasons. Later he modified his view, noting the desirability of having students from all over the republic and from different social backgrounds able to join in a common experience of learning in the capital. He had had this experience himself as a youth from Campeche, and he clung to it with a bittersweet nostalgia. He also questioned Díaz Covarrubias's sharp distinction between instruction and education, arguing

[48] For a characteristic French discussion, see Charles Robin, "Des Rapports de l'éducation avec l'instruction," *La Philosophie positive* 17 (1876): 25–48, 161–91, 305–36; 18 (1877): 5–18. An added difficulty in terminology is that the more neutral *enseñanza* (French *enseignement*), as in the famous article 3: *La Enseñanza es libre*, does not have an English cognate and is hard to translate. "Education" is probably the best translation, although "teaching" is more literal (and more awkward).

[49] Sierra, "Libertad de instrucción," *El Federalista*, 30 April 1875 (*Obras*, 8:34); Díaz Covarrubias, *Instrucción pública* (1875), pp. clvi–clxix. This discussion was reprinted as "El Internado" in *Revista positiva* 2 (1902): 477–82.

that the two were intertwined. Instruction by the state, he said, is constantly modifying the education that comes from the family. For example, the teaching of the scientific method, which rejects miracles, is an indirect refutation of supernatural religion. One must realize, he added, that "the study of the sciences influences the discipline of the mind and that this discipline in turn influences the formation of character." And concluding, he asserted: "No, instruction is not the whole of education, it is only the most noble part of it." In discussing the value of patriotic celebrations promoted by the government, Sierra went even further by expressing his conviction that the state had a "mission, . . . that of educator of the people."[50]

Gabino Barreda did not address the question of education versus instruction directly, but his position was perhaps the clearest of the three. Quoting Comte, he envisioned the ENP system as one of education derived from the scientific method as opposed to mere instruction. This conception is revealed in his praise of the Jesuits, in his characterization of the professor's "social mission," and in his insertion of the elements of Comte's religion of humanity into his philosophy of education. Still Barreda was unclear about the precise role of the state. Even though the ENP was an official school, and even though Barreda as early as 1863 spoke of the state as educator, there always remained in his philosophy of education the influence of Comte's ideal of distinct temporal and spiritual powers in society.[51]

This leads us to the third issue brought to the surface by the student revolt of 1875, the overall relation of higher education to the state. Besides the abolition of the *internado*, the students called for a "free university," one that in some undefined way would be independent of the state. For them such an institution was the implementation of article 3 of the principle of *enseñanza libre*. For Sierra, article 3, taken together with article 4 that established freedom of profession and employment was the impetus for the "constant advancement of higher education through lib-

---

[50] Sierra, "El Internado," *El Federalista*, 14 December 1875 (*Obras*, 8:58); "Educación e instrucción," *El Federalista*, 23 November 1875 (*Obras*, 8:50–52); "Las Fiestas de la república," *El Federalista*, 21 September 1875 (*Obras*, 8:37). Sierra mixed the two terms in his educational writings, except when he was making an explicit effort to distinguish between them. It should be noted that between 1868 and 1875, 49 percent of ENP students came from outside the Federal District: Dias, "Conformación social," p. 261.

[51] Agustín Aragón insisted that Barreda adhered consistently to the Comtean ideal, a conviction that made him hostile to the *internado*: see Aragón, "Un Documento histórico," *Revista positiva* 5 (1905): 238. Aragón's argument is not totally convincing because Barreda's sympathy for the Jesuits and his emphasis on the need for education versus instruction would suggest support for the *internado*. Francisco Cosmes, a strong advocate of the *internado*, cited Barreda's opposition to it as the one defect in his otherwise admirable education plan of 1867: *Historia*, 1:134–38.

erty." He went on to assert that "independent" higher education "is the true key to any system of free education," and he cited as a model the creation in Germany of "free universities subsidized by the state." He voiced strong criticism of the 1875 education bill, which by eliminating the Junta Directiva de Instrucción Pública would have transferred the authority of the faculty (for example, to set degree and license requirements) directly to the executive power.[52] Though Sierra's call for a free university, like that of most of the students, was derived from liberal and constitutional premises, it did not necessarily conflict with the ideas of positivists. Though Barreda was curiously silent on the student strike of 1875, his disciple Miguel S. Macedo, one of its leaders, made a revealing retrospective comment. The objective of the strike, he said in 1877, was no less than:

> the emancipation of science from the tutelage of the state, just as it has been emancipated from the church. This emancipation is totally in accord with the social regime of positivism, which looks to the savant not only when he occupies the podium, but also when he is elevated to the first rank of authority, entrusted with the direction of society.[53]

Perhaps the origins of the idea of the autonomous university in Mexico must be sought in positivism, that is, in the Comtean conception of the spiritual power as well as in the liberal ideals of the Constitution of 1857.

In the midst of the controversy of 1875 over the goals and the organization of higher education, Justo Sierra and Gabino Barreda experienced their only direct confrontation, a now-famous polemical interchange. Although it pertained more directly to history and politics than to education, the debate pointed up further Sierra's early ambivalence toward positivism as well as some significant differences in the two men's assumptions. The debate also demonstrated the close relation between educational policy and politics, a theme we will return to in chapter 6. The interchange grew out of Sierra's "historical rectifications," made on an incidental analogy that appeared in the course of an essay by Barreda on primary education. After generally agreeing with Barreda's argument that public primary education ought to be made obligatory nationwide, Sierra reacted sharply to his statement that arbitrary methods of primary instruction were the same as those used by Mohammed or Robespierre in imposing their dogmas, "theological" in the first case, "ontological" (or "metaphysical") in the second. According to Barreda, both had resorted

[52] Sierra, "Libertad de instrucción," *El Federalista*, 30 April 1875 (*Obras*, 8:34–36); "La Instrucción secundaria en el proyecto de plan de estudios," *El Federalista*, 26 October 1875 (*Obras*, 8:45).

[53] Macedo, "Ensayo sobre los deberes recíprocos de los superiores y de los inferiores," *Anales*, p. 226 (17 July 1877).

to the "substitution of superhuman authority for conviction based on utility," that is, on facts and experience. In short, their method was "believe or I'll kill you." Barreda went on to assert, to the great consternation of Sierra, that "the bloody Robespierre is the Mohammed of ontological politics, just as Mohammed is the Robespierre of theological politics." The subsequent polemic filled five articles, though little more was said about primary education.[54]

Sierra strongly objected to Barreda's comparison of Mohammed to Robespierre. Without denying the evils of the reign of terror, Sierra defended Robespierre for his compassion and moderation in comparison with the ultraterrorists, those who finally executed him. Sierra also defended "the irreproachable austerity of [Robespierre's] life and his terrible but immense love for the French Revolution, *alma parens* of the modern world." Moreover, Robespierre was more the utilitarian than the ontologist; he instituted the terror more to implement liberty and democracy than because of his belief in the supreme being, that is, in Barreda's "superhuman authority." The historical detail on the revolution introduced by Sierra is impressive. Sierra had attended the French Lycée in Mexico City on first coming from Campeche in 1861–62 and had devoured Lamartine's *Les Girondins*, which he later called "the Bible of fifteen-year-old revolutionaries." He had "breathed" the "atmosphere" of the revolution since he was young, he said; his reasoning had "marched forward, like the battalions at Jemmappes, to the beat of the *Marseillaise*." The revolution was the source of his "philosophical and social convictions"; it nourished his youthful passion for "liberty and justice."[55] Though Sierra's interpretation of the French Revolution was to change markedly within two years, his youthful romantic attachment to its ideals never entirely left him.

The historical debate brought to the surface many of Sierra's general questions about positivism, and these appear scattered throughout his articles. For example, he objected to Barreda's tone, that of a "combative savant" who pins labels such as "ontologist" or "metaphysician" on his opponents; it is "the fanaticism of antifanaticism." Moreover, such ab-

---

[54] Barreda, "Algunas ideas respecto de instrucción primaria" (*El Federalista*, 15 August 1875), *Opúsculos*, pp. 171–72. Obligatory primary education was a part of the 1872 proposal and gained increasing support in the next few years. Curiously enough, it was one issue on which Guillermo Prieto, the great antagonist of the ENP, and Barreda agreed. For further discussion of the issue, see chap. 7.

[55] Justo Sierra, "Rectificaciones históricas. Robespierre y el Dr. Barreda II," *El Federalista*, 25 January 1876 (*Obras*, 9:63–70). The reference to Lamartine's *Les Girondins* appeared in "El Maestro Altamirano" (1889), *Revista nacional*, 2:16 (*Obras*, 3:382). On Sierra's school days, see Claude Dumas, "Justo Sierra y el liceo franco-mexicano," pp. 531–40; idem, "La República universal de Justo Sierra," *Historia mexicana* 14 (1965): 416–22; idem, *Justo Sierra*, 1:23–25.

struse labels probably disguise Barreda's true enemies, in plainer language the "spiritualist liberals." Sierra was clearly uneasy. He said that though he was no metaphysician, he did defend the conclusions of the spiritualists, which incidentally were the same as those of the utilitarian Mill, namely, "that man's freedom . . . is the final objective of social institutions." Sierra was not willing to accept Barreda's assertion that the advance of civilization had naturally brought about the decrease of individual liberty and the increase of individual obligation; or, as Barreda had expressed it in 1863: "Liberty, in all phenomena, organic or inorganic, consists of being fully subject to the laws that determine them." When an object is subject to the law of gravity, it is said to "fall freely." These were Comtean assumptions that Sierra could never fully embrace.[56]

Justo Sierra's transition from critic of the National Preparatory School to apologist for it and for its educational philosophy reached a climax in the critical year 1877. Although it was less dramatic than the transition in his politics, which we examined in chapter 3, the two were intimately related. Four months after the political upheaval of late 1876, Sierra received his first appointment in the ENP as professor of history and chronology. As a recent adherent to the legalistic cause of José María Iglesias, he was at pains to justify his acceptance of the post and thus his acceptance of the revolutionary and unconstitutional government of Porfirio Díaz. As we have seen, he did so at the end of June, principally on pragmatic and "scientific" grounds, in arguments that foreshadowed the political concepts of the next few years.

On 8 September 1877 Sierra delivered a remarkable apologia to science before the students of the Preparatoria assembled for the annual distribution of prizes. The recent defender of Robespierre began his oration by evoking the death of Condorcet—the prophet of progress, human perfectibility, and science triumphant—on the guillotine. "Today [in Mexico], as in the year 1793 [in France], the ephemeral effigy of liberty [which had been placed above the guillotine] signifies negation." By contrast, the *Preparatoria* and the new generation it produces signify "affirmation" and faith in the future. Like Condorcet, continued Sierra in his exhortation to the students, "you speak of the inexorable laws of order and progress. Great and simple is your secret: science." The tone of Sierra's address was religious but his terminology was Judeo-Christian and not Comtean. By means of the graduated curriculum of the ENP, "a ladder higher and firmer than Jacob's," he continued, science can lead us to penetrate the mysteries of the universe and to glorify God. Sierra left the

[56] Sierra, "Rectificaciones históricas I," *El Federalista*, 28 December 1875 (*Obras*, 9:61–62); Barreda, "Algunas ideas," *Opúsculos*, pp. 165–66; "De la Educación moral," ibid., p. 113.

students with the charge of "the Nazarene to his disciples: 'Go forth and teach.' " We the faculty are passing on to you the "torch of science. . . . Take it . . . and illuminate the future."[57]

Sierra's transition was now complete. He was no longer a detached critic of the new educational system. He now spoke as one personally committed to the school's mission of training an elite that could bring about what he called "renovation"—religious, social, and political. He also spoke with confidence as a new spiritual leader, if not the titular leader, of the Preparatoria. His distinctive contribution to the school, apart from defending it in the momentous controversy that was to follow, was to expand gradually the place of history in the curriculum. In 1874 he had deplored history's virtual omission. He had attacked the bill of 1875 that would have made sociology a required subject and history a voluntary one. The two were inextricably connected, he said; sociology is none other than the "natural history of society," and its place should be central. Soon after his appointment in April 1877 he again lamented the disregard for history in an eloquent open letter to Genaro Raigosa, who was seeking advice on a text to use in the Instituto de Zacatecas. Sierra was at that moment preparing his own text on ancient history, soon to be published in installments; and this immersion in the writing of history was an integral part of Sierra's political and philosophical transition of 1877.[58] Whereas Barreda had approached higher education from the perspective of medicine and the physical sciences, Sierra approached it from the perspective of poetry, law, and history. Though both extolled science and both can be called positivists, the differences between them were significant.

[57] Sierra, "La Escuela preparatoria," *La Libertad*, 6 January 1878; (*Obras*, 5:19–23); also in *El Mundo científico*, 12 January 1878. Not only was the publication of the speech delayed but also the ceremony itself, presumably because of the political crisis. The prizes being presented were for the year 1876. For further insights on Sierra's ideas at this point, see O'Gorman, "Justo Sierra," pp. 180–82 and passim.

[58] Sierra, "La Enseñanza de la historia," *El Federalista*, 26 October 1875 (*Obras*, 8:47–50); "La Cátedra de historia general en la escuela preparatoria. A Genaro Raigosa," *La Época*, 23 May 1877 (not in *Obras*). Sierra's concerns met a favorable response in two subsequent pieces of legislation: one, a regulation for the public primary schools on 12 January 1879 by which history was to be taught in each of the three years instead of in only one (Dublán and Lozano, *Legislación*, 13:728–30); two, a congressional decree of 20 April 1880 establishing in the ENP a new obligatory course in the history of Mexico (*Revista de la instrucción pública*, 1:103–03 [May 1, 1896]). For further discussion of Sierra's *Compendio de la historia de la antigüedad*, see pp. 32–33.

CHAPTER 6

The Great Textbook Controversy

THE DISPUTE OVER the National Preparatory School, which had simmered throughout the 1870s, suddenly boiled over in 1880 and engulfed the Mexico City intellectual elite. Once again positivists were put on the defensive, this time not by a hostile Congress, but by a ministry determined to redirect or to abolish the positivist curriculum. The opponents of positivism were clearly encouraged by the departure of Barreda in 1878 as well as by the conciliatory politics of President Díaz. In his varied ministerial appointments and in his support of Manuel González as candidate for president, Díaz avoided identifying himself exclusively with the *La Libertad* group and with its advocacy of scientific politics and positivist education. The enemies of positivism were also probably encouraged by José María Vigil's vigorous defense of classic political liberalism and by the preelection efforts to reconstruct the "Liberal party."

The controversy began when the logic text by Alexander Bain, adopted by the Preparatory School for 1881, was rejected by executive decision and replaced by the Spanish translation of Guillaume Tiberghien's *Logique*. The Chamber of Deputies reacted immediately; swayed by Justo Sierra's eloquence, it summoned the Minister of Justice Ignacio Mariscal to explain his action. Mariscal was able to avoid the interpellation and the confrontation with Congress by agreeing to reconsider his decision; but then on 14 October he reiterated his decision, justifying it in a lengthy memorandum to the Junta Directiva de Instrucción Pública.[1] On 3 November the antipositivist Vigil was appointed to replace the positivist Parra as professor of logic, a position Vigil continued to hold until 1892. With the inauguration of President González on 1 December 1880, Ezequiel Montes became minister of justice and by the following April he had proposed a new plan of studies, which, like the congressional proposals of the early 1870s, would have eliminated the ENP and relegated the teaching of preparatory subjects to the various professional schools.[2]

---

[1] *Diario de los debates*, 10th congress, 1:276–79 (session of 30 September 1880), which includes Sierra's speech (also *Obras*, 8:55–59). Congress withdrew the interpellation the next day after Deputy Hammeken reported his conversation with Mariscal. The Mariscal memorandum appeared in the *Diario oficial* of 19 November (also in Díaz y de Ovando, *Escuela*, 2:150–52).

[2] Ezequiel Montes, "Proyecto de ley orgánica de la instrucción pública en el Distrito Federal," *Diario oficial*, 21–25 April 1881; also in *Diario de los debates*, 10th congress, 4

The Montes plan was not presented to the Chamber of Deputies until September, but in the meantime the two ministerial initiatives had unleashed an intense and wide-ranging debate in the press. Tiberghien, metaphysics, spiritualism, and ultimately political liberalism were defended by Hilario Gabilondo, Vigil, and Altamirano in *La República*; Bain, the ENP, positivism, and scientific politics were upheld by Sierra, García, Cosmes, Hammeken, and Parra in the *El Centinela español* and *La Libertad*. Gabilondo was perhaps the most hardy of the combatants; during October and November 1880 he was responding regularly to three different antagonists. The controversy turned more broadly philosophical in late 1881 and early 1882, reaching a climax in the articles by Vigil in his *Revista filosófica* and by Parra in his *El Positivismo* and in *La Libertad*. It then subsided later in the year when yet another Minister of Justice, Joaquín Baranda (appointed 13 September), persuaded the ENP to consider a recently published (and presumably less controversial) philosophy text by Paul Janet.

The public debate over the teaching of logic had its reflection within the Junta de Profesores of the ENP. The junta's recommendation of Bain in July 1880 (by a vote of thirteen to seven) was the first instance since 1869 in which any debate or vote on the adoption of texts had appeared in its minutes.[3] From 1869 through 1876 Mill's text was the one chosen; Bain was substituted for it beginning in 1877. Opponents of positivism had clearly made headway within the junta by 1880, but they did not prevail until 1883. Tiberghien's text, though presumably used by Vigil after his appointment, was never officially approved by the junta, in large part because of Sierra's continuing opposition. In fact in July 1882 the junta (at Sierra's behest) approved a new and supposedly "neutral" text by the positivist Luis E. Ruiz.[4] It was ultimately rejected by Minister Baranda and the junta acquiesced. The minister's choice, as we have seen, was Janet, which was finally approved without discussion in July 1883.

It should be noted that virtually all decisions on logic texts taken by the junta included the phrase "and oral lessons," which suggests that much of the teaching of logic depended on professorial interpretation rather than on a close reading of the text by students. It is difficult to

vols. (Mexico, 1880–98), 3:34–73 (19 September 1881). Montes said he purposely delayed submission of the plan to Congress in order to allow for public debate.

[3] Archivo Histórico de la Universidad, Preparatoria, Actas de la Junta de Profesores, vol. 23, p. 85 (7 July 1880). The junta generally met twice a year, once to distribute prizes and once in June or July to approve texts for the following year.

[4] Luis E. Ruiz, *Nociones de lógica* (Mexico, 1882). The book was also published serially in *La Libertad* from 23 May through 29 June. For the debates within the junta from 1881 through 1883 and the actions taken, see Archivo Histórico de la Universidad, 23:95–126.

imagine students ages thirteen to eighteen reading Mill or Bain in English or French. (No accessible Spanish translation of Mill and none at all of Bain existed.) Tiberghien's work did exist in a translation by the Mexican José María Castillo Velasco; but it was more a treatise than a text and it was filled with abstruse passages that were probably incomprehensible to most students—a point frequently made by Justo Sierra. The Ruiz text was a simplified adaptation of Bain and thus more appropriate, but by mid-1882 the tide was moving against positivism. Janet, which had appeared in Spanish in 1882, was lucid but it was lengthy and probably still too difficult. In short, more than is usually the case, students were probably learning logic and philosophy from the teacher rather than from texts.[5] However, even if they were little read, the texts played the symbolic role in the controversy.

Much of the debate of the early 1880s was an elaboration of arguments that had been put forth during the previous decade. However, they were given a new focus and intensity by vigorous and substantial statements made by Ignacio Mariscal and Ezequiel Montes. These ministers in their actions and in their words were responding to what they saw as strong public sentiment against government imposition of a philosophy that undermined moral principles and religious belief. Mariscal said the choice was between two systems of logic or philosophy, Bain's, which encouraged an "absolute skepticism" toward the foundations of religion, and Tiberghien's "rational deism," which did not favor any "specific sect" but left the student free to accept the beliefs of his parents or to form his own. Sierra had argued on 30 September like Barreda in 1868 that deism was itself a religious system ("a theology of the Phrygian cap"), and that the only appropriate text for a country in which church and state were separate was one that made no mention of religion whatsoever. Though acknowledging the possibility that Bain might not be directly hostile toward religion, Mariscal nonetheless reiterated his principal point, the need to respond to parental concerns. State instruction simply cannot impart a "disdainful skepticism" toward "what is called metaphysics"; for, upon it "the great majority of the human species base their religion, their ethics, their hopes for beyond the grave, and their aspirations for the

---

[5] Bain's *Logic: Deductive and Inductive*, over seven hundred pages in length, was published in London in 1870 (French ed.: 2 vols., 1875). Mill's *A System of Logic* appeared in French in 1866–67. A fragment was published in one volume in Spain in 1853, but it was probably never used in Mexico. Tiberghien, *Lógica: la ciencia del conocimiento*, 2 vols. (Mexico, 1875–78), 1st ed. (Paris, 1865). Paul Janet, *Traité élémentaire de philosophie à l'usage des classes* (Paris, 1879). The Spanish edition published in 1882 by Bouret in Paris and Mexico City was 896 pages. Even Ruiz acknowledged that in the teaching of logic the teacher was probably more important than the text: Ruiz, *Nociones*, p. 5.

ideal and the infinite." Mariscal even suggested that the rapid growth of Catholic schools was due to public rejection of positivism.

Although Montes also noted the "veritable alarm in society," he based his argument against positivism and the preparatory school on an extensive survey of Mexican education beginning with the Calmecac of the Aztecs. Montes emphasized continuity, and as O'Gorman has noted, he showed a remarkable sympathy for colonial education and for the plan of studies of the centralist government of 1843. He argued that the 1867 plan was an overreaction to the defects of the old university, eliminating philosophy from the curriculum, "denying the absolute principles on which ethics (*las ciencias morales*) are founded," and "reducing science to pure experimental observation."[6] Montes (1820–83) was a contemporary of Barreda and a Juárez liberal, but unlike Barreda he was a jurist not a scientist, educated at San Ildefonso and a professor there in its halcyon days, the early 1850s under Rector Sebastián Lerdo de Tejada. He asserted nostalgically that the old system had produced a "phalanx of patriots," whereas the new system will produce "men who scornfully term the idea of *patria* a metaphysical abstraction" and who will sacrifice higher ideals to the pursuit of personal gain. Students are being exposed to "the disastrous influences of atheistic and materialist doctrines, left without any moral guide" for their lives. Though Montes did not ignore careerist complaints against the "excessive agglomeration of subjects," his justification for abolishing the positivist system was clearly more lofty and principled than was that of the early 1870s.

What for Ezequiel Montes was the preservation of educational continuity was for Justo Sierra an assault upon "the intellectual progress of our country." Sierra seized upon the minister's nostalgia for the plan of 1843 as an attempt "to sell us as reform a set of old ideas and practices that seemed buried forever in the nearly century-old dust of the ministerial archives." We might as well revive the Pontifical University! The minister's plan can be summed up in one word: "retrogression." But Sierra's three articles did more than ridicule the Montes plan; they consisted primarily of a reasoned and detailed exposition of the uniform and encyclopedic preparatory curriculum, based on Comte's hierarchy of the sciences (which "conforms to the laws of mental development"), capped by logic and ethics. The values that Montes cherishes, wrote Sierra, can be best enhanced by the best possible education, one whose principal objective is "to form men who know how to think, who know how to study, in short who are not strangers to the foundations of modern progress."[7] That

[6] O'Gorman, "Justo Sierra," p. 189; Montes, "Proyecto de ley," *Diario de los debates*, 10th congress, 3:60.

[7] Sierra, "El Plan de estudios del Señor Montes," *El Centinela español*, 28 April, 1, 5 May 1881, republished in *La Libertad*, 29 April, 3, 7 May 1881 (also in *Obras*, 8:82–97).

positivism was equivalent to progress was also central to the rhetoric of Telesforo García and Jorge Hammeken. García's principal question was: "Does the metaphysical system better guarantee progress than the experimental system?" The answer for García was as obvious as it was for Hammeken, who envisioned "a new and unexplored world" of treasures that would be opened up to the imagination from "the study of phenomena." Recently returned from Europe, Hammeken affirmed with examples that the positivist system "is the one that must predominate in this new and luminous civilization."[8]

By late 1881 the concrete questions that had given rise to the debate were still unresolved and the educational conflict had reached a stalemate. The Montes plan was buried in a congressional committee, never to emerge. The antipositivist José María Vigil was installed in the preparatory school, but he was teaching logic without a text. As if determined to break the stalemate, the two professors of logic, the displaced Porfirio Parra and the newly appointed Vigil, joined battle; and the question of the texts became submerged in a larger philosophical dispute. Parra was uneasy with the notion that the controversy was over philosophy, adhering to the standard positivist position that the fifth-year course based on the texts by Mill and Bain was a course in scientific method, a generalization upon the methods of the individual sciences. Sierra had attacked Tiberghien's text in September 1880 as being less logic than metaphysics, drawn from the incomprehensible system of the German philosopher Krause; and he quoted choice passages to prove his point. García and Hammeken had done likewise, but they had also defended "positive philosophy." Yet Parra tried (not always successfully) to avoid the term philosophy because of its association with metaphysics and religion.

Not to be guided by his opponent, Vigil insisted that the conflict was indeed philosophical and that positivism was equivalent to "sensualism" or "empiricism." In fact, by mid-1882 as he was turning his support from Tiberghien to Janet, he said that the debate was not between positivism and metaphysics (or Krausism), but between positivism and "spiritualism." Parra in a sense conceded the point, but his target was "eclecticism," which he said was tantamount to intellectual anarchy. Such anarchy could only be corrected by proper method, by system, by coordination, in short by true "intellectual education." The mention of anarchy brought forth Vigil's substantial discussion of "positivist anar-

---

[8] García, *Polémica filosófica* (the pamphlet of 1881, composed of the articles from October and November 1880 discussed in chap. 2, n. 5); Hammeken, "La Filosofía positiva y la filosofía metafísica," a series of five articles in *La Libertad* from 14 October to 2 November 1880 (Díaz y de Ovando, *Escuela*, 2:113–38).

chy," that is, the conflicts among major positivists.[9] Both combatants were drawing liberally upon contemporary European sources, as were their colleagues. Therefore, to understand better the significance of the controversy for Mexican education and politics we must examine it within a broader comparative context.

Vigil's move away from Tiberghien to Janet symbolized a shift in intellectual orientation among antipositivists in Mexico from Spanish Krausism to French spiritualism. The positivists accused Vigil of merely following fashion, but the matter went deeper than that. The educational debate of the early 1880s was one instance in which the Spanish intellectual experience was less relevant than the French for nineteenth-century Mexico. Evidence of Krausism in Mexico is slight, brief, and superficial by comparison to that of spiritualism. Whereas French philosophical and educational controversies had considerable reverberations in Mexico, those of Spain did not. The explanation lies partly in the peculiarity of Spanish intellectual life during the midcentury decades, partly in timing, and partly in the means of intellectual diffusion.

The spectacular impact on Spain of German idealism in the form espoused by the obscure philosopher Karl Christian Friedrich Krause (1781–1832) is a much studied subject.[10] Krause's ideas were propagated in Spain by Julián Sanz del Río, who was appointed to be the first professor of the history of philosophy at the University of Madrid in 1843 on the condition that he prepare for the post by two years of study abroad. Sanz del Río's intellectual pilgrimage took him first to Paris, where he found the reigning eclecticism of Victor Cousin superficial, then to Brussels, where Krause's disciple Heinrich Ahrens taught the philosophy of law, and finally (on Ahrens advice) to Heidelberg, the fount of Krause's teachings. On his return from Germany, Sanz del Río spent a decade in retreat, mastering and translating Krause and Ahrens. Sanz del Río's exceptional influence at the University of Madrid began in 1857 and lasted until his death in 1869. His *Ideal de la humanidad para la vida* (1860), an adaptation of *Urbild der Menschheit* (1811), Krause's most important

[9] "La Educación intelectual" was the title of Parra's major contribution to the debate, a series of nineteen articles in *La Libertad* from 10 December 1881 to 4 April 1882. Vigil's "La Anarquía positivista" appeared in *Revista filosófica*, 1 May, 1 June 1882, pp. 49–58, 65–74. Unfortunately I have been unable to locate Parra's fortnightly *El Positivismo*, announced in *La Libertad* on 27 December 1881 and mentioned frequently by Vigil. It probably contains much that was reprinted elsewhere, but perhaps also some that was not.

[10] See Juan López Morillas, *The Krausist Movement and Ideological Change in Spain, 1854–1874* (Spanish edition 1956; Cambridge, 1981); Vicente Cacho Viu, *La Institución libre de enseñanza* (Madrid, 1962); Pierre Jobit, *Les Éducateurs de l'Espagne contemporaine* (Paris, 1936). For the institutional context, see Antonio Álvarez de Morales, *Génesis de la universidad española contemporanea* (Madrid, 1972); also the note by Joan Connelly Ullman in *Comparative Studies in Society and History* 26 (1984): 367–70.

(and practical) work, has been described as the "book of hours" of several student generations. Sanz del Río's career as student and teacher coincided with and was a vital part of the rationalist struggle to renovate Spanish academic and intellectual life, beginning with the creation of the centralized University of Madrid in 1836 and culminating in the educational experiments that followed the September revolution of 1868.

However, it was not primarily through Sanz del Río that Krausism reached Mexico, but through Guillaume Tiberghien (1819–1901), a Belgian student of Ahrens and longtime professor at the Free University of Brussels. A number of Tiberghien's works were translated in Spain between 1872 and 1875, the same year that volume one of his *Lógica* appeared in Mexico. Tiberghien was popular with "the disciples of Sanz del Río's students," in part because he presented Krause's ideas more clearly than did the master himself and in part because he emphasized the eclectic and conciliatory features of Krausism, such that it became a compromise between idealist philosophy, religious dogmas, and results from the natural sciences. In short, Tiberghien was popular in Spain at the very time when "a new and fearsome enemy was coming up from behind," that is, when Krausism was being challenged by positivism.[11]

Curiously enough, the only serious exposition of Krausism in Mexico appeared in Telesforo García's *Polémica filosófica*, the purpose of which was to reveal in detail its total inadequacy as a philosophy for Mexican youth. The Spanish-born García, who came to Mexico in 1865 at the age of twenty-one, had probably studied with Sanz del Río during the heyday of his influence in Madrid. In refuting Gabilondo's assertion that he was a Comtean (though not that he was a positivist), García acknowledged that the Krausist concept of "the evolution of humanity as a living and conscious organism"—later modified by the empiricism of Herbert Spencer—had been an important element in his intellectual formation.[12] In Mexico García moved from Krausism to positivism, as did many of his contemporaries in the peninsula, for example, the critic Manuel de la Revilla, several of whose articles appeared in *La Libertad*.[13] Although

[11] López Morillas, *Krausist Movement*, p. 41. On Tiberghien in Spain, see Cacho Viu, *Institución*, pp. 380–83 (including a list of his works that appeared in Spanish translation).

[12] García, *Polémica*, p. 22, 29; (published first in *El Centinela*, 11, 25 November · 1880). Gabilondo's accusation appeared in *La República*, 26 October 1880 (Díaz y de Ovando, *Escuela*, 2:128).

[13] García's pamphlet, *La España y los españoles* (Mexico, 1877) still showed some traces of Krausism (see p. 240). Revilla's "Las Modernas Tendencias de la ciencia en su relación con la política" appeared in *La Libertad*, 22, 24 May 1879. It argued that positivism in France, Italy, and Spain was supporting a "conservative, opportunist, or governmental democracy." Revilla (1846–81) might possibly have been a friend of García from student days. The Catholic newspaper *El Nacional* commented on 2 December 1893 on García's transition from Sanz del Río to Spencer.

García regarded with some favor his own exposure to Krause's philosophy at a time when it was subjected to "highly rigorous examination" and made more rational by Sanz del Río, he had nothing but scorn for Tiberghien, whom he accused (perhaps wrongly) of perpetuating the more fantastic, obscure, and arbitrary aspects of Krause's thought.

García identified these aspects by way of presenting a brief summary of Krause's doctrine of "harmonic rationalism." It begins with internal consciousness of the self as the basis of knowledge; it proceeds to the distinction between the self and the non-self, which appears at the initial moment of thinking; and it culminates in the harmonizing of these necessary opposites by means of the "intuitive sense of being." This intuitive sense is derived from God, who is at once indemonstrable and capable of being grasped through mental effort. García berated Gabilondo and his colleagues for ignoring these complexities of Krause (or Tiberghien). For example, he said it was wrong to use Krause to affirm "the absolute idea of human liberty," when Krause himself "never tires of emphasizing the *finite liberty* of man in its dependence on the infinite liberty of God."[14] Much of García's critique was directed toward Krause's panentheism as a "pious" system, "capable of leading men toward the divine life." Sierra characterized it as deism, but both agreed that it was a religious system that should not be taught in secular state schools. Tiberghien's special interest was the philosophy of religion, which probably is one reason why García found Tiberghien's version of Krausism so "fantastic" compared with that of Sanz del Río. In fact, the Mexican edition of the *Lógica* omitted many of his religious passages out of deference to the views of orthodox Catholic parents.[15]

At the heart of the positivists' objections to Krausism was their hostility to the German idealist conception of science (*Wissenschaft*) as the single and total structure of human knowledge that embraced philosophy and its constituent elements. The positivist conception of science as knowledge was limited to what could be derived from the observation and measurement of phenomena. When the Spanish Krausists fought for the

[14] García, *Polémica*, p. 24. The positivists all complained about Krausist prose, as have most other commentators. Arnulf Zweig writes: "The obscurity of [Krause's] style is awesome; he expressed himself in an artificial and often unfathomable vocabulary that included such monstrous neologisms as *Or-om-wesenlebverhaltheit* and *Vereinselbganzweseninnesein*—words which are untranslatable into German, let alone into English": *Encyclopedia of Philosophy*, 8 vols. (New York, 1967), 4:363.

[15] See the report of Junta Directiva de Instrucción Pública to Minister Mariscal, dated 12 November 1880 (Díaz y de Ovando, *Escuela*, 2:150), which said passages that "could be thought to favor a specific religion" had been omitted. A cursory comparison of vol. 1 of the French edition of 1865 with the Castillo Velasco translation (1875) verifies the junta's contention: several passages demonstrating panentheism have been deleted, especially in the concluding section. On Krause's concept of panentheism, see Jobit, *Éducateurs*, 1:204–12.

"freedom of science" in the Spanish university, they meant it in the German sense in which the experimental sciences were subordinated to philosophy. When Tiberghien defined logic as "the science of knowledge in general and especially of scientific knowledge, that is, 'the science of science,'" positivists regarded such a definition as a metaphysical misnomer.[16]

We need not necessarily agree that "Sanz del Río and his followers were the first to immerse the Spanish mind in modern rationalism" in order to discern Krausism's different role in Spain and in Mexico.[17] In Spain Krausism was a profound and general movement affecting intellectual, academic, and even political life, as opposed to traditional Catholic influences in the university system within a confessional state. Moreover, Krausism preceded positivism, which did not make its appearance in Spain until the early 1870s. Krausism reached its height in Spain at the time of the Mexican Reforma, which marked the formal triumph of the secular state and its legal separation from the church. Except for the unusual case of Telesforo García, Krausism entered Mexico after positivism had been the official philosophy of a reformed system of higher education for more than a decade. Therefore, it was used to oppose an already-established positivism, a reversal of its role in Spain. The Spanish Krausists of the 1860s were as yet scarcely aware of positivism. Though Krausism did enter Mexico by way of Spain, it came primarily through a Belgian interpreter who was cognizant of positivism's long-established place in the French-speaking world. Tiberghien's Krausism was in part a critique of positivism and could be used as such by Mexican opponents of the ENP curriculum. But it was also a critique that had affinities with French spiritualism, although it was rooted in a different philosophic tradition. Thus the move by Vigil and his colleagues from Tiberghien to Janet, from Krausism to spiritualism, came naturally and easily, particularly when the latter was already well-established in Mexican intellectual life.

Spiritualism was probably the dominant philosophy of nineteenth-century France, if one regards "philosophy" as what was espoused by professional philosophers and taught in the French university. Spiritualism is viewed in the Anglo-Saxon philosophical world as a distinctly "French" movement; indeed, there is no entry for it in English-language encyclopedias.[18] "Spiritualism" was the term preferred by Victor Cousin (1792–

[16] Tiberghien, *Lógica*, 1:18, quoted by Gabilondo in *La República*, 9 November 1880 (Díaz y de Ovando, *Escuela*, 2:142).

[17] The assertion is by López Morillas in *Krausist Movement*, pp. 9–10.

[18] For example, in the *Encyclopedia of Philosophy*. Nor does the term appear in Maurice Mandelbaum's *History, Man, and Reason* (Baltimore, 1971). Mandelbaum argues that there were two principal and continuing currents of philosophic thought in nineteenth-century

1867) for his philosophical system, often called "eclecticism"; and it became principally identified with his followers, men such as Paul Janet,
Elme-Marie Caro, Étienne Vacherot, and Jules Simon, all of whom were
well-known in Mexico after 1867. Like his younger contemporary and
great antagonist, Auguste Comte, Cousin sought a principle of organization for a world whose spiritual bonds had been broken by the great revolution. Rejecting eighteenth-century "materialism" or "sensualism" as
critical and destructive, he made his starting point introspection, or "intelligent reconstruction" through observation of the human mind. Despite its critique of eighteenth-century thought, Cousin's eclectic system
was built upon a sensitivity to the history of philosophy as well as to contemporary foreign doctrines, notably German idealism. Cousin and even
more his spiritualist followers looked upon their philosophy as one of
matter and of mind, as an effort to reconcile materialism and idealism.
Spiritualists saw ideas as derived both experimentally from sensations
and from consciousness, which they termed the "intimate sense" and which
they equated with reason. In addition, for them the French word *esprit*
(Spanish, *espíritu*) meant "spirit" as well as "mind," and this dual meaning suggested a relation between mind and a higher immaterial substance, the infinite, or God.

Cousin enjoyed immense popularity during the 1820s at a time when
Comte was struggling for an audience, and his eclecticism became the
official philosophy taught in the schools during the July Monarchy.[19] Because of his eminence, Cousin never felt it necessary to confront Comte's
positivism directly and he became increasingly out of touch with the
quickening pace of the natural sciences. However, his spiritualist followers were forced to come to grips with both. The result was that the midcentury decades, the years of the Second Empire, were years of philosophic dissention in which writers became emotionally involved in
pursuing "the big questions." Moreover, in the conflict between positivism and spiritualism in France, positions often became confused, even in
the work of a single writer. One of those writers, frequently cited (by
both sides) in Mexico, was Vacherot, who wrote in 1858 that his goal was
to "express . . . the metaphysical idea of our century, a simple and natural idea, in harmony with the progress of the positive sciences."[20] After

Europe, metaphysical idealism and positivism. French spiritualism (or eclecticism) scarcely
figures in his discussion. It is treated, however, by J. H. Randall, Jr., *The Career of Philosophy*, 2 vols. (New York, 1965), 2:440–49, whose approach is by national schools.

[19] Doris S. Goldstein, " 'Official Philosophies' in Modern France: the Example of Victor
Cousin," *Journal of Social History* 1 (1968): 259–79. See also Alan B. Spitzer, *The French
Generation of 1820* (Princeton, 1987), chap. 3.

[20] W. M. Simon, "The 'Two Cultures' in Nineteenth Century France: Victor Cousin and
Auguste Comte," *Journal of the History of Ideas* 26 (1956): 45–58. Charlton, *Positivist*

1870 in France, positions became hardened and spirtualism became increasingly a defense of idealist principles against an ascendant positivism. This shift from ambiguity to greater rigidity also took place in Mexican philosophical discourse from the 1870s to the early 1880s.

We have already noted traces of French spiritualism during the 1870s, even among those who were soon to become leading positivists. After his conversion to positivism, Jorge Hammeken y Mexía recalled his "spiritualist" days on *La Tribuna*, when he translated Janet's balanced and judicious assessment of the political philosophies of the French revolutionary era. Sierra's early critique of the curriculum of the National Preparatory School—that it was too exclusive, that it did not take proper cognizance of liberty and human personality, that it overlooked the history of philosophy—reflected concerns clearly drawn from French spiritualism. His ambivalence toward the ENP is more easily understood when viewed within the context of the ambiguities of midcentury philosophical debate in France. Like Janet and Vacherot, Sierra tried to reconcile idealist principles with the imperatives of the natural sciences. Though he had become an ardent positivist by the late 1870s, he never completely abandoned his earlier spiritualist inclinations. In fact, Sierra's entire intellectual career from 1867 to 1910 construed in philosophical terms may be seen as one of continuing tension between idealism and positivism, the best model for which can be found in nineteenth-century France.

While Hammeken and Sierra turned away from spiritualism, José María Vigil turned increasingly toward it to strengthen his antipositivist position. As we have seen, he quoted liberally from Caro's defense of natural rights and democracy in his debate of 1878 with Sierra over "old" versus "new" liberalism. Vigil's attachment to Caro led him to translate for his *Revista filosófica* (1882) the second half of Caro's essay on Littré, which has been called "the most comprehensive attempt by a member of Cousin's school to refute positivism."[21] Scattered throughout the *Revista* were fourteen vaguely identified articles by leading members of the

---

Thought, pp. 11–23; Étienne Vacherot (1809–97), *La Métaphysique et la science, ou principes de métaphysique positive*, 2d ed., 3 vols. (Paris, 1863), 1:xxxv. In the 1880 debate Hammeken quoted "the eminent metaphysician" Vacherot's acknowledgement of the strength of positivism: *La Libertad*, 16 October 1880 (Díaz y de Ovando, *Escuela*, 2:117–18). Gabilondo used the same Vacherot article to demonstrate the vitality of the metaphysical spirit, despite positivism: *La República*, 19 October 1880 (Díaz y de Ovando, *Escuela*, 2:119–120). The article in question was Vacherot, "Les Trois États de l'esprit humaine," *Revue des deux mondes* 15 August 1880, pp. 856–92.

[21] Simon, " 'Two Cultures,' " p. 51n. The Caro selection was "Émile Littré, II: La Philosophie positive, ses transformations, son avenir," *Revue des deux mondes*, 1 May 1882, pp. 5–46. As in the case of many *Revue* articles, the two parts were published soon afterwards as a book. It should be noted that the translation appeared exactly two months after the original, indicating the rapid distribution of the *Revue* and fast work done by Vigil.

French philosophical and academic establishment, taken from Adolphe Franck's famous spiritualist compendium, the eighteen-hundred-page *Dictionnaire des sciences philosophiques*.[22] In fact, the initial item in Vigil's periodical was a lengthy discussion of "philosophy" by Franck himself. Quite apart from the content of Vigil's own articles, his work of translation is impressive evidence of his immersion in French spiritualism. It comes as no surprise that as professor of logic in the ENP he would urge the adoption of Janet's new text.

The contents of Vigil's *Revista filosófica* point up the difficult question of intellectual diffusion. There is abundant evidence that individuals such as Vigil, Sierra, Hammeken, and Parra were steeped in French literary and philosophical culture and were also well-versed in French history and politics. We know that Barreda and Hammeken spent time in France, but among the individuals discussed in this book, they were exceptions. We know little specifically about what Mexicans read and in what form. Biographical information, personal correspondence, inventories of personal libraries, even intellectual reminiscences are scanty or nonexistent. We know virtually nothing about the book and periodical trade in nineteenth-century Mexico, for example, which European publications were sold, in what quantities, and for what prices. In writings by Mexicans, quotations, translations, and direct arguments taken from European sources were certainly better identified after 1867 than they were earlier in the century; yet even during our period documentation was haphazard at best.

What then, from fragmentary and impressionistic evidence, can we say about the means of diffusion of these ideas? Except for occasional Spanish translations and works of Spanish authors, French was the principal language of culture for the Mexican elite. For example, they read Mill, Bain, Spencer, and Darwin in French translations. Though many works by European authors obviously circulated and were read in Mexico, it is probable that much of what was known of European intellectual life came from the pages of the *Revue des deux mondes*. The *Revue* was a massive fortnightly publication to which many of the major figures of French phi-

---

[22] Adolphe Franck, ed., *Dictionnaire des sciences philosophiques par une société de professeurs et de savants*, 2d ed. (Paris, 1875). 1st ed. 1843–53, in 6 vols. Franck (1809–93) was a leading member of Cousin's "philosophical regiment" who held a chair at the Collège de France from 1854 to 1881. A few of the other contributors whose articles Vigil translated were: Émile Saisset (1814–63), Émile-Auguste-Edouard Charles (1826–97); Pierre-Ernest Bersot (1816–80), and Jacques-Albert-Félix Lemoine (1824–74). All held prestigious academic posts. Among other translations in the *Revista* were Caro's "La Réligion positiviste," taken from his *Études morales sur le temps présent*, 4th ed. (Paris, 1879) and an excerpt from Louis Liard, *La Science et la métaphysique* (1879). Liard (1846–1917) was also a spiritualist. He was a vice-rector of the University of Paris and was prominent in the movement to reform that institution.

losophy, letters, politics, and science made regular contributions, in the best French tradition of *haute vulgarisation*. Though the *Revue* tended to be Orleanist in its politics and spiritualist in its philosophy, it did not exclude other viewpoints. For example, Littré wrote important articles, as did democrats like Janet and Caro. The *Revue* also brought to its readers penetrating reviews of German and English works and essays on intellectual movements in those countries. Its longevity and stability, its intellectual quality, and its accessibility made the *Revue* especially attractive to Mexicans.[23]

As we have seen in chapter 2, the Spanish connection is of great importance in understanding the nature of scientific politics (or conservative-liberalism) in Mexico. Emilio Castelar's fortnightly commentary on Spanish and European politics, which ran in *El Monitor republicano* from 1867 to 1896 (and briefly in *La Libertad*), was a vital source of information and opinion for Mexicans. They also looked to Castelar because he was a determined republican and yet not a radical, as he revealed during his brief term as president of the republic in 1873. Castelar's effort to institute strong republican government in the face of anarchy was an important model for advocates of scientific politics. Personal and emotional ties to Spain and Spaniards were strong among members of the *La Libertad* group.

However, in the realm of philosophy and higher education, Spanish experience and Spanish writings were less relevant to the Mexicans than were French models. Philosophical idealism was significant in Mexico, but principally in its French eclectic or spiritualist form and not in its German Krausist form through the Spain of Sanz del Río. The brief popularity of Tiberghien's works in Mexico was due to their late arrival in Spain, to his familiarity as a Belgian with French positivism, and thus to the affinity of his critique with that of the French spiritualists. It should also be noted that Emilio Castelar was not a Krausist, though he was at one with them in the university struggle against the government in the 1860s. He had studied in Madrid a decade earlier, several years before Sanz del Río began teaching. Although Castelar was not a philosopher, his philosophical orientation appears to have been toward French spiritualism. In fact, he was occasionally cited by the Mexican opponents of positivism in the debates of the early 1880s.[24] The strength of French

---

[23] See *Le Livre du centenaire. Cent ans de vie française à la revue des deux mondes* (Paris, 1929). The *Revue* was also a stronghold of literary romanticism.

[24] See Vigil's quotation (in an attack on Luis E. Ruiz) of a passage from Castelar's speech to a recent pedagogical congress in Madrid urging respect for religious belief while teaching the findings of modern science: *Revista filosófica*, 1 August 1882, p. 112. Two years earlier *El Monitor* (18 May 1880) devoted nearly five full pages (plus effusive commentary) to Castelar's inaugural lecture to the Academia de la Lengua. The lecture carried a similar mes-

philosophical culture in nineteenth-century Mexico is not unlike its strength in Spain itself, except for the remarkable, short-lived intrusion of German idealism.

Let us return to the Mexican controversy, which reached its climax in 1882 with the interchange between the two professors, Vigil and Parra. Though Parra's defense of positivist "intellectual education" restated much of what Barreda had written a decade earlier, it diverged from Barreda in three respects. The first was that Parra directed himself specifically against "eclecticism," a natural result of the philosophical incursion we have just examined. The second was that Parra's positivism was less Comtean and more heterodox than was Barreda's; that is, Parra put less emphasis than Barreda had on social reconstruction and moral regeneration, and none at all on the religion of humanity. The third was that Parra came to grips with the issue of psychology, whereas Barreda ignored it. Psychology was a problem for positivists because of Comte's disdain for it as a science. For his part, Vigil, now steeped in some of the major documents of French spiritualism, was able to exploit the schisms that existed within the enemy camp. In doing so he effectively challenged the philosophical basis of the National Preparatory School.

Parra's series of nineteen articles was a classic positivist presentation, even if he was less orthodox than Barreda. The first four articles, devoted to an attack on eclecticism, were followed by a discussion of each of the three, and only three, systems that could legitimately guide the "education of the intellect *(inteligencia)*"—the scholastic, the rationalist or metaphysical, and the positive. As might be expected, ten articles of the series were devoted to the last of the three systems; yet Parra did recognize the worth of the first two. Scholasticism "was a happy synthesis, which for a long time satisfied doubts and produced a uniformity of opinions," thus restraining anarchy in thought. Its defect was that it followed only the deductive method, which led to the conviction that reason could acquire knowledge of absolutes without the aid of observation and experience. Despite the good intentions of the scholastic system, the result was a tyranny over thought and the impossibility of establishing any properly constituted science. It fell to Bacon and Descartes, said Parra, to tear down the old synthesis and to reconstruct philosophy using sounder materials, experiment and mathematics. Bacon's method led to the establishment of the sciences. Descartes's "pure metaphysical method" also had its value, principally "to facilitate the transition from the old regime to the new," but it suffered from "subjectivism" and encouraged anarchy.[25]

---

sage. Hennessy identifies a strain of "Hegelian historicism" in Castelar's thought, which would have been compatible with French eclecticism: Hennessy, *Federal Republic*, p. 80.

[25] Parra, "Educación intelectual" (nos. 5–9), *La Libertad*, 10 January–7 February 1882.

Parra's respect for scholasticism and metaphysics as "pure" systems contrasted with his disdain for eclecticism, which he said reigned in the Preparatoria. The eclectics have an almost superstitious reverence for varied philosophical systems. They seem to be saying that because "errors are nothing but half-truths" and because no proposition is absolutely false, "no error should be rejected." It makes little sense, argued Parra, to preserve in the ENP curriculum the "encyclopedic hierarchy instituted by Comte," while throwing out "scientific logic." Parra regarded Tiberghien's text as essentially an eclectic choice, administered as a kind of metaphysical antidote to the supposed "particles of base materialism" that were poisoning "naive adolescents." The result, he concluded, is a hopeless permissiveness being perpetuated by the "partisans of the non-systematization of education."[26]

The key word in Parra's argument was "system," the basic ingredient that made education more than mere instruction. Of the three systems, he said, it is essential to choose one, not to mix them as the eclectics are doing. Given this premise and the defects of scholasticism and rationalism, the only choice for Parra was positivism, the system that communicated useful knowledge as well as disciplined the intellect by means of the scientific method. The program is modest, he asserted, in the sense that it makes no attempt "to know the essence of things"; yet the results are "magnificent." Though the only basis of solid knowledge is facts, science is more than "the arid and sterile enumeration of specific cases"; it consists of the coordination of facts, "linking them by means of fruitful generalizations," and arriving at "clear and precise notions." Parra emphasized more than did Barreda that the positivist system was not deterministic. "Uniformity of laws is compatible with variation of results"; theory is compatible with practice. He proceeded to suggest how specific laws of phenomena could be suppressed or manipulated, how the powers of probability and prediction could be developed in order to bring about socially useful results. Having been trained as a physician, his examples were drawn mostly from medicine: to wit, if we could learn the laws governing yellow fever, we could eradicate the disease. Parra concluded characteristically with a jab at metaphysics by reiterating the limits of science. Its method makes no effort to know the unknowable, to explain the unexplainable.[27]

Vigil's two principal arguments—the first that positivism was despite

[26] Ibid. (nos. 1–4), 10–28 December 1882.

[27] Ibid. (nos. 10–19), 15 February–4 April 1882. Parra's conclusion was an extension of the argument presented in his student paper of 1877 dismissing those who sought "first causes": Parra, "Las Causas primeras," *Anales*, pp. 49–67. He may have borrowed the term "intellectual education" from Herbert Spencer, *Education, Intellectual, Moral, and Physical* (1860). First Spanish edition, 1878.

Parra's protestations a philosophy equivalent to empiricism or sensualism, and the second that as a philosophy positivism was defective because of basic conflicts among its major adherents—were closely related. Beneath Vigil's rhetoric was a basic idealist conviction derived from the French spiritualists that it was impossible to separate philosophy from metaphysics. "Metaphysics is to philosophy what philosophy is to the other sciences: the object and center of all its investigations, the trunk that supports and gives life to all its branches."[28] So wrote Franck in an article translated and reprinted by Vigil from the *Dictionnaire des sciences philosophiques*. Since positivists like Parra rejected the claim of metaphysics that it was possible to discover principles of explanation more fundamental than those derived from observation, and since they did not even place philosophy among the sciences (and indeed had abolished the term from the ENP curriculum), there was little common ground on which to debate. For example, when Vigil asserted repeatedly that the experimental method, however appropriate it might be for the "sciences of observation," was totally inappropriate for the "moral and philosophical sciences," Parra's response was only an uncomprehending "why?"[29]

Vigil's two-part "Positivist Anarchy" consisted primarily of translated passages, in the first part from Herbert Spencer's "Reasons for Dissenting from the Philosophy of M. Comte," and in the second from Mill's famous essay on Comte and from Littré's rejoinder in defense of the master.[30] What interested Vigil most was the disagreement among the three positivists on the question of cause. While Comte, according to Spencer, denied the possibility of "investigation on what are called causes, be they first or final," the latter insisted that the scientific method led ultimately to the "consciousness of cause." This consciousness of cause, added Spencer, "can be abolished only by abolishing consciousness itself." Vigil was delighted by Spencer's footnote that by virtue of this opinion, "it is clear that I cannot be what he [Comte] calls a positivist."[31] The question arose again in the debate between Mill and Littré over the nature of the "unknowable," that is, the supernatural origin of the universe. Whereas Mill

[28] *Revista filosófica*, 1 February 1882, p. 9.

[29] Vigil, in ibid., 1 May 1882, p. 50, 58; Parra, "La Pseudo-anarquía positivista I," *La Libertad*, 31 May 1882.

[30] The documents Vigil used were Herbert Spencer, *Classification des sciences*, 4th ed. (1st edition 1872; Paris, 1881), pp. 95–106 ("Pourquoi je me sépare d'Auguste Comte,"); John Stuart Mill, *Auguste Comte et le positivisme*, 2d ed. (1st. ed, 1868, Paris, 1879); Émile Littré, "La Philosophie positive: M. Auguste Comte et M. J. Stuart Mill," *Revue des deux mondes*, 15 August 1866, pp. 829–66.

[31] *Revista filosófica*, 1 May 1882, pp. 53–54. I have quoted from Spencer, "Reasons" (1864), in *Essays: Scientific, Political, and Speculative*, 3 vols. (*Works*, 1891 ed., 21 vols.), 2:127–28.

left open the existence of the supernatural and like Spencer saw it as a point on which science and religion might conceivably be reconciled, Littré asserted (interpreting Comte) that what could not be known by the scientific method was absolutely inaccessible to the human mind. Vigil concluded that Littré had "excommunicated" Mill from the "Comtean guild," further proof of "positivist anarchy."[32] Without taking sides himself, Parra dismissed Vigil's dissection of these disagreements as mere "sophistry," a misuse of the cherished positivist concept of intellectual anarchy. What exists in these debates, countered Parra, is a simple difference of opinion on the application of the scientific method, not on the method itself. They are differences that could exist among individuals within any school of thought.[33]

Throughout his essay Vigil repeatedly used the labels "sensualism" and "empiricism," adding that in the dispute between Mill and Littré the former revealed himself to be a semiatheist, the latter an atheist. Soon after publishing it, Vigil published Caro's critique of Littré, asserting that it not only demonstrated the "radical vices" of positivism but also "why it [positivism] is in open contradiction with the spirit and tendencies of Mexican society."[34] Far more congenial to Mexican society, he might have added, were the convictions with which Paul Janet concluded his text, soon to be adopted in the National Preparatory School. After acknowledging the existence of a philosophy in each of the sciences, Janet reaffirmed that philosophy proper had "its own domain," which developed from "internal sense," self-knowledge, or consciousness. Moreover, continued Janet, philosophy has relations not only with the natural sciences, but also with the most elevated functions of the human soul— poetry and religion—which have as their final object the ideal and the divine. "The philosopher thinks, the religious man believes and worships, the poet sings and dreams; but a single breath, a single God, inspires (*anima*) all three."[35]

In his case for the positivist system of education, Porfirio Parra gave special importance to "the law of association of mental states" as developed by British psychologists. In doing so, he was broaching the definition and place of psychology, a major point of controversy between posi-

---

[32] *Revista filosófica*, 1 June 1882, pp. 72–74. On the dispute between Littré and Mill, see Charlton, *Positivist Thought*, pp. 61–66. Sierra (in his spiritualist phase) quoted Littré on the "unknowable" (see chap. 5, n. 43).

[33] Parra, "Pseudo-anarquía I-III," *La Libertad*, 31 May, 1–2 June 1882.

[34] Vigil, in *Revista filosófica*, 1 July 1882, p. 96. Vigil also referred to (but did not emphasize) Comte's religion of humanity as a point of contention among positivists. He cited Mill's attack and inserted a translation of Caro's "La Réligion positiviste" from *Études morales sur le temps présent* (Paris, 1855 [4th ed. 1879]) in his *Revista filosófica*, 1 January, 1 February 1883, pp. 177–89, 192–206.

[35] Janet, *Tratado*, pp. 870–78. The passage quoted was Janet's final sentence.

tivists and spiritualists. The adoption of Alexander Bain's *Logic* in the ENP had brought the issue to the fore, because Bain represented the culmination of the tradition of British empirical psychology dating back to John Locke and recently introduced into France. Bain regarded "psychological data" as the "groundwork of logic," and he began his text with a brief summary of relevant principles drawn from his major life work of establishing psychology as an independent science.[36] Vigil attacked repeatedly the implications of empirical psychology, focusing his attention on the text by Luis E. Ruiz, whom he accused of producing an abridged version of Bain. According to Vigil, the terms "mind" and "psychology" were now robbed of their philosophical significance and what remained was "a psychology without soul and a mind without substance." The positivists were proclaiming "the absolute impossibility of knowing the mind as more than a series of material phenomena."[37]

The Mexican debate over psychology had its origins in a major difference between Comte and Cousin. One point of departure for Comte's whole system was his refusal to treat internal mental experiences, the results of introspection, as facts, which in turn for Cousin were the basis of the scientific method. For Comte, introspection was simply unscientific. In his classification he made psychology a mere branch of physiology and he rejected traditional logic as being based on overly vague generalities.[38] Parra, following Mill, Spencer, and Bain, admitted Comte's error and clearly accepted psychology as a separate science, as did Sierra. For Vigil, this departure by Parra was only further proof of the anarchy that reigned in the positivist camp. Vigil's attack on the new experimental psychology brought him back to his central rhetorical point, namely that the positivists were ultimately placing morality and ethics on a "purely sensual basis" and were eliminating God "as principle of all that exists, both in the subjective and in the objective realms."[39]

Throughout the educational and philosophical controversy of the early 1880s ran the thread of politics. Although political and educational issues had remained separate in the debates of the previous decade, they came together abruptly in 1880. On 23 September, four days before the exec-

[36] Parra, "Educación intelectual" (nos. 12–13), 24 February, 1 March 1882. The entry of experimental psychology into France is usually dated at 1870, the year Théodule Ribot published his *La Psychologie anglaise contemporaine*: see Charlton, *French Positivism*, pp. 83–85; Gabriel Compayré, introduction to Alexander Bain, *Logique: déductive et inductive*, 2 vols. (Paris, 1875). On Bain's psychology, see George S. Brett, *History of Psychology*, ed. R. S. Peters (London, 1953), pp. 441–50.

[37] Vigil, in *Revista filosófica*, 1 July, 1 October, 1 December 1882, pp. 95, 133, 167.

[38] See Simon, *European Positivism*, pp. 27, 122–25; idem, " 'Two Cultures,' " pp. 47–49; Compayré, introduction to Bain, *Logique*, 1:34.

[39] Parra, "Pseudo-anarquía III," 2 June 1882; Sierra, "Plan Montes," 3, 7 May 1881 (*Obras*, 8:90, 96); Vigil, in *Revista filosófica*, 1 August, 1 December 1882, pp. 110, 169.

utive decision to substitute Tiberghien's logic text for Bain's, Juan A. Mateos proposed in the Chamber of Deputies that all nationalized ecclesiastical buildings still in the charge of foreign clergy or of the Jesuits be closed forthwith and put up for public auction. A week later, Francisco Cosmes responded in *La Libertad*, accusing Mateos of still living in 1861, of still haranguing against "clerical tyranny" long after the battle against it had been won, and of wantonly attacking the right of the Jesuits to propagate their ideas in a free country. The old orator of the Reforma can rest assured, concluded Cosmes, that "the liberal conquests are well protected by a new generation, which possesses a philosophical method less vulnerable to clerical attacks than that of the metaphysicians of the era of the Constitution of 1857."[40] Cosmes was immediately seconded by Telesforo García, while Mateos and the "old guard" liberals were defended by Ignacio M. Altamirano and Hilario Gabilondo. Justo Sierra in turn responded to Altamirano in an open letter of 13 October. Altamirano took note of the juxtaposition of the two issues, the logic text and the heritage of the Reforma, but it was García's series of articles that most dramatically joined the political debate of the late 1870s to the philosophical questions raised by the substitution of textbooks.[41]

The political themes that emerged in the educational and philosophical controversy of the early eighties were not new. They reflected the continuing conflict between scientific politics and doctrinaire liberalism and they can be found in the exchanges between Sierra and Vigil two years earlier. However, the joining of political and educational debate and the onset of a new presidential administration produced subtle but significant changes in the character of the controversy, if not in the ideas expressed. Scientific politics had emerged in the aftermath of factional turmoil as an argument for strong government and constitutional revision. Its advocates were a group of young journalist-intellectuals seeking official status for the new doctrine in a regime whose bases of support were shaky. Although *La Libertad* received a government subvention, and although Díaz restrained his ultra supporters of 1876, the *tuxtepecanos netos*, the president also resisted identifying himself exclusively with the advocates of the new doctrine. Pragmatic political reconciliation seemed to be the

[40] Cosmes, "Una Ley reformista," *La Libertad*, 1 October 1880. The Mateos proposal can be found in *Diario de los debates*, 10th congress, 1:219.

[41] García's articles first appeared in *El Centinela español*, 10 October, 4, 11, 25 November 1880, a year later as *Polémica filosófica*, and in two subsequent editions as *Política científica y política metafísica* (see chap. 2, n. 5; pp. 175–77). The Sierra letter was dated 9, but first appeared in *La República* on 12 October (and the next day in *La Libertad*). It should also be noted that the translator of Tiberghien, José María Castillo Velasco (1820–83), was another "old guard" liberal who had served on the drafting committee for the Constitution of 1857. He was later minister of *gobernación* in 1871–72.

guiding principle of the first Díaz regime, a principle that was perpetuated in the presidency of Manuel González.

We have noted in chapter 3 the decline of liberal constitutionalist opposition to the government after 1880, exemplified by the cases of José María Vigil and the newspaper *El Monitor republicano*. Vigil's ideas themselves did not change in 1880, but his relationship to the regime did. When he defended classic liberal ideas against Sierra, Parra, García, or Hammeken, he did so as the newly appointed professor of logic in the ENP and as director of the national library, in support of the antipositivist ministerial initiatives of Ignacio Mariscal and Ezequiel Montes. Vigil was no longer an outsider and thus his defense of liberalism became more generalized and philosophical, less focused on what he had seen earlier as a specific threat to the Constitution of 1857. For their part, the advocates of scientific politics were put on the defensive as positivists because of the resurgence of doctrinaire liberalism in the Ministry of Justice and Public Instruction. Nonetheless, they did not turn against the regime, because many of their assumptions were now influencing policy in other areas. For instance, Manuel Fernández Leal, Barreda's close friend who had taught math at the ENP from 1868 to 1878, was now serving as subsecretary of *fomento*. In summary, after 1880 political debate not only became tied to the controversy over higher education, but it became further confused by renewed consensus within the liberal establishment. Put another way, both parties to the debate had in effect established a presence within the state apparatus itself.

The subordination of the political to the educational controversy after 1880 meant that the explicitly positivist dimensions of scientific politics were more subject to debate than they had been earlier. Whereas Comte had rarely been mentioned by the editors of *La Libertad* or by Vigil in 1878–79, his political judgments were now frequently discussed, as his ideas on education had been for more than a decade. A key word in the polemical exchanges of the early eighties was "absolutism." García characterized the new generation of scientifically oriented youth as rejecting both the "absolutism of divine right" and the "absolutism of the rights of man," to which Gabilondo replied that García was merely applying Comte's theories to the political realm. Comte's "only absolute is that all is relative," that all truths must emanate from the observation of phenomena.[42] His doctrine led him, charged Gabilondo, to support both the French republic in 1848 and the Second Empire in 1852; both "were phenomena of the political and social order, and consequently were rel-

[42] García, *El Centinela*, 10 October 1880 (also *Polémica*, p. 12); Hilario Gabilondo, "La Lógica de Tiberghien en la Escuela Nacional Preparatoria," *La República*, 22, 29 October 1880 (Díaz y de Ovando, *Escuela*, 2:123, 135); also *La República*, 13, 14 October; 10 November (Díaz y de Ovando, *Escuela*, 2:112–13, 145).

ative." Gabilondo made much of Comte's support of Napoleon III and of his high regard for Julius Caesar and low regard for the Greeks. García did not defend Comte's later politics, but instead he pointed out the "progressive" political affiliations of heterodox positivists like Littré and Spencer. The burden of Gabilondo's rhetoric, however, was on the defense of his own set of absolutes—God, country, and liberty—which he said were being undermined by positivism. In fact, he emphasized them so much that *La Libertad* called him *"el caballero de los tres absolutos"* and even coined the verb *gabilondear*.[43]

Although his views were more reasoned and substantial than Gabilondo's, José María Vigil also pointed to Comte's absolutism, and concluded categorically in 1882 that "positivist and liberal are contradictory terms." Making the connection between philosophy and politics in the manner of the French spiritualists, he went on to assert that "positivism, like any sensualist doctrine, degrades man . . . and leads necessarily to skepticism, materialism, atheism, and despotism."[44] Porfirio Parra, who had always been less political than Sierra or García, never responded directly to Vigil, but instead he introduced his discussion of "intellectual education" with a familiar positivist view of Mexican political history. He stressed the "mental disequilibrium" that existed in Mexico because of the abrupt transition in 1810 from absolutism to democracy. More favorable toward "the greatest revolution in history" than Comte had been, Parra contrasted Mexico's colonial ignorance with Europe's long mental preparation for 1789, which had begun with Luther's break from the medieval church. The result in Mexico, he said, has been a kaleidoscopic series of changes since independence. Instead of basing political changes on an "exact study of our society," every politician "attempted to shape the nation as if it were soft wax to the mold of his own opinions."[45] Parra went on to specify the social and moral evils of the existing intellectual anarchy (guided philosophically by eclecticism), which could only be corrected by proper method and proper system in education.

As might be expected, Justo Sierra, the historian, addressed Mexican political history far more specifically and sympathetically than did Parra, the physician and logician. Yet their positivist criteria were similar. Sierra was responding respectfully to Ignacio Altamirano, his predecessor at the ENP and literary mentor of the Juárez years, who had resigned from *La Libertad* in protest against attacks by Leopoldo Zamora and Cosmes on the liberals of the Reforma. Sierra disarmed his correspondent, acknowl-

[43] See the heated exchanges of March and April 1882 in *La Libertad* and *La República*, summarized by Díaz y de Ovando in *Escuela*, 1:112–15.

[44] Vigil, in *Revista filosófica*, 1 November 1882, p. 156; also p. 131. Vigil was discussing the logic text by Ruiz.

[45] Parra, "Educación intelectual" (no. 1), 10 December 1881.

edging that the attacks were extreme and that Altamirano was right to resign; but he then proceeded to justify them in substance if not in style. He assured Altamirano that his attachment to positivist method would never lead him to denigrate the revolution of Ayutla and the Reforma; but he then suggested that their leaders were guided by an "eminently subjective notion" and an "egoistic sentiment," that they held to impractical "metaphysical conceptions," and that they hated the past. On the other hand, continued Sierra, we have a profound respect for the past, the entire past, Catholic and feudal as well as revolutionary. Even though the ideas of the reformers were "alien to any scientific observation of reality," they did pave the way "for the definitive arrival of an organic, positive, and scientific period," which, added Sierra, is now being solidified by a system of education built on the "ascending hierarchy of the sciences."

Sierra's patronizing argument was cast in strongly generational terms, a central feature of the rhetoric of scientific politics after 1878. In concluding he lauded Altamirano as the "mentor of the new generation," just as he was the "spoiled child of the generation that is now passing."[46] Both Sierra and Parra avoided political prescriptions, or any call for strong government or constitutional revision, which is perhaps further evidence that some of the assumptions of scientific politics had found their way into the González administration.

In the midst of the textbook controversy Justo Sierra issued a formal proposal for the creation of a "national university." It was to be an independent corporation made up of the major professional schools, the National Preparatory School, and a yet-to-be-created Escuela Normal y de Altos Estudios. The university would be governed by a director general and his council, composed of directors and professors of the various schools, plus student representatives. This body (*cuerpo universitario*) would establish the curriculum, grant degrees, and appoint and dismiss professors (under certain conditions). The university would be constituted as a juridical person with the right to acquire and dispose of property within the limits of the constitution. Though independent, the institution was to be intimately tied to the government, its source of funding. The autonomous functions of the university would be carried out within the general provision that the executive was to "define and regulate" the powers of university authorities and to exercise "vigilance" over its inter-

---

[46] Sierra, in *La Libertad*, 13 October 1880 (*Obras*, 14:62–66). Altamirano announced his resignation, directed to Sierra, in *La República* on 9 October, specifically in reaction to an article of 7 October by "Timón" (Leopoldo Zamora) in *La Libertad*. Cosmes also responded to Altamirano in tones similar to Sierra's; but several younger positivists, headed by Luis E. Ruiz, Porfirio Parra, and Manuel Flores, were more deferential. See "Una Carta del Sr. Cosmes" and "Un Remitido importante," in *La República*, 12 October 1880.

nal affairs. Its director general was to be appointed by the president. Curricular changes voted by the *cuerpo universitario* would be subject to suspensive executive veto; after a year they could be instituted, but only by two-thirds vote. Finally, under Sierra's plan the government was to modify immediately the existing curriculum for preparatory studies, restoring it essentially to the positivist plan of 1867–69.[47]

Sierra's proposal was prompted by Ignacio Mariscal's intervention in the professorial selection of logic texts, and it brought forth once again the relation between the state and higher education. Sierra was forced to elaborate his position on this issue by Enrique M. de los Ríos, a student of Altamirano, who questioned how Sierra's proposed university could be funded by the government and still maintain its independence. Sierra's response was elaborate and complex, but he did make it clear, as he had in 1875, that he regarded the role of the state as fundamental. He introduced his proposal by saying that in general he was a partisan of state action when that was necessary to advance social organization, and yet that as a "member of the liberal positivist school," he viewed all that led to the normal replacement of government action by individual action as a sign of progress. Citing Spencer, he saw these two processes, "integration" and "differentiation," as complementary. In proposing a national university, Sierra maintained that his objective was to free the "teaching functions" from the government, thus eliminating the "paternal dominion" (*patria potestad*) it presently exerted over "science." While arguing that "the propagation of science" should be freed from the state and left under the direction of a "technically competent body," Sierra nonetheless recognized that at the present stage of evolution the state must "impell society to constitute itself under the regime of science." In short, progress demanded an "interpenetration" of the state and public instruction.[48]

Sierra asserted that Germany provided the inspiration for his proposed national university. In doing so, he was responding to the immense prestige of the German university and was following a general tendency in Europe and America to look to it as a model for the reorganization of higher education. With the foundation of the University of Berlin in 1810 by Wilhelm Von Humboldt and the spread of its system to the other Ger-

[47] Sierra, "La Universidad nacional," *El Centinela español*, 10 February 1881 (*Obras*, 8:65–69), introduced in the Chamber of Deputies (with minor modifications) as a *proyecto de ley* on 7 April (ibid., pp. 333–37).

[48] Sierra, "El Gobierno y la universidad nacional," *La Libertad*, 5, 25 March 1881 (*Obras*, 8:77–82). The first Ríos statement, an exercise done in the elocution class of the law school, appeared in *La República*, 27 February 1881. The second statement appeared on 10 March and is reprinted in *La Universidad de Justo Sierra*, ed. Juan Hernández Luna (Mexico, 1948), pp. 147–51.

man states by 1830, universities came to be organized around the ideal, drawn from classical philology and philosophy, of science (*Wissenschaft*) as the organic totality of knowledge. In the university, studies were to be pursued freely in search of a single truth, rather than for practical objectives; and the separate disciplines in separate departments were to be brought together by philosophy. *Wissenschaft* in effect meant systematic scholarship, rather than science in the Anglo-American sense. Research and teaching, in a climate of "academic freedom," were a unity; and only the productive scholar could be an ideal teacher. The academic coherence of each German university and of the system as a whole had great appeal, in part because it appeared to stand in sharp contrast to the other great European public system, the all-embracing, yet internally incoherent, University of France, established by Napoleon in 1807. The new German system had been established in the dark days of Napoleonic occupation, and the ideals of German university and German national state were integrally connected. Thus the German universities acquired their unique character as state-guided and -funded, yet academically autonomous, institutions.[49]

The superiority of German higher education came to be recognized in France after 1870, and under German influence the several faculties of arts and sciences were finally formed into "universities" in 1896. The Spaniard Julián Sanz del Río returned from Heidelberg in 1844, impressed with the autonomy of the German university from both church and state; and he and his Krausist followers devoted themselves to establishing the "freedom of science" in the University of Madrid. Forced outside the university, one of those followers, Francisco Giner de los Ríos, founded in 1876 the privately funded and quasi-autonomous Institución Libre de Enseñanza. However, it failed as a school of higher learning largely because the government refused to validate its titles and degrees.[50] In Mexico, besides Sierra's references to the German model, first in 1875 and then again in 1881, it also appeared in an anonymous argument for a "free university," written probably in 1875 and finally published in *El Nacional* in November 1880 as a contribution to the ed-

[49] See Hajo Holborn, *A History of Modern Germany*, 3 vols. (New York, 1959–64), 2:479–84; also Friedrich Paulsen, *The German Universities and University Study* (New York, 1906), a clear and eloquent if idealized appreciation of the system. Recent research has emphasized that continued evocations of Humboldt's ideal after 1860 (as perpetuated in accounts such as those by Paulsen and Holborn) masked a growing tension within the universities between the natural sciences and philosophy. See Charles E. McClelland, *State, Society, and University in Germany, 1700–1914* (Cambridge, 1980). Sierra, like other observers of the day, was of course unaware of this tension.

[50] Cacho Viu, *Institución*, p. 486.

ucational debate.[51] In short, Sierra's resort to the model of the German university for Mexico was not unique; and it was probably based more on general reputation than on direct study. There is little other evidence that Sierra was attracted to German thought and culture.

We have noted that the idea of a free university was first presented in April 1875 by students in rebellion against outmoded pedagogy and government interference in their extracurricular life. Using *"enseñanza libre"* as their banner, the students won broad and varied support, including the young Comtean positivist Miguel S. Macedo, the old liberal Altamirano, and the then-spiritualist Justo Sierra. What brought these varied supporters together was the conviction that higher education should have some corporate integrity and thus some immunity from whimsical government intervention. Yet there was no suggestion, except possibly by Macedo, that higher education should be detached from the government. Sierra argued consistently that the modern state was a progressive force, by which he meant its promotion of the secular and scientific spirit. The modern state has never condemned the Galileos of this world, he asserted. Its universities have struggled against "theological tradition"; they "have been the normal school of the modern mind."[52]

Like the French liberals of the nineteenth century, Sierra took education by the state for granted as the only alternative to education by the church. The issue of church education arose less frequently in Mexico after 1867 than in France because church and state were legally separate, but the issue was qualitatively similar in the two countries. By contrast, the persistent influence of the church within the state and thus within the University of Madrid made the Spanish situation extreme and therefore less pertinent to Mexico. It is revealing that Sierra never mentioned the Institución Libre de Enseñanza, and that, except for one reference by Enrique M. de los Ríos, it went virtually unnoticed during the controversy over higher education in Mexico.[53]

Edmundo O'Gorman has argued that Sierra proposed the national university in 1881 as a way to "save positivism" from a hostile government. It is true that Sierra's proposal did provide for an official positivist pre-

[51] "La Universidad libre" (eleven articles), *El Nacional*, 30 October, 2, 4, 6, 9, 11, 16, 20, 23, 25 November, 4 December 1880. The preface (30 October) stated that they were written during the last part of the Lerdo administration. The plan proposed was somewhat similar to Sierra's except that it called for suppression of the ENP. See also the commentary by Díaz y de Ovando, *Escuela*, 1:91–94.

[52] Sierra, "El Gobierno y la universidad nacional," 5 March 1880 (*Obras*, 8:78).

[53] I have found only two short descriptive notices in *La Libertad*, 27 December 1881 and 19 July 1882. Ríos referred to an article in *La República* (8 March 1881), a full description taken from a Spanish source. It should be noted that despite its failure as a school of higher learning, the Institución had great success for over a generation as a force for progressive education on the secondary level.

paratory curriculum to be embedded within a quasi-autonomous university, giving positivism double protection against attack. But seen within the context of local precedents and foreign influences, the proposal went beyond positivism and spoke to larger issues in Mexican higher education. Sierra's university aroused little immediate interest; it was overshadowed by the polemical controversy over philosophy and religion and the bill died in a legislative committee. However, in part because it did speak to broader issues, Sierra's idea had a reincarnation in somewhat different form as the National University of Mexico. Or, as O'Gorman put it, in 1910 a transformed Sierra "revived [the university] in order to surmount [positivism]."[54]

By mid-1883 the philosophical controversy had subsided, leaving the conflict over educational policy unresolved. The Montes plan to eliminate the National Preparatory School had failed, as had Sierra's proposal to insulate it from further danger. The positivist curriculum remained largely intact, except for some dilution of the science requirements for future lawyers and except for the critical fifth-year course in logic, which was being taught by positivism's most vigorous opponent, José María Vigil.[55] By appointing Joaquín Baranda as minister of justice in September 1882, the government seemed to signal its intention to extend the policy of reconciliation to education. The controversy was effectively ended with the adoption of Janet's text, under pressure from Baranda. Even Porfirio Parra resigned himself to Janet, which he found less offensive than Tiberghien. In Spain, Tiberghien was regarded as sympathetic to modern science by comparison with Krause, but he was clearly less sympathetic than Janet. Whereas Tiberghien's critique of positivism was sharply polemical, Janet's was based on reasoned analysis.[56] The changing climate in Mexican education and politics was sensed by the quasi-official La Patria on the second anniversary of Barreda's death. Because of his work, said the paper, an enlightened and prudent "new generation" is entering political life, as the country approaches an era of "order, peace, and progress."[57]

During the subsequent decade there were two periods during which

[54] O'Gorman, "Justo Sierra," p. 201.

[55] A Ministry of Justice circular of 21 January 1881 reinstated the changes made in 1873 (see chap. 5, n. 38), notably the elimination of chemistry and natural history for future lawyers, adding instead a third year of Latin, Revista de la instrucción pública, 1 May 1896, 1:99–100.

[56] Parra, "Educación intelectual" (nos. 3–4), 17, 28 December 1881. He cited Barreda's maxim, "we must be intolerant in theory and tolerant in practice," as his guide. Cf. Tiberghein, Lógica, 1:6–16 and Janet, Tratado, pp. 870–72.

[57] La Patria, 21 February 1883 (Díaz y de Ovando, Escuela, 2:183). It should be noted that José María Vigil contributed nearly two editorials a week (though not these two) to La Patria between 1 January 1883 and 24 January 1884. See below, p. 241.

the Preparatoria again became the subject of public controversy. At these times the earlier issues reemerged, but these debates lacked their earlier vigor and urgency. The first episode took place in 1885 when a new director of the ENP established a professorial commission to consider curricular changes. The second took place in 1891 when the curriculum was thoroughly examined by the second National Congress of Public Instruction, convened by Minister Baranda. The result of both episodes was favorable to the traditional preparatory school system. In 1885 the status quo of 1883 was reaffirmed; in 1891 the classic program of 1869 was reinstated, ushering in fifteen years of unchallenged positivism in Mexican higher education.

The first episode came in the aftermath of the crisis of November 1884, the decision by the González government to recognize the longstanding British debt. One victim of the crisis was Justo Sierra, who was serving as interim director of the preparatory school following the resignation of Alfonso Herrera the previous August. Preparatory students protested the government's action on the debt as unpatriotic and then turned their wrath against Sierra when he sided with the government. Amid rumors that the new president, Porfirio Díaz, might close the school, Vidal Castañeda y Nájera was appointed director on 20 January 1885. The student upheaval raised the general question of discipline, curricular as well as extracurricular, and Castañeda's commission addressed the gradual erosion of the uniform program under continual pressure from career-minded students and parents. The Junta de Profesores upheld the principle of curricular uniformity but agreed that it was more prudent to work internally toward that goal than to propose new legislation. The other major question addressed by the commission was the neglect of literary studies, and especially of Latin, in the overall curriculum. The junta showed less harmony on this issue, and the positivists won out over the more humanistically oriented committee. The addition of a sixth year to the curriculum was also proposed, but it was rejected as impractical in the face of popular sentiment.[58]

Two months after the Castañeda commission had concluded its work, the annual selection of texts brought philosophical contention once again

[58] The two committee reports, dated 23 March and 15 June 1885, plus subsequent discussion can be found in Archivo Histórico de la Universidad, 23:157–90. The first report was also reprinted in *El Tiempo* on 5 April (Díaz y de Ovando, *Escuela*, 2:216–17). The spokesmen for the commission were Vigil and Rafael Ángel de la Peña. For Peña's commentary on the second report, see *Explicación razonada que el profesor . . . presenta al ciudadano director de la escuela nacional preparatoria de las modificaciones a la ley de instrucción pública propuestas por los catedráticos de la misma escuela* (Mexico, 1886). In response to student insubordination a lengthy and detailed set of regulations governing conduct in the ENP was issued on 31 March 1885: *Revista de la instrucción pública*, 1 June 1896, 1:165–69.

to the surface. On this occasion the positivists, notably Manuel Flores, José María Gamboa, Eduardo Garay, and Justo Sierra challenged the re-adoption of Janet, which in turn was defended vigorously by Vigil and by Rafael Angel de la Peña. Although the positivists prevailed in the Junta de Profesores, the government, which had published the pro-Janet speeches, overruled the junta, resorting apparently to a recent change in the regulatory legislation.[59] The speeches themselves were a thorough-going restatement of Vigil's spiritualist arguments of 1882—that positiv-ism equaled sensualism and thus was antireligious, that positivism was vitiated as a philosophy by major disagreement among its advocates, and that positivism was antithetical to liberalism as a political doctrine. Vigil also restated the spiritualist conception of psychology and asserted in op-position to Flores that the subject must be introduced in the fifth-year class before, rather than after, formal logic. In the course of his defense of Janet, Vigil admitted a "deplorable fact" long noted by the positivists, namely that "anarchy" reigned in preparatory teaching. It was quite true, he said, that in his logic class he had to counteract "with metaphysics" the positivist principles established by Garay in the physics course.[60] However, Vigil did not suggest that the positivist curriculum should be abolished, perhaps because he feared that such a suggestion would only encourage those careerists who wanted no uniformity at all, positivist or otherwise.

Both the government and the faculty of the preparatory school may have had further incentive to perpetuate the educational status quo be-cause of the resurgence of militant Catholicism, led by an unrestrained press. Joining the long-lived *La Voz de México* were *El Centinela católico* (1880–84) and *El Tiempo* (1883–1912). The latter was directed by Victo-

---

[59] José María Vigil and Rafael Ángel de la Peña, *Discursos pronunciados por . . . en las juntas de catedráticos celebrados en la escuela nacional preparatoria los días 27 y 31 de agosto y 1 y 4 de septiembre de presente año, con motivo de la designación de texto para la clase de lógica* (Mexico, 1885). The Mariscal memorandum of 14 October 1880 (see pp. 171–72) was inserted as an appendix to the pamphlet, clearly to justify the government's rejection of the majority decision against Janet. An addition to the regulatory law of 1869 was issued on 10 August 1885, explicitly empowering the minister to make the final decision on ENP texts: Dublán and Lozano, *Legislación*, 17:305–06. This legislative change was ap-parently unrelated to the deliberations of the Castañeda commission.

[60] Vigil and Peña, *Discursos*, pp. 36–37. It should be emphasized that the government did not include the positivists' speeches in the pamphlet, nor to my knowledge do they appear elsewhere. There were also references to philosophical debates in March at the Liceo Hidalgo between Vigil and Parra, but I have found no texts. The government's ac-tions suggest its desire to perpetuate the status quo, that is, a modified positivist curriculum and a spiritualist logic course. Further evidence of this policy is the government's apparent refusal to accept Vigil's resignation as professor of logic, presented in a letter to the Ministry of Justice dated 5 September. See the text in Agraz García de Alba, *Biobibliografía*, pp. 170–71.

riano Agüeros (1854–1911), who came to be a leading spokesman and publisher for the new Catholic generation. *El Tiempo* followed the upheaval in the ENP and the curricular reform efforts of 1885 closely, and it delighted in encouraging student grievances and in identifying conflicts between positivists and spiritualists.[61] These conflicts had of course diminished considerably since 1882, when Vigil had seemed on occasion to make common cause with Catholics against the positivist virus. In his *Revista filosófica* he even published an antipositivist discourse by Célestin-Joseph Félix (1810–91), a renowned French Jesuit preacher.[62]

By 1885 Catholics had totally rejected Vigil's earlier efforts to gain their acceptance for the logic course by demonstrating his respect for religion. Though *El Tiempo* rated positivism worse than Janet's spiritualism, it attacked as inconsistent all efforts by Vigil to defend the eclectic ENP curriculum. Moreover, it regarded Vigil's close colleague, the remarkable liberal Catholic Peña, as an apostate. *El Tiempo* found absurd Peña's argument that the committee report on the curriculum was compatible with the Catholic faith.[63] Even less restrained than the articles in *El Tiempo* was a diatribe against positivism by José de Jesús Cuevas, who had been a leader of the Sociedad Católica in the early 1870s and a stalwart of the Catholic press.[64] This hardening of the Catholic position was bound to enhance the growing ideological consensus within the liberal establishment.

After five quiet years, the National Preparatory School again became the subject of public discussion at the two national congresses of public

[61] For example, *El Tiempo*'s series on the Castañeda commission's reports in April and May (Díaz y de Ovando, *Escuela*, 2:216–31).

[62] Célestin-Joseph Félix, "La Negación positivista y su valor científico," *Revista filosófica*, 1 April, 1 May, 1883, pp. 225–34, 241–51. The speech had been published the year before by the Catholics and had aroused much commentary in the press, including six articles by Jorge Hammeken y Mexía, who noted the strange alliance: "El Padre Félix y la metafísica mexicana," *La Libertad*, 31 March–12 May 1882. On Vigil and the Catholics, see also *Revista filosófica*, 1 March, 1 May 1882, pp. 32, 62–63.

[63] *El Tiempo*, 25 April 1885 (Díaz y de Ovando, *Escuela*, 2:229). Vigil defended his association with "the theologian" Peña against positivist skeptics by saying that they agreed on philosophy but not on theology: Vigil and Peña, *Discursos*, p. 53. Peña's career was unusual and deserves further study. He graduated in theology from the Pontifical University in 1860, then turned to science and literature and taught math and grammar at the ENP after 1868. He published a highly regarded grammatical treatise in 1898. In 1892 he proposed to the new archbishop of Mexico, Próspero María Alarcón, that more modern science be injected into seminary training for priests: Peña, "Exposición razonada del plan de estudios para el seminario conciliar de México," *Obras* (Mexico, 1900), pp. 1–67. Peña (1837–1906) was even accorded a sympathetic obituary in the *Revista positiva* 6 (21 May 1906): 318–19.

[64] Cuevas, "El Positivismo en México," *La Voz de México*, 20 October 1885 (also published as a pamphlet in Zacatecas). On Cuevas (1842–1901), see José de Jesús Cuevas, *Obras* (Mexico, 1898), pp. v–xix.

instruction. The purpose of the congresses, as set forth frankly by Joaquín Baranda in his call to governors to name delegates, was to bring uniformity to public education at all levels, correcting the "lamentable anarchy" that existed in the laws and systems of the several states. Setting the context for the educational deliberations, Baranda extolled the prevailing climate of peace and identified the state as the agent of modern democratic progress. Economic and social problems are being solved, he continued, by "a new and extraordinary program in our history, which subordinates politics to administration and sterile theories to immediate facts and beneficial results."[65] First on Baranda's agenda, as we will see in chapter 7, was the extension of free and obligatory primary education, legislated for the Federal District in 1888, to the entire country. This was the exclusive work of the first congress, which met from 1 December 1889 to 31 March 1890, leaving for the second congress (29 November 1890 to 28 February 1891) the consideration of other levels of education. In effect, the second congress directed its attention primarily toward preparatory instruction. Its uniform extension throughout the nation became a minor issue and was readily approved. More significant was the traditional question of curricular organization and the philosophy that should guide it. The result of these deliberations was an overwhelming victory for positivism, a vindication of the classic program of 1869.

We will recognize in Baranda's rhetoric the themes of scientific politics, as expressed for example in the manifesto of the National Liberal Union of 1892. The organization of public education by the congresses formed an integral part of the program of administration, reconciliation, and development that had taken form in 1878 and reached its culmination in the early 1890s. The role of science in this program was elaborated further in the initial report of the committee on preparatory instruction, chaired by Porfirio Parra. Arguing in familiar fashion the need for a uniform Comtean curriculum (and mixing its metaphors), the committee referred to science as both the "cement" and the "alma mater" of contemporary civilization. Today, it continued, all is decided in the name of science, just as all was decided in the name of reason in the eighteenth century or of God in the sixteenth. Scientific education also had more specific political benefits: "Those who love each other in the schoolrooms as brothers will not be combatants in fratricidal conflicts, but will become friends and collaborators in the peaceful tasks of society (*la vida social*)."[66]

---

[65] Baranda, circular to state governors (1 June 1889), *Debates del [primer] congreso nacional de instrucción pública* (Mexico, 1889 [sic]), pp. i–iii.

[66] Report of committee on preparatory instruction (4 February 1890), ibid., pp. 236–42 (Díaz y de Ovando, *Escuela*, 2:287–91). The initial committee report was presented, but not discussed, in the first congress. A later report, made to the second congress, was more

In the eyes of the committee, these "friends and collaborators" consti-tuted the "enlightened classes," which must create laws and institutions, promote industry and commerce, and advance science, arts, and letters. Just as the nation needs a people to be led, it also needs those "who know how to lead." Parra and his committee brought together the Porfirian politics of reconciliation with the educational elitism of the Preparatoria's founders.[67]

We have seen that there were two curricular issues that fueled the controversy over higher education for two decades. The first was whether or not there should be a uniform set of preparatory studies, based on the hierarchy of the sciences, to be pursued by all students, regardless of their career objectives. The second was the nature of the course in logic (philosophy) and its placement in the curriculum. The second congress dealt decisively with both issues. It was evident by 1889 that even apart from the logic course there had been considerable erosion in the uniform preparatory curriculum over twenty years. The requirements for would-be lawyers, physicians, and engineers varied considerably, in response to both practical and ideological pressures; and the changes were being made piecemeal in sometimes obscure laws and directives.[68] It was also evident from Minister Baranda's call to the state governors and from the complexion of the delegates that the government had moved since 1885 from the acceptance of the status quo to support for positivist uniformity. Both the committee and the congress itself were dominated by Prepara-toria stalwarts, dedicated to reinstating the now-traditional curriculum. Parra chaired the committee and Justo Sierra presided over both con-gresses. Manuel Flores and Luis E. Ruiz were both committee members and officers of the second congress. In fact, of the nine men who made up the committee on preparatory instruction, at least six had strong ENP and positivist ties.[69]

---

specific, but quoted several general passages from the earlier one: *Segundo Congreso na-cional de instrucción pública* (Mexico, 1891), pp. 106–17 (session of 13 January 1891).

[67] Ibid., p. 107. One important theme of scientific politics, constitutional reform, was not relevant to educational organization and thus did not appear in the deliberations of the congress.

[68] See chap. 6, n. 55. A decree of the Ministry of *Fomento* dated 16 May 1883 established rigorous scientific requirements for would-be engineers, at the expense of humanistic sub-jects, especially Latin: *Revista de la instrucción pública* (1 May 1896, 1:102). A summary of the existing preparatory requirements accompanied the ministry's "questionnaire" of 19 November 1889, which was designed to guide the deliberations of the congress: *Diario del hogar*, 6 December 1889 (Díaz y de Ovando, *Escuela*, 2:286).

[69] Besides the three men mentioned, R[icardo?] Aguilar had been a prize-winning student in 1872; Emilio G. Baz had held various faculty positions since 1872; Miguel Schulz had entered the ENP in 1868, taught geography beginning in 1882, and was interim director in 1901. Of the other three members, Alberto Lombardo (b. 1844) attended San Ildefonso before the ENP was founded and was a signer of the Liberal Union manifesto; Rosendo

The objections raised to reinstating the uniform curriculum were weak by comparison with the forceful case made for it. Ramón Manterola accused the committee of following Comte too slavishly and proposed instead a "simultaneous" curriculum in which the various sciences would be introduced gradually from the first year along with mathematics. Such a system would provide students who abandoned their studies after two or three years some exposure to the sciences and not just to abstract mathematics.[70] In rejecting Manterola's proposal, Parra restated his standard case for good method, for true education as opposed to scattered instruction. He was clearly more concerned with those who completed their studies than with those who did not. In addition, he made it more explicit than he had earlier that he and his colleagues rejected Comte's second period of "mental derangement." We are not Comteans, said Parra, but "eclectics" [!], drawing from the "best interpreters of science," beginning with Comte in his first period. Nonetheless, the uniform and hierarchical program that was adopted by the congress was basically Comtean, with the important addition of psychology, which reflected, according to Sierra, the "growing influence of English doctrines."[71]

In establishing a uniform curriculum there had always been the problem of literary and humanistic studies and it reemerged in the second congress. The Parra committee acknowledged that the urgent need to give the sciences a fundamental place in the curriculum had led in 1869 to the slighting of literary studies, a fact confirmed in Barreda's writings.[72] Antipositivists had regularly attacked the downgrading of the humanities, especially Latin, and we have noted that the amount of required Latin constituted one of the major variations within the existing curriculum by 1889. The committee's proposal to eliminate Latin met some opposition, but it passed easily following Justo Sierra's persuasive intervention. For him Latin was simply a "dead language," appropriate as the capstone of literary studies or as part of the career training for lawyers and doctors, but not appropriate for general preparatory education in a scientific world.[73]

Pineda was a *Científico* of 1893 who was educated in Oaxaca and thus had no ENP ties; I have been unable to identify Francisco Gómez Flores.

[70] For Manterola's speech and proposal, see *Segundo Congreso,* 7 February 1891, pp. 353–60. Manterola (1848–1901) was a prominent educator and journalist who was serving as director of the Escuela Normal. He had written on Hegelian philosophy and defended it at the Liceo Hidalgo against both Parra and Vigil. See Emeterio Valverde Téllez, *Crítica filosófica* (Mexico, 1904), pp. 409–30, where Manterola is identified as an "eclectic."

[71] Parra, in *Segundo Congreso,* 31 January 1891, p. 282; Sierra, in his closing speech of 28 February 1891, ibid., p. 470 (*Obras,* 5:135). Psychology was included in the logic course and not taught separately.

[72] *Debates del [primer] congreso,* 4 February 1890, p. 240 (Díaz y de Ovando, *Escuela* 2:290).

[73] Sierra, in *Segundo Congreso,* 3 February 1891, pp. 332–39 (*Obras,* 8:262–67, an abbre-

The Parra committee also proposed a sixth year in the curriculum to accommodate humanistic studies, including more English and Spanish; but much of the extra time was to be taken up by other subjects, such as hygiene, physical education, and lectures in sociology. The most important gain for the humanities, the expansion of history, had come gradually as a reaction from many quarters to Barreda's disinterest in the subject. The principal champion of history had been Justo Sierra, and undoubtedly his prestige influenced the inclusion of a respectable historical component in the proposed curriculum.[74] In sum, despite some concessions to literary and humanistic studies, the positivists of the second congress made it clear that their basic goal was to reinstate scientific education in the sense generally envisioned by Gabino Barreda.

As we might expect, the most contentious issue in the deliberations of the second congress was the nature and placement of the logic course. Nonetheless, the discussions were mild by comparison with earlier ones and represented in effect the completion of the controversy of the early 1880s. After a decade in retreat the positivists were again dominant and Parra's committee made a forceful and articulate reformulation of their argument. The abstract rules of logic must be learned after specific exposure to the fundamental sciences. Logic is a study of scientific method in the abstract, which, added the committee, must "preside over and determine all our mental activity, in the laboratory and in the home, in the classroom and in the public arena."[75] Despite the committee's positivist report, its initial summary proposal stated only that logic (undefined as to content) would conclude preparatory studies. Then, as if sensing their advantage in the congress, the positivists submitted on 3 February a revised proposal: Logic would consist of "the systematization of the methods of the sciences, with the complete exclusion of any theological or metaphysical concept."[76] Three days later in *El Universal*, Parra deplored the existing logic course, which was drawn from "contemporary French eclecticism, an essentially mixed form of philosophizing." Concluding his public case, Parra announced that very soon the congress would consider reform, that is, "placing [teaching] in harmony with the state of contemporary knowledge."

The boldness of the positivists provoked one significant rejoinder in

---

viated version). Sierra also justified the elimination of Latin in his closing speech: *Segundo Congreso*, 28 February 1891, p. 472 (*Obras*, 5:136–37). There remained in the curriculum one third-year course in Greek and Latin "roots."

[74] The congress approved history for each of the last three years and increased it from three to six hours above the committee proposal for the sixth year: *Segundo Congreso*, 9 February 1891, p. 370. Barreda's disinterest in history probably was due more to his personal orientation toward medicine and the physical sciences than to the influence of Comte. Comte put emphasis on history and the historical method (see p. 214).

[75] Ibid., 13 January 1891, p. 112.

[76] Ibid., p. 298. The revised proposal was passed fifteen to three without debate.

the congress, by Andrés Díaz Millán, and a predictable response in the press by José María Vigil, who was not a delegate but was still serving as professor of logic. In language reminiscent of earlier debates, Díaz Millán attacked the exclusivism of the revised committee resolution. If there are two (or more) competing schools of logic, he said, then they should both (or all) be taught. By eliminating all theological or metaphysical concepts from teaching, the state would in effect be giving one system official status; for whatever Parra and his colleagues may say to the contrary, positivism is a philosophical system. An official positivism would eliminate any idea of God as cause and any abstraction or general idea as a basis for our constitution. Díaz Millán went on to compare positivism with "Christianity in the epoch of Constantine." It has reached the seat of power, and "tomorrow, like Catholicism, it may come to tyrannize our minds (*puede ser el tirano de las conciencias*)."[77] Díaz Millán's case was forceful, but without effect. He had been absent when the committee's revised proposal was approved and his attempt to have the matter reconsidered was ruled out of order by President Justo Sierra.

Parra could not let such a strong case go unanswered, even if it would not affect the actions of the congress. His reply, as before, was that the proposed course was one in logic, not philosophy, and that by endorsing it the state would only be endorsing the teaching of neutral scientific method. It would not in any way be imposing a religious belief or a philosophic doctrine.[78] Díaz Millán made no rebuttal but left the task to Vigil, who defined metaphysics and philosophy, defended his course as not in conflict with anything taught before it in the curriculum, and said that Janet's system of philosophy was not mixed, but "radically rationalist." Like Díaz Millán he emphasized the exclusiveness of the experimental method; it negated Man's reason, "the faculty of the absolute, without which there would be no high ideals, no progress, no liberty, no morality, no science." Vigil's rebuttal brought a further response from Parra, who devoted four more articles to an elaboration of his argument.[79]

Despite Vigil's vigorous words, his final exchange with Parra had a quality of routine and even of resignation. The question of the logic course had already been settled in the congress, where Justo Sierra in his concluding address presented an eloquent summary of the now victorious positivist position. Vigil acknowledged Sierra's eloquence in one

---

[77] Díaz Millán, in ibid., 12 February 1891, p. 378. He mentioned the religion of humanity and referred its establishment in Brazil.

[78] Parra, "El Señor Díaz Millán," *El Universal*, 17 February 1891.

[79] Vigil, "Un Plan de estudios," *El Universal*, 20–21 February 1891: "Al Sr. Doctor Parra," ibid., 6 March 1891. Parra, "Método científico," ibid., 25–26 February 1891; "Al Señor Lic. Vigil," ibid., 11, 20 March 1891. These articles were preceded by three others (30 January–24 February), revealing further the ascendancy of the positivist position.

last defense of spiritualism, but the case was closed. Within two weeks there was a report that Parra would be giving oral lessons in logic from Bain and within a few months there was another that he was preparing his own text. In May 1892 came the news that Vigil had moved from logic to literature and that his replacement would be the positivist José María Gamboa.[80] Thus ended the philosophical controversy that was born with the National Preparatory School and came of age in the great textbook debate of 1880.

José María Vigil's defense of spiritualism in 1891 against the positivists might be compared with *El Monitor republicano*'s defense of the pure constitution against the *Científicos* in 1893. Both efforts represented the last stand of doctrinaire liberalism against the growing consensus within the post-Reforma political and educational establishment. During the first decade the conflict over higher education remained generally apart from politics. Ironically, the new educational system, guided by a philosophy that was theoretically antithetical to liberalism, was given official status in 1867 by a government that was the incarnation of the heroic liberal struggle. It was only with the assertion of a new political doctrine in 1878 that educational and political issues became joined and that the antiliberal implications of positivism became fully apparent. The philosophical debate of the early 1880s between spiritualists and positivists also became a political debate over the nature of Mexican liberalism. Yet because of the policy of factional reconciliation, the debate never questioned the González regime itself. Vigil may have defended the constitution as a political dissident in 1878, but by 1881 he was defending spiritualism and liberal principles as an insider, supported by the minister of justice.

Positivism was indeed a "fearsome enemy," to use López Morillas's phrase, because those who embraced it never denied their liberalism. We need only cite the example of Justo Sierra's transformation in the 1870s from spiritualist to positivist, from constitutional legalist to constitutional revisionist. Through it all he remained first and foremost a liberal. As liberalism became reinterpreted through science and as the new interpreters, strengthened by the growing cadre of graduates of the National Preparatory School, increasingly found their way into the circles of government, the vigor of doctrinaire liberalism within the establishment

[80] The reports appeared in *El Partido liberal*, 3 March 1891 and in *El Diario del hogar*, 25 September 1891 (Díaz y de Ovando, *Escuela*, 2:297, 300). The appointments were noted in *El Diario del hogar*, 31 May 1892 (Díaz y de Ovando, *Escuela*, 2:301). Gamboa was also a *Científico* of what I have called the "second echelon" (see p. 126). It should be noted that Vigil was probably diverted in the late 1880s from defending philosophy by the task of writing vol. 5 of *México a través de los siglos*, published in 1889.

diminished. After the mid-1890s it could only find expression on the outside.

By 1892 positivism had regained its status as Mexico's official philosophy of preparatory education. The basic elements of Barreda's curriculum were reaffirmed, though much of his Comtean vision was put aside by the more heterodox Porfirio Parra and Justo Sierra. Barreda's emphasis on scientific education as a means of moral regeneration and his flirtation with Comte's religion of humanity had little appeal for the leaders of the second National Congress of Public Instruction. In addition, they found a place for psychology, which Barreda had ignored. The curriculum adopted in 1891 was finally written into law with some modifications in 1896. The leader in this effort was Ezequiel A. Chávez (1868–1946), a Preparatoria graduate of 1886 and later a professor, who was rising to prominence in the Ministry of Justice. Besides writing the revised plan for preparatory studies, Chávez also directed the voluminous *Revista de la instrucción pública mexicana*, an important element in Minister Baranda's continuing program of educational organization.[81] There was turmoil in the ENP during the mid-nineties when students resisted the martial discipline imposed by Director Castañeda y Nájera, but the school regained equanimity after 1901 under the respected leadership of Manuel Flores and Porfirio Parra. Perhaps the culmination of positivism came in 1903 with the adoption and publication of Parra's two-volume *Nuevo Sistema de lógica*, a synthesis of his work of twenty-five years.[82] But the reign of positivism was short, for it had now become the new orthodoxy; and like any orthodoxy, it was vulnerable to free intellectual inquiry.

[81] The new *ley de enseñanza preparatoria en el distrito federal*, dated 19 December 1896, can be found in *Revista de la instrucción pública* (1 January 1897), 1:609–14. The law followed a series of discussions presided over by Chávez and recorded in the *Revista*, which began publication on 15 March 1896. It ran until 1903 and then continued as *Boletín de instrucción pública* until 1911. The Chávez plan of 1896 incorporated the 1891 recommendations but compressed the program into eight semesters. It was changed to six years in 1901.

[82] For details of the conflict within the Preparatoria during 1895–96, see Díaz y de Ovando, *Escuela*, 1:186–99. On Parra's text, see Zea, *Positivismo*, pp. 386–93.

CHAPTER 7

Positivism, Liberalism, and Society

THE YEARS AFTER 1867 saw the rise of positivism as the predominant set of social ideas in Mexico, just as positivist philosophy came to guide the reorganization of higher education and positive or scientific politics became the prevailing concept of government. As we have demonstrated, positivist ideas met strong resistance from both Catholics and liberals, yet by the 1890s their ascendancy seemed sure. Above all, positivism proclaimed that the age of science had arrived in Mexico, a message that was irresistible as the regime of Porfirio Díaz reached maturity. Positivist social theory was of course closely related to positivist philosophy and to scientific politics, and we have touched upon it frequently in the preceding pages. Yet we must probe further its principal elements in order to understand better the assumptions of the intellectual and governing elite of Porfirian Mexico and how these assumptions affected social policy.

The principal elements of positivist social theory can be found in the thought of Auguste Comte and Herbert Spencer. I will give further attention to the specifically social ideas of these "twin pillars" of European positivism, particularly those of Spencer, and I will compare the two and weigh their relative importance in Mexico. Another important element of positivist social theory was the evolutionary biology of Charles Darwin and particularly the doctrine of "Social Darwinism," a term that has become a universal catchword for late nineteenth-century social attitudes. A final element was the historical school of law, which if it was not explicitly positivist did share many positivist assumptions. Formulated originally by the German jurist Friedrich Carl Von Savigny, it was interpreted for Mexico by the French constitutional theorist Edouard Laboulaye. We have seen that Laboulaye's historical constitutionalism was an important ingredient of the emerging scientific politics; it was also significant in Mexican social thought.

Comte and Spencer provided the basis for widely held general assumptions about man and society in the late nineteenth century. Most salient was the notion that society was a natural organism, subject like all of nature to evolution or change over time. Man as an individual was an integral part of this changing organism and his ideas, beliefs, and behavior could not be understood in the abstract but only in relation to society as a whole. This understanding could come about only through science, that is, through observation of social phenomena, through experimentation, and through a search for social laws. In short, there could and must be a science of society that followed the procedures and the objectives of the science of nature. According to both Comte and Spencer, progress was the highest social law, the virtual equivalent of evolution or development; and their message was one of optimism, improvement, and even (in the case of Comte) the regeneration of the human species. Beyond these generalities, the differences in their ideas were more critical and significant for Mexico than were the similarities, and it is to those differences that I will soon turn.

Comte's work was interpreted in Mexico at least a decade before that of Spencer, in part because Comte was older and began to publish a generation earlier, but also because he was French. Whereas Pedro Contreras Elizalde and Gabino Barreda had been exposed to Comte and even knew him personally in Paris as early as 1848, few Mexicans went to England and there is no evidence of similar encounters by Mexicans with Spencer. We have noted in chapter 5 that Mexico's first Comtean essay, Barreda's *De La Educación moral*, appeared in 1863, whereas the years 1874–75 probably mark the entry of Spencer's thought into Mexican intellectual life. Only a few Mexicans read Spencer in English and it seems clear that most learned of him through France, where his work arrived surprisingly late. The first French translation of Spencer appeared in 1871, but it was not until 1874 with the widely publicized French edition of *The Study of Sociology* that Spencer found a Mexican audience. From that time on Spencer's place was secure, and he rapidly became the most frequently cited European social theorist in Mexico, as he was throughout Spanish America.[1]

Understanding the reception of Darwinism in Mexico involves at least two distinct questions. The first is when and how Darwin's works reached Mexico and the second involves the way his ideas were used by Mexicans. Darwin was a naturalist and not a social theorist; our principal concern is not with the impact of his ideas on Mexican biology, but rather

---

[1] Comte was born in 1798, Spencer in 1820. Spencer's *First Principles* (1862) was published in French in 1871, *The Study of Sociology* (1873) appeared as *Introduction à la science sociale* (1874). The latter was the occasion for an important essay by Paul Janet, "La Science sociale et la philosophie anglaise," *Revue des deux mondes*, 1 November 1874, pp. 81–110, which undoubtedly helped to disseminate Spencer's ideas in Mexico. There was also the earlier essay by Auguste Laugel, "Les Études philosophiques en Angleterre," ibid., 15 February 1864, pp. 930–57, a long review of *First Principles*, as well as Théodule Ribot's *La Psychologie anglaise* (1870). It is unlikely that these two publications were much noticed in Mexico, but I do not claim to have done exhaustive research on the matter. Spencer's first work, *Social Statics* (1851), was never translated into French or Spanish, and his early essays were not translated until the late 1870s. Nothing of Spencer appeared in Spanish before 1878.

with their application to social thought. Since the latter question goes beyond Mexico and entails the general problem of whether Social Darwinism was derived more from Darwin himself or from other sources, we will defer that question and turn first to the seemingly more straightforward issue of transmission.

As Roberto Moreno has shown, Darwinism was probably first known in Mexico in the early 1870s and it was not formally cited until 1875, when Justo Sierra referred at least twice to Darwin and Wallace's "magnificent law of transformism." It may be, as Moreno suggests, that Darwin was known more through *The Descent of Man* (1871) than through *The Origin of Species* (1859), because of the greater shock produced by the *Descent* among Catholics. The religious implications of the theory of human origins were the subject of much controversy in the Mexican press, beginning in 1878 when *La Voz de México*, *El Centinela católico*, and *La Ilustración católica* debated the brothers Sierra and other editors of the newly founded *La Libertad*. In fact, Porfirio Parra, *La Libertad*'s young science editor, felt obliged to remind the Catholic polemicists that Darwinism was quite different from the positivism of Mill, Bain, Comte, and even of Spencer, and that most positivists greeted "the Darwinian hypothesis" with skepticism and even hostility. Because of positivism's official status in higher education, early Catholic opposition to Darwinism in Mexico was probably less significant than the controversy it aroused in positivist circles.[2]

The key to understanding Darwin's impact in Mexico, as is the case with so many other instances of intellectual transmission, lies in the fact that he was known through French sources. Darwin was slow to be accepted in France, not because of Catholic opposition but because there was deeply entrenched scientific resistance to the theory of the transformation of species, resistance particularly by the academician Georges Cuvier and his followers to the ideas of the Chevalier de Lamarck. Moreover, French supporters of *transformisme* (the French always preferred the term to "evolution") came to regard Darwin as merely reviving and perpetuating Lamarck's theories of the years 1800 to 1820 rather than introducing ideas that were new and revolutionary. The *Origin* caused little stir in France when it was first published and a French edition did not appear until 1862. Finding no scientist who would undertake a translation, the publisher turned to Clémence Royer, an intelligent writer on economic and social questions. Royer was a convinced transformist of strong anticlerical views, and she added a polemical preface of nearly fifty pages to the book along with numerous notes and commentaries through-

[2] Moreno, *Polémica*, pp. 17–42. Parra's article appeared in *La Libertad* on 20 October 1878.

out the text. Moreover, she changed the subtitle in order to point up Darwin's contribution to the idea of progress. Darwin did not object to the translation itself, but after the appearance of the third edition (1870)—which included additional opinionated comments—he sought another translator, both for the *Origin* and for the newly published *Descent*. Yet he was still unable to find an eminent scientist to take on the project.[3]

Many of the features of the French debate over Darwin were replicated in the first major Mexican discussion of Darwin's ideas which took place in the Asociación Metodófila "Gabino Barreda" during February and March 1877. The discussion began with a brief sympathetic paper presented by Pedro Noriega, a medical student, and this was followed by a long negative critique of Darwin's theory by Barreda, interspersed with shorter pro-Darwinian statements by Noriega's fellow students, Parra and Manuel Flores.[4] Barreda refused to accept Darwin's work as representing a true "scientific theory." According to Barreda, it was impressive at the descriptive level, but Darwin did not prove the laws he supposedly deduced from observed facts. Barreda questioned at length Darwin's unproved assertion that only the most useful organs were transmitted and noted his failure to account for useless organs or monstrosities. Barreda found Lamarck's more modest theory superior, because it simply emphasized the "gradual diversification of living species" and the inheritance of characteristics acquired by interaction with the environment rather than positing the emergence of new species through the process of natural selection.[5]

Like the French critics before him, Barreda particularly objected to Darwin's metaphorical language, the use of phrases such as "natural selection" or the "struggle for life," which he said became substitutes for scientific rigor. He kept reminding his students that the subject of their meetings was "method" and "logic," and he seemed to have them in mind when he asserted:

> In effect, if anything favors and explains the notable success of the transformist hypothesis, it is the brilliant style of the author [Darwin], aided by an incomparable wealth of details which, wrapped in and embellished by continual met-

[3] See Robert E. Stebbins, "France," in Glick, *Comparative Reception*, pp. 117–67; also Linda L. Clark, *Social Darwinism in France* (University, Alabama, 1984), pp. 9–28. Royer's original subtitle was *Ou Des Lois du progrès chez les êtres organisés*; Darwin's was *By Means of Natural Selection or The Preservation of Favored Races in The Struggle for Life.*

[4] *Anales*, pp. 97–186 (sessions 25 February–18 March). Text also in Moreno, *Polémica*, pp. 45–124.

[5] *Anales*, pp. 119–20 (Moreno, *Polémica*, pp. 63–64).

aphors, form a most seductive description of organisms as a whole and in their infinite variety.[6]

Barreda ended his discourse with a number of references to European Darwinists and their critics, all of whom were prominent in the French debates of the 1860s and 1870s. For example, he expressed some sympathy for the view of Cuvier's successor, Flourens, that Darwin's work had a propagandistic and proselytizing quality. According to Darwin's disciples, one must either accept transformism or be regarded as "a fanatic and a retrograde." To prove his point Barreda quoted from Royer's preface to her translation of the *Origin*: " 'The doctrine of Darwin is the rational revolution of progress, which places itself in logical opposition to the irrational revelation of the fall. . . . As for me, my choice is made; I have chosen progress.' " Büchner and Haeckel made similar assertions, said Barreda; for them accepting Darwin has become a matter of faith, not science. At the same time, even transformists such as Huxley and Topinard continued to emphasize the hypothetical character of Darwin's conclusions.[7] Thus, the best that can be said is that Darwinism is superior to finalist and theological doctrines. "If some day," concluded Barreda, "a satisfactory theory on the origin of species is formulated, Darwin will doubtless be considered one of its most illustrious precursors."[8]

The debate over Darwinism demonstrates first of all that Barreda (and perhaps his students as well) were transferring to Mexico both the documents and the terms of the debate in France. It should be noted, for example, that the word *transformismo* was used almost exclusively in their discussions; the term *evolución* rarely appeared. Second, Barreda seemed to be fighting a losing battle, for he found himself challenged by his two most prominent students, Parra and Flores, who showed themselves to be "seduced" by Darwin. Perhaps they found his metaphors and his style (and Royer's eloquent preface) more engaging than Barreda's rigorous (and austere) positivist logic. Perhaps they were already developing, as Parra suggested to his Catholic critics the following year, a flex-

[6] *Anales*, p. 181 (Moreno, *Polémica*, pp. 119–20).

[7] On Pierre-Marie-Jean Flourens, see Stebbins, "France," p. 130. Barreda probably used the third edition of Darwin's *De L'Origine des espèces* (Paris, 1870), in which Royer's preface to the first edition was reprinted (quoted passage from the final paragraph, p. lxxi). A Darwinist essay by the German materialist philosopher Ludwig Büchner appeared in French in 1869, Ernst Haeckel's *Histoire de la création des êtres organisés d'après les lois naturelles* in 1874. Barreda cited Thomas Huxley's *Les Sciences naturelles* (Paris, 1877), a translation of *Lay Sermons*, and Paul Topinard's *L'Anthropologie* (Paris, 1876). He also mentioned Jean-Louis Armand Quatrefages de Breau, who wrote a series of influential articles on transformism in the *Revue des deux mondes* (1869) that were probably read in Mexico.

[8] *Anales*, p. 186 (Moreno, *Polémica*, p. 124).

ible and heterodox positivism that was departing from their mentor's rigidities. Finally, although the 1877 debate gives us a good insight into the process by which Darwin's ideas were transmitted to Mexico, it tells us little of how they were used in social thought. The debaters concerned themselves solely with the scientific and methodological aspects of *The Origin of Species*.

The historical and comparative school of law, like the more prominent elements of positivist social theory, did not flower in Mexico until after 1867. Though there were indications that the assumptions of the historical school affected Mariano Otero in the 1840s, the effect was weak when compared for example to its effects in Argentina and Chile. As we have suggested, Mexico's Reforma, the great ideological conflict of the mid-century decades, served as an intellectual watershed, deferring the shift away from natural law and doctrinaire constitutionalism. The historical school argued that law was not an abstract entity arbitrarily set down by the legislator and having a separate existence, but that it was organically connected to society and its development.[9] Such assumptions did much to erode the faith in constitutional ideals, an erosion that we have traced in chapter 3 from the *convocatoria* of 1867 and the subsequent campaign to reinstitute a senate to *La Libertad*'s program of constitutional reform. We have noted the role of Edouard Laboulaye's history of the United States, translated in Mexico in 1870, in the Senate campaign. At their origin, French positivism and the German historical school of law shared an antipathy toward the arbitrary social and legal changes imposed by the French Revolution; they also shared a common emphasis on the organic evolution of society. Thus the advocates of scientific politics, as social evolutionists, could draw from Laboulaye, the French follower of the German school, as well as from Comte and Spencer.[10] Like Laboulaye, they rejected both democracy and dictatorship and favored a strong constitutional government based "empirically" on the preservation of a conservative social order.

In examining positivist social ideas in Mexico after 1867, we must recall one of the basic themes of this study, namely the growth of positivism within a political climate governed by an all-embracing liberal myth. Liberalism was triumphant in 1867, and political success thereafter required formal adherence to the liberal creed embodied in the Laws of Reform and the Constitution of 1857. In short, the ideas we are examining were those of a liberal establishment, and in part our problem is to discern the

---

[9] See Hermann Kantorowicz, "Savigny and the Historical School of Law," *Law Quarterly Review* 53 (1937): 326–43.

[10] Laboulaye wrote *Essai sur la vie et les doctrines de Frèdéric Charles de Savigny* (Paris, 1842), republished in *Études contemporaines sur l'Allemagne et les pays slaves* (Paris, 1856—and three further editions to 1872).

relation between positivism and liberalism in Mexican social thought. Of the two principal elements of positivist social theory, the works of Comte and Spencer, which one was more congenial to the Mexican liberal heritage? The prevailing view, established by Leopoldo Zea's studies in the 1940s of Mexican positivism, is that Spencer was the more influential author in Mexico because his ideas provided a better rationale for the interests of the Mexican "bourgeoisie," the group I have preferred to call the liberal establishment. Without necessarily rejecting Zea's conclusion let us reexamine the question of influence, beginning not with the interests of a supposed ascendant or hegemonic class, but with the ideas themselves, the positivism of Comte and Spencer.

There were two principal differences in the social thought of Comte and Spencer that were relevant to their impact in Mexico. One involved their conceptions of the social organism and its relation to the individuals that composed it. The other involved their conceptions of the process of evolution itself. Besides these theoretical distinctions, Comte and Spencer presented their ideas differently, which affected their comparative receptions and use in Mexico. Moreover, the relation of the ideas of Comte and Spencer to other currents of positivist social (or potentially social) thought—notably Darwinism and the historical school of law—differed. These then are the intertwined general considerations that guide our inquiry.

Both Comte and Spencer drew their conceptions of the social organism from biology; however, Comte used biology, or more properly physiology, to elucidate man's original nature, whereas Spencer used biology as a model for society in all of its aspects. We have noted in chapter 5 that Comte drew upon the physiological research of his day to demonstrate that altruism was a more fundamental human trait than egoism, and that social feeling was a stronger force than conflict between individuals. However, Comte only cautiously advanced the analogy between nature and human society, and he rejected the idea that sociology was derived from biology. For Spencer, on the contrary, human society was merely an extension of nature and the study of sociology was dependent on biology.[11]

Fundamental to Spencer's view of the social organism was the idea that society was simply an aggregation of individuals. "There is no way of coming at a true theory of society," he wrote in his first book, "but by inquiring into the nature of its component individuals." He began all three of his major sociological works with atomistic assumptions drawn

---

[11] Comte, *Cours*, 4:229; Herbert Spencer, *The Study of Sociology* [1873] (Ann Arbor, 1961), chap. 14 ("Preparation in Biology"). Spencer gave Comte credit for setting forth "the connexion between the Science of Life and the Science of Society" (ibid., p. 299).

from his early exposure to Benthamite utilitarianism, religious noncon-
formity, and laissez-faire economics. These assumptions guided his entire
thought, even though they often conflicted with the very notion of social
organism itself. Comte's assumptions about society were never atomistic.
When referring to the peculiarities of the social organism, Comte used
terms like "fundamental consensus," "harmony," and "solidarity"; and he
argued the necessity in sociology as in biology of proceeding from the
whole to the parts. Though he was less inclined than Spencer to apply
biological notions to social theory, he ultimately developed a more coherent concept of social organism.[12]

The process of social evolution was far more naturalistic for Spencer
than it was for Comte. Spencer saw the change from the homogeneous
to the heterogeneous, from the simple to the complex, as universal
throughout nature. Its explanation lay in the fact that "every active force
produces more than one change—every cause produces more than one
effect." Spencer's sociological writings were studded with astronomical,
physical, geological, and zoological analogies. In Comte, "the positive
theory of social progress," while clearly related to the physical and biological sciences, seemed to take the form of a distinct inquiry, what he
called "the dynamic study of the collective life of humanity." Comte's
basic analogy was between the stages of the human mind (theological,
metaphysical, and positive) and the stages of society. Progress for him
was progress in the way men thought, individually or collectively, and
thus rationally ordered their environment. For Spencer, progress was the
improvement in the way men adapted to inevitable changes in their circumstances. "Progress is not an accident, not a thing within human control, but a beneficient necessity" was his famous statement.[13]

Comte in his positive philosophy put great emphasis on method, on
the classification of the sciences based on their increasing complexity, a
classification that Spencer explicitly rejected. Comte's thought lent itself
most directly in Mexico (and thoughout Latin America) to reorganizing
higher education, to introducing a universal system for applying the scientific method to the study of phenomena. Spencer was less interested
in method and more interested in demonstrating by example the law of
evolution. He provided voluminous details on the variety of peoples and

[12] The Spencer passage is from *Social Statics* (1851), p. 16, quoted in J. W. Burrow,
Evolution and Society: A Study in Victorian Social Theory (Cambridge, 1968), p. 199. For
Comte's argument, see *Cours*, 4:182–89. Comte acknowledged, however, that in the "inorganic" sciences one should properly proceed from the parts to the whole. See also John
C. Greene, "Biology and Social Theory in the Nineteenth Century: Auguste Comte and
Herbert Spencer," *Critical Problems in the History of Science*, ed. Marshall Clagett (Mad-
ison, 1959), p. 441, and W. M. Simon, "Herbert Spencer and the 'Social Organism,' " *Journal of the History of Ideas* 21 (1960): 294–99, two valuable essays.
[13] Herbert Spencer, "Progress: its Law and Cause" (1857), *Essays on Education and
Kindred Subjects* (London, 1911), p. 176, 195; Comte, *Cours*, 4:168.

races, their customs, behavior, and mental characteristics. Comte's "progress of humanity" was more abstract and became in effect the progress of the European white race. Spencer's thought had a descriptive ethnographical dimension that was lacking in Comte, and he helped Mexicans focus attention on the peculiarities of their society within the universal scheme of evolution.

On the other hand, Comte had a greater appreciation for history than did Spencer, which enhanced the appeal of his thought in Mexico. One way that Comte distinguished sociology from biology was in its use of the historical method, "the historical comparison of the several consecutive stages of humanity" and the influence of one generation on the next. Because Spencer saw the progress of humanity as coextensive with progress in nature, he thought it unimportant to study the facts of human history. "A true theory of humanity," he wrote, is to be studied "in the facts you see around you and in the general laws of life." He said he was a "lover of history; but it is the history of the Cosmos as a whole."[14] At the apex of Spencer's unilinear vision of progress was the European society of his day, and particularly that of industrial and individualistic England. Comte characterized nineteenth-century Europe as a society in transition, governed by intellectual and thus social anarchy; and he looked to science to provide the means of organizing it once again as it had been in the Middle Ages into a collective and hierarchical whole. Whereas Spencer idealized the society of his day, Comte criticized it as transitory.

The differences between Comte and Spencer's social thought come into sharper relief when examining their relation to Darwinian biology and particularly to Social Darwinism. As we have noted, Comte construed biology more as physiology than as natural history. He rejected Lamarck's theory that organisms were continuously transformed by their interaction with the environment and clung instead to Cuvier's doctrine of the fixity of species. He died two years before the publication of *The Origin of Species*, so that he could not have been influenced as was his Mexican disciple Barreda by the debate over Darwinism in France and the consequent revival of Lamarck's development hypothesis. Spencer, on the other hand, was a convinced Lamarckian who adopted as did Darwin both the theory of the transformation of species and of the transmission by inheritance of acquired characteristics.[15]

Spencer added to Lamarck's theories the idea of social selection. Drawing from the *Essay on the Theory of Population* by Malthus, he

[14] Comte, *Cours*, pp. 236–37; Spencer, letter to Edward Lott (1852), quoted in Greene, "Biology and Social Theory," p. 432.

[15] See J. D. Y. Peel, *Herbert Spencer: the Evolution of a Sociologist* (New York, 1971), pp. 146–53; George W. Stocking, Jr., "Lamarckianism in American Social Science, 1890–1915," in *Race, Culture, and Evolution. Essays in the History of Anthropology* (New York, 1968), pp. 238–41.

argued that the pressure of population on the means of subsistence had brought progress by ensuring the survival of those who were most intelligent and skillful in each generation. In his own essay on population (1852), Spencer coined the phrase the "survival of the fittest," which Darwin later applied to the world of nature. Though Darwin did not discuss man in the *Origin*, he was aware of the social implications of his theory of natural selection, implications that were seized upon and applied by numerous writers after 1859 and ultimately by Darwin himself (with some caution) in *The Descent of Man* in 1871.[16] To what extent Darwin himself was a Social Darwinist is much debated, but it seems clear that the ideas of Spencer and Darwin were mutually reinforcing. It is also clear that the key notion of Social Darwinism—the natural selection of the individuals, groups, and races most fit to survive in the universal struggle for existence—permeated Spencer's social thought but was antithetical to that of Comte. Therefore the vogue of Social Darwinism in Mexico (and throughout Latin America) after 1870 was a demonstration of the influence of Spencer and not of Comte.

To conclude these general considerations, we should note briefly that Comte's engagement in history and historical method made his thought more compatible than Spencer's with the historical and comparative school of law, a lesser but nonetheless significant ingredient of positivist social theory. The historical school of law was one of the sources of evolutionary social theory that was unrelated to biology and to the developmental hypotheses of Lamarck, Darwin, or Spencer.[17] Although the French legal interpreter Laboulaye was basically a liberal, something that could never be said of Comte, Laboulaye's critique of doctrinaire constitutionalism and popular sovereignty, his elitism, and his acceptance of a significant role for the state in society brought him into the same realm of discourse as Comte. The Mexicans found it difficult to join the virulent individualism of Herbert Spencer, which was tied to the Darwinian notion of natural struggle, with the benign organicism of the historical school of law. They found the marriage easier in the case of Comte. Keeping in mind these broad and admittedly complex questions, let us now turn to the evidence from Mexico itself.

While we can identify with confidence the increase in positivist as-

---

[16] Richard Hofstadter, *Social Darwinism in American Thought, 1860–1915*, rev. ed. (Boston, 1955), p. 39; John C. Greene, "Darwin as a Social Evolutionist," *Journal of the History of Biology* 10 (1977): 11–27. Greene draws his conclusions from annotations Darwin made before and after 1859 in books and reprints in his personal library. See also the revisionist examination of Spencer's Social Darwinism in Robert C. Bannister, *Social Darwinism: Science and Myth in Anglo-American Social Thought* (Philadelphia, 1979), chap. 2.

[17] See Burrow, *Evolution and Society*, chap. 5, on Sir Henry Maine, the English jurist who was strongly influenced by the German school. Though Maine had no discernible impact in Mexico, Burrow's account is useful because it points up the contribution of the historical school of law to evolutionary theory in England independent of Darwinism.

sumptions in social thought after 1867, it is a difficult and perhaps un-profitable task to distinguish specifically those that are derived from Comte and those from Spencer. In general, Comte's overt influence seems to have been limited to the reflections on society by Gabino Barreda, the founder of the National Preparatory School, those of a small group of his disciples and students between 1867 and 1877, and after 1900 those of the orthodox positivist Agustín Aragón. By contrast, once Spencer's writings were known in Mexico in the mid-1870s (almost simultaneously with those of Darwin), he was continuously referred to and frequently quoted by a variety of individuals on numerous social questions. Spencer captured and articulated the yearning by intellectuals and the educated public to relate society to life in the broadest sense, and he became a symbol of the age not only in Mexico but throughout the Atlantic world. He was far more frequently referred to and quoted than Comte ever was, which leads us to the initial conclusion that his influence in Mexico must have been greater than Comte's. Yet in certain more subtle, qualitative ways, as we have already suggested throughout this study, Mexican social thought and policy bore a Comtean stamp. Finally, in identifying the incursion of positivist ideas, we must keep in mind the continuing strength of liberalism in the post-Reforma era.

Gabino Barreda's explicit social commentary was sparse. However, his most frequently cited passages revealed a distinctly Comtean approach to wealth and property, in sharp reaction to the liberal and vaguely socialist Nicolás Pizarro, who in his text on ethics extolled Christ's maxim that to gain perfection a man should distribute his goods among the poor. While perhaps having some merit in Roman times, said Barreda, such a practice today would bring ruin to our industrial society. Capital should not be condemned as such; rather it should be seen as a powerful source of progress. Barreda distinguished between capital for mere personal gain and capital "as a public force that society has placed in the hands [of the rich] for the common welfare and progress." In the proper moral environment (presumably with the triumph of positivist ethics) the rich would become aware of their responsibilities. Once wealth and work are viewed properly as social functions, as indispensable to "collective life" as circulation and digestion are to individual life, then the "fierce antipathy" of the proletarian poor for the capitalist rich and the "stupid disdain" of the rich for the poor would yield to cooperation. "Regulate property rather than destroy it, humanize the rich rather than impoverish them: These are the objectives to which modern moralists and philosophers should turn their efforts!"[18]

Barreda's Comtean argument was developed in more detail by his stu-

[18] Barreda, "Informe presentado a la junta directiva de estudios" (1868?), Opúsculos, pp. 127–28. On Pizarro, see above, p. 149.

dent Miguel S. Macedo in an essay on social ethics given before the Asociación Metodófila in 1877. Rigorously pursuing the "positive method"
and relentlessly defining his terms, Macedo set out to demonstrate the
"reciprocal duties of superiors and inferiors." Those who are superior—
women in the moral sphere, the rich in the social sphere, savants in the
sphere of science— should command the veneration, respect, and grati-
tude of their inferiors in each sphere. Reciprocally, those who are superior must use that superiority to serve humanity. Like Barreda, Macedo
deplored conflicts between capitalists and proletarians, which could be
overcome by an infusion of positive morality. Although the objectives of
strikes are often justified, serving "to impress on the superior the importance of cooperation by the inferior," in practice they bring social disrup-
tion and misery. In short, Macedo found strikes mostly "anarchical."
Shifting from the industrial workplace to more familiar ground, he asserted that the favorable outcome of the student "strike" of 1875 was due
to the entry into the ENP of the "ideas of a new science and a new ethics."
The students (of whom he was a leader) were able to "stop at the edge of
the abyss of anarchy and to pursue the path of morality, calling in the
name of progress for beneficial reforms."[19]

Permeating the formalistic observations of Barreda and Macedo was
Comte's ideal of a paternalistic society built upon accepted moral and
social hierarchies in which property would be social in nature and thus
necessarily regulated by the state. It would be a society in which "live
for others," the formula of positive ethics, would reign; in which "revolutionary pride" would give way to social solidarity; in which rights would
give way to duties, egoism to altruism. Despite the influx of Spencerian
and Darwinian ideas of natural struggle and survival, some of these Comtean assumptions lingered on in Mexican social thought.[20]

In contrast to the aloof and apolitical social theorizing of Barreda's Aso-

[19] Macedo, "Ensayo sobre los deberes recíprocos," *Anales*, p. 226 and passim. Macedo
like Barreda quoted several passages from Comte without identifying them. Lacking a thorough knowledge of Comte's many dense volumes, it is impossible to identify the source of
specific quotations, in fact it is difficult even to determine what of Comte the Mexicans
actually read. For a convenient summary of Comte's social ethics, see Lévy-Bruhl, *Philosophy*, pp. 319–32.

[20] Unfortunately, Macedo, who became a leading jurist, a *Científico*, and even a subminister, wrote little after 1877 that was not technical and legal. Nonetheless, his *La Criminalidad en México. Medios de combatirla* (Mexico, 1897), a speech before the second Con-
curso Científico Mexicano, reveals few naturalistic assumptions about society, quite in
contrast, for example, to Julio Guerrero, *La Génesis del crimen en México. Estudio de psiquiatría social* (Mexico, 1901). Macedo's approach to crime prevention was to isolate delin-
quent elements and to control them rather than to identify the social causes of crime. Barreda's approach had been similar. See Barreda, "El Congreso penitenciario de Estokolmo"
(1878), *Revista positiva* 12 (1912): 22–42, 49–75. Barreda attended as the Mexican delegate
before taking up his diplomatic post in Germany.

ciación Metodófila were the engaged arguments of Justo Sierra's *La Libertad* group, in which the program for national reconstruction through scientific politics was buttressed by social assumptions drawn from Spencer and Darwin. Random examples from *La Libertad* point up the editors' impulse to disseminate the new doctrines of biological and social evolution. These include the already noted impassioned defense led by Santiago Sierra of Darwin's theory of human origins against the attacks of the Catholics. The death of Darwin in 1882 was the occasion for a series of five articles assessing his scientific work.[21] In early 1879 Barreda's former student Luis E. Ruiz submitted a fragment in Spanish of Spencer's *Education*, along with some enthusiastic comments.[22] He would have preferred, he said, to treat readers of *La Libertad* to "all [!] the works of the distinguished English philosopher." On 14 December 1882, the entire front page was devoted to a long article from the *New York Sun* discussing Spencer's *Descriptive Sociology*.[23] Telesforo García and Carlos Olaguíbel occasionally referred to Spencer in support of removing burdensome taxes on industry. What does our manufacturing industry do, asked Olaguíbel, if not to produce (in Spencer's terms) "an infinite number of heterogeneous effects" in science, art, agriculture, and commerce?[24] *La Libertad* regarded itself as being in the vanguard of positivism, Spencerian and Darwinian as well as Comtean.

In order to demonstrate the general use of Spencer by the "new generation," let us turn once again to its leader, Justo Sierra. Sierra took on positivist ideas including those of Spencer about 1877, an intellectual transition that paralleled his political transition from José María Iglesias to Porfirio Díaz. We noted in chapter 2 that Sierra's presentation of scientific politics was infused with evolutionary terminology. He construed

---

[21] "Un Juicio sobre Darwin," *La Libertad*, 15 June–7 July 1882. Interestingly enough, the anonymous and technical articles disputed many of Darwin's findings. Other than in this series, his death was hardly mentioned in the Mexican press. See notices in Moreno, *Polémica*, pp. 361–63.

[22] Ruiz, in *La Libertad*, 7–9 January 1879; also 19 February, a favorable commentary on a recent regulation for the national primary schools for girls issued by Protasio Tagle, the minister of justice, whom Ruiz claimed was "imbued with Spencer's doctrines." Ruiz probably worked from the first French edition (1878) of Spencer's *Education* (1860). Characteristically he ended his comments on Spencer with a quotation from Comte, stressing the need for more method and less doctrine, more education and less instruction.

[23] Spencer's *Descriptive Sociology, or Groups [Cyclopedia] of Sociological Facts; Representing the Constitution of Every Type and Grade of Society, Past and Present, Stationary and Progressive*, 10 [folio] vols. (New York and London, 1873–1910), was a massive compilation, "free of all speculations and hypotheses," begun by Spencer and continued by others. It revealed Spencer's view of history as descriptive sociology. The Mexican translator of the article was Felipe Cazenueve, a frequent commentator on North American topics.

[24] Olaguíbel in *La Libertad*, 14 September 1878; T. García in ibid., 8 January 1878.

society in biological terms, subject to the laws governing all organisms—natural selection, the struggle for existence, and progress from the homogeneous to the heterogeneous.

One problem Sierra addressed in 1878 and 1879 was the proper relationship between the individual and society in a nation that sought reconstruction and strength after years of revolution, debilitating civil dissention, and threats from abroad. He addressed this problem as a liberal patriot, heir to the heroic midcentury struggles to institute constitutional liberties and a secular society against foreign enemies, domestic reactionaries, and traitors. He also addressed this problem in the terms of Auguste Comte, as an intellectual entering an organizing period of history, one that demanded a scientific or positive philosophy to replace the metaphysical or negative philosophy of the critical period just passed, a period that had witnessed the destruction of the colonial regime but also had brought revolution and civil war. Sierra began from the premise, imposed, he said, by "inflexible" scientific laws, that "the individual and society are two great organic realities that cannot be separated." Following Spencer's principle of simultaneous integration and differentiation, he asserted that as society becomes more highly organized, the individual inevitably broadens his activity.

However, throughout his general reflections on society appeared the very un-Spencerian idea of the positive role of the state. While claiming to be an individualist in the sense that he placed human rights ultimately above state power, he also rejected individual liberty as an absolute principle, calling it mere "verbal liberty." Absent from Sierra's theorizing is any trace of Spencer's frequent diatribes against government regulation and against intervention in social questions, such as appear in *The Study of Sociology*. In contrast to Spencer, Sierra explicitly tied the increase in individual activity to the development and greater precision of "the sphere of social action, whose primary representative is the state." Of course, these statements were embedded in *La Libertad*'s main argument, namely that authority must be strengthened to overcome anarchy and to ensure economic progress. In addition, Sierra referred frequently to the threat of the United States, which was particularly truculent during the late 1870s. In fact, he used the phrase "struggle for existence" primarily to characterize the extreme weakness of the Mexican organism in confrontation with "the marvelous collective animal" to the north. For Sierra this natural imbalance demanded the strengthening of central authority, the nervous force that directed the muscular force of external defense.[25]

[25] Sierra in ibid., 10 May 1878, 3 January 1879 (*Obras*, 4:145–46, 182); also Sierra in *La Libertad*, 14 February, 6 September 1878, 4 February (*Obras*, 4:142, 163, 212–13). See

In understanding Sierra's use of Spencer, we are again aided by evidence from France. An interchange between Sierra and Manuel Sánchez Mármol ("Candido") brought forth the name of Alfred Fouillée, the independent French philosopher who attempted to reconcile deterministic evolutionary theory with liberty and free will. At issue between Sierra and Sánchez Mármol was the persistent question of the extent to which strong central authority could be justified by biological laws as applied to the social organism. Fouillée, interpreting Spencer, had argued that the individual "cells" of the organism, guided by "ideas," could spontaneously achieve "consensus" or social order and therefore should not be coerced by the "directive organ." Sierra found Fouillée's arguments as advanced by Sánchez Mármol exaggerated, and he claimed that such a spontaneous consensus was impossible in a weak organism like Mexico.[26] The disputants' use of Fouillée's complex interpretation was confused, but the fact that it was read and debated points up the relevance of his concerns to them.

In sum, Sierra was eclectic in his use of Spencer, resisting his extreme individualism and his intense antipathy toward the state. Sierra juxtaposed Spencer's naturalistic view of society to the more Comtean concepts that made up scientific politics. With these theoretical matters in mind, let us now turn to selected issues facing the liberal establishment, the status of the Indian in society and the related policy questions of obligatory public education and colonization by foreigners.

Positivism affected Mexican social thought pertaining to the Indian in two ways. The first was to focus the attention of intellectuals and policymakers on the racial peculiarity and diversity of their society. A premise of positivism, exemplified in the program of scientific politics, was that the country's problems could be approached scientifically by careful investigation of the facts, leading to empirically derived conclusions and thus to social policy. The second effect of positivism that pertained to the Indian was to place Mexican society in a broader scheme in accord with

---

also *La Libertad* articles (not by Sierra) of 23 May 1878 and 7 October 1879, and others cited on pp. 32–34.

[26] Sierra in *La Libertad*, 3 September 1879 (*Obras*, 4:238–40) responding to Sánchez Mármol in *La Patria*, 27 August. The unidentified Fouillée article was "L'Organisme sociale," part one of "L'Histoire naturelle des sociétés humaines ou animales," *Revue des deux mondes*, 15 July 1879, pp. 370–405. It was a review of several evolutionary works, principally Spencer's *Principes de sociologie* (1878) and *Essais de politique* (1879). On Fouillée (1838–1912) and Spencer, see Clark, *Social Darwinism*, pp. 55–56. Sierra came to be increasingly sympathetic to Fouillée's concept of "thought-force" (*idée-force*): Force is an act of consciousness; conversely every idea is a force that can be realized in action. See examples, p. 229 (1883); Sierra, "Discurso en el acto de inauguración de la universidad nacional de México" (22 September 1910), *Obras*, 5:45. However, in 1879, as a recent convert to positivism, Sierra regarded Fouillée as too "spiritual" [sic].

universal social laws like the law of evolution and its components. Although positivists did not regard the two orientations as being in conflict, there was a tension between them that helps to elucidate social thought and policy. Was Mexican society, whatever its racial peculiarities, pursuing a natural and universal course determined by biologic or environmental factors that ultimately limited the effects of policy? Or could policymakers, cognizant of the particular Mexican reality, bring about change, even in defiance of recognized social or racial laws? To this tension derived from positivism can be added another element that guided social policy, namely an intense consciousness of the nation's unique history since 1810. The movement for independence and the Reforma were often viewed after 1867 as two stages of an ongoing social process, a struggle for national autonomy, first against Spain, secondly against the remnants of the colonial regime. The Indian and mestizo majority of the population had participated in both.

Justo Sierra put the Indian population at 38 percent in 1885; others put it as high as 60 percent. More signficant than the precise figure was the growing perception among late nineteenth-century observers that Indians were a major component of the population who could not be ignored. Nonetheless, concern for the Indians and "the racial question" developed slowly after 1867, despite an Indian president (Juárez) and recent popular adherence to the heroic liberal struggle. Pre-Reforma liberals had tried to ignore the Indians. They denigrated Mexico's Aztec past and construed nationality in creole terms. Following the doctrine of equality under the law, they even attempted in vain to eliminate the term "Indian" from official parlance and often resorted to the phrase "the so-called Indians" (*los llamados indios*) in parliamentary discussions. Their favored remedy for the Indian problem was racial "fusion" through European colonization. There was a longstanding liberal prejudice against communal property and the Constitution of 1857 left it vulnerable to encroachment by landowners. Conservatives took a more paternalistic view of the Indians, extolling colonial policies of racial separation and social control; but ultimately they showed no more engagement in the issue than the liberals.[27] An exception to this indifference was the scholar Francisco Pimentel, who in 1864 drew a bleak and realistic picture of the degradation of the Indians. Although Pimentel served the Maximilian regime, his remedies were distinctly those of the earlier creole liberals: the union of In-

---

[27] Sierra, "México social," *Revista nacional* 1 (1889): 16 (*Obras*, 9:128). Sierra's overall figures, taken from Antonio García Cubas, were: Europeans and creoles, 1.98 million (18.96 percent); Indians, 3.97 million (38.02 percent); mestizos, 4.49 million (43 percent); total, 10.44 million. For a detailed account of the pre-Reforma view of the Indian see my *Mexican Liberalism*, chap. 7.

dians and whites through immigration; individual proprietorship; and the elimination of the word race, "in fact as well as in law."[28]

Post-Reforma views of the Indian in society varied, but amid the diversity was a clear continuity from earlier decades grounded in midcentury romantic erudition and embellished by public commemoration. The investigation of Indian languages by Pimentel and by Manuel Orozco y Berra in the 1860s was continued by Antonio García Cubas in the seventies and eighties. Alfredo Chavero's massive volume on ancient Mexico (1888) profited from the earlier ethnohistorical research of José Fernando Ramírez, as well as from that of Orozco y Berra. Even before 1867, the government recognized Cuauhtemoc the last of the Aztec emperors as a national hero, thus preparing the way for the impressive monument constructed at the crossroads of the new Mexico City between 1877 and 1887.[29]

Pimentel's dark assessment of present-day Indian misery went unrevised in the subsequent decades, although later accounts tended to be more cursory than his. In 1874 Eduardo Ruiz compared the Indians politically to the helots of Sparta and socially and religiously to "the pariahs of India." Their dismal situation, he added, continues unchanged despite liberal policies since independence. In 1878 José María Vigil attributed Indian degradation to "our lengthy civil conflicts," but by 1883 he was emphasizing geographic and material separation from other races. For Justo Sierra, Spanish colonization had imposed a seemingly "incurable passivity" on the Indian by a policy that oscillated between "oppression and tutelage, between the exploitation of the Indian as an animal and his protection as a perpetual minor." There followed Sierra's much-quoted conclusion that "the social problem of the Indian race is a problem of nutrition and education." Vicente Riva Palacio was more detached and scientific, using Darwin to argue that the unique dental structure of pure Indians (the lack of a canine tooth or its replacement by a molar) demonstrated an advanced evolution. However, since this uniqueness was

[28] Francisco Pimentel, "Memoria sobre las causas que han originado la situación actual de la raza indígena de México y medios de remediarla," *Obras completas*, 5 vols. (Mexico, 1903–04), 3:148.

[29] Francisco Pimentel, *Cuadro descriptivo de las lenguas indígenas de México o tratado de filología mexicana* (1862–65); Manuel Orozco y Berra, *Geografía de las lenguas y carta etnográfica de México (1864) and Historia antigua y de la conquista de México* (1880–82); Antonio García Cubas, *The Republic of Mexico in 1876* (1876) and *Cuadro geográfico, estadístico, descriptivo e histórico de los Estados Unidos Mexicanos* (1885). Ramírez edited numerous ethnographical sources during the 1850s and 1860s. Chavero wrote vol. 1 of *México a través de los siglos*. On the planning of the statue to Cuauhtemoc at the junction of Paseo de la Reforma and Avenida Insurgentes, see Barbara Tenenbaum, "Murals in Stone—The Paseo de la Reforma and Porfirian Mexico, 1873–1910," paper presented at The Seventh Conference of Mexican and U.S. Historians, Oaxaca, 1985.

not evident among those of mixed race, Riva Palacio implied that the mestizo was emerging as more Spanish than Indian. In 1893 *El Siglo XIX* asserted that the Indian race, imprisoned by nature, would in time be conquered and annihilated by the white race. However, when challenged by *El Partido liberal*, the editors retreated, saying that they meant absorption by the mestizo, not outright extinction. An anti-Darwinist view came from Agustín Aragón, the orthodox positivist, in 1900. Excoriating the elite for their scorn of the Indian, he asserted in paternalistic Comtean terms that "the Indian population sustains us" as "cannon-fodder" in war and as the "proletariat" in peace. "Our existence rests exclusively on [the Indian]," he concluded.[30]

While general commentaries on the Indian were surprisingly few, the post-Reforma liberal establishment as in earlier years took sharp notice when rural peoples normally regarded as docile turned violent. Rural rebellions from midcentury until 1880 were both numerous and varied in nature. For example, there was an extensive guerrilla movement of nearly two decades led by Manuel Lozada in western Jalisco, which became entangled in the national civil war and only ended with the capture and execution of Lozada by government troops in 1873. There was the denouement of the caste war of Yucatán, in which Mayan Indians, after their defeat in the early 1850s, retreated into the interior of the peninsula and held out for the rest of the century, aided by arms from British Honduras. There were the continuing attacks by the nomadic tribes or *indios bárbaros* of the north and the fierce resistance of the more settled Yaquis of Sonora, broken finally by the extension of political control and by economic development, as the region turned from a remote frontier into a border with Mexico's rapidly expanding neighbor. There were also the many smaller agrarian rebellions of peons, villagers, and *rancheros* against landowners throughout the heavily populated central highlands, which reached a crescendo between 1840 and 1880 and then declined thereafter. The Mexico City elite, while always sensitive to news of rebellion, were poorly informed and largely insensitive to the variety of

---

[30] Ruiz, "Estado social de los indios," *La Tribuna*, 8 January 1874; Vigil, in *El Monitor republicano*, 15 October, 14 November 1878, and in *La Patria*, 11 March, 19 July 1883; Sierra, "México social," *Revista nacional* 1 (1889): 14–15 (*Obras*, 9:126–27); Vicente Riva Palacio, ed., *México a través de los siglos*, 5 vols. (Barcelona and Mexico, 1888–89), 2:472–77 (also in Moreno, *Polémica*, pp. 247–56); "El Progreso y el indio," *El Universal*, 8, 10 November 1893; Agustín Aragón (1900), "El Territorio de México y sus habitantes," in Sierra, *México*, 1:26, 30. For post-1867 views of the Indians, see also Luis González y González, "El Subsuelo indígena," Cosío Villegas, *Historia moderna*, 3:149–76; Martin S. Stabb, "Indigenism and Racism in Mexican Thought: 1857–1911," *Journal of Inter-American Studies* 1 (1959): 405–23; T. G. Powell, "Mexican Intellectuals and the Indian Question, 1876–1911," *Hispanic American Historical Review* 48 (1968): 9–36; William D. Raat, "Los Intelectuales, el positivismo y la cuestión indígena," *Historia mexicana* 20 (1971): 412–27.

rural protests and to the range of grievances they entailed. Observers in the capital tended to refer to all rural rebels as Indians and to juxtapose indiscriminately such terms as socialist, communist, caste war, and barbarism.[31]

To characterize the response of the liberal establishment to rural rebellion, let us examine the case of the state of Hidalgo, which experienced widespread upheaval in late 1877 and early 1878, just as the editors of *La Libertad* were launching their program of scientific politics in Mexico City. The rebellion throughout the southern section of the state had been preceded by an earlier uprising in 1869–70, which may have been abetted by recent zealous efforts to implement the *ley Lerdo* of 1856, a provision of which called for the alienation of communal village lands to individuals. In addition, it appears that some village property had been appropriated by neighboring haciendas as *terrenos baldíos* (unclaimed lands) under a decree of 1863. The earlier resistance produced several leaders, the most important being Francisco Islas, who articulated village grievances in at least two manifestos. After a lull of seven years, the region was again in turmoil. Old grievances came to the surface in part due to unfulfilled promises of municipal autonomy in the revolt of Tuxtepec that brought Porfirio Díaz to power. Haciendas were attacked and lands taken and distributed among the Otomí villagers of the region. Moreover, Islas reemerged as the spokesman for the rebels and by early 1878 he was submitting statements of village grievances to Mexico City newspapers. Islas asserted that the villagers were simply recovering previously usurped lands and then seeking a dialogue with the affected landowners and justice from the courts. "Is there in all this even the germ of communism?" he asked, referring to the epithet often used in the establishment press. Islas did suggest, however, that the rebellion might spread if a new Morelos should emerge from "the bosom of the Indian race."[32]

Throughout the century Indian rebellions had inevitably brought coalescence to the intellectual and governing elite that was often sharply

[31] Leticia Reina, *Las Rebeliones campesinas en México, 1819–1906* (Mexico, 1980), p. 41. Reina documents some forty major and twenty-five minor rebellions in the center, south, and southeast of the country, virtually all of them before 1880. For a vigorous general interpretation and a synthesis of the rapidly growing literature on agrarian violence, see John Tutino, *From Insurrection to Revolution in Mexico, Social Bases of Agrarian Violence, 1750–1940* (Princeton, 1986).

[32] For details on the earlier rebellion in Hidalgo, see T. G. Powell, *El Liberalismo y el campesinado en el centro de México, 1850–1876* (Mexico, 1974), pp. 141–44; also Reina (on both), *Rebeliones*, pp. 139–43. The Islas statement appeared in *El Hijo del trabajo*, 27 January 1878 (quoted in Reina, *Rebeliones*, p. 137). Two others appeared in *La Libertad* on 19 January and 13 February 1878. In the latter, Islas referred to a pamphlet he was publishing, but I have been unable to locate it.

divided on political questions. So in 1878 *La Libertad* and *El Monitor republicano*, soon to be at odds over Mexico's constitutional heritage, responded with unanimity to the events in Hidalgo. At first *La Libertad* took a less alarmist view than its rival, printing the appeals of Francisco Islas and dismissing *El Monitor*'s fear of a new caste war and an assertion of Indian nationality. "Since the idea of *patria* does not exist in the indigenous past," said the editorialist, "it is impossible for the Indians to rise up in the name of this idea." Within a month *La Libertad* was warning that although the Indians were fighting today for "a few hundred square yards (*varas*) of ground," tomorrow they would want "the destruction of the white race." Both *El Monitor* and *La Libertad* acknowledged that there might be legitimate local grievances to be investigated and the latter even suggested purchasing lands from *hacendados* and selling them to villagers. But both newspapers agreed that force ("the only recourse civilization has against barbarism") must precede adjudication and reforms. The Indians have little idea of property and are threatening an "irresponsible (*inconsciente*) communism." In short, for *La Libertad* they were an unintelligent race that could not comprehend reason or justice.[33]

Throughout 1878 the elite of the capital watched events in Hidalgo closely along with other rebellions in Michoacán and Mexico and especially a series of attacks on haciendas at San Bernabé, just south of the city. But by early 1879 peace was restored and both newspapers were taking a broader view of rural violence and the means to quell it. Vigil suggested large-scale development projects to employ rural people. *La Libertad* placed the problem within its program of scientific politics. To ignore the threat of "social war," it argued, and to concern ourselves only with enervating "Byzantine" political struggles is "to commit national suicide (*lesa-nación*)." *La Libertad* called for vigorous government action that could "count on the efficient cooperation of the conservative elements of society, directly interested in combatting the danger that threatens us."[34]

The reaction of the liberal establishment to rural rebellion in the late 1870s was reminiscent of the creole reaction to the revolt of Miguel Hidalgo in 1810 and to the caste wars of 1847–49. It was the response of an intellectual and governing elite to attacks upon property and the estab-

---

[33] "Juvenal" (Enrique Chávarri) in *El Monitor*, 25 January 1878; *La Libertad*, 26 January, 24 February 1878. *La Libertad*'s spokesman might have been the hispanophile Francisco Cosmes, editorial secretary at this time, or Telesforo García. It probably was not Justo Sierra.

[34] The San Bernabé incident took place 10–13 November 1878 and drew comments by Vigil in *El Monitor* on 20 November and by *La Libertad* on 14, 19, 20 November 1878 and 14 January 1879. *La Libertad*'s general article, "La Guerra social," appeared on 3 March 1879.

lished social order by culturally segregated, racially distinct, and "unciv-
ilized" peoples. There is little indication that this response was affected
by the Social Darwinist ideas that were just entering the country. However, we can detect in their thinking the elements of scientific politics
infused with positivism (including assumptions of the historical school of
law): strong government, social order, work instead of politics—a formula
for progress sure to be upheld by "the conservative elements," men of
property protecting their interests and those of the nation. In fact, scientific politics as applied to rural rebellion was more than a detached set
of ideas; it underlay a successfully implemented policy in the countryside
after 1880, producing a thirty-year period of "agrarian compression."[35]
However, the elite response to the "Indian problem" was only in part
political repression, economic development, and racial denigration. Once
violence was quelled and the fear of race war dissipated, broader social
initiatives came to be debated and legislated—obligatory public education and colonization by foreigners. Both programs had roots in the liberal tradition but were revived with new vigor in the age of positivism.

Although the campaign to solidify the principle of gratuitous obligatory
primary education did not mature until after 1880, its precedents can be
traced back at least to a short-lived decree of 1842. The constitution-makers of 1856–57 circumvented the issue, probably because their orientation was more libertarian than statist and because they were reluctant to
confront "the clerical monopoly" of education directly. Article 3 of the
constitution stated simply that *"la enseñanza es libre,"* which inhibited
state surveillance or control and opened up, as we have seen, a large area
for interpretation and debate by a subsequent generation. With the surge
of statist anticlericalism, however, during the years 1859 to 1863 came
the law of 15 April 1861 that placed primary education "under federal
inspection" by the Ministry of Justice and Public Instruction.

By 1867, after a decade of civil and ideological strife, the idea of "the
state as educator (*el estado docente*)" emerged as an integral part of triumphant liberalism. The law of 2 December 1867 provided not only for
the establishment of a state-controlled preparatory school, but also (in a
cursory way) for a system of primary education in the Federal District,
which was to be publicly funded, gratuitous "for the poor," and obligatory. However, such a system remained little more than an officially recognized idea during the subsequent decade, in part because of general
opposition from within the liberal establishment to state control but also

---

[35] Florencia Mallon has recently argued for the strong impulse toward social control by
both liberals and conservatives in the face of popular dissidence during the civil war years
of the 1850s. See Florencia Mallon, "Peasants and State Formation in Nineteenth-Century
Mexico: Morelos, 1848–1858," *Political Power and Social Theory* 7 (1988): 1–54. The phrase
"agrarian compression" is from Tutino, *From Insurrection to Revolution*, chap. 8.

because the major educational preoccupation was with training a scientifically oriented elite in the new National Preparatory School. In practice, primary education was left to the municipalities and remained woefully underfunded. Moreover, primary education meant education for the Indian population, and, as we have seen, awareness of the sociological realities of the country was slow to take form in the years after 1867.[36]

Nonetheless, the principle of obligatory primary education gained broad and articulate support during the regime of Sebastián Lerdo de Tejada. It appeared as one of the articles in the several plans to "reform" public education advanced by opponents of the Preparatoria from 1872 to 1875. They accepted the principle despite their argument that the state-controlled preparatory school contradicted article 3. Obligatory education was also upheld vigorously by Lerdo's positivist-oriented Minister of Justice José Díaz Covarrubias. He devoted the opening section of his extensive report of 1875 on public instruction to the subject, refuting the view that it constituted "an offense to individual liberty and to the independence of families." With the notable exception of France, he continued, obligatory education has been adopted by many countries as well as by several Mexican states. In fact, France will soon cease to be a world leader if it does not adopt it. The principle was also enthusiastically endorsed by both Gabino Barreda and Justo Sierra, despite sharp philosophical differences between them in their polemical interchanges of 1875. The various arguments of these years in favor of obligatory education reveal the combining of liberal and Comtean positivist precepts and demonstrate one instance in which Comte's thought was more relevant to the Mexican liberal tradition than Spencer's. It should also be noted that the statements of the 1870s were remarkably abstract in tone. It is difficult to find in them any reference to Mexico's Indian population.[37]

Although Barreda focused his attention almost entirely on the Preparatoria, he did make it clear where he stood as a positivist on obligatory primary education. It cannot properly be attacked as an infringement of individual rights, he argued, because the progress of civilization demands that liberties gradually give way to duties. Thus the obligation to educate one's children is like the obligation to do military service or to pay taxes.

[36] On the precedents for obligatory primary education, see Josefina Vázquez, *Nacionalismo y educación en México* (Mexico, 1970), pp. 27, 44–48. On primary education after 1876, see Héctor Díaz Zermeño, "La Escuela nacional primaria en la ciudad de México, 1876–1910," *Historia mexicana* 29 (1979): 59–90; Moisés González Navarro, *El Porfiriato, Vida social*, Cosío Villegas, *Historia moderna*, 4:529–56. For further details on legislation see Ernesto Meneses Morales, *Tendencias educativas oficiales en México, 1821–1911* (Mexico, 1983).

[37] For the educational plans of 1872–75, see pp. 155–57; for the ideas of Díaz Covarrubias, pp. 146, 163; for the Barreda-Sierra polemic, pp. 165–67.

They are the responsibilities of "social existence." From a "scientific" as well as from a "purely practical and empirical" point of view, "obligatory primary instruction is a question of convenience and of social stability." Central to Barreda's view of education, as we have seen in chapter 5, was the Comtean idea of "cultivating" pupils instead of letting them go totally to nature. Cultivation meant instilling a sense of universal morality by means of which altruistic or "good" inclinations would replace those that are egoistic or "bad." It was like cultivating or "educating" a flower not to produce thorns. Who would ever defend the "natural rights of the flower?" asked Barreda.[38]

Barreda's epigraph, a statement by Comte that education is the art that "perfects action by improving the agent," also served as the point of departure for Justo Sierra. Musing on the issue of education as a moral force in society, Sierra introduced several paragraphs from Spencer's recently published *Introduction à la science sociale*, which attacked the idea that the spread of education would reduce crime and improve the populace. Sierra acknowledged Spencer's point that a direct correlation between science and morality was absurd and that education should not be regarded as a social panacea. Such a view is adhered to by those who "do not have the slightest idea of the social organism" and of the slow process of evolution. However, Sierra concluded that he ultimately disagreed with Spencer's strictures and that he agreed instead with Comte and Barreda's faith in education. All citizens must learn certain moral precepts "in order to standardize (*normar*) their political and social conduct." Moreover, added Sierra, a democratic people must be able to fill out electoral ballots.[39] Sierra's favorable response to Barreda may have been influenced by Paul Janet's recent critical review of Spencer's *Science sociale* in which the French democrat and spiritualist philosopher attacked the deterministic and antigovernment implications of Spencer's thought.[40] Janet referred particularly to the example of obligatory education, which was being debated actively in France. We find in these early arguments by Barreda and Sierra for state-enforced primary education the fundamental intellectual orientation that guided it, the conflu-

---

[38] Barreda, "Algunas ideas respecto de instrucción primaria," *Opúsculos*, pp. 159–68, 174–76. On the use of *instrucción* vs. *educación* during the 1870s, see pp. 162–64.

[39] Sierra, "Necesidad de la instrucción primaria," *El Federalista*, 7 December 1875 (*Obras*, 8:52–56). The quotes from Spencer can be found in *The Study of Sociology*, pp. 329–32. Sierra cited the title as *Introducción a la ciencia social*, a clear indication that he had read the French version. No Spanish translation of the work existed in 1875.

[40] See Janet, "La Science sociale," pp. 83, 104, 109–10. My supposition that Sierra probably read Janet's essay in the *Revue des deux mondes* is based on other direct references to the journal, on the appearance of a translation of Janet's essay on the French Revolution in *La Tribuna* (see pp. 84–85), and on Sierra's defense of French revolutionary principles in his debate with Barreda. He was clearly struggling over positivism vs. spiritualism in 1875.

ence of reformist liberalism and Comtean positivism adapted to the Mexican milieu.[41]

Succumbing first to legislative confusion and then to the political confusion of the years 1876–77, obligatory primary education was revived as a proposed constitutional amendment by Justo Sierra in October 1880.[42] Because the philosophical battle lines between positivists and spiritualist liberals were now being drawn over the scientific curriculum of the National Preparatory School, Sierra's strategy was to emphasize the agreement of both camps on the "single objective" of abolishing national "ignorance." Like those who hold to "metaphysical" ideas, said Sierra, we positivists also defend the "right of the child to education"; but for us it is not an "absolute" right, but rather one that is "useful and [socially] convenient." The committee presenting the revised proposal went further and stressed the rights of the state: "Man must belong to the state from birth through his primary education." Again as in the 1870s the measure was approved by the Chamber of Deputies (this time unanimously), only to languish in the Senate.[43] However, public debate continued in the 1880s, stimulated by a new awareness of the social realities of the country. This awareness had been sharpened by the rash of rural rebellions of the late 1870s and was buttressed intellectually by the diffusion of Spencerian ideas. The grounds of the argument shifted from the freedom of teaching versus state control to the value of educating the Indian. This shift was revealed particularly in the frequently cited debate between Sierra, supported by the "old" liberal, Ignacio M. Altamirano, and Sierra's positivist colleague, Francisco Cosmes.[44]

The debate was touched off by Altamirano's praise for a thoroughgoing

[41] I say "adapted," because Comte's ideal was not precisely state-controlled education but education under the spiritual power, which he saw as coextensive with the state. In fact, primary education was to be conducted in the home under maternal direction. A summary of Comte's ideas on primary education can be found in "Discours" (1848), *Système*, 1:170–79 (*General View*, pp. 189–98). On the spiritual power and state control see pp. 152–53.

[42] Obligatory education was part of the law approved and passed on to the Senate on 11 December 1875 (see chap. 5, n. 37). A new proposal, extending obligatory education to the entire nation, was introduced on 4 April 1876. Debate followed on whether Congress had the authority to legislate for the entire country in the case of an issue that had not been provided for specifically in the constitution. On April 6 the proposal was returned to committee to be reintroduced as a constitutional amendment. There it apparently remained until revived by Sierra in 1880. See *Diario de los debates*, 8th congress, 1st ser., 2:19–38.

[43] Sierra's original proposal of 7 October 1880 can be found in ibid., 10th congress, 1:314, the revised proposal (and committee argument) of 30 September 1881 in ibid., 3:340–43 (*Obras*, 8:159–60n., 337–41). Sierra's argument is in *Diario de los debates*, 10th congress, 3:691–93 (*Obras*, 8:159–62). The revised measure was approved and passed on to the Senate on 29 October 1881: *Diario de los debates*, 10th congress, 3:693–94.

[44] The three-sided debate took place in fourteen articles in *La Libertad*, 14 February–15 March 1883.

set of regulations for obligatory public education passed in January 1883 by the state of Puebla. For Cosmes, this was one more example of trying (as had the constitution-makers) to impose "alien institutions" in defiance of Mexico's sociological reality. While obligatory schooling might have some justification in the Federal District, where the "white race" and "civilization" predominate, it has none at all in the mountains and forests where the "immense mass of the indigenous population is imprisoned." Moreover, continued Cosmes, the Indian regards his son as "a species of work animal that provides him useful services," and schooling would mean depriving the family of its means of survival. The only relevant education for the Indian would be in agricultural techniques, taught during nonwork hours, when the Indian often turns to drink. The state could thus "correct his vices and educate him at the same time." Citing Spencer, Cosmes argued that the improvement of the Indian must depend on the development of industry, transportation, and communications, which would bring him into contact with civilization. In short, for Cosmes evolutionary material changes stimulated by governmental action must precede spiritual changes; to reverse this natural process by arbitrary legislation was utopian.[45]

Sierra responded sharply to Cosmes's determinism: He was carrying Spencer's ideas to their extreme, advancing a "theory of systematic inactivity . . . contrary to the dignity of our species." Sierra said he preferred the position of Comte and Littré that "a society (*estado social*) is the more modifiable by human action the more complex it becomes." Sierra also argued for the power of legislated ideals in guiding the evolution of society. He noted Fouillée's effort like his own "to transform metaphysics, basing it on experimentalism," that is, to find a philosophical middle ground between idealism and deterministic positivism.[46] The position of Cosmes in this debate was notable for its absence of biological racism derived from Social Darwinist assumptions. Though he denigrated Indian culture and though he seemed to doubt the Indian's inherent ability to benefit from schooling, his principal argument focused on environmental, not biological, obstacles. In responding to Altamirano, Cosmes insisted that he too was a good liberal but that he wanted a "practical liberty," not simply a liberty of the "written law." For his part, Sierra

[45] Cosmes in ibid., 16 February, 1, 8 March.

[46] Sierra in ibid., 6 March (*Obras*, 8:112–14). On Sierra and Fouillée, see p. 219. Like Janet, Fouillée criticized Spencer's determinism. On this occasion, Sierra cited Fouillée's *L'Idée moderne du droit* (1878). Sierra also referred to the debates over the universal education laws recently passed (1879–82) in France under the leadership of the positivist Jules Ferry. Sierra said that many of Cosmes's objections were similar to those espoused in France. On the French legislation, see Evelyn M. Acomb, *The French Laic Laws, 1879–1889* (New York, 1941).

concluded by acknowledging that the law of obligatory education would be difficult to apply and that its application should be based on "the special conditions of the indigenous race."

Despite suggestions of compromise in the exchanges between Sierra and Cosmes, Sierra adhered doggedly to the ideal of educating the Indian. As the campaign for explicit federal legislation on obligatory education reached its climax in the late 1880s, Sierra abandoned his earlier efforts to amend the constitution and now settled for a detailed law pertaining to the Federal District and territories, which he introduced on 8 October 1887. Again as in 1880 Sierra emphasized the agreement of diverse philosophical parties on universal education, including Henri-Gabriel Didon, a renowned French cleric. The most serious opposition, maintained Sierra, comes from those who carry Spencerian individualism to the extreme and conceive of the state solely as "judge and policeman." While acknowledging the validity of such a role in some future industrial age as envisioned by Spencer, Sierra saw it as distant for countries like Mexico, "which organize themselves slowly and painfully." By attacking the obstacles to organization, the Mexican state "actually multiplies the active liberty of each individual." The debate itself was vigorous, even though the opponents were few. Faustino Michel stressed the contradiction between *enseñanza obligatoria* in the law and *enseñanza libre* in the constitution. Juan Bribiesca regarded the measure as utopian. Alfredo Chavero opposed penal sanctions for noncompliance. José María Gamboa saw the monopoly on education merely shifting from clerics to a few normal school graduates. After prolonged discussion including orations in favor of the measure by *reformista* liberals Juan A. Mateos and Guillermo Prieto, it was approved overwhelmingly by both houses of Congress the following year.[47]

Opposition to the measure came not only from constitutional liberals defending article 3 but also from those who, like Cosmes earlier, questioned the educability of the Indian. Emilio Pimentel, a lawyer from Oaxaca and later a *Científico*, supported the measure in general but opposed the specific inclusion of "elements of the fundamental sciences of observation and experimentation" among the list of subjects to be taught. The ignorance and backwardness of the Indian race is so profound, argued

[47] Henri-Gabriel Didon (1840–1900) was an influential French Dominican who wrote particularly on educational questions. Sierra quoted a passage from *Les Allemands* (1884), a work on German universities. The text of the original proposal from the education committee, which Sierra chaired, can be found in *Diario de los debates*, 13th congress, 4 vols. (Mexico, 1888–90), 3:164–70. The law in its final form (25 May 1888) is in Dublán and Lozano, *Legislación*, 19:127–29. The eleven sessions of debate ran from 25 November to 7 December 1887, when the measure passed on to the Senate (*Diario de los debates*, 13th congress, 3:461–685).

Pimentel, that Indians do not have even the most rudimentary knowledge upon which scientific instruction could be based. Or as Rodolfo Sandoval put it, we must not begin by trying "to make the Indians doctors in natural science."[48]

Pimentel's skepticism elicited from Sierra a spirited defense of the Indian's aptitude "for assimilation, imitation, and observation," evident since the days of the sixteenth-century missionaries. We simply cannot distinguish on either rational or constitutional grounds between the capability of the races of the country. To do so, asserted Sierra, would be to condemn "to perpetual ostracism this race to which we owe part of our blood and part of our glories, [that is,] the conquest of our institutions." In the face of skepticism about universal education, Sierra inevitably invoked the heroic liberal tradition, as he did pointedly on 26 November: "This is a law of social redemption that was actually decreed by Juárez, one that the Ocampos and the Ramírez would have signed in blood."[49]

With the passage of the law of 1888 the principle of obligatory primary education was finally vindicated. It is significant that the final speaker to defend the bill in the Chamber of Deputies was Joaquín Baranda, the minister of justice and public instruction. He essentially closed the debate by asserting that the executive regarded the principle as vital to the nation, despite difficulties of implementation. Within a year Baranda had convened the first National Congress of Public Instruction and was charging the delegates to make educational uniformity the primary subject of their deliberations. A key question guiding the discussions, which took place from 1 December 1889 to 31 March 1890, was whether or not the 1888 law for the Federal District and the territories should become the national model. Since most of the delegates were proponents of uniformity and centralization, this issue was not strongly contended. The lengthy debates of both the first and second congresses focused instead on educational philosophy, pedagogical theory, curricular details, and questions of implementation. Although Justo Sierra who presided over both congresses emphasized that their role was only to make recommendations, these were clearly official gatherings whose conclusions would be tantamount to policy. In closing the first congress, Sierra told the delegates that they might be known in the future as the "constitution-makers of public education."[50]

[48] Pimentel in the session of 2 December (ibid., pp. 606–09); Sandoval in the session of 28 November (ibid., p. 505).

[49] Sierra in the sessions of 5 December and 26 November (ibid., p. 646, 491 [Obras, 8:212, 180]).

[50] Sierra in the session of 31 March 1890 (Debates del [primer] congreso, p. 587 [Obras, 5:126]). The one aspect of uniform education that did engender debate was whether the designation "secular" (laico) should be included, as in the Jalisco law (modeled, said Sierra,

Given the official impetus and the composition of the delegates, it is no surprise that the theme of unification dominated the rhetoric of the congress. Miguel F. Martínez, speaking for the obligatory education committee, said that the "most important" point to be made for a national system was political, the need for intellectual and moral unity to complement fiscal unity and legal codification. Moreover, he added, "it is time to complete the work of the apostles of the Reforma." For Sierra, ever closer economic ties both national and international demanded that the centrifugal forces of cultural heterogeneity "be transformed into cohesion." Reiterating familiar Spencerian themes, Sierra added that "we are only a gathering of men trying to apply the scientific method to the problems of public education." Universal education, promoted by the state as "organ," is a need of society as a "living organism" even more than it is a right. Francisco Bulnes interpreted Spencer in his own fashion, suggesting that at the present stage of Mexico's evolution, "homogeneity" did not mean backwardness; centralization in education, like dictatorship in government, was a precondition of future "heterogeneity." Cosmes was again the major dissenting voice in the congress, arguing in his minority report (*voto particular*) that a unified system would violate the rights of states. But his voice was lost, for as we have seen in previous chapters the centralizing tenets of scientific politics were clearly in the ascendancy by 1890.[51]

The question of educating the Indian was debated in the first congress, though less so in this official gathering than earlier. Cosmes supported by Manuel Gómez Portugal again stressed the obstacles to implementing uniform education that stemmed from racial, climatic, and financial differences between the states. While some states are progressive, he said, others have "populations which are victims of religious fanaticism and ignorance." But such dissent was greeted by strong rhetoric from all sides, from old and new liberals, *reformistas* and future *Científicos*. Mateos said race was a "biological question that must not be considered by

---

on the French law of 1882), or omitted, as in the law for the Federal District. Sierra saw the term as superfluous in Mexico, where (unlike France) the church and state were separate. Moreover, *laico* in a Mexican law might mean prohibiting religious teaching in private as well as in public schools, which Sierra regarded as a threat to religious freedom. Sierra was overruled and ultimately acceded to the majority view, saying that he would, like Minister Baranda, interpret *laico* to mean "neutral." See Sierra in the sessions of 20 December 1889 and 31 March 1890 (*Debates del [primer] congreso*, p. 70, 582 [*Obras*, 8:224–26; 5:119]). There were frequent references in the debates as there had been earlier to the French legislation of 1879–82.

[51] Martínez in the session of 10 December 1889 (*Debates del [primer] congreso*, p. 20); Sierra in the session of 20 December (p. 68–69 [*Obras*, 8:222]) and session of 31 March 1890 (p. 581 [*Obras*, 5:118–19]); Bulnes and Cosmes in the session of 20 December 1889 (p. 66, 59).

us." Moreover, he continued, "the children of different areas do not constitute a difference of race; for me, all are from the Mexican family and all have the same aptitude." Martínez argued for the committee that Indians "are capable of rivaling whites and mestizos in the struggle for knowledge." Ramón Manterola agreed, adding that differences of race and culture were merely transitory and could be leveled by education. In a sharp rejoinder to Genaro Raigosa's suggestion that Juárez might have opposed certain aspects of uniform education, Rosendo Pineda responded: "No, gentlemen! Juárez would have come here to vote with us for the positive and complete vindication of the Indian race, that race which is the foundation (*como el fondo*) of our nationality." However inadequate the provisions were for implementing the measure, the principle of nationwide obligatory primary education was clearly affirmed by the first National Congress of Public Instruction.[52]

Within six years of the close of the first congress the regulation of primary education in the Federal District passed from the legislative to the executive branch and a new federal bureaucracy was put in place. The revised regulatory law of 3 June 1896 established the Dirección General de Instrucción Primaria within the Ministry of Justice, headed by the positivist educator Luis E. Ruiz. The lingering authority of the municipalities over primary education gave way to administrative centralization. The states soon followed the example of the Federal District and the foundation was laid for the modern state-controlled system of primary education, a process comparable to what took place (at the same time) in preparatory school education. The organization of public education was an important element in the triumph of scientific politics by the 1890s.[53]

The debates over obligatory education took place in an increasingly positivist intellectual environment. After 1880 Spencerian and Darwinian ideas sharpened the sense of race and helped direct the discussion to-

[52] Cosmes in the session of 13 December 1889 (*Debates del [primer] congreso*, pp. 26–27); Goméz Portugal and Mateos in the session of 20 December (pp. 48–51, 57); Martínez in the session of 10 December (p. 17); Manterola in the session of 20 December (pp. 39–40); Pineda in the session of 22 January 1890 (p. 208).

[53] On the bureaucratization of primary education, see Mary Kay Vaughan, *The State, Education, and Social Class in Mexico, 1880–1928* (De Kalb, 1982), pp. 57–66. The congressional authorization (28 May 1890) for the executive to regulate the 1888 law was followed by the regulatory law of 21 March 1891 (Dublán and Lozano, *Legislación*, 20:135–36; 21:24–37). The regulations were revised (3 June 1896) to include the Dirección General de Instrucción Primaria (ibid., 26:223–42). The ministry's rationale for the Dirección General ("in order that [primary education] may be disseminated and attended to uniformly, under a single scientific and administrative plan") can be found in *Memoria . . . de justicia e instrucción pública*, 1892–96 (Mexico, 1899), pp. 326–28. Presumably the bureaucratic route to uniform national primary instruction was pursued in part because of earlier congressional resistance to constitutional change.

ward the Indian as the potential recipient of general schooling. Francisco Cosmes took a deterministic outlook from Spencer and argued that redemption of the Indian must be left to natural evolutionary forces. Emilio Pimentel implicitly shared these views, but his argument was more traditional, perpetuating colonial attitudes toward *la gente sin razón*. Absent in the assumptions of both skeptics was evidence of biological racism, that is, a belief in the inherent inferiority of the Indian independent of environmental circumstances. Nor did the Darwinian notion of the struggle for racial survival enter into their arguments.

Justo Sierra's campaign also developed within a positivist framework. Although he began from the premise that society was an organism subject to the exigencies of the law of evolution, his orientation was more Comtean than Spencerian. As an advocate of scientific politics, he rejected Spencer's noninterventionist state. Like Gabino Barreda, he adhered to the concept of *el estado docente*, the state as the inculcator of common moral and civic virtues to all citizens. But he also held to universal education as an ideal, one that might (in the terms of Fouillée) actually guide the evolutionary process. In the face of deterministic skepticism about obligatory education, Sierra (along with Mateos, Martínez, and Pineda) called up the heroic liberal tradition. He passionately defended the mid-century reformers and even praised the constitution-makers, whom he had frequently attacked as "metaphysicians" in political debates. Sierra was a reluctant democrat, but in defending universal education he did speak as a liberal patriot, recognizing the Indian roots of the Mexican "mestizo family" and the participation of Indians in Mexico's liberal struggle to liquidate the colonial past and to achieve national autonomy. If administrative centralization guided by the tenets of scientific politics was one impetus for the establishment of obligatory education, reaffirmation of the liberal myth was the other.

Even more than obligatory education, colonization by foreigners was advanced in nineteenth-century Mexico as a solution to the social question. The settlement and cultivation of unoccupied lands by European immigrants would create a class of small property-holders comparable to the yeoman farmers of the United States or to the French rural bourgeoisie. Small property-holders would bring democracy to a feudal society made up of latifundia and backward Indian communities. The strength of liberal enthusiasm for colonization is demonstrated by its persistence, despite the loss of Texas and the vast regions of the northwest to expanding North American settlement. In fact the war of 1847 actually brought forth new colonization plans to secure the now-reduced frontiers against further invasion. The caste wars of the late forties provided another impetus. As Mora put it in 1849, colonization could bring about "the fusion of all races and colors" and prevent future Indian rebellions.

A government colonization bureau was established in 1846, but general legislation failed to emerge in the pre-Reforma period, largely because of congressional disputes over provisions for religious toleration.[54]

Interest in colonization continued strong in the Constituent Congress of 1856–57, but the critical determinant of post-Reforma colonization policies was the wartime decree "on the occupation and alienation of unclaimed lands (*terrenos baldíos*)" of 20 July 1863, issued by the beleaguered Juárez government in San Luis Potosí. The decree provided for individual claims not to exceed twenty-five hundred hectares; it set prices for public lands in the various states; and it established a rudimentary mechanism for surveying and demarcating the claims. Moreover, it explicitly abrogated "the provisions of former legislation which declared public lands inalienable." The decree reflected the spirit of article 27 of the constitution and of the reform laws alienating corporate property, that is, it reaffirmed individual property both as an absolute right and as a stimulus to economic development. It also reflected, like the decrees on church property, the government's need for funds in a time of fiscal crisis. There was no specific reference to colonization in the law, but thereafter policies on colonization and on *baldíos* became intertwined. The colonization laws of 1875 and 1883 in effect joined the provisions of the 1863 land law to procedures for encouraging settlement by foreigners. As Wistano Luis Orozco the principal critic of Porfirian land policies wrote in 1895, the later laws "completely ignored any legislative precedent (*monumento*) other than the Juárez law."[55]

"To attract to our extensive and unpopulated territory the greatest possible number of honest and industrious colonists . . . is certainly one of the duties of any enlightened government, especially in a nation like ours, so rich in natural resources but lacking the necessary hands to exploit them." Such was the unquestioned sentiment of the post-Reforma liberal establishment, articulated anew by Vicente Riva Palacio, minister of *fomento* for the Díaz regime in December 1877. Riva Palacio's report to Congress was brief, because despite high enthusiasm and a prolifera-

---

[54] For a brief account of postindependence ideas on colonization, see my *Mexican Liberalism*, pp. 179–80, 211–12, 241–42, 247; for a more comprehensive account see Dieter G. Berninger, *La Inmigración en México, 1821–1857* (Mexico, 1974).

[55] For the ideas of the constitution-makers on colonization, see Jacqueline Covo, *Las Ideas de la reforma en México, 1855–1861* (Mexico, 1983), pp. 377–89. The 1863 law *sobre ocupación y enajenación de terrenos baldíos* can be found in Dublán and Lozano, *Legislación*, 9:637–40. A decree of 22 July set land prices (pp. 641–42). Article 27 of the 1863 law stated: *Queda derogada desde esta fecha la disposición de las leyes antiguas, que declaran imprescriptibles los terrenos baldíos.* For Orozco's statement, see Wistano Luis Orozco, *Legislación y jurisprudencia sobre terrenos baldíos*, 2 vols. (Mexico, 1895), 1:658. Orozco argued at length that the Juárez law and its successors subverted the traditional principle that all lands were vested in the state.

tion of projects, colonization had made little headway during the previous decade. A vague provisional law had been passed in May 1875 authorizing the executive to issue contracts; but as with obligatory education, a colonization policy did not mature until after 1880.[56] Nonetheless, a rationale for future policy (which ignored the land question) appeared in the program of scientific politics as presented by *La Libertad* in the months following Riva Palacio's report. Justo Sierra put the matter in medical terms, diagnosing Mexico as "anemic." The nation "carries an impoverished blood in its veins," producing skepticism, lack of energy, resistance to what is useful, and premature aging. The condition can "only be corrected," he continued, "by great quantities of iron, supplied in the form of railroads, and large doses of strong blood, supplied in the form of immigration." The efforts of Minister Riva Palacio won *La Libertad*'s praise; they appeared to be part of a "homogeneous" and "complete plan, dictated by an approach that was truly scientific."[57]

The long-awaited legislation came in December 1883 when the Chamber of Deputies approved without debate a proposal introduced two years earlier by Manuel Fernández Leal, the positivist subminister of *fomento*. The law clearly subordinated colonization to the demarcation of *terrenos baldíos*. Both surveying and colonizing the land was to be carried out by private companies that would receive for their efforts one-third of the land that they identified. The law was the product of the fever for economic development of the 1880s, an implementation of one aspect of scientific politics.[58] Colonization like literacy became tied to the

---

[56] *Memoria presentada . . . por el secretario de estado y del despacho de fomento, colonización, industria y comercio*, December 1876–December 1877 (Mexico, 1877), p. 441. The law of 31 May 1875 can be found in Dublán and Lozano, *Legislación*, 12:742–43. The colonization committee introduced two laws on 21 November 1874, but advised the briefer provisional one because of the need for quick action: *Diario de los debates*, 7th congress, 3:614–21. The latter was passed unanimously on 28 May 1875 (ibid., 4:612). On colonization during the Restored Republic, see González y González, "El Hombre y la tierra," Cosío Villegas, *Historia moderna*, 3:129–46; for the Porfiriato, see González Navarro, *Porfiriato*, pp. 134–53, 187–205; also idem, *La Colonización en México, 1877–1910* (Mexico, 1960).

[57] Sierra in *La Libertad*, 4 February 1879 (*Obras*, 4:211–12); *La Libertad*, 14 November 1878. Phraseology similar to Sierra's can be found in the *Diario oficial*'s editorial of 23 July 1878.

[58] The 1883 law was introduced by Fernández Leal on 29 April 1881: *Diario de los debates*, 10th congress, 2:625–29. The committee recommended a virtually unchanged version (*Diario de los debates*, 11th congress, 4 vols. [Mexico, 1882–92], 3:289–93) on 29 November 1883. It was passed unanimously and officially promulgated on 15 December: Dublán and Lozano, *Legislación*, 16:663–67. Curiously, José María Vigil was a member of the colonization committee; Porfirio Parra, his philosophical combatant of 1882–83, proposed immediate passage of the law. They apparently kept philosophy and land policy in separate compartments! On the developmental impulse during the González administration, see Don M. Coerver, "The Perils of Progress: the Mexican Department of Fomento during the Boom Years, 1880–1884, " *Inter-American Economic Affairs* 31 (1977): 41–62.

expansion of railroads, telegraphs, agriculture, and mining. Though often presented in the language of the new organicism, colonization policy was decisively guided by the traditional liberal doctrine of individual property, reinforced in the age of positivism more by Herbert Spencer's individualism than by Auguste Comte's collectivism. Though Comte's social conception of property ultimately had its impact on policy in Mexico, that impact was not evident during the nineteenth century. The earlier liberal ideal of creating a rural bourgeoisie through colonization vanished, subverted by the limitations of liberal theory as well as by the realities of Mexican society. Although liberals consistently favored small properties, they had no theoretical defense against excessive private accumulation. The much-lamented result of the 1883 law, abetted by another of 1894, was that it alienated vast amounts of public and communally held land to large landholders and to speculators (the notorious *compañías deslindadoras*) but did little to settle European colonists on small properties in rural Mexico.[59]

Although colonization as a social program was a failure, the discussion of it did reveal important assumptions concerning the bases and the future of Mexican society. As we have seen, one persistent argument was that an incursion of European immigrants would improve the nation through a better racial mixture. Earlier advocates of colonization like Mora and Pimentel had spoken of "fusion"; by the 1870s it was common to talk of "improving the blood." In 1874 Justo Sierra surveyed world history as a history of colonization. None of the supposedly unified peoples, he wrote, had developed without immigration and a "crossing of the races." He reiterated the argument in 1876, lauding the "cosmopolitan theory" put forth by the Argentines by which the country's health would spring from "the transfusion into our veins of the virile blood of

One measure of the government's role in the boom was the fact that the *Memorias de fomento* expanded to three volumes for December 1877–December 1882 and to five volumes for January 1883–June 1885.

[59] The revised land law of 26 March 1894, effectively freed those acquiring *baldíos* from the obligation to colonize, thus temporarily acknowledging the failure of government-promoted colonization efforts. The law also removed the previous limitation of 2,500 hectares on individual claims. Later laws of 1902 and 1909 abrogated these revised provisions, returning to the premises of 1875 and 1883. According to González Navarro, in 1908 there were 8,481 colonists in Mexico, about 4–5,000 of them foreigners. The total number of foreign residents (in 1910) was 116,527. By comparison, there were 221,915 Mexicans living in the United States. In the period from 1877 to 1910, 38,774,280 hectares were alienated as *baldíos*, 52 percent of which were granted to or purchased by the surveying companies. The amount of land alienated was of course far less in the heavily populated central states than elsewhere. See González Navarro, *Colonización*, pp. 12–14, 36, 123; idem, *Porfiriato*, pp. 195–96. The developmentalist rationale for the 1894 law by Manuel Fernández Leal, who was now a full minister, can be found in *Memoria . . . de fomento, colonización e industria . . . 1892 a 1896* (Mexico, 1897), pp. 1–12; the text of the law is on pp. 133–35.

other nations." Despite the continuity of racial mixture as a theme, we can note a subtle shift of assumptions from the 1840s to the 1870s and 1880s. Whereas earlier advocates of colonization had adhered to a creole concept of nationality, a kind of whitening ideal, later advocates regarded the Indian roots of the nation more positively—as did proponents of obligatory primary education. While the newer view was far from universal, it steadily gained strength within the liberal establishment. Moreover, it was drawn from Mexican experience and it contradicted the strictures on racial mixture that were common in European social thought.[60]

One interesting expression of this changing view of racial mixture appeared in a series of articles by Luis Alva. Writing in 1882 while the colonization law was being considered in Congress, Alva's theme was mixed colonies, that is, the advantage of introducing into colonies of foreigners one-third to one-half Indian families. Alva extolled the Indian qualities of industry, hospitality, gentleness, and knowledge of the land; and he deplored the misery and exploitation to which the race had been subjected since the destruction of the "Great Tenochtitlán." Though commonly regarded as "equal to the ass," an "imbecile," good only as a servant or a slave, the Indian "is perhaps the best element of our population." Unfortunately, continued Alva, little improvement has come about since independence. "Now that peace leaves us time to meditate, the great problem we have to resolve is the redemption of the Indian"; let us turn him from a "poor pariah" into a "true citizen." Rejecting the idea that there was a racial basis for intelligence, Alva asserted that "race disappears in the face of humanity." Intermarriage will bring a "better race" within fifty years; "for it is known that any race is improved by crossing, if carried out under good conditions." Alva was vague about the "conditions," but he did suggest Irish Catholics as good candidates. Alva's basic point was that mixed colonies would be the best way "to keep alive national spirit, institutions, and customs." Alva's articles were lyrical in tone and reflected the rosy optimism of the González years. He juxtaposed economic development under Carlos Pacheco, minister of *fomento*, to the redemption of the Indian through mixed colonies and through education. Uncritical as his views were they did signify a distinct departure from the traditional creole concept of nationality.[61]

[60] Sierra in *El Federalista*, 22 August 1874 (*Obras*, 4:295), responding to Hilarión Frías y Soto who argued that the Romans, the French, and the Spaniards were "unified" peoples, and the stronger for it; Sierra in *El Federalista*, 17 May 1876 (*Obras*, 4:353). The articles were prompted by discussion of the 1875 colonization law.

[61] Alva's thirteen articles, "La Colonización y la raza indígena," ran in *La Libertad* from 7 June to 20 July 1882. They were numbered one through twelve, plus one that was unnumbered (24 June). In 1893 Alva was an editor of *El Monitor republicano* and a doctrinaire liberal opponent of the *Científicos* until his death on 1 December (see pp. 113–15). We

In an era of heightened sociological and racial consciousness, the programs for colonization by foreigners and universal education inevitably brought to the surface the perennial question of national identity. If the new awareness of the Indian, stimulated in part by the heroic popular struggle of the Reforma, undermined the creole concept of nationality, what, then, of the Spanish roots of Mexico? Could they still be defended and if so, by whom? The traditional defenders, the political conservatives, had lost their credibility after 1867, and liberals had always been ambivalent at best toward the Spanish heritage. The defense of Spain was left primarily to the Spaniards themselves, who, as we have seen, had regained a significant place in Mexican economic and intellectual life by the 1870s. In this context the Spanish colonization of Mexico became the subject of a voluminous journalistic controversy in mid-1875 between *La Colonia española* and the *Diario oficial*. The polemic was provoked by Adolfo Llanos y Alcaraz, the pugnacious editor of *La Colonia*, who praised the colonization law of 1875 but urged an additional article, which would "relegate the word 'foreigner' to oblivion," and "national susceptibility" to "the graveyard of historical curiosities." Llanos went on to glorify Spain, "which left in America part of its vitality (*savia*), a part of its grandeur." Spain never treated Mexico "with the harshness of the conquistador"; rather, she brought "all her wisdom." Mexico as "New Spain," continued Llanos y Alcaraz, "was always the favorite child, preferred even to Spain herself." Clearly, Spanish immigrants should not be regarded as foreigners.

The *Diario oficial* was at first restrained in its response, appearing to shrug off the deliberately provocative assertions of *La Colonia*. The ignorance and fanaticism of the colonial era, said the *Diario*, were not a "crime" of Spain but of the times; what is important is that they were rectified, first by heroic struggle and the implanting of liberal institutions and more recently by peace and economic progress. The way is now cleared for effective colonization; yet Mexicans, as descendants of Aztecs as well as of Spaniards, can never eliminate the term foreigner or abandon national susceptibility. But *La Colonia* persisted in its exaltation of past Spanish grandeur and its denigration of present Mexican backwardness, and the polemic escalated into some eleven hundred pages of vintage black-white legendry. Llanos y Alcaraz showed his colors as a controversialist by publishing the polemic followed by two other volumes, one of which was directed to Europeans and entitled "Don't Come to America." The latter was presented in part as a protest against a stamp

---

know little else about him. Alva's forceful advocacy of mixed colonies was novel, but the idea itself was not. Both the 1875 and 1883 laws offered a government subsidy to native colonists, that is, "families or individuals of pure Indian race" in 1875, "Mexican families" in 1883.

tax (*ley del timbre*), levied since the early seventies on the consumption of manufactures. Llanos argued that it discriminated against Spanish entrepreneurs. He was finally expelled from the country in 1879, with the encouragement of the Spanish minister himself. His excesses antagonized not only the Mexicans but also the Spanish community.[62]

The controversy of the mid-1870s continued as *La Voz de México* reacted to Llanos y Alcaraz; *La Voz* was answered in turn by Telesforo García, a more measured defender of Spanish civilization in America. In a somewhat confusing intellectual transition from Krausist idealism to Spencerian positivism, García posited the evolution of the human spirit through a struggle of peoples as organisms, which he said had led progressively to the realization of order in the cosmos, of unity in variety. Thus, "the immigration of the Spanish race to America is born of an imperative necessity, of a law of progress." García argued that each race had its own role to play in history and he proceeded to recite a long list of Spanish achievements in all fields of endeavor, which presumably had enriched Mexican culture. He also defended the present-day Spanish residents of the country whose economic contributions he claimed were vital to Mexico's prosperity. We have noted in chapter 2 the close ties that existed between the Mexican advocates of scientific politics and Spain, ties both intellectual and personal. García as a leader of the Spanish community and as a proprietor of *La Libertad* was perhaps the key link in this connection. Therefore it would be a mistake to overestimate the significance of the controversy of the 1870s over the Spanish roots of Mexican identity. Nonetheless it remained an issue that in the hands of polemicists could easily arouse passion.[63] It continues to be such an issue to this day.

[62] *Polémica entre el diario oficial y la colonia española sobre la administración vireynal en Nueva España y la colonización en México*, 2 vols. (Mexico, 1875). The editors of the *Diario oficial* were Darío Balandrano and Andrés C. Vázquez. The dated articles reprinted in the *Polémica* ran from 16 June to 21 September 1875. They were followed by thirty-five undated *La Colonia* articles, further responding to the *Diario oficial* (*Polémica*, 2:257–674). The other volumes by Llanos y Alcaraz were *No Vengáis a América. Libro dedicado a los pueblos europeos* (Mexico, 1876), made up mostly of articles reprinted from *La Colonia* (1874–76); and *Origen del plajio en México; polémica sostenida por el periódico la colonia española con varios órganos de la prensa mexicana* (Mexico, 1877), made up of articles (1874) by Llanos and by Niceto de Zamacois, refuting *El Federalista*'s contention that kidnapping was a Spanish import, initiated by José María Cobos, a Spanish general who fought for Maximilian. On the activities of Llanos and his expulsion, see Luther N. Steward, Jr., "Spanish Journalism in Mexico, 1867–1879," *Hispanic American Historical Review* 45 (1965): 422–33; also *La Libertad*, 10 June and 30 July 1879, commentaries on the matter by Telesforo García. There was also strong anti-Spanish sentiment in the history texts of the day: see Vázquez, *Nacionalismo*, pp. 69–79.

[63] García, *España* (1877), pp. 31–32. García took as a personal insult the attack by *La Voz* on the typical Spaniard who arrived poor, married a woman of good family, and accumu-

If one catalyst for Mexico's growing preoccupation with national identity was Spain, the other was the United States. In the postindependence period the institutions and society of the northern neighbor had served as a model for liberals, even though the ideas for achieving liberal goals were drawn principally from sources more akin to Mexican traditions, namely from France and reformist Spain. The vision of the United States as a liberal utopia persisted through the Reforma, despite the threat posed to Mexican existence by the loss of half its territory to North American aggression.[64] Once again in the seventies and eighties Mexican advocates of universal education and colonization by foreigners had before them the marvelous experience of the United States, as did the promoters of rapid economic development.

No one expressed this renewed emulation of North American achievements more openly than José María Vigil, the classic liberal who was drawn into the González administration and who became a prolific editorialist for the quasi-official *La Patria* in 1883. Week after week Vigil depicted with an easy optimism and a remarkable liberality the social and economic growth of the United States and the entry of American capital and entrepreneurs into Mexico. Mexico should not regard the United States as a threat, argued Vigil. If Mexico wants to fulfill its destiny, "it must follow resolutely the example before its eyes; at hand is the model it must imitate in everything." Vigil dismissed fears that a flood of immigrants and capital might undermine Mexico's "supposed character as a Latin nation." After all, the United States has not lost "its moral identity, despite the heterogeneous elements which have gone into its formation." Vigil even envisioned a "radical evolution . . . which might end up by absorbing [Mexico's] present inhabitants into a superior entity," phrases that came dangerously close to predicting annexation. However, it should be noted that Vigil did not include Indian policy among the North American achievements to be imitated. He emphasized Indian participation in the Revolution for Independence and the Reforma, and he was a strong advocate of universal education.[65]

---

lated a fortune as a merchant. As for *La Voz's* charge that Spaniards had nowhere to go but Mexico, García produced statistics to show that there were fewer Spaniards in Mexico (6,380) than in Sardinia (p. 28). García's pamphlet was published by Santiago Sierra's press. On García and the *La Libertad* group, see pp. 47–49. The controversy over Spanish colonization reemerged in 1894 when Francisco Cosmes asserted on 16 September that Hernán Cortés was the "true father" of the *patria*: Francisco Cosmes, *La Dominación española y la patria mexicana* (Mexico, 1896), pp. 7–8. The pamphlet consisted of a number of articles from *El Partido liberal* plus an enthusiastic preface by García.

[64] I have argued these points further in *Mexican Liberalism*, chap. 6. See also Donathon C. Olliff, *Reforma Mexico and the United States: A Search for Alternatives to Annexation, 1854–1861* (University, Alabama, 1981), a revealing study.

[65] Vigil in *La Patria*, particularly 4 and 11 January, 25 February, 11 March, 19 July 1883.

In strong contrast to Vigil's bland and optimistic view of North American penetration of the 1880s was the alarm sounded by his frequent opponent, Justo Sierra. Sierra was not replying specifically to Vigil but to those "who believe that our well-being consists of becoming Northamericanized." It is a view, he said, that even attracted the Lerdos, the Ocampos, and the Juárez—the great liberal patriots of the Reforma generation. Sierra went on to identify three forms of threatening "Americanism," the legal, the economic, and the cultural. According to Sierra, the age of "legal Americanism" had now passed. It was the product of an "essentially metaphysical education" that looked to the imposition of abstract North American constitutional principles as the basis of "our regeneration." Since 1867 by careful study and modification we have begun to adapt the constitution "to our needs," such that "republic is not the synonym of anarchy," "federation is combined with a rational centralization," and "indvidual liberty does not turn into social dissolution." In short, said Sierra, we are cautiously pursuing "the reformist spirit in the conservative sense (we give the word its scientific meaning)."

Sierra was in effect summarizing the program of scientific politics of 1878, identifying its precedents in the *convocatoria* of 1867. He pointed to the adoption of the Senate and the partially completed work of codification and then to the reforms yet to be accomplished, such as extension of the presidential term, the irremovability of judges, and the immediate issue of the day, obligatory education. In the legal and institutional realm, Sierra maintained that the country had "abandoned Americanism" for "a Mexicanism that is eclectic and at the same time practical." Sierra saw the country as now entering the era of "economic Americanism," full of illusions about the unlimited benefits of economic expansion. Although he doubted that railroads and agriculture would bring the expected profits either to Mexicans or Americans, he acknowledged that "we have crossed the Rubicon" (or better said, American railroads are crossing the Bravo), and that there was no turning back. Mexico's problem now was to avoid becoming "a protectorate, which every Mexican will be obliged to resist, by law and by the rifle."[66]

Even greater than the economic threat was the cultural threat, "perhaps the most dangerous form" of Americanism, the "attempt at moral and intellectual annexation." Sierra was particularly alarmed by Governor Evaristo Madero's intended contract with Baptist missionaries to establish three normal schools in Coahuila. The implications of the project struck at the heart of Sierra's most cherished cause, the strengthening of the nation through a distinctively Mexican universal education. Sierra fully acknowledged the dynamic and progressive role of Protestantism in

[66] Sierra, "Americanismo I," *La Libertad*, 22 December 1883 (*Obras*, 8:133–36).

history, but he feared that its spread among the general population might lead to an excessive admiration for the United States, particularly in this era of economic penetration. Sierra saw self-interest competing with liberty in the American character. The United States "is the offspring of two great birds of prey, England and Germany," and Mexico could well become the next victim. Thus, turning over "the most delicate part of our education," the training of teachers, "to a Protestant sect," poses a threat to our language and customs. The central government must intervene, concluded Sierra, even if to do so is unconstitutional: "The supreme law is the preservation of the *patria*."[67]

The fear of Americanization brought forth Sierra's deepest thoughts about national identity, thoughts that point up further a critical dimension of the relationship between liberalism and scientific politics in late nineteenth-century Mexico. Sierra was no apologist for the Spanish colonial heritage. He adhered to the heroic liberal tradition, beginning with the Hidalgo revolt of 1810 and ending with the victory of Juárez over Maximilian and the conservatives. He was strongly anticlerical and he lamented the stagnation of the Catholic Church. He admired Protestantism and the United States as symbols of liberal progress in the modern world. Yet as a Mexican patriot, he instinctively reacted against imitation and sought Mexico's identity in elements that would differentiate it from Protestant North America. Sierra, like his fellow advocates of scientific politics, sought a "conservative-liberalism," which found its political models in republican France and Spain and its theoretical foundations in the positivism of Auguste Comte and in the historical constitutionalism of Edouard Laboulaye.

Sierra also absorbed the new race consciousness of Spencer and Darwin, but he adapted it to the Mexican milieu. Although he disagreed sharply with Francisco Cosmes over the feasibility of universal education, their views converged when the subject of cultural Americanism arose in their debate. Each spoke in his own way of the need for reviving the traditional mission spirit of Catholicism to ward off alien influences; each juxtaposed Catholicism, Mexican nationality, and the Latin race. Cosmes was blatantly hispanophile; he perpetuated the earlier creole concept of nationality and like the resident Spaniards he tied Mexican identity to Spain. Sierra, like most of the liberal establishment, sought nationality in the "mestizo family," in the convergence of Indian and Hispanic

---

[67] Sierra, "Americanismo II. Un Proyecto de escuelas anexionistas," *La Libertad*, 27 December 1883 (*Obras*, 8:136–39). For a much less alarmist view of the potential influence of Protestantism on the Indian population, see Federico Mendoza y Vizcaino in *El Monitor republicano*, 26 July 1883. Mendoza was a doctrinaire liberal critic of the González regime (see pp. 69–70).

traditions. Yet, unlike José María Vigil and many other liberals, he was not mesmerized by North America. In the face of the Anglo-Saxon challenge, Justo Sierra's instinct was "to conserve the Latin spirit of our nationality," a spirit that was informed ultimately by religious values. It is an instinct that has deep roots in Mexico.[68]

[68] Cf. Sierra in *La Libertad*, 6 March 1883 (*Obras*, 8:114) with Cosmes in *La Libertad*, 14 March. Sierra's well-known phrase, "the mestizo family," appeared in "México social," *Revista nacional* 1 (1889): 19 (*Obras*, 9:131). Like most social commentators of the day, Sierra used the term "race" freely, both in its anthropological and its historical sense. A race in nineteenth-century parlance could be either a physically non-European group, such as the Indians of Mexico; or it could be simply a nationality or people, such as the "Spanish race" or the "Latin race," developing over time and distinguished from others by geography, language, or religion. I have discussed these concepts further in "Political and Social Ideas," pp. 397–400.

CHAPTER 8

Conclusion: The Legacy

THE CENTRAL THREAD of this study is the political ideas of the intellectual and quasi-governmental elite of the post-Reforma generation in Mexico. Since these ideas developed in a philosophical climate infused with positivism, I have also explored positivism itself, not only for its effect on political thought but also as the principal element in the refashioning of Mexican higher education and in the formulation of social thought and policy. Although these discussions of educational and social ideas occupy separate chapters, they never stray very far from politics. The main political issues continually reappear and serve to integrate the study as a whole. The political thought of the era is best characterized as a triumphant and official liberalism, in contention with positivist concepts and yet gradually transformed by them. In short, the book treats the intellectual assumptions of the liberal establishment of the late nineteenth century, years in which ideological consensus prevailed despite factional conflict and continuous and often acrimonious debate. One measure of this consensus was the recurring rhetorical theme of Liberal party unity, which accompanied the policies of Presidents Díaz and González to reconcile former partisans of Juárez, Lerdo, and Iglesias and finally to glorify Benito Juárez as the consummate liberal and national hero.

The key to the transformation of liberalism was the appearance of the doctrine of scientific politics, hinted at by Gabino Barreda in 1867 but first systematically enunciated in 1878 by a "new generation" of journalist-intellectuals in the newspaper *La Libertad*. The doctrine of scientific politics was drawn from French positivism of the 1820s and constituted a critique of classic liberal and democratic ideas, now branded as "revolutionary" and "anarchical," products of the "metaphysical" mentality of an age gone by. The new "positive" age must be guided by "science," and policies must be built upon observation, experiment, and facts, not upon dogmas and abstractions. Administration by scientifically educated experts must replace traditional politics as the basis of effective government. In presenting these ideas, men such as Justo Sierra, Francisco Cosmes, and Telesforo García saw themselves as "new" liberals, superseding the "old" liberals of the Reforma era. Their specific program was to strengthen government through constitutional reform, and they looked to the fledgling regime of Porfirio Díaz to implement this program.

Though the intellectual origins and much of the terminology of scientific politics must be sought in the positivism of Henri de Saint-Simon and Auguste Comte, widely generalized in European thought by the 1870s, more immediate inspiration came from the contemporary conservative republics of France and Spain, led by Jules Simon, Adolphe Thiers, and Emilio Castelar. The Third French Republic was a stable constitutional regime implanted in the aftermath of foreign war and sociopolitical conflict. Castelar's short-lived presidency of the First Spanish Republic in 1873 was a gallant effort to impose strong government in the face of anarchy. Likewise the regime of Porfirio Díaz could bring order out of the chaos of 1876, seen by the men of *La Libertad* as the culmination of two decades of "revolution." The leaders of the French and Spanish republics were "conservative-liberals," and conservative-liberalism became the banner of *La Libertad*, the correlate of scientific politics.

The principal argument of this book is that the advocates of scientific politics of 1878 and their heirs, the *Científicos* of 1893, must be regarded as constitutionalists and not merely as apologists for the authoritarian regime of Porfirio Díaz. Their program of 1878 was to strengthen government through constitutional reform, not to put aside or to subvert the constitution in the name of science. A lengthened presidential term, a suspensive veto, restricted suffrage, the retention of a senate, a separate vice-presidency, and life tenure for judges—these changes would make the constitution conform to social reality and would avoid the need to suspend it at moments of crisis. *La Libertad*'s call for constitutional reform sparked a debate in 1878 and 1879, principally between Justo Sierra and José María Vigil, who doggedly defended the Constitution of 1857 in its pure form. The debate was not one between positivists and liberals or between subverters and defenders of the constitution, but one between two groups of constitutionalists, indeed two groups of liberals, the conservative-liberals (or advocates of scientific politics) and the doctrinaire or classic liberals. In short, this debate like others examined in this book took place within the liberal establishment that emerged after 1867.

To demonstrate the argument that scientific politics must be seen as a form of constitutionalism, it has been necessary to break with chronology and pursue three interrelated inquiries. First we explored the circumstances surrounding the *convocatoria* of 1867, the calling of elections and the restoration of constitutional government following the decade of civil war. Second, we examined the political activities and ideas of the *La Libertad* group before the founding of the newspaper in 1878, especially their fervent support of the cause of José María Iglesias in 1876 and their reappraisal of it the following year. Third, we looked ahead to the founding of the National Liberal Union in 1892 and the vigorous constitutional debate that ensued over the irremovability of judges, a debate that involved many of the issues and some of the individuals of 1878.

In the case of the constitutional reforms called for in the *convocatoria* and the debate surrounding them we found numerous precedents for 1878. In the name of "constitutional balance," Sebastián Lerdo, the author of the *convocatoria*, advocated what was in effect a perpetuation of the strong wartime presidency of Benito Juárez. Francisco Zarco's commentary in the leading newspaper *El Siglo XIX* revealed the ambivalence of a former doctrinaire constitutionalist toward the advance of centralizing administration. A particularly notable precedent for 1878 was the official campaign of the late 1860s and early 1870s to reinstitute a senate. Influenced by the French constitutional theorist Edouard Laboulaye, the argument for a senate contained the anomalous combination of "interests" versus excessive democracy, legal guarantees against "dictatorship," and enhanced central state authority. Laboulaye was a historical rather than a doctrinaire constitutionalist, an elitist rather than a democrat, a former supporter of the Orleanist monarchy who vigorously opposed Napoleon III and ultimately became a stalwart of the Third Republic. His orientation was an important ingredient of scientific politics. The men of *La Libertad*, citing Laboulaye, could call themselves liberals yet propose a reform of the constitution in a "conservative sense."

In the second case, we discovered that the future editors of *La Libertad* began their political careers as exaggerated constitutionalists, opposing Lerdo's reelection and supporting Chief Justice Iglesias's legalistic claim to the presidency in 1876. Their transition to scientific politics came in the critical year 1877, a transition year in which their constitutionalism was tempered by the new political imperatives of the Díaz military victory. The experience of Justo Sierra and his reflections upon it are particularly revealing.

In the third and most decisive case we could identify scientific politics as constitutionalism in the program of the Liberal Union of 1892, also led by Justo Sierra. Sierra's manifesto restated the administrative and centralizing principles of scientific politics, but it emphasized even more the need for constitutional reform, this time to limit, not enhance, the authority of Porfirio Díaz. The arguments from science were similar to those put forth in 1878; but in the changed circumstances of 1892–93 strong constitutional government meant vigorous institutions to restrain personal executive power. In the complex debate of 1893 over the permanency of judges, the constitutional reformers were dubbed "*científicos*," which marked the origin of a notorious and variously defined group. Though the *Científicos* failed in 1893, they tried again in 1903, this time calling for political parties to provide continuity in the face of increasingly precarious personal government by an aged president. Their second effort, led by Francisco Bulnes, was a kind of denouement. It aroused little debate and apparently less support than the first. Thus the scientific politics of 1878 from precedents in the *convocatoria* of 1867 to its climax in the episode of 1892–93 and its denouement in 1903 had a strong constitutionalist component, despite the disdain for constitutions, indeed for liberalism itself, present in traditional positivist theory as espoused by Saint-Simon and Comte.

In the constitutional debates that took place within the liberal establishment from 1867 to 1893, those upholding the classic or doctrinaire position became increasingly ineffective. Before 1867 *reformista* liberals like Francisco Zarco or José María Vigil could be both constitutionalists and anticlerical reformers; they could support both limited and enhanced central authority; they could be both antistatists and statists. Moreover, in the ideological struggle against monarchy and corporate privilege, liberals could equate democracy or popular sovereignty with both the wartime dictatorship of Benito Juárez and the Constitution of 1857 in its pure form. However, with the restoration of the republic and the triumph of liberalism, the imperative was no longer struggle but rather reconciliation and orderly material reconstruction.

In an era of growing ideological consensus, the doctrine of popular sovereignty came into disrepute. It was held to be the basis for a dangerous democracy, identified with rebellion, anarchy, and revolution. Thus Francisco Zarco was forced to accept the implications of the *convocatoria* of 1867 and the "relaxation" of the constitution in the face of regional rebellions. José María Vigil's defense of the pure constitution in 1878–79, associating it with the "school of Rousseau, parent of unconditional democracy," had limited impact. So did his effort to identify the men of *La Libertad* with the old conservatives. As conciliatory scientific politics gained ground during the first presidency of Porfirio Díaz, Vigil's message could easily be branded metaphysical and passé. Vigil did find a personal haven in the González regime after 1880, but he turned from overtly political to philosophical debate, attempting to uphold classic liberalism indirectly by attacking positivism in higher education.

Even less effective than Vigil's indirect defense of classic liberalism was the defense of the pure constitution by the editors of *El Monitor republicano* in the three-sided debate of 1893. The *Científicos* as constitutionalists had appropriated one major argument of the doctrinaire liberals and the defenders of Porfirio Díaz another. The *Científicos* called for the limitation of excessive executive authority, while those who portrayed Díaz as a potential social reformer used popular sovereignty to argue the need for democratic Caesarism. After 1893 the doctrinaire liberals, now branded "Jacobins" by their opponents, no longer had a place within the intellectual and governmental establishment and were forced to go underground.

To demonstrate further the relationship between positivism and liberalism in the political ideas of the post-Reforma generation, we have had to move beyond the concept of scientific politics and its constitutionalist component to the more purely philosophical dimensions of the relationship. The positive philosophy of Auguste Comte as a theory of knowledge and even as a program for the moral regeneration of society had its greatest impact in the establishment of the Escuela Nacional Preparatoria, directed by Gabino Barreda. The curriculum of the school, which was required of all preprofessional students, was based on Comte's hierarchy of the sciences. Moreover it made the scientific method its guiding principle and suppressed the initial course in "philosophy" in favor of a final course in "logic," or scientific reasoning. As a part of the logic course, Barreda even suggested replacing traditional Christian ethics with Comte's secular ethics of humanity, that is, the cultivation of the altruism and social benevolence appropriate to a scientific age.

Although the new school and its required curriculum had the official sanction of the Juárez and Lerdo regimes, it was subject to continuous attacks on both practical and philosophical grounds, from inside and outside the government, by liberals and Catholics and by students and parents. Catholics attacked what appeared to be official support for atheism. Liberals opposed a state-imposed curriculum in the name of freedom of teaching (according to article 3 of the constitution). Students and parents objected to required courses that were not directly relevant to professional training. Much of the attack on the Preparatoria from within the liberal establishment was based on an idealist resistance to positivist empiricism, a resistance drawn from French spiritualist philosophy of the school of Victor Cousin. This resistance was particularly notable in Justo Sierra's writings of 1874 to 1877, which expressed ambivalence toward the school and its exclusivist view of philosophy as scientific method. Like the French spiritualists, Sierra attempted to reconcile metaphysics and science, to preserve spiritual liberty and free will in the face of the new determinism. However, Sierra made a philosophical transition from spiritualism to positivism in 1877 that paralleled his political transition from constitutional legalism to scientific politics and from Iglesias to Díaz. In 1877 Sierra took a professorship at the ENP and thereafter became an ardent defender of the school and its positivist curriculum.

Despite the kinship between positive philosophy and emerging scientific politics, the educational and political arguments followed separate though parallel courses through the 1870s. Gabino Barreda, the progenitor of positivism in Mexico, was essentially apolitical, as were his disciples. However, politics and educational philosophy did come together after 1880 in the great debate over the choice of logic texts for the ENP. Should it be the positivist text by William Bain or the idealist text by Guillaume Tiberghien, a Belgian disciple of the German philosopher Krause? This seemingly arid issue led to an elaborate polemic in the Mexico City press between positivists and idealists (both Krausist and spiritualist), and it drew in the advocates of scientific politics and the doctrinaire liberals. The basic theoretical conflict between positivism and liberalism came to the surface, particularly in the exchanges between Porfirio Parra and José María Vigil. Vigil argued as did the French spiritualists from whom he drew that positivism posed a serious threat to classic liberal principles. However, since both groups now had a strong presence in the regime of Manuel González, the political discussion remained generalized and became subordinated to educational and philosophical issues. The constitution was not mentioned and the regime itself went unquestioned.

Following a temporary standoff on the ENP curriculum issue during the later 1880s, positivism once again gained ascendancy in official educational circles. Justo Sierra was elected to preside over the two National Congresses of Public Instruction of 1889 to 1891 and positivist delegates carried the debates. The second congress reaffirmed the basic elements of the curriculum of 1867–69, and scientific logic won out over spiritualist philosophy. Nonetheless, what emerged in 1891 was not the more orthodox Comtean ideas of Gabino Barreda, but rather a more heterodox positivism as espoused by Sierra and Parra. The second congress ignored Barreda's flirtation with Comte's religion of humanity and his call for scientific education as a means of moral regeneration. It also found a place for psychology (rejected by Comte and Barreda) and a more ample place for history. The victory of positivism in higher education coincided with the ascendancy of scientific politics. The educational congresses were followed directly by the 1892 convention of the National Liberal Union. It was clear from the rhetoric of these gatherings that the reaffirmation of positivist higher education was an integral part of the agenda of scientific politics. The scientific training of a cohesive elite was central to the program of administration, reconciliation, and development that reached its culmination in the early 1890s. Moreover, José María Vigil's weak defense of spiritualism in a final exchange with Porfirio Parra in 1891 can be juxtaposed to *El Monitor*'s ineffective defense of the pure constitution in 1893 as representing the decline of doctrinaire liberalism within the establishment.

I have concluded my discussion of the complex relationship between liberalism, positivism, and scientific politics by examining the assumptions that underlay social thought and policy. To do so I had to establish the relative influences of the various elements of positivist social theory, namely, the thought of Auguste Comte and Herbert Spencer, Social Darwinism, and, tangentially, the historical school of law, as interpreted by Laboulaye. In pursuing these positivist and quasi-positivist ingredients of Mexican social thought, it was necessary to reiterate that positivism entered a political climate governed by a pervasive liberal myth. The heritage of liberal thought infused with the heroic and popular patriotism of the midcentury decades had a leavening influence on the formation of Porfirian social ideas. Viewed in another way, my specific problem was to discern which of the two principal ingredients of positivist social theory, the ideas of Comte or those of Spencer, was more congenial to Mexico's liberal heritage. I approached this problem by first discussing general social attitudes, especially those toward the Indian population and toward rural rebellions. Then I turned to two important and much-debated policy questions, obligatory primary education and colonization by foreigners (including the related issue of *terrenos baldíos* or unclaimed lands).

By any quantitative measure, Herbert Spencer was more influential in Mexican social thought than Auguste Comte. After 1875 when his ideas (along with those of Charles Darwin) entered Mexico, he was far more widely cited than Comte. Moreover Spencer's concept of progress as the adaptation by individuals to changes in the environment, his ethnographic orientation, and his popularization of the Darwinian concepts of natural selection and the struggle for existence made him especially attractive to a generation imbued with a sharpened race consciousness and a fever for economic development. The only evidence of overt Comtean influence came in the formalistic social theorizing of Gabino Barreda and his early disciple Manuel S. Macedo. Comtean ideas, such as a paternalism based on accepted social and moral hierarchies, social solidarity as opposed to "revolutionary pride," an emphasis on duties versus rights, on altruism versus egoism, and even a social view of property were advanced by Barreda and Macedo, but in the abstract, without reference to the ethnic realities of Mexican society. They were not enunciated further until Agustín Aragón became the spokesman for a sectarian orthodox positivism after 1900. Yet despite the proliferation of Spencerian and Social Darwinist influences, I would argue that in certain subtle and qualitative ways, Mexican social thought and policy bore a Comtean stamp.

This Comtean strand can be discerned in the general social assumptions of the advocates of scientific politics, particularly those of Justo Sierra. To be sure, *La Libertad*'s program for social reconstruction was infused with Spencerian evolutionary terminology and a biological conception of society. Yet Sierra saw the individual and society as "the two great organic realities that cannot be separated," in contrast to Spencer's extreme individualism. Moreover, throughout Sierra's thought runs the very un-Spencerian idea of the positive role of the state. Spencer's tirades against state action and regulation were ignored (and even on occasion criticized) by Sierra, just as they were by Spencer's French interpreters. More specifically, in the campaign for universal primary education Comtean influence was manifest in the notion of "cultivating" students and instilling in them a sense of universal morality. For Barreda and for Sierra after him, the key agent in the educational process was *el estado docente*, the state as the inculcator of civic and moral virtues in all citizens. This fundamental concept, in contrast to Spencer's idea of letting students be educated by nature, revealed the confluence of Comtean positivism and reformist liberalism in Mexican social thought.

Turning specifically to the question of the Indians, I would also argue that after 1867 attitudes and policy were guided more by traditional liberalism infused with Comtean ideas than by either Spencerian or Darwinist concepts. As in the pre-Reforma period, the Indian question drew little attention from the metropolitan elite except during periods of rebellion. When rural violence did erupt, for example in the state of Hidalgo in 1877–79, the response of the liberal establishment was reminiscent of the creole reaction to Miguel Hidalgo's insurgency of 1810 or to the caste wars of 1847–49. Political differences were put aside as advocates of scientific politics and doctrinaire liberals alike called for vigorous government action against the threat of "barbarism" and "social war," for recruitment of the "conservative elements of society" to defend property, and in general for promotion of "work" (or economic development) instead of internecine politics. While many of the assumptions of scientific politics were made manifest in the response to Indian rebellions, recently arrived Social Darwinist notions of inevitable racial struggle and biological superiority and inferiority were not. In fact, even in the 1880s and early 1890s, Social Darwinism made slow headway as an intellectual basis for important policy initiatives affecting the Indians.

In large part the campaign to legislate universal primary education became during the 1880s a debate over the educability of the Indians. Francisco Cosmes and other skeptics argued from Spencerian determinism that redemption of the Indians must be left to natural evolutionary forces, but absent from their argument was evidence of biological racism, that is, a belief in the inherent inferiority of the Indians independent of environmental circumstances. Nor did the Darwinian notion of the struggle for racial survival appear in their rhetoric. The leading proponent of obligatory education, Justo Sierra, also developed his campaign within a positivist evolutionary framework, but his orientation was more Comtean than Spencerian. He refuted Spencer by adhering to *el estado docente*, but he also held to universal education as an ideal, one that might actually guide the evolutionary process. Moreover, in the face of deterministic skepticism, Sierra along with liberals of various political persuasions acknowledged the participation of Indians in Mexico's popular struggle of the Reforma and called up the heroic liberal tradition. He characterized the successful 1888 measure extending obligatory education to the Federal District as "a law of social redemption . . . that the Ocampos and the Ramírez would have signed in blood." The extension of state-controlled obligatory education to the entire nation by the first National Congress of Public Instruction in 1890 was guided in large part by the dictates of ascendant scientific politics, that is, by the impulse toward "uniformity" and administrative centralization. It was also guided by the powerful liberal myth.

The flawed policy of promoting the colonization of Mexico by European immigrants was also a traditional liberal inspiration, buttressed by the fundamental doctrine of private property. In this instance liberal socioeconomic doctrines were reinforced by Spencerian individualism rather than by Comtean collectivism. Colonization policies became subordinated to a series of measures designed to make unoccupied lands available for economic development, either by individuals or by "surveying companies" (as provided in the law of 1883). The traditional liberal ideal of small property-holders (whether Indian villagers or foreign colonists) as the key to rural progress was subverted by an officially condoned appropriation of *baldíos* and of village lands by large property interests. Although colonization was a failure, the discussion of it did reveal important assumptions about the bases and future of Mexican society. One persistent argument for colonization had been that an incursion of Europeans would improve society through a better racial mixture. However, from the 1840s to the 1870s there was a shift from a creole concept of nationality to a more positive view of the Indian roots of nationality. It was drawn from Mexican experience and it contradicted the denigration of racial mixture common in European Social Darwinism. This positive view of the Indian, and particularly of racial mixture, was prominent in the writing of Justo Sierra, but it was also elaborated by the doctrinaire liberal Luis Alva in an unusual series of articles in 1883 advocating "mixed colonies."

The debates on colonization and on universal education led inevitably to the general question of Mexican national identity. There were the perennial (and perhaps superficial) polemics over the Spanish component of Mexican nationality, but the most significant catalyst for reflection on the question of identity in a climate of rapid economic development was the United States. One tendency, exemplified by José María Vigil in the early 1880s, was to be mesmerized by North American material progress and to take a benign view of any and all influences from the United States. The advocates of scientific politics were more wary. In 1883 Justo

Sierra sounded the alarm by pointing to the triple threat of "American-ism"—legal, economic, and cultural. At the heart of his concern was that by blindly imitating American institutions and values, Mexico would sac-rifice its cultural integrity. Like his fellow advocates of scientific politics, Sierra sought a defense against legal Americanism in French and Spanish conservative-liberalism. He sought Mexican social origins in the "mestizo family"; but his instinct was also "to conserve the Latin spirit of our na-tionality," a spirit that was rooted in Catholic resistance to missionary Protestantism. Thus we return to a central theme of our studies, namely that Mexican liberalism, whether in its classic early nineteenth-century form or in its late nineteenth-century transformation, was continental in orientation. Its intellectual inspiration and political models were drawn from France and Spain and adapted to Mexican circumstances.

It will be obvious to the reader that Justo Sierra looms large in this book. He was clearly the preeminent intellectual of Porfirian Mexico and any effort to untangle the complexities of Mexican thought brings us re-peatedly back to Sierra. He was the leader of both the *La Libertad* group and the *Científicos*. Although the two were distinct cohorts, Justo Sierra did provide an all-important link between 1878 and 1893. After 1878 he became a chief defender of the National Preparatory School and its posi-tivist mission against liberal and Catholic critics, and he deserves much of the credit for the reaffirmation of its scientific curriculum by the early 1890s.

Sierra epitomized the continental orientation of the Mexican liberal establishment. His early education was steeped in the romance of the French Revolution that he defended so vigorously against Gabino Bar-reda in 1875. The philosophy of Sierra's twenties was French spiritual-ism, and the ambivalence of his mature years between positivism and idealism reflected the experience of French philosophy in the nineteenth century. He looked to the French Third Republic as a political model. Sierra's tie to Spain was more personal, perhaps more visceral. His fa-ther-in-law was a pillar of the Spanish colony in Mexico City. He main-tained a lifetime intimacy with Telesforo García, the chief promoter of the Hispano-Mexican bond. His religious convictions had deep Spanish roots. He held Emilio Castelar, the soul of late nineteenth-century Span-ish liberalism, in great esteem. Finally, he ended his life as minister plenipotentiary to the *madre patria*. Sierra, of course, also looked be-yond France and Spain. His early plan for an autonomous national uni-versity was overtly of German inspiration. The influences of John Stuart Mill, Charles Darwin, and particularly of Herbert Spencer were impor-tant to him, but the evidence suggests that Sierra like others of his gen-eration viewed the German University and British thought through a French prism.

Yet, Sierra was no mere transplanted European intellectual. He was the "high priest of the liberal *patria*" during the Porfiriato.[1] Through his histories he codified the official civic religion of the post-Reforma years. His dogged campaign to establish the principle of obligatory primary education bears testimony not only to his educational vision but also to his conviction that the nation had Indian as well as Hispanic roots and that the result was a mestizo society. He was the one Porfirian figure whose reputation was to survive the onslaught of the Revolution and gain a secure place in the pantheon of national heroes. His *Evolución política del pueblo mexicano* remains the country's most revered history, as much for its message as for its style. Any consideration of the legacy of late nineteenth-century thought for the contemporary era must acknowledge the centrality of Sierra.[2]

Nonetheless I have resisted the temptation (admittedly with some ambivalence) to frame this study as Mexican liberalism in the age of Sierra. To do so would have been to distort the range, the chronology, and the complexity of late nineteenth-century Mexican political ideas. Sierra's expressed political consciousness dates from about 1874, whereas the precedents for scientific politics and its constitutionalist component must be sought in the *convocatoria* of 1867 and in the subsequent campaign for a senate—that is, before the entry of Sierra into the political arena. To understand the relationship between positivism and liberalism in higher education the focus must first be on Gabino Barreda and not on Sierra. Moreover, in the philosophical and quasi-political debates of the early 1880s, Telesforo García, Jorge Hammeken y Mexía, Porfirio Parra, and José María Vigil attract our attention more than does Sierra. To be sure, Sierra presided over the ascendancy of both positivist education and scientific politics in the early 1890s, the moment when the Liberal party became in Sierra's words a *partido de gobierno*. However, with the break-up of the liberal establishment (a subject beyond the limits of this study), Sierra began his administrative career as the ministerial organizer of the state-directed educational system, which culminated in the found-

---

[1] The phrase is that of David Brading, who in the most recent of his perceptive essays on Mexican political culture points up Sierra's role in perpetuating the efforts of Ignacio M. Altamirano: David A. Brading, "Liberal Patriotism and the Mexican Reforma," *Journal of Latin American Studies* 20 (1988): 47–48.

[2] The apotheosis of Justo Sierra probably began with the first integral edition of Sierra's history of 1900–02 published by La Casa de España en México in 1940 with an introduction by Alfonso Reyes. As noted earlier, the present title, *Evolución política*, first appeared with that edition. Between 1912 and 1940 there were only fragmentary Sierra publications. His *Obras completas* in fourteen volumes, directed by Agustín Yáñez (who also provided an eloquent biography), were published in 1948, the centennial of Sierra's birth. The reconstruction of Sierra was undoubtedly a significant dimension of the intellectual "act of consciousness" (*toma de conciencia*) of the 1940s.

ing of the national university. Although that administrative career from 1901 to 1910 marked the climax of Sierra's life and thought, consideration of it would have led me away from the central conceptual issues of this study. Those issues are too complex to find their epitome in the ideas of one man.

I have alluded frequently to the break-up of the liberal establishment during the decade-and-a-half before 1910. One symptom of this break-up was the ineffectiveness of the Jacobins or doctrinaire liberals in 1893, followed by the cessation in 1896 of the two stalwarts of the liberal press since the 1840s, *El Siglo XIX* and *El Monitor republicano*. Another symptom was the failure of the *Científicos* to limit the authoritarian and personal power of Porfirio Díaz. After 1893 the constitutionalist component of scientific politics receded, despite a vain effort to reassert it in the second National Liberal Union of 1903. The advocates of scientific politics were confident in 1892 that the Liberal party had at long last turned from a party of revolution into a party of government, but by 1903 personal government had supplanted establishment parties of any kind. The *Científicos* became thoroughly reconciled with the regime at the expense of their program to provide governmental continuity through institutions. Forced out of the establishment, doctrinaire liberalism found refuge after 1900 in the clandestine clubs, in the rebellious Partido Liberal Mexicano of 1905, and ultimately in the antireelectionist movement of Francisco I. Madero. The regime had hardened, the establishment had narrowed, the ideological consensus had faded, and Mexico was on the way to revolution.

Any effort to identify the legacy of scientific politics for post-1910 Mexico must focus on the ideology of the Madero revolution and of the subsequent constitutionalist movement of Venustiano Carranza, which had triumphed over other revolutionary factions by 1917. Madero has traditionally been portrayed as the "apostle of democracy" whose popular program of effective suffrage and no-reelection revived the liberalism of the Reforma and Restored Republic following the long Díaz dictatorship. Madero, then, was heir to the liberal and democratic opposition to Díaz, which persisted depite harrassment and occasional repression. This interpretation is implicit in the work of Jesús Reyes Heroles (although he omitted treatment of the Porfiriato), and it was forcefully presented by Daniel Cosío Villegas, as we noted in chapter 1. Madero's "innocent thesis" of 1910, the "belief that political life, liberty, and democracy were of greater value even than order" and material progress, became the point of departure for Cosío's critique of the Neo-Porfiriato of the 1940s and his decision to study the Porfiriato itself.[3] Therefore Cosío construed

[3] Cosío Villegas, "La Crisis de México" (1947), in *Extremos americanos* (Mexico, 1949), p. 14.

Madero's political ideology as a mix of the constitutionalism of 1857 and popular sovereignty kept alive by Zarco, Vigil, *El Monitor republicano*, Emilio Vázquez, and other opposition journalists.

Recent efforts to reexamine the Madero movement have not only emphasized its indifference to agrarian problems and its repudiation of *zapatismo*, but also its internal compromises with the old regime. Alan Knight points out that despite Madero's liberal constitutionalist critique of the Porfiriato, he had only admiration for the economic growth achieved by Díaz. John Womack, Jr., even refers to the emergence in 1911 of a "Madero-*Científico* government."[4] Does this evidence not suggest the continuity of scientific politics in the ideology of the Madero regime? If we accept the argument that scientific politics had a constitutionalist component and was itself a variety of liberalism, can we not infer the presence of this component after 1910? This is not to deny the strong democratic impulse in the Madero revolution or the clear resurgence of classic liberalism following its expulsion from the establishment in the 1890s, but only to suggest that *maderismo* as a liberal movement might have been more complex than we have supposed.

Traces of scientific politics were even stronger in the Carranza regime. As we noted in chapter 1, Arnaldo Córdova's demolition of the liberal myth and his efforts to seek the origins of an ideology of capitalist economic development in the post-Reforma period posits a perpetuation of the ideas of the *Científicos* in the guiding assumptions of the Carranza era. Similarly, Knight argues for the persistence of a "developmentalist liberalism" of Porfirian origin (analogous to what I have called scientific politics), which "came out of the Revolution stronger than ever, among other reasons, because of its new revolutionary and populist seal."[5] Capitalist development was certainly part of the "ethos" of the Carranza regime, but so was constitutionalism. Cosío Villegas and others have pointed out that Emilio Rabasa, a latter-day advocate of scientific politics, exerted a strong influence on the formulation of the Constitution of 1917. Rabasa was more than an apologist for the authoritarian presidency; he also maintained a faith in historical constitutionalism, the buttress of an

---

[4] Alan Knight, "El Liberalismo mexicano desde la reforma hasta la revolución (una interpretación)," *Historia mexicana* 35 (1985): 84; John Womack, Jr., "The Mexican Revolution, 1910–1920," *Cambridge History of Latin America*, 5:85. François-Xavier Guerra also emphasizes Madero's *Científico* ties, but in other respects his recent magisterial study reaffirms the democratic character of the *maderista* revolution. He argues that the "democratic fiction" (the divergence between the principles of the constitution and political practice) maintained since 1857, dissolved in 1910. In his view, the imaginary "people" of the nineteenth century became real people, giving Madero a new legitimacy: François-Xavier Guerra, *Le Mexique. De L'Ancien Régime à la révolution*, 2 vols. (Paris, 1985).

[5] Knight, "Liberalismo," p. 69; also idem, *The Mexican Revolution*, 2 vols. (Cambridge, 1986), 2:494–96.

enlightened elite. "The dictators have completed their task," he concluded in 1912, "the constitutional stage must follow."[6] His goal was to bring the written and real constitutions into harmony, to solidify the reign of political institutions and liberties in concert with a strong and effective administration dedicated to reconstruction and economic development. If the Carranza era marked the emergence of the quasi-authoritarian revolutionary state, scientific politics was clearly one of its elements.

We will recall that one feature of the constitutional debate of 1893 was the appearance of a vigorous "scientific" argument for democratic Caesarism or presidential populism, put forth in opposition to the proposal by the *Científicos* for irremovable judges. Francisco Cosmes and Carlos Olaguíbel split from their former colleagues and identified major social problems that could only be addressed by a reformist state headed by an authoritarian Porfirio Díaz. Irremovable judges, they said, would only uphold the social status quo. In making their argument the advocates of democratic Caesarism revived the doctrine of popular sovereignty, ineffective since it had been used to justify the wartime dictatorship of Benito Juárez. Despite our natural tendency to dismiss this argument as pure opportunism on the part of Cosmes and Olaguíbel, it did have intellectual logic and substance and it may have affected the legacy of scientific politics. Perhaps it even provided a precedent for the tendency toward presidential populism that also emerged with Carranza and has persisted intermittently to our day.

To pursue further the legacy of late nineteenth-century thought, we must go beyond scientific politics and consider other aspects of the relationship between positivism and liberalism. Did the philosophical contention between spiritualism (idealism) and positivism (empiricism) that was at the heart of the debates over the National Preparatory School and its scientific curriculum have repercussions after 1910? Did positivist social thought persist through the revolutionary decade or was it repudiated by the programs of social reform?

Scholars have tended to treat politics and philosophy after 1910 as separate categories. Historians of ideas identify a philosophical revolt against positivism coincident with the Revolution and led by the intellectuals of the Ateneo de la Juventud, such as Pedro Henríquez Ureña, José Vasconcelos, and Antonio Caso. Though the activities of the Ateneo were disrupted by the violence of the early revolutionary years, a new idealism took hold in the recently established national university, particularly through the teaching and writings of Caso. Thus began a reorientation of Mexican culture in which positivism gave way to humanism and to a revival of metaphysics and culminated in the philosophical and literary search for identity in the 1940s.

But did this movement intersect with political thought? Córdova has argued that the philosophical "spiritualism" of the Ateneo tradition remained on the margin of political life, isolated in the university. What persisted in official circles among such intellectuals as Andrés Molina Enríquez, Luis Cabrera, and José Covarrubias was positivism—which Córdova maintains should be regarded as the "philosophy" of the Revolution.[7] I am persuaded that there was a continuity of positivism during the revolutionary decade (indeed, it formed part of the continuity of scientific politics), but less so that the new idealism became marginalized. More probably, positivism and idealism continued to interact in politics and in higher education after 1910, just as they had earlier. Justo Sierra, the mentor of the *ateneístas*, was moving away from positivism (or returning to his earlier idealism) during the last years of his life. Vasconcelos as a philosophical idealist became a committed *maderista* and participated in the revolutionary convention of 1914–15, before beginning his wanderings abroad. He seems to have repudiated positivism, except in aspects of his social thought. On the other hand, two important intellectuals (and later politicians) of the famous generation of 1915, Manuel Gómez Morín and Vicente Lombardo Toledano, appear to have retained positivist leanings, despite the influence of Antonio Caso.[8] Seen comparatively, the philosophical transition from positivism to the new idealism was a broad and gradual Latin American phenomenon between 1900 and 1920 that involved much ambivalence and often intersected with politics. This transition also took place in Mexico, despite the uniqueness of its revolutionary experience.[9]

In the realm of social thought we can also discern the continuity of late nineteenth-century patterns, despite the popular and radical challenges of the Revolution. To be sure, colonization by foreigners as a social panacea was finally laid to rest and the notorious policy of alienating *terrenos baldíos* to individuals and surveying companies was repudiated. None-

---

[7] Arnaldo Córdova, "¿Espiritualismo o positivismo? La Filosofía de la revolución mexicana," Mexico, Centro de Estudios Latinoamericanos (UNAM), Avances de investigación, no. 14 (1975). I prefer the more general term "new idealism" to "spiritualism." The chief influences on the Ateneo were from Émile Boutroux and Henri Bergson, who had moved beyond the earlier French spiritualism.

[8] See Enrique Krauze, *Caudillos culturales en la revolución mexicana* (Mexico, 1976), a dual biography of Gómez Morín and Lombardo Toledano. Gómez Morín, as architect of Mexico's new banking system in the 1920s, emphasized *técnica* as opposed to politics and envisioned himself as a new Limantour. Lombardo Toledano revealed positivist assumptions in 1922 as director of the ENP and as the author of a study in legal theory. See Córdova, "¿Espiritualismo o positivismo?" pp. 20–23.

[9] I have argued this point in more detail in "Political and Social Ideas," pp. 414–28.

theless, many intellectuals after 1910 held to the basic evolutionary assumptions of positivism, conditioned by midcentury reformist liberalism. Andrés Molina Enríquez, author of the positivist study *Los Grandes Problemas nacionales* (1909), became the most influential advisor on official agrarian policy from 1915 to 1920. Like Sierra he advanced the mestizo concept of nationality and rejected biological racism. He also regarded property as evolving naturally from communal holdings to the higher form of individual tenure. At the same time he saw the need for state protection of the weaker Indian communal entity as a temporary measure. Thus the positivism of Molina Enríquez, like that of Sierra, was in some respects more Comtean than Spencerian, particularly in its conception of state and society. Sierra became the architect of a state-controlled educational system dedicated to cultivating moral and civic virtues in the masses; Molina Enríquez became the architect of the communal *ejido*, endowed with legal status and patronized by the state.[10]

Even the nativism (*indigenismo*) that emerged with the Revolution remained largely within an optimistic evolutionary framework, by contrast for example with the radical concept of Indian regeneration espoused by José Carlos Mariátegui in Peru. This was the case with the ideas of Manuel Gamio, a Ph.D. trained at Columbia University who directed the government's Department of Anthropology after 1917. It was also the case with José Vasconcelos. As minister of education in 1921, he gave official support to the implementation of Gamio's theory of "integral education"—archeological excavation at Teotihuacán tied to instruction of the local Indian populace, always with an eye to the revival and preservation of traditional arts and crafts. Vasconcelos's vision of America as the cradle of the "cosmic race" assumed both the incorporation of the Indians into Mexican society and their ultimate Europeanization.

Moving nearer to the present day and returning to the principal theme of this study, scientific politics as a form of constitutional liberalism, can we not find evidence of its legacy in the recent attempts to inject "democracy" into Mexican political life? The main historical model for contemporary reformers, one vigorously evoked a generation ago by Daniel Cosío Villegas, is the program of Francisco I. Madero. "Effective suffrage, no-reelection" remains a noble and undeniable principle to guide political reform in a postrevolutionary era. But the recent efforts to modify the political system also bring to mind the agenda of the *Científicos*, traces of which can be discerned in the ideology of Madero. In both in-

---

[10] In justifying article 27 of the Constitution of 1917, Molina Enríquez acknowledged that its spirit was "collectivist" as opposed to the "individualism" of 1857. He claimed that this change merely reflected the Comtean concept (unknown in 1857) that societies were "living organisms." See Andrés Molina Enríquez, "El Artículo 27 de la constitución federal," *Boletín de la secretaría de gobernación* 1 (1922): 6.

stances we note the existence of a powerful political myth, the myth of liberalism in the 1890s and the myth of the continuing revolution now. Thus in both instances debate and reform proposals emerged from within the establishment, from within the intellectual and quasi-governmental elite—the liberal establishment then, the "revolutionary" establishment now. In both instances reform has been limited to politics. One objective of scientific politics—strong centralized administration, guided by a technocratic elite and oriented toward capitalist economic development—was taken for granted then and continues to be taken so now, at least up to the most recent national elections.

The concern of the *Científicos* was personal government; the concern of reformers today is overweening executive power, expressed through an increasingly exclusionary political system. The *Científicos* looked to institutions to bring constitutional balance to government, and by 1903 they were calling for true political parties. They even suggested the formation of a new conservative party. But it was a vain hope, for the liberal myth had appropriated political life and rendered party conservatism unviable. The *Científicos'* problem may still be the problem of today. Are institutional limitations on authority and a competitive party system possible in a nation that still adheres to a unifying political myth?

Bibliography

THIS BOOK is based almost entirely on published sources, some readily available, other more obscure. The challenge in studying the history of political ideas in Latin America is not so much to ferret out heretofore-unknown materials, but to discern assumptions that are sometimes elusive and intractable, even in materials that are well known. The sources used include the writings of politically oriented intellectuals (and their private correspondence where available), public debates (particularly in the Chamber of Deputies and the National Congresses of Public Instruction), ministry reports, and legislation. Since I am studying the ideas of the liberal establishment from 1867 to the early 1890s, most of the documents were either officially approved or tolerated. In this era of political reconciliation and ideological consensus, the suppression of dissident opinion was less prevalent than is often assumed.

Much intellectual expression both political and philosophical first appeared in newspapers and in occasional periodicals, at least until the coming of industrial journalism in 1896. Therefore the leading newspapers and periodicals of Mexico City have been the most valuable single source for this study. Although some of the texts were reprinted in pamphlets or in book form, I have usually had to return to the originals to date texts exactly, to establish context, or even occasionally to compare different printed versions of a text. Nonetheless, I have been greatly aided in my work by several compilations of documents of the era, especially the *Obras completas* (1948) of Justo Sierra, directed by Agustín Yáñez, and the collection of articles from the press pertaining to the Escuela Nacional Preparatoria (1972), edited by Clementina Díaz y de Ovando. In these and a few other cases I have cited both the original and the more accessible source of a given document for the benefit of both specialized and less specialized readers. The original dates and circumstances of publication and in some cases the subsequent publication history of a given text are important data in the history of ideas, and I have tried to provide such data where it is pertinent.

The most extensive repository of Mexican newspapers is the Hemeroteca Nacional, moved in recent years from the old Jesuit compound on the Calle del Carmen to the grand new quarters south of the university. I have also located valuable newspapers and periodicals in the Hemeroteca de Hacienda, the Archivo General de la Nación, and the Biblioteca de México. I have also found obscure pamphlets and books of the era in these institutions, as well as in the Centro de Estudios de Historia de

México Condumex, the Lafragua Collection of the Biblioteca Nacional, the Benson Latin American Library of the University of Texas, the Bancroft Library of the University of California at Berkeley, the New York Public Library, Widener Library of Harvard University, the Library of Congress, and the University of Iowa Library. I have utilized a few manuscript materials pertaining to the ENP in the Archivo Histórico de la Universidad and some biographical materials in the Archivo Histórico Matías Romero and the Archivo de la Secretaría de Relaciones Exteriores. Generally speaking, biographical information on lesser-known figures, especially those later branded as *porfiristas* or *Científicos*, is hard to come by.

European materials, French, Spanish, and English (in French translation) have been vital to this project. Some key texts are readily accessible, but many others cited or quoted by the Mexicans (though often identified poorly or not at all) proved difficult to track down. Many appeared in French journals that circulated in Mexico, especially the *Revue des deux mondes*. Fortunately, the University of Iowa Library boasts a complete run of this all-important periodical. Other French translations of key English works read by the Mexicans were found in a variety of libraries in the United States. The translations often contain revealing introductory or editorial comments. Spanish works and especially translations into Spanish were far fewer and apparently less available in Mexico than were the French ones. However, the importance of the Spaniard Emilio Castelar for this study led me to Madrid, where I made use of the extensive Castelar materials in the Biblioteca Nacional. Finally, mention should be made of the magnificent late nineteenth- and early twentieth-century encyclopedias for identifying European writers who were known to the Mexicans but are little known today. Especially valuable were *La Grande encyclopédie, Grand Dictionnaire universel du xix siècle* (Larousse), and *Enciclopedia universal ilustrada europeo-americana* (Espasa-Calpe).

The alphabetical list that follows consists of most of the items cited in the text and the footnotes. I have included in the list a few articles from newspapers and journals, especially ones in series, which are of particular importance and not reprinted elsewhere. Otherwise I have listed only the newspaper or periodical itself. The Justo Sierra texts listed do not appear in the *Obras completas*. I have only listed Barreda writings that are not included in the *Opúsculos* (1877) or in the *Anales de la asociación metodófila "Gabino Barreda"* (1877).

Abelove, Henry, et al., eds. *Visions of History*. New York: Pantheon, 1984.
Acomb, Evelyn M. *The French Laic Laws, 1879–1889*. New York: Columbia University Press, 1941.

Acta de las audiencias [de la suprema corte de justicia] en que se trató del proyecto de la reforma constitucional sobre la vicepresidencia de la república. Mexico: Díaz de León, 1881.

Adame Goddard, Jorge. *El Pensamiento político y social de los católicos mexicanos, 1867–1914.* Mexico: Universidad Nacional Autónoma de México [UNAM], 1981.

Agraz García de Alba, Gabriel. *Biobibliografía general de don José María Vigil.* Mexico: UNAM, 1981.

Altamirano, Ignacio M. *Discursos.* Mexico: Ediciones Beneficios Públicos, 1934.

Alva, Luis. "La Colonización y la raza indígena." Nos. 1–12. *La Libertad.* 7 June to 20 July 1882.

Álvarez de Morales, Antonio. *Génesis de la universidad española contemporanea.* Madrid: Instituto de Estudios Administrativos, 1972.

Anderson, Rodney D. *Outcasts in Their Own Land: Mexican Industrial Workers, 1906–1911.* De Kalb: Northern Illinois University Press, 1976.

Anales de la asociación metodófila "Gabino Barreda." Mexico: Dublán y Chávez, 1877.

Aragón, Agustín. *Essai sur l'histoire du positivisme au Mexique. Le Docteur Gabino Barreda.* Mexico and Paris [1898?].

———. "El Territorio de México y sus habitantes." *México, su evolución social.* Ed. Justo Sierra. 2 vols. in 3. Mexico: Ballescá, 1900–02, 1:1–32.

Arbousse-Bastide, Paul. *La Doctrine de l'éducation universelle dans la philosophie d'Auguste Comte.* 2 vols. Paris: Presses Universitaires de France, 1957.

Archivo de la Secretaria de Relaciones Exteriores, L–E–1910, expediente H/131 "884–903"/7192; 521,23 (46): sección 43, caja 4, expediente 482 [43–4–48].

Archivo Histórico de la Universidad, Preparatoria, Actas de la Junta de Profesores. Vol. 23.

Archivo Histórico Matías Romero, nos. 22430, 22737, 23884.

Arnáiz y Freg, Arturo. "El Liberalismo mexicano y su significación social." *Cuadernos americanos* 27 (1968): 86–95.

El Artista. 3 vols. Mexico, 1874–75.

Bain, Alexander. *Logic: Deductive and Inductive.* New York: Appleton, 1874. 1st ed. 1870.

———. *Logique: déductive et inductive.* 2 vols. Trans. Gabriel Compayré. Paris: Germer-Ballière, 1875.

Bannister, Robert C. *Social Darwinism: Science and Myth in Anglo-American Social Thought.* Philadelphia: Temple University Press, 1979.

Barreda, Gabino. "El Congreso penitenciario de Estokolmo" (1878). *Revista positiva* 12 (1912): 22–42, 49–75.

———. "Discurso . . . en la apoteosis de Don Leopoldo Río de la Loza" (15 November 1877). *Boletín de instrucción pública* 8 (1907): 447–69.

———. "Instrucción pública" (1872). *Revista positiva* 1 (1901): 257–340.

———. *Opúsculos, discusiones y discursos.* Mexico: Dublán y Chávez, 1877.

Barrera Fuentes, Florencio. *Historia de la revolución mexicana. La Etapa precursora.* 2d ed. Mexico: Instituto Nacional de Estudios Históricos de la Revolución Mexicana, 1970.

Batis, Huberto, ed. *Índices de El Renacimiento*. Mexico: UNAM, 1963.

Bazant, Jan. *Antonio Haro y Tamariz y sus aventuras políticas, 1811–1869*. Mexico: El Colegio de México, 1985.

Berninger, Dieter G. *La Inmigración en México, 1821–1857*. Mexico: Secretaría de Educación Pública, 1974.

Berry, Charles R. *The Reform in Oaxaca, 1856–1876*. Lincoln: University of Nebraska Press, 1981.

El Bien público. Mexico, 1 August 1876–12 October 1876.

Blanco y negro. Revista ilustrada. Madrid, 30 May 1899.

Boletín oficial del gobierno interino de los Estados Unidos Mexicanos. Guanajuato, Querétaro, Celaya, 2 November–15 December 1876.

Borah, Woodrow. "Latin American History in World Perspective." In *The Future of History*. Ed. Charles F. Delzell. Nashville: Vanderbilt University Press, 1977, pp. 151–72.

Boutmy, Émile. *Taine, Scherer, Laboulaye*. Paris: A. Colin, 1901.

Brading, David A. "Liberal Patriotism and the Mexican Reforma." *Journal of Latin American Studies* 20 (1988): 27–48.

Brandt, Joseph A. *Toward the New Spain*. Chicago: University of Chicago Press, 1933.

Brett, George S. *History of Psychology*. Ed. R. S. Peters. London: Allen and Unwin, 1953.

Breymann, Walter N. "The *Científicos* and the Collapse of the Díaz Regime. A Study in the Origins of Mexican Revolutionary Sentiment, 1903–1910." *Proceedings of the Arkansas Academy of Sciences* 8 (1955): 192–97.

———. "The *Científicos*: Critics of the Díaz Regime, 1892–1903." *Proceedings of the Arkansas Academy of Sciences* 7 (1955): 91–97.

Bryan, Anthony T. "Mexican Politics in Transition, 1900–1913: the Role of General Bernardo Reyes." Ph.D. diss., University of Nebraska, 1970.

———. "Political Power in Porfirio Díaz's Mexico: A Review and Commentary." *The Historian* 38 (1976): 648–68.

Bulnes, Francisco. *Defensa y amplición de mi discurso pronunciado el 21 de junio de 1903 ante la convención nacional liberal*. Mexico: El Mundo y El Imparcial, 1903.

———. *Discurso pronunciado por el Sr. ingeniero D. Francisco Bulnes delegado del estado de Morelos, en la sesión del 21 de junio de 1903, presentado y fundando la candidatura del señor general Porfirio Díaz*. Mexico: Tipografía Económica, 1903.

———. *Juárez y la revolución de Ayutla y de reforma*. Mexico: Murguía, 1905.

———. *Porvenir de las naciones hispano americanas ante las conquistas recientes de Europa y los Estados Unidos*. Mexico: Nava, 1899.

———. *El Verdadero Juárez y la verdad sobre la intervención y el imperio*. Mexico: Bouret, 1904.

Burrow, J. W. *Evolution and Society: A Study in Victorian Social Theory*. Cambridge: Cambridge University Press, 1968.

[Cabrera, Luis]. *Obras políticas del Lic. Blas Urrea*. Mexico: Nacional, 1921.

Cacho Viu, Vicente. *La institución libre de enseñanza*. Madrid: Rialp, 1962.

Caro, Elme-Marie. "La Démocratie devant la morale de l'avenir. Les nouvelles théories sur le droit naturel." *Revue des deux mondes*, 1 November 1875, pp. 5–36.

——. "Émile Littré, II: La Philosophie positive, ses transformations, son avenir." *Revue des deux mondes*, 1 May 1882, pp. 5–46.

——. "Emilio Littré. La Filosofía positiva, sus transformaciones, su porvenir." *Revista filosófica* (1882), pp. 81–92, 97–108, 112–24.

——. "La Religión positivista." *Revista filosófica* (1882), pp. 177–89, 192–206.

——. "La Réligion positiviste." *Études morales sur le temps présent*. 4th ed. Paris: Hachette, 1879. 1st ed. 1855.

Carreño, Alberto María. *La Real y Pontificia Universidad de México, 1536–1865*. Mexico: UNAM, 1961.

——, ed. *Archivo del General Porfirio Díaz*. 30 vols. Mexico: Elede, 1947–51.

Casasús, Joaquín. *Historia de la deuda contraída en Londres*. Mexico: Imprenta del Gobierno, 1885.

——, ed. *La Reforma monetaria en México*. Mexico: Hull, 1905.

Case, Robert. "Resurgimiento de los conservadores en México—1876–1877." *Historia mexicana* 25 (1975): 204–31.

Castelar, Emilio. *Correspondencia de Emilio Castelar, 1868–1899*. Ed. Adolfo Calzado. Madrid: Est. Typográfico, 1908.

——. *Cuestiones políticas y sociales*. 3 vols. Madrid: A. de San Martín, 1870.

——. *Discursos parlamentarios*. Ed. Carmen Llorca. Madrid: Narcea, 1973.

——. *La Fórmula del progreso. Ideas democráticas*. Madrid: Casas y Díaz, 1858.

——. *Historia del descubrimiento de América*. 2d ed., 2 vols. Madrid: González, 1894.

——. *Obras escogidas*. 7 vols. Madrid: San Martín, 1922–23.

——. "Prólogo" to Adolfo Thiers, *Historia de la revolución francesa*. 4 vols. Barcelona: Montaner y Simón, 1876–79, 1:i–clx.

——. *Recuerdos y esperanzas*. 2 vols. Madrid: A de San Martin, n.d.

El Centinela español. Mexico, 1 December 1879–29 April 1883.

Charlton, D. G. *Positivist Thought in France During the Second Empire, 1852–1870*. London: Oxford University Press, 1959.

——. *Secular Religions in France, 1815–1870*. London: Oxford University Press, 1963.

Chase, Myrna. *Elie Halévy: An Intellectual Biography*. New York: Columbia University Press, 1980.

Claggett, Helen L., and David M. Valderrama. *A Revised Guide to the Law and Legal Literature of Mexico*. Washington: Library of Congress, 1973.

Clark, Linda L. *Social Darwinism in France*. University: University of Alabama Press, 1984.

Cockcroft, James D. *Intellectual Precursors of the Mexican Revolution, 1910–1913*. Austin: University of Texas Press, 1968.

Coerver, Don M. "The Perils of Progress: the Mexican Department of Fomento during the Boom Years, 1880–1884." *Inter-American Economic Affairs* 31 (1977): 41–62.

————. *The Porfirian Interregnum: The Presidency of Manuel González of Mexico, 1880–1884*. Ft. Worth: Texas Christian University Press, 1979.

Coker, F. W. *Organismic Theories of the State*. New York: Columbia University Press, 1910.

Comte, Auguste. *Cours de philosophie positive*. 5th ed. 6 vols. Paris: Schleicher Frères, 1907–08. 1st ed. 1830–42.

————. *General View of Positivism*. Trans. J. H. Bridges. New York: Speller, 1957.

————. *Système de politique positive*. 3rd ed. 4 vols. Paris, 1890. 1st ed. 1851–54.

Constant de Rébeque, Benjamin. *Cours de politique constitutionnelle ou collection des ouvrages publiés sur le gouvernement représentatif*. 2d ed. 2 vols. Paris: Guillaumin, 1872.

Córdova, Arnaldo. "¿Espiritualismo o positivismo? La Filosofía de la revolución mexicana." Mexico: Centro de Estudios Latinoamericanos (UNAM), Avances de investigaciones, no. 14, 1975. Unpublished paper.

————. *La Ideología de la revolución mexicana. La Formación del nuevo régimen*. Mexico: Era, 1973.

Cosío Villegas, Daniel. *La Constitución de 1857 y sus críticos*. Mexico: Hermes, 1957.

————. *Extremos de América*. Mexico: Tezontle, 1949.

————. *Historia moderna de México*. 9 vols. in 10. Mexico: Hermes, 1955–72.

Cosmes, Francisco G. *La Dominación española y la patria mexicana*. Mexico: El Partido Liberal, 1896.

————. *Historia general de Méjico, continuación de la de Don Niceto de Zamacois*. 4 vols. (vols. 21–24). Barcelona: Araluce, 1901–1902.

————. "Un Poeta extraviado entre los positivistas. El Sr. Sierra y su discurso sobre inamobilidad del poder judicial." *El Siglo XIX*, 14, 15, 19, 27, 30 December 1893.

Covo, Jacqueline. *Las Ideas de la reforma en México, 1885–1861*. Mexico: UNAM, 1983.

Cuevas, José de Jesús. *Obras*. Vol. 1. Mexico: Agüeros, 1898.

————. "El Positivismo en México." *La Voz de México*, 20 October 1885.

Darío, Rubén. *Obras completas*. Vol. 22. Madrid: Mundo Latino, 1917.

Darwin, Charles. *The Descent of Man, and Selection in Relation to Sex*. London: Murray, 1871.

————. *The Origin of Species*. Rev. ed. New York: Appleton, 1860.

————. *De L'Origine des espèces*. Trans. Clémence Royer. 3d ed. Paris: Guillaumin, 1870. 1st ed. 1862.

Debates del [primer] congreso nacional de instrucción pública. Mexico: El Partido Liberal, 1889 [sic].

La Democracia. Madrid, 21, 25 February 1865.

Diario de los debates. Cámara de diputados, 3rd to the 18th congresses. Mexico. 1862–98.

Diario de los debates. Senado, 16th congress. Mexico, 1893–94.

Diario de sesiones de las cortes constituyentes de la república española. 4 vols. Madrid: J. Antonio Garcia, 1874.

Diario oficial del gobierno. Mexico, 1867–1914.

Dias, Geralda. "Conformación social y política de la escuela nacional preparatoria." Ph.D. diss., El Colegio de México, 1979.

Díaz Covarrubias, José. *La Instrucción pública en México.* Mexico: Imprenta del Gobierno, 1875.

Díaz y de Ovando, Clementina. *La Escuela nacional preparatoria.* 2 vols. Mexico: UNAM, 1972.

Díaz Zermeño, Héctor. "La Escuela nacional primaria en la ciudad de México, 1876–1910." *Historia mexicana* 29 (1979): 59–90.

Dublán, Manuel, and José María Lozano, *Legislación mexicana.* 34 vols. Mexico, 1876–1904.

Duguit, Leon, and Henri Monnier. *Les Constitutions et les principales lois politiques de la France.* 4th ed. Paris: Pichon, 1925.

Dumas, Claude. *Justo Sierra et le Mexique de son temps, 1848–1912.* 3 vols. Lille: Université de Lille III, 1975.

———. "Justo Sierra y el liceo franco-mexicano. Sobre la educación en México, 1861–1862." *Historia mexicana* 16 (1967): 31–40.

———. "La República universal de Justo Sierra." *Historia mexicana* 14 (1965): 416–22.

La Época. Mexico, 1 May 1877–30 December 1877.

Eros, John. "The Positivist Generation of French Republicanism." *Sociological Review* new series, 3 (1955): 255–77.

F.N.V. "La Ciencia positiva." *La Revista eclesiástica.* Puebla, 1 August 1868.

———. "El Positivismo." *La Revista eclesiástica.* Puebla, 25 July 1868.

El Federalista. Mexico, 2 January 1871 until 1878.

El Foro. Periódico de jurisprudencia y de legislación. Mexico, 1 June 1873–25 June 1895.

Fouillée, Alfred. "L'Histoire naturelle des sociétés humaines ou animales." Part I. "L'Organisme sociale." *Revue des deux mondes,* 15 July 1879, pp. 370–405.

———. *L'Idée moderne du droit.* Paris: Hachette, 1878.

Franck, Adolphe, ed. *Dictionnaire des sciences philosophiques par une société de professeurs et de savants.* 2d ed. Paris: Hachette, 1875. 1st ed. 1843–53.

Frías y Soto, Hilarión. *Carta de . . . al Sr. diputado Francisco Bulnes.* Mexico: Central, 1903.

Fuentes Mares, José. "La Convocatoria de 1867." *Historia mexicana* 14 (1964): 423–44.

García Granados, Ricardo. *La Constitución de 1857 y las leyes de reforma en México, Estudio histórico-sociológico.* Mexico: Tipografía Económica, 1906.

———. *Historia de México desde la restauración de la república en 1867 hasta la caída de Porfirio Díaz.* 4 vols. Mexico: Botas, 1923–28.

García, Telesforo. *Considerations sur la guerre européene.* Mexico: Imprenta Franco Mexicana, 1916.

———. *La España y los españoles en México.* Mexico: S. Sierra, 1877.

————. *Polémica filosófica.* ¿*Garantiza mejor el progreso el sistema metafísico que el sistema experimental?* Mexico: La Libertad, 1881.

————. *Política científica y política metafísica.* Mexico: Fomento, 1887.

Gillispie, Charles C. "The Work of Élie Halévy: A Critical Appraisal." *Journal of Modern History* 22 (1950): 232–49.

Girard, Louis. "Political Liberalism in France, 1840–1875." In *French Society and Culture Since the Old Regime.* Ed. E. M. Acomb and M. L. Brown, Jr. New York: Holt, Rinehart, 1966, pp. 119–32.

Glick, Thomas F., ed. *The Comparative Reception of Darwinism.* Austin: University of Texas Press, 1974.

El Globo. Mexico, 28 June 1867–31 October 1869.

Goldstein, Doris S. " 'Official Philosophies' in Modern France: the Example of Victor Cousin." *Journal of Social History* 1 (1968): 59–79.

González Navarro, Moises. *La Colonización en México, 1877–1910.* Mexico: Estampillas y Valores, 1960.

————. *El Porfiriato. Vida social.* Vol. 4 of *Historia moderna de México.* Ed. Daniel Cosío Villegas. Mexico: Hermes, 1957.

————. "Los Positivistas mexicanos en Francia." *Historia mexicana,* 9 (1959): 119–29.

González y González, Luis. "El Hombre y la tierra." *Historia moderna de México.* Vol. 3. Ed. Daniel Cosío Villegas. Mexico: Hermes, 1956, pp. 3–146.

————. "El Subsuelo indígena." *Historia moderna de México.* Vol. 3. Ed. Daniel Cosío Villegas. Mexico: Hermes, 1956, pp. 149–325.

Gortari, Eli de. *La Ciencia en la historia de México.* Mexico: Fondo de Cultura Económica, 1963.

Greene, John C. "Biology and Social Theory in the Nineteenth Century: Auguste Comte and Herbert Spencer." In *Critical Problems in the History of Science.* Ed. Marshall Clagett. Madison: University of Wisconsin Press, 1959, pp. 419–46.

————. "Darwin as a Social Evolutionist." *Journal of the History of Biology* 10 (1977): 1–27.

Guerra, François-Xavier. *Le Mexique. De L'Ancien Régime à la révolution.* 2 vols. Paris: L'Harmattan, 1985.

Guerrero, Julio. *La Génesis del crimen en México. Estudio de psiquiatría social.* Mexico: Bouret, 1901.

Guzmán, León. *Cuestiones constitucionales. El Sistema de dos cámaras y sus consecuencias.* Mexico: Imprenta del Comercio, 1870.

Hale, Charles A. "The History of Ideas: Substantive and Methodological Aspects of the Thought of Leopoldo Zea." *Journal of Latin American Studies* 3 (1971): 59–70.

————. "The Liberal Impulse: Daniel Cosío Villegas and the *Historia moderna de México.*" *Hispanic American Historical Review* 54 (1974): 479–98.

————. "Liberalismo mexicano." *Historia mexicana* 12 (1963): 457–63.

————. *Mexican Liberalism in the Age of Mora, 1821–1853.* New Haven: Yale University Press, 1968.

————. "Political and Social Ideas in Latin America, 1870–1930." In *Cambridge*

History of Latin America. Ed. Leslie Bethell. 5 vols. Cambridge University Press, 1984–86, 4:367–441, 637–43.

———. "The Reconstruction of Nineteenth Century Politics in Spanish America: A Case for the History of Ideas." *Latin American Research Review* 8, 2 (1973): 53–73.

Halévy, Élie. *The Growth of Philosophic Radicalism*. London, Faber, 1928. 1st ed. 1901–04.

———. "Saint-Simonian Economic Doctrine" (1907–08). In *The Era of Tyrannies*. New York: New York University Press, 1966.

Hammeken y Mexía, Jorge. "La Filosofía positiva y la filosofía metafísica." *La Libertad*, 14 October–2 November 1880.

———. "La Philosophie positive au Mexique. Lettre . . . a M. Littré." *La Philosophie positive* 20 (1878), 194–213.

Hennessy, C. A. M. *The Federal Republic in Spain*. London: Oxford University Press, 1962.

Hernández Luna, Juan, ed. *La Universidad de Justo Sierra*. Mexico: UNAM, 1948.

Hofstadter, Richard. *Social Darwinism in American Thought, 1860–1915*. Rev. ed. Boston: Beacon, 1955.

Holborn, Hajo. *A History of Modern Germany*. 3 vols. New York: Alfred A. Knopf, 1959–69.

Iglesias, José María. *La Cuestión presidencial en 1876*. Mexico: Filomena Mata, 1892.

———. *Estudio constitucional sobre facultades de la corte de justicia*. Mexico: Díaz de León y White, 1874.

Janet, Paul. "La Filosofía de la revolución francesa." *La Tribuna*, 14–24 February 1874.

———. *Histoire de la science politique dans ses rapports avec la morale*. 3d ed. 2 vols. Paris: Alcan, 1887. 1st ed. 1852.

———. "La Philosophie de la révolution I." *Revue des deux mondes*, 1 January 1872, pp. 42–73.

———. "La Science sociale et la philosophie anglaise." *Revue des deux mondes*, 1 November 1874, pp. 81–110.

———. *Traité élémentaire de philosophie a l'usage des classes*. Paris: Délagrave, 1879.

———. *Tratado elemental de filosofía*. Mexico and Paris: Bouret, 1880.

Jobit, Pierre. *Les Éducateurs de l'Espagne contemporaine*. 2 vols. Paris: Boccard, 1936.

Kantorowicz, Hermann. "Savigny and the Historical School of Law." *Law Quarterly Review* 53 (1937): 326–43.

Katz, Friedrich. "Mexico: Restored Republic and Porfiriato, 1867–1910." In *Cambridge History of Latin America*. Ed. Leslie Bethell. 5 vols. Cambridge: Cambridge University Press, 1984–86, 5:3–78, 831–35.

Ker, Anita M. *Mexican Government Publications*. Washington: Government Printing Office, 1940.

Knapp, Frank A. *The Life of Sebastián Lerdo de Tejada, 1823–1889*. Austin: University of Texas Press, 1951.

————. "Parliamentary Government and the Mexican Constitution of 1857: A Forgotten Phase of Mexican Political History." *Hispanic American Historical Review* 33 (1953): 65–87.

Knight, Alan. "El Liberalismo mexicano desde la reforma hasta la revolución (una interpretación)." *Historia mexicana* 35 (1985): 59–91.

————. *The Mexican Revolution.* 2 vols. Cambridge: Cambridge University Press, 1986.

Knowlton, Robert J. *Church Property and the Mexican Reform, 1856–1910.* De Kalb: Northern Illinois University Press, 1976.

Krause, K. C. F. *Ideal de la humanidad para la vida.* Trans. and ed. Julián Sanz del Río. Madrid: Galiano, 1860.

Krauze, Enrique. *Caudillos culturales en la revolución mexicana.* Mexico: El Colegio de México, 1976.

Laboulaye, Edouard. *Histoire des États-Unis.* 6th ed. 3 vols. Paris: Charpentier, 1877. 1st ed. 1855–66.

————. *Historia de los Estados Unidos.* 2 vols. Trans. Manuel Dublán. Mexico: Imprenta del Gobierno, 1870.

Lemoine, Ernesto. *La Escuela nacional preparatoria en el período de Gabino Barreda, 1867–1878.* Mexico: UNAM, 1970.

Lévy-Bruhl, Lucien. *The Philosophy of Auguste Comte.* London: Swan Sonneshein, 1903.

La Libertad. Mexico, 5 January 1878–31 December 1884.

Limantour, José Yves. *Apuntes sobre mi vida política.* Mexico: Porrua, 1965.

Littré, Émile. *Auguste Comte et la philosophie positive.* 2d ed. Paris: Hachette, 1864.

————. "La Philosophie positive: M. Auguste Comte et M. J. Stuart Mill." *Revue des deux mondes,* 15 August 1866, pp. 829–66.

Le Livre du centenaire. Cent ans de vie française a la revue des deux mondes. Paris: Hachette, 1929.

López Morillas, Juan. *The Krausist Movement and Ideological Change in Spain, 1854–1874.* Cambridge: Cambridge University Press, 1981. Spanish ed. 1956.

López-Portillo y Rojas, José. *Elevación y caída de Porfirio Díaz.* 2d ed. Mexico: Porrua, 1975. 1st ed. 1921.

Llanos y Alcaraz, Adolfo. *No Vengáis a América. Libro dedicado a los pueblos europeos.* Mexico: La Colonia Española, 1876.

————. *Origen del plajio en México: polémica sostenida por el periódico la colonia española con varios órganos de la prensa mexicana.* Mexico: La Colonia española, 1877.

Llorca, Carmen. *Emilio Castelar.* Madrid: Biblioteca Nueva, 1966.

Macedo, Miguel S. *La Criminalidad en México. Medios de combatirla.* Mexico: Fomento, 1897.

————. "Ensayo sobre los deberes recíprocos de los superiores y de los inferiores." *Anales de la asociación metodófila "Gabino Barreda"* (1877), pp. 213–29.

Mallon, Florencia. "Peasants and State Formation in Nineteenth-Century Mexico: Morelos, 1848–1858." *Political Power and Social Theory* 7 (1988): 1–54.

Mandelbaum, Maurice. *History, Man, and Reason.* Baltimore: Johns Hopkins University Press, 1971.

Manero, Antonio. *El Antiguo Régimen y la revolución.* Mexico: La Europea, 1911.

Mantecón Navasal, José Ignacio, et al. *Bibliografía general de don Justo Sierra.* Mexico: UNAM, 1969.

Manuel, Frank. *The New World of Henri Saint-Simon.* Cambridge: Harvard University Press, 1956.

Marañon, Gregorio. "Efemérides y comentarios" (1952). *Obras completas.* 2d ed. 10 vols. Madrid: Espasa Calpe, 1968–77, 9:587–91.

María y Campos, Alfonso de. "Los Científicos y la reforma monetaria de 1905." *Estudios políticos* 5 (1979): 157–87.

———. "Porfirianos prominentes: Orígenes y años de juventud de ocho integrantes del grupo de los científicos, 1846–1876," *Historia mexicana,* 34 (1985): 610–61.

McClelland, Charles E. *State, Society, and University in Germany, 1700–1914.* Cambridge: Cambridge University Press, 1980.

McMahon, T. J. "The Spanish Immigrant Community in Mexico City During the Porfiriato, 1876–1911." Ph.D. diss., University of Notre Dame, 1974.

Memoria de hacienda y crédito público, 1877–78. Mexico: Imprenta del Gobierno, 1879.

Memoria presentada . . . por el secretario de estado y del despacho de fomento, colonización, industria y comercio, December 1876–December 1877. Mexico: Imprenta del Gobierno, 1877.

Memoria . . . de justicia e instrucción pública. 1869, 1892–96. Mexico: Imprenta del Gobierno, 1870, 1899.

Meneses Morales, Ernesto. *Tendencias educativas oficiales en México, 1821–1911.* Mexico: Porrua, 1983.

Mill, John Stuart. *A System of Logic, Ratiocinative and Inductive, Being a Connected View of the Principles of Evidence, and Methods of Scientific Investigation.* 2 vols. London: Parke, 1843.

———. *Auguste Comte and Positivism.* Ann Arbor: University of Michigan Press, 1961. 1st ed. 1865.

———. *Auguste Comte et le positivisme.* Paris: Baillière, 1868.

Miño Grijalva, Manuel, et al. *Tres Aspectos de la presencia española en México durante el Porfiriato.* Mexico: El Colegio de México, 1981.

Molina Enríquez, Andrés. "El Artículo 27 de la constitución federal." *Boletín de la secretaría de gobernación* 1 (1922): 1–124.

———. *Los Grandes Problemas nacionales.* Mexico: Carranza, 1909.

El Monitor republicano. Mexico, 14 February 1846–31 December 1896.

Monroy, Guadalupe. "Instrucción pública." *Historia moderna de Mexico.* Vol. 3. Ed. Daniel Cosío Villegas. Mexico: Hermes, 1956, pp. 643–743.

———, ed. *Archivo histórico de Matías Romero. Catálogo descriptivo.* 2 vols. Mexico: El Banco de México, 1965–70.

Moody, Joseph N. *French Education Since Napoleon.* Syracuse: Syracuse University Press, 1978.

Moreno, Roberto, ed. *La Polémica del darwinismo en México. Siglo XIX*. Mexico: UNAM, 1984.

El Mundo científico. Revista de las ciencias y de sus aplicaciones a las artes y a la industria. 2 June 1877–26 January 1878.

El Nacional. Mexico, 1 July 1880–31 August 1900[?].

Niblo, Stephen R. "The Political Economy of the Early Porfiriato: Politics and Economics in Mexico, 1876–1880." Ph.D. diss., Northern Illinois University, 1972.

Niemeyer, E. V., Jr. *El General Bernardo Reyes*. Monterrey: Universidad de Nuevo León, 1966.

O'Gorman, Edmundo. "Justo Sierra y los orígenes de la universidad de México, 1910" (1949). *Seis Estudios históricos de tema mexicano*. Xalapa: Universidad Veracruzana, 1960, pp. 145–201.

Olliff, Donathon C. *Reforma Mexico and the United States: A Search for Alternatives to Annexation, 1854–1861*. University: University of Alabama Press, 1981.

Orozco, Wistano Luis. *Legislación y jurisprudencia sobre terrenos baldíos*. 2 vols. Mexico: El Tiempo, 1895.

Osborne, Thomas R. "The Recruitment of the Administrative Elite in the Third French Republic, 1870–1905: the System of the École Libre des Sciences Politiques." Ph.D. diss., University of Connecticut, 1974.

Otero, Mariano. *Ensayo sobre el verdadero estado del la cuestión social y política que se agita en la república mexicana*. Mexico: Cumplido, 1842.

Parra, Porfirio. "La Ciencia en México." *México, su evolución social*. 2 vols. in 3. Ed. Justo Sierra. Mexico: Ballescá, 1900–02, pp. 418–66.

———. "La Educación intelectual." Nos. 1–19. *La Libertad*. 10 December 1881–4 April 1882.

———. *Nuevo Sistema de lógica inductiva y deductiva*. 2 vols. Mexico: Tipografía Económica, 1903.

———. "La Pseudo-anarquía positivista I–III." *La Libertad*. 31 May, 1, 2 June 1882.

El Partido liberal. Mexico, 15 February 1885–29 August 1896.

La Patria. Mexico, 15 March 1877 until 1914.

Paulsen, Friedrich. *The German Universities and University Study*. New York: Macmillan, 1906.

Paz, Ireneo. *Los Hombres prominentes de México*. Mexico: Patria, 1888.

Peel, J. D. Y. *Herbert Spencer: the Evolution of a Sociologist*. New York: Basic Books, 1971.

Peña, Rafael Ángel de la. *Explicación razonada que el profesor . . . presenta al ciudadano director de la escuela nacional preparatoria de las modificaciones a la ley de instrucción pública propuestas por los catedráticos de la misma escuela*. Mexico: Díaz de León, 1886.

———. "Exposición razonada del plan de estudios para el seminario conciliar de México" (1892). *Obras*. Mexico: Agüeros, 1900, pp. 1–67.

Perry, Laurens B. *Juárez and Díaz: Machine Politics in Mexico*. De Kalb: Northern Illinois University Press, 1978.

Peza, Juan de Díos. *Memorias, reliquias y retratos*. Paris: Bouret, 1901.

Pi-Suñer Llorens, Antonia. *El Sexenio revolucionario español (1868–1874) ante el gobierno y la prensa mexicana durante la república restaurada*. Mexico: UNAM, 1984.

———, ed. *México y España durante la república restaurada*. Mexico: Secretaría de Relaciones Exteriores, 1985.

Pimentel, Francisco. "Memoria sobre las causas que han originado la situación actual de la raza indígena de México y medios de remediarla" (1864). *Obras completas*. 5 vols. Mexico: Tipografía Económia, 1903–04, 3:7–149.

Piza, Agapito. "Historia parlamentaria de la cámara de senadores," in *Diario de los debates*. Senado, 8th congress, 3 vols. Mexico: Imprenta del Gobierno, 1882, 1:5–46.

Pizarro, Nicolás. *Catecismo de moral*. Méjico: Fuentes, 1868.

Polémica entre el diario oficial y la colonia española sobre la administración vireynal en Nueva España y la colonización en México. 2 vols. Mexico: Políglota, Hospicio de San Nicolás, 1875.

Ponteil, Félix. *Les Institutions de la France de 1814 à 1870*. Paris: Presses Universitaires de France, 1966.

Potash, Robert A. "Historiography of Mexico Since 1821." *Hispanic American Historical Review* 40 (1960): 383–424.

Powell, T. G. *El Liberalismo y el campesinado en el centro de México, 1850–1876*. Mexico: Secretaría de Educación Pública, 1974.

———. "Mexican Intellectuals and the Indian Question, 1876–1911." *Hispanic American Historical Review* 48 (1968): 19–36.

El Precursor. Mexico, 8 October 1874–8 April 1876.

Prida y Arteaga, Ramón. *¡De La Dictadura a la anarquía!* 2d ed. Mexico: Botas, 1958. 1st ed. 1918.

Proceso. Mexico. 25 March 1985.

Quevedo y Zubieta, Salvador. *Mexico, Recuerdos de un emigrado con prologo de Don Emilio Castelar*. Madrid: Sucesores de Rivadeneyra, 1883.

Quintana, José Miguel. *Lafragua, político y romántico*. Mexico: Editorial Academia Literaria, 1958.

Quirk, Robert E. *The Mexican Revolution, 1914–1915*. Bloomington: Indiana University Press, 1960.

Raat, William D. "Agustín Aragón and Mexico's Religion of Humanity." *Journal of Inter-American Studies and World Affairs* 11 (1969): 441–57.

———. "The Antipositivist Movement in Prerevolutionary Mexico, 1892–1911." *Journal of Inter-American Studies and World Affairs* 19 (1977): 83–98.

———. "Los Intelectuales, el positivismo y la cuestión indígena." *Historia mexicana* 20 (1971): 412–27.

———. "Leopoldo Zea and Mexican Positivism: A Reappraisal." *Hispanic American Historical Review* 48 (1968): 1–18.

———. *El Positivismo durante el porfiriato, 1876–1910*. Mexico: Secretaría de Educación Pública, 1975.

Rabasa, Emilio. *La Constitución y la dictadura*. 3d ed. Mexico: Porrua, 1956. 1st ed. 1912.

————. *Evolución histórica de México*. 2d ed. Mexico: Porrua, 1956. 1st ed. 1920.

Ramírez, Ignacio. *Obras*. 2 vols. Mexico: Fomento, 1889.

Randall, J. H., Jr. *The Career of Philosophy*. 2 vols. New York: Columbia University Press, 1962–65.

La República. Mexico, 15 February 1880–31 December 1885.

Reina, Leticia. *Las Rebeliones campesinas en México, 1819–1906*. Mexico: Siglo XXI, 1980.

El Renacimiento. Periódico literario. Mexico, 1869, 1894.

Renan, Ernest. "L'Instruction supérieure en France" (1864). *Oeuvres completes*. 10 vols. Paris: Calman-Lévy, 1947, 1:69–97.

Revista filosófica. Mexico, 1 February 1882–1 August 1883.

Revista de la instrucción pública mexicana. 5 vols. 15 March 1896–15 December 1902.

Revista nacional de letras y ciencias. 2 vols. Mexico, 1889–90.

Revista positiva. 14 vols. Mexico, 1901–14.

Reyes de la Maza, Luis. "Nicolás Pizarro, novelista y pensador liberal." *Historia mexicana* 6 (1957): 572–87.

Reyes Heroles, Jesús. "Estudio preliminar" to Mariano Otero, *Obras*. 2 vols. Mexico: Porrua, 1967, 1:1–190.

————. *El Liberalismo mexicano*. 3 vols. Mexico: UNAM, 1957–61.

Rice, Jacqueline Ann. "The Mexican Political Elite: Life Patterns of the Delegates to the 1892 Union Liberal Convention." Ph.D. Diss., University of California at Los Angeles, 1979.

Riva Palacio, Vicente. *Cuentos del general*. Ed. Clementina Díaz y de Ovando. Mexico: Porrua, 1968.

————, ed. *México a través de los siglos*. 5 vols. Barcelona and Mexico: Ballescá, 1888–89.

Robin, Charles. "Des Rapports de l'éducation avec l'instruction." *La Philosophie positive* 17 (1876): 25–48, 161–91, 305–36; 18 (1877): 5–18.

Ross, Stanley R., ed. *Is the Mexican Revolution Dead?* 2d ed. Philadelphia: Temple University Press, 1975.

Ruggiero, Guido de. *History of European Liberalism*. London: Oxford University Press, 1927.

Ruiz Castañeda, María del Carmen. "La Universidad libre (1875), antecedente de la universidad autónoma." *Deslinde*, 110 (1979): 1–35.

Ruiz, Luis E. *Nociones de lógica*. Mexico: La Libertad, 1882.

Saint-Simon, Claude-Henri de. *Du Système industriel*. 3 vols. (1821). In *Oeuvres*. Vol. 3. Paris: Anthropos, 1966.

Schmitt, Karl M. "Catholic Adjustment to the Secular State: the Case of Mexico, 1867–1911." *Catholic Historical Review* 48 (1962): 182–204.

————. "The Díaz Conciliation Policy on State and Local Levels, 1876–1911." *Hispanic American Historical Review* 40 (1960): 513–32.

Schulte, Josephine. "Gabino Barreda y su misión diplomática en Alemania, 1878–1879," *Historia mexicana* 24 (1974): 230–52.

Scott, John A. *Republican Ideas and the Liberal Tradition in France, 1870–1914.* New York: Columbia University Press, 1951.

Segundo Congreso nacional de instrucción pública. Mexico: El Partido Liberal, 1891.

Sierra, Carlos J., ed. *José María Vigil.* Mexico: Club de Periodistas, 1963.

Sierra, Justo. "A Carlos Olaguíbel." *La Época,* 24 June 1877.

——. "La Cátedra de historia general en la escuela preparatoria. A Genaro Raigosa." *La Época,* 23 May 1877.

——. "Un Consejo al presidente." *La Libertad,* 6 September 1879.

——. "La Constitución y el plan de Tuxtepec." *La Época,* 29 July 1877.

——. "El Derecho individual y un opúsculo del Sr. Lancaster Jones." *La Libertad,* 29 April 1879.

——. "España libre. A Emilio Castelar." *El Monitor republicano,* 30 March 1873.

——. "El General Burnside y México." *La Libertad,* 30 July 1879.

——. *Obras completas.* 14 vols. Mexico: UNAM, 1948–49.

——. "La Protesta del plan de Tuxtepec." *La Época,* 27 June 1877.

——, ed. *México, su evolución social.* 2 vols. in 3. Mexico: Ballescá, 1900–02.

El Siglo XIX. Mexico, 8 October 1841–14 May 1863; 15 July 1867–15 October 1896.

Simon, Walter M. *European Positivism in the Nineteenth Century.* Ithaca: Cornell University Press, 1963.

——. "Herbert Spencer and the 'Social Organism.'" *Journal of the History of Ideas* 21 (1960): 294–99.

——. "The 'Two Cultures' in Nineteenth-Century France: Victor Cousin and Auguste Comte." *Journal of the History of Ideas* 26 (1956): 45–58.

Sinkin, Richard N. "The Mexican Constitutional Congress 1856–1857: A Statistical Analysis." *Hispanic American Historical Review* 53 (1973): 1–26.

——. *The Mexican Reform, 1855–1876. A Study in Liberal Nation-Building.* Austin: University of Texas Press, 1979.

Sosa, Francisco. *Biografías de mexicanos distinguidos.* Mexico: Fomento, 1884.

Spencer, Herbert. *Classification des sciences.* Paris: Ballière, 1872.

——. "Classification of the Sciences" (plus appendix, "Reasons for Dissenting from the Philosophy of M. Comte"). *Essays: Scientific, Political, and Speculative.* 3 vols. In *Works.* 21 vols. New York: Appleton, 1891, 14:74–144. 1st ed. 1864.

——. *Descriptive Sociology, or Groups [Cyclopedia] of Sociological Facts; Representing the Constitution of Every Type and Grade of Society, Past and Present, Stationary and Progressive.* 10 vols. New York and London: Williams and Norgate, 1873–1910.

——. *Education. Intellectual, Moral, and Physical.* New York: Appleton, 1920. 1st ed. 1860.

——. *First Principles.* 6th ed. New York: Appleton, 1907. 1st ed. 1862.

——. *Introduction à la science sociale.* Paris: Baillière, 1874.

——. *Principles of Sociology.* 3 vols. New York: Appleton, 1898. 1st ed. 1876–97.

———. "Progress: its Law and Cause" (1857). *Essays on Education and Kindred Subjects*. London: Dent, 1911.

———. *Social Statics*. London: Chapman, 1851.

———. *The Study of Sociology*. Ann Arbor: University of Michigan Press, 1961. 1st ed. 1873.

Spitzer, Alan B. *The French Generation of 1820*. Princeton: Princeton University Press, 1987.

Stabb, Martin S. "Indigenism and Racism in Mexican Thought: 1857–1911." *Journal of Inter-American Studies* 1 (1959): 405–23.

Stebbins, Robert E. "France." *Comparative Reception of Darwinism*. Ed. Thomas F. Glick. Austin: University of Texas Press, 1974.

Steward, Luther N., Jr. "Spanish Journalism in Mexico, 1867–1879." *Hispanic American Historical Review* 45 (1965): 422–33.

Stocking, George W., Jr. "Lamarckianism in American Social Science, 1890–1915." In *Race, Culture, and Evolution. Essays in the History of Anthropology*. New York: Free Press, 1968, pp. 234–69.

Taine, Hippolyte A. *Origines de la France contemporaine*. 6 vols. Paris: Hachette, 1876–94.

———. "Psychologie du jacobin." *Revue des deux mondes*, 1 April 1881, pp. 536–59.

Tamayo, Jorge L., ed. *Benito Juárez, Documentos, discursos y correspondencia*. 15 vols. Mexico: Secretaria del Patrimonio Nacional, 1964–70.

Tena Ramírez, Felipe. *Derecho constitucional mexicano*. 11th ed. Mexico: Porrua, 1972.

Tenenbaum, Barbara. "Murals in Stone—The Paseo de la Reforma and Porfirian Mexico, 1873–1910." Paper presented at the Seventh Conference of Mexican and U.S. Historians, Oaxaca, 1985.

Tiberghien, Guillaume. *Lógica: la ciencia del conocimiento*. 2 vols. Trans. José María Castillo Velasco. Mexico: Librería Madrileña, 1875–78.

———. *Logique: la science de la connaissance*. 2 vols. Paris: Librairie Internationale, 1865.

El Tiempo. Diario católico. Mexico, 1 July 1883 until circa 1912.

La Tribuna. Mexico, 1 January 1874–18 February 1874.

Tutino, John. *From Insurrection to Revolution in Mexico. Social Bases of Agrarian Violence, 1750–1940*. Princeton: Princeton University Press, 1986.

U.S. Congress, Senate. *Investigations on Mexican Affairs, Preliminary Report and Hearing of the Committee on Foreign Relations*. 66th Congress, 2d Sess., on Res. 106. Washington, D.C.: Government Printing Office, 1920.

Ullman, Joan Connelly. Note, in *Comparative Studies in Society and History* 26 (1984): 367–70.

El Universal. Mexico, 1 July 1888–5 December 1901.

La Universidad libre. Mexico, 26 May 1875–30 June 1875.

Uno más uno. Mexico, 25 March 1985.

Vacherot, Étienne. *La Métaphysique et la science, ou principes de métaphysique positive*. 2d ed. 3 vols. Paris: Chamerot, 1863.

————. "Les Trois États de l'esprit humaine." *Revue des deux mondes*, 15 August 1880, pp. 856–92.

Valadés, José C. *El Porfirismo, historia de un régimen*. 3 vols. Mexico: Robredo, Patria, 1941–48.

Vallarta, Ignacio. *Cuestiones constitucionales. Votos . . . [1878–82]*. 4 vols. Mexico: A. García, 1894–96.

Valverde Téllez, Emeterio. *Apuntaciones históricas sobre la filosofía en México*. Mexico: Herrero, 1896.

————. *Bibliografía filosófica mexicana*. 2 vols. León: Rodríguez, 1913.

————. *Crítica filosófica*. Mexico: Díaz de León, 1904.

Vaughan, Mary Kay. *The State, Education, and Social Class in Mexico, 1880–1928*. De Kalb: Northern Illinois University Press, 1982.

Vázquez, Emilio. *La Reelección*. Mexico: Cerca de Santo Domingo, 1892.

————. *La Reelección indefinida*. Mexico: Orozco, 1890.

Vázquez, Josefina. *Nacionalismo y educación en México*. Mexico: El Colegio de México, 1970.

Verduin, Arnold E. ed. *Manual of Spanish Constitutions, 1808–1931*. Ypsilanti, University Lithoprinters, 1941.

Vigil, José María. "La Anarquía positivista." *Revista filosófica*, 1 May, 1 June 1882, pp. 49–58, 65–74.

————, and Rafael Ángel de la Peña. *Discursos pronunciados por . . . en las juntas de catedráticos celebrados en la escuela nacional preparatoria los días 27 y 31 de agosto y 1 y 4 de septiembre de presente año, con motivo de la designación de texto para la clase de lógica*. Mexico: Imprenta del Gobierno, 1885.

Villada, José V. ed. *La Reelección del presidente de la república y gobernadores de los estados. Memorandum acerca de la reforma de los artículos 78 y 109 de la constitución mexicana*. Mexico: Villada, n.d. [1887?].

La Voz de México. Diario político, religioso, científico y literario de la 'Soc. Católica.' 17 April 1870–1908.

Walker, David W. "Porfirian Labor Politics: Working Class Organizations in Mexico City and Porfirio Díaz, 1876–1902." *The Americas* 37 (1981): 257–89.

Weeks, Charles A. *El Mito de Juárez en México*. Mexico: Jus, 1977.

Wheat, Raymond C. *Francisco Zarco. El Portavoz liberal de la reforma*. Mexico: Porrua, 1957.

Womack, John, Jr. "The Mexican Revolution, 1910–1920." In *Cambridge History of Latin America*. Ed. Leslie Bethell. 5 vols. Cambridge: Cambridge University Press, 1984–86, 5:79–153, 835–45.

————. *Zapata and the Mexican Revolution*. New York: Alfred A. Knopf, 1969.

Yáñez, Agustin. *Don Justo Sierra*. Mexico: UNAM, 1948.

Zarco, Francisco. *Historia del congreso extraordinario constituyente, 1856–1857*. 3d ed. Mexico: El Colegio de Mexico, 1956.

Zea, Leopoldo. *El Positivismo en Mexico*. Fondo de Cultura Económica, 1968. 1st ed. in 2 vols., 1943–44.

Zwieg, Arnulf. "Karl Christian Friedrich Krause." *Encyclopedia of Philosophy*. 8 vols. New York: Macmillan, 1967, 4:363–65.

Index